If there is a truth, it is that truth is a stake in the struggle.
—Pierre Bourdieu

Everybody's an authority
In a free land
—Bob Mould

'Milner has ... such a terrific job, riddling the book with absorbing characters and ... views and fossicking diligently for those illuminating nuggets ... [he] is laudably lucid on the technicalities of how music works ... one of the many things that this fascinating book will make you ponder, most intriguingly, is the question of whether – given that we treat it so disrespectfully – we really like music all that much' *New Humanist*

'This engrossing book is a history of recording technology and an examination of the high-fidelity fallacy ... *Perfecting Sound Forever* is an unashamedly anoraky book. As an unashamed anorak, that's high praise' *Literary Review*

'This is such a gorgeous book. I cannot recommend this book highly enough' Rhod Sharp, BBC Radio 5 Live, *Up All Night*

'Fascinating ... a rich blend of commerce, ideology, technology and creativity' *Sunday Times*

'Lively, passionate and ever-questioning ... the book is pieced together with such energy and spirit that you often forget you're reading about sound waves. From Edison's tone test techniques to Spector's Wall of Sound, this is an accessible, well-informed and unique perspective' *Record Collector*

'Milner's appreciation of music is wide and deep ... [his] passionate love of music resonates throughout, and he provides illuminating answers to questions that are poorly understood. The blurb claims that *Perfecting Sound Forever* "will change the way we think about music" and, when the din dies down, you find that it has' *Guardian*

'A compelling and thoroughly rewarding read for any music freak fascinated by the recording and manipulation of sound ... [Milner] covers a phenomenal number of seismic shifts in our sonic landscape' *Time Out*

Perfecting Sound Forever

The Story of Recorded Music

Greg Milner

GRANTA

Granta Publications, 12 Addison Avenue, London W11 4QR

First published in Great Britain by Granta Books, 2009
First published in the United States by Faber and Faber, Inc., 2009
This paperback edition published by Granta Books, 2010

Grateful acknowledgment is made to Simon Howson for permission
to print the images on pages 281 and 286.

A CIP catalogue record for this book
is available from the British Library.

3 5 7 9 10 8 6 4

ISBN 978 1 84708 140 7

Text designed by Jonathan D. Lippincott

Printed and bound in Great Britain by CPI Group (UK) Ltd, Croydon, CR0 4YY

Contents

Liner Notes

The story goes that, late in his life, Guglielmo Marconi had an epiphany. The godfather of radio technology decided that no sound ever dies. It just decays beyond the point that we can detect it with our ears. Any sound was forever recoverable, he believed, with the right device. His dream was to build one powerful enough to pick up Christ's Sermon on the Mount.

On the most basic level, Marconi was wrong. Sound is just change in air pressure that we interpret as information. The air is disturbed, but it always rights itself. The air always wins. But to say that a sound dies implies that it was once alive, and that's not quite right, either. Sound waves are energy, and in our universe energy is never created or destroyed—it just changes form. The energy of a sound wave is absorbed by the air molecules until we can't hear it anymore, but nothing has really died. And if death never occurred, doesn't it stand to reason that the sound lives on somehow?

Raw sound may not have much of a shelf life, but Marconi's theory surely does. It survives as a low-level urban legend, bandied about in dorm rooms and Internet forums. I thought it was true before I even knew who Marconi was, and I have no idea where I learned it. Maybe you've always believed it, too. Its survival attests to a universal desire and anxiety. Our time on Earth is fleeting, the impressions we leave on it are ephemeral, but maybe there is a part of us that can outlast this dust-to-dust. Maybe our complete history is all around us. We just need to learn how to read it.

We don't have Marconi's magic sound-reviver, but we do have recordings, those documents of the air pressure changes before the energy is swallowed up forever. We've had them since Thomas Edison's phonograph, the first machine ever to capture that mechanical energy and reproduce it later, seemingly *creating energy* in a world that forbids it. Maybe the phonograph was the most utopian invention in human history up to that point. While Marconi's dream lies dormant, the Edisonian dream lives on.

This is a book about the evolution of that dream, and its effect on music. It is not an exhaustive history of recording technology or the art of record production, although those subjects play a large role in this story. And it's certainly not about every sonic innovator who's ever committed music to tape, disk, or hard drive. It is an attempt to find some of the important fault lines in the narrative of "recorded history"—the points where people with access to the technology decided that *this* was how recordings should sound, and *this* is what it means to make a record. Ultimately, this is the story of what it means to make a recording of music—a *representation* of music—and declare it to be music itself.

As for Marconi's dream—it remains just that. Here in the early twenty-first century, there's no sign of progress on that front. But who knows—maybe in a few hundred or thousand or million years one of our descendants will discover that Marconi was right. Legions of microphones will then comb the ether, extracting every musical sound made by anyone, anywhere, ever. It will be the ultimate box set. By then, I imagine we'll download music directly into our minds. Still, I hope it gets released on vinyl.

Perfecting Sound Forever

Intro: "Testing, Testing . . ."

The turntable of the talking machines is comparable to the potter's wheel: a tone-mass is formed upon them both, and for each the material is preexisting. But the finished tone/clay container that is produced in this manner remains empty. It is only filled by the hearer.
—Theodor Adorno

The first thing the universe did was cut a record.

For 400,000 years after the big bang, all of creation was a hot, dense, soupy substance that trapped light. It also conducted sound. The pressure from the initial blast pushed on pockets of hot gas. The gas resisted and pushed back. The resulting vibrations filled the cosmos with the sound of celestial bells.

In the same manner that a handful of stones scattered in a pond generates overlapping ripples, the sound waves that caused the cosmic hum spread out through space as ripples of excess matter. It was in these ripples that galaxies were most likely to form. As the universe cooled, the matter was frozen in place. Sound now traveled much slower than light. Astronomers refer to this as the period when the universe "recombined." They could just as well say "remixed."

The initial recording session took about a million years. One of the songs it produced was us (the rough tracks, anyway). Like the sound waves inscribed in the grooves of a vinyl record, we live in the galactic ripples. Our prehistory is frozen sound.

Or maybe a compact disc is a better model for who we are. Unlike a phonograph's stylus, which moves from the disc's edge to its center, the laser that reads a CD begins at the center and moves outward. The primordial sound wave of the big bang is now around 500 million light-years across, reverberating throughout the still-expanding universe. The tone is too faint and low to be heard without the most sensitive equipment, but it's out there and all around us. The final mix isn't complete, and we don't know how the record ends.

Around 13.7 billion years later, Thomas Alva Edison, working in his laboratory in West Orange, New Jersey, shouted "Mary Had a Little Lamb" into a mouthpiece. The sound was etched onto wax paper and played back, making Edison the first human being to record a sound and reproduce it. A few months later, he unveiled the first phonograph, which he used to record a remake of the poem, this time onto tinfoil. And on a Friday evening thirty-eight years after that, an Edison phonograph convinced several hundred people in nearby Montclair that a recording could sound like life itself.

The concert was by invitation only. If you were there, it was because someone at the Phonograph Sales Company, the local purveyor of Edison audio products and the sponsor of the event, thought you were among a better class of people. The featured performers were the contralto Christine Miller, the violinist Arthur Walsh, and the flutist Harold Lyman. As people filed into the hall of the Montclair Club on September 17, 1915, the real headliner was already onstage, front and center: an Edison Diamond Disc Phonograph in a wood cabinet.

The Diamond Disc Phonograph was no ordinary "talking machine," a term that Edison considered an insult to what was nothing less than a musical instrument. He and his hand-picked research team had spent years developing it, doing hundreds of tests and making countless adjustments to arrive at a machine that sounded perfect. They had even invented a new type of resin for the discs themselves. The Diamond Disc Phonograph was perfect because it "disappeared" every time you played it. The machine was a neutral conduit. It heard everything, and added and subtracted nothing, issuing music so pure that Edison was confident it could withstand the toughest challenge.

Tonight's concert was billed as a "tone test."

Verdi E. B. Fuller, the head of the phonograph division at Edison's company, walked onstage. "Ladies and gentlemen," he said, "the mere fact of sound reproduction no longer has novelty, but there has lately been developed by Mr. Edison a new art of recording and re-creating all forms of sound. You are invited here to listen to a new sound-recreating instrument in which Mr. Edison's new art is embodied."

The invitations had mentioned something about this, some sort of comparison between the live voice and its reproduced facsimile. Fuller told the audience that Edison's machine could "hear" as sensitively as the human ear, and could therefore reproduce a sound that was indistinguishable from the original. "I shall demonstrate to you that the characteristic tone of every musical instrument can be faithfully re-created," he said, adding, "The reproduction of the human voice is equally faithful."

Fuller brought Miller onstage and cued up a recording of her singing "O Rest in the Lord," an aria from Mendelssohn's *Elijah*. The record began, and Miller let it play for a while. She began singing along with it, and then stopped. There were audible gasps from the audience. It was uncanny how closely Miller's recorded voice mirrored the sounds coming from her mouth onstage. The record continued playing, with Miller onstage dipping in and out of it like a DJ. The audience cheered every time she stopped moving her lips and let the record sing for her. Then she did the same thing with a recording of herself singing Liddle's "Abide With Me."

She took a break and Fuller introduced Walsh, who soloed over a recording of *Ave Maria*. After Lyman took his turn, Miller returned to sing "Ah! Mon Fils" and some Scottish folk songs. Lyman and Walsh performed together, and then it was time for Miller's finale. Fuller put on a recording of Miller singing Foster's "The Old Folks at Home." Her voice issued forth, loud and strong, from the phonograph's bell . . .

> Way down upon the Swanee River,
> Far, far, away
> That's where my heart is yearning ever,
> Home where the old folks stay

The Miller onstage began to sing with the Miller in the machine. As the mechanical Miller sang, flesh-and-blood Miller continued her bait-and-switch. The audience craned forward to see when her lips stopped moving. It was the only way they could tell when she wasn't singing. As the song neared its end, at a point when both Millers were singing, the audience received one final surprise. The stage lights went down. The audience was now staring into darkness as the music continued. Only their ears could guide them, and their ears failed them. The lights came up, and there was Miller, her mouth frozen in a smile.

When had she stopped singing?

The crowd went wild.

What happened that night in Montclair was repeated thousands of times between 1915 and 1925, in cities and towns of all sizes, first in the United States and later around the world. In 1920 alone, the peak year of the tests, twenty-five sets of artists performed two thousand tests. The tone test procedure was always the same—artists signed to Edison's record company performed for free, accompanied by their recorded voices emitting from the bell of a Diamond Disc Phonograph—and the goal was always the same: to prove that the Edison Diamond Disc Phonograph had reached the apex of audio perfection, by fooling listeners into thinking they were hearing the real thing.

Tone tests were eventually held in towns too small to host professional musicians. For some people, a tone test was their first major live music event; for many others, it was the first time they'd been invited to hear expensive recorded sound and to think about it critically. Like hardcore bands in the early eighties going wherever a punk kid could book an American Legion hall, the tone tests would come to you (probably playing in those same American Legion halls), as long as there was a local Edison dealer willing to do some legwork.

Some whispered then, and many more would concur today, that trickery made the tone tests work. One of the cardinal rules of the tests was that the phonograph should always be running; it was the musicians who started and stopped as it played continuously. Anna Case, an opera singer and Edison recording artist who performed at the most famous tone test, at Carnegie Hall in 1920, is generally credited with launching the tone-test concept a few years earlier, when she dropped by an Iowa record store that happened to be playing one of her records, and performed a duet with herself. "When I walked in the door, I started singing with the record and making my voice sound exactly like it," she recalled almost sixty years later. This became a key tenet of the tests. While the phonograph played, the singer would strive to imitate the sonic characteristics of the record, such as the "pinched" quality it lent to voices. This was a subtle inversion of the whole point of the tone tests, which was to show that it could imitate life perfectly. In practice, the tone tests posited the sound of the machine as the baseline, and subsumed the sound of "reality" within it.

It took a real effort by the performers to maintain the illusion that the machine was dominant. Even at a large event like Carnegie Hall, a human voice could dwarf the Diamond Disc. "I remember I stood right by the machine," Case said. "The audience was there, and there was nobody on stage with me. The machine played and I sang with it. Of course, if I had sung loud, it would have been louder than the machine, but I gave my voice the same quality as the machine so they couldn't tell."

Vocal tricks undoubtedly explained some of the tone tests' success, but we should consider the constantly playing phonograph as less a trick than a manifesto. The phonograph had begun as a means to document a musical performance, to offer a representation of the "real," but Edison was telling the world that this equation no longer held. From now on, recordings would not sound like the world; the world would sound like recordings.

In the fall of 2005, ninety years after the Montclair tone test, I went searching for its echoes. The loudest reverberation could be found a few miles up the Garden State Parkway from Montclair and the Oranges, in Michael Fremer's basement. Fremer is a writer who often reviews high-end audio equipment, the editor of MusicAngle.com, and an early anti-CD gadfly who still preaches the gospel in his "Analog Corner" column in *Stereophile*. Fremer invited me to his house to hear the Caliburn, a new turntable made by the Australian company Continuum Audio Labs. He said it was the best turntable he had ever heard—and at $90,000, it happened to be the most expensive turntable ever made.

The many minds that developed the Caliburn include more than just audio experts. There was the guy who builds vacuum control mechanisms for particle accelerators, who applied his knowledge to the Caliburn's external vacuum unit. There was the expert in magnetic circuits who devised a unique method of driving the platter, and the metallurgist who in consultation with the *Journal of Metals* "editorial advisor for magnesium" came up with the precise alloy for the chassis, deemed optimal for damping energy and minimizing vibrations. An aeronautical engineer led the design team, which used advanced three-dimensional shape-optimization software—originally developed to study stresses in aircraft wings and fuselages—to determine everything from where to place the feet to how best to isolate the platter. Artificially intelligent reshaping algorithms were used to design the tonearm, which works on a diamond pivot system used in advanced aircraft instruments. A computerized external control unit constantly monitors the entire system.

The Caliburn itself really costs only $65,000. The extra $25,000 gets you the optional but highly recommended "Castellon"—a chromed aluminum stand designed for the turntable and its components, and the product of as much advanced technology as the components. The goal of the team that designed it was to prevent any—and they mean *any*—external vibrations from impacting the system. If there were a way to make a 160-pound turntable float in space, completely divorced from the corrupting vibrations of the material world, they would have found it. Instead, they used two opposing magnetic plates that levitate the shelf on which the turntable rests, augmented by other methods that Continuum won't reveal, but which are rumored to be so sophisticated that manufacturers of dark-matter detectors are interested.

Continuum is an appropriate name, because there is a direct link between the Caliburn in Fremer's basement and the Diamond Disc that wowed the audience in nearby Montclair nearly a century earlier. Continuum's stated goal—"release every last nuance of recorded information without adding additional artifacts"—describes exactly what Edison wanted to do. He believed that a perfect recording could provide music that was truer, purer, realer than the musical event it documented. It could provide a direct link to the music's essence, collapsing the real and metaphorical distance between the singer onstage and the listener in the audience. Like the Caliburn practically hovering on the Castillon, the Diamond Disc could capture only the vibrations of the music, not the unwanted vibrations of the material world. It could release everything and add nothing.

Edison was just as certain as Continuum that he was very close to this exalted state. This mutual belief is no more an indictment of Edison's naïveté than it is of Continuum's hubris, because the quest is fundamentally quixotic. We can never be certain that we have drawn out every last bit of reality from a recording. The proof is in the ongoing analog-versus-digital debate. From the earliest days of digital audio, advocates of digital have been able to "prove" objectively, by a comparison of waveforms, that they have perfectly captured and preserved music. But there was a time when many people believed that the Diamond Disc was perfect, and who is to say they were wrong? Perhaps in another hundred years Continuum's perfect sound will seem as quaintly imperfect as Edison's does today.

To understand how this schism can occur, consider that Continuum and Edison are linked not only by their goals but also by the technology used to achieve them. Like any analog audio device, the Caliburn builds on the same technology Edison used to record "Mary Had a Little Lamb" on wax paper. Edison's voice caused a diaphragm to vibrate. This diaphragm was attached to a stylus that responded to these vibrations by etching a pattern into wax paper. This pattern was "analogous" to—and therefore an "analog" of—the sound waves that caused the diaphragm to vibrate. During playback, the stylus followed that pattern, causing the diaphragm to create vibrations that re-created—shakily, but clearly enough—the original sound waves in the air. A vinyl LP played on a Caliburn is a copy of a master disc that was created by a stylus responding to the vibrations created by the sound of a master tape. During playback, the Caliburn's stylus traces these analog grooves to re-create an analog of the original sounds on the master tape.

For all the advanced technology of the Caliburn, the biggest difference between it and the Diamond Disc is the presence of electricity. The grooves on a Diamond Disc were the direct result of sound waves exerting force on a diaphragm. The playback stylus similarly caused vibrations, which were naturally amplified by the phonograph's horn. The Caliburn, like any modern turntable, works by turning the vibrations of the stylus on the record's grooves into a series of fluctuating voltages. Picked up by an amplifier, this current causes your speaker cones to vibrate in a way that mimics the original sound wave. Though separated by more than a century, both machines operate on the same basic analog principles.

In the early twentieth century, this distinction between acoustic and electrical recordings seemed significant. Edison, for example, hated the idea of electrical recording. Acoustic versus electrical was the original recording dialectic, with proponents of the former arguing for the purity and transparency of the acoustic process, against the supposedly corrupting effects of the electrical. Today, with acoustic recording a distant historical memory, acoustic versus electrical has become analog versus digital. The analog mind-set, of which the Caliburn is an extreme example, argues for the "purity" of a vinyl disc—made and played using electrical analog methods—against the supposed corruption of even the most carefully manufactured compact disc played on the most sophisticated CD player.

Edison was on the wrong side of history, although he didn't know it. If you own a Caliburn, you are on the wrong side of history, and you're proud of it. Although you advocate a technology that Edison despised, it is you who are the Edisonian. You are even more marginalized than Edison, and you pay for the privilege. You're like a tribe forced onto a reservation, speaking a dying language while the world speaks digital Esperanto.

Fremer is fluent in both tongues. He played me the Caliburn in his basement crammed with records, CDs, and audio equipment. He'd set up a system with a total value of more than $200,000, including a $12,000 preamp, a $31,000 phono preamp, and a $23,000 amplifier. The pair of speakers, which each stood several feet high, cost $45,000. Even the cables connecting all of this were worth a few thousand dollars.

He cued up an Irma Thomas record and dropped the needle. She started singing about how time was on her side, yes it was, and it sounded like . . . what, exactly?

Well, it didn't sound like Irma Thomas was standing in front of me. It was more like it sounded the way Irma Thomas was supposed to sound. The sound was *total*. If there was a way to inhabit the music, to live in it, this was what it was like.

Fremer spent the next few hours putting on records—Steely Dan, Roy Orbison, Elvis Presley, Elvis Costello, Shellac, the Smiths, Bruce Springsteen, the Rolling Stones, XTC, the Clash—one after another. Most of these were records I'd heard before, but I realized I had never *really* heard them. Nirvana's *Nevermind* had never sounded fiercer; that two-note guitar phrase that leads into the chorus of "Smells Like Teen Spirit" was like an air-raid siren. The snare crack that begins the bridge on Elvis Costello's "Accidents Will Happen" did the proverbial leap out of the speakers. Shellac's "Prayer to God," recorded to emphasize the three-dimensional sense of musicians playing together in a room, now seemed to both stretch the space between them and make them sound more intimately connected. Oddly, hearing the Smiths' "How Soon Is Now?" was most revelatory. Johnny Marr's unrelenting tremolo effect made the room shimmer. A recurring riff in the song that I'd always assumed was played on a piano now revealed itself to be somebody hitting a vibraphone so hard you could hear the mallet swing through the air.

But did it sound "live"? Would the Caliburn pass a tone test? No, and I don't think that anyone with twenty-first-century ears would think otherwise. If nothing else, the sound of the stylus on vinyl—a mechanical reality that even $90,000 cannot completely eliminate—would be a giveaway. Although the sound of the live Springsteen album Fremer put on uncannily re-created what it's like to be in the middle of a loud rock show—the Caliburn could handle all the distortions and overtones so that even the lack of clarity seemed realistic—imitating the sound of "reality" didn't seem like the point. When listening to something designed to extract every bit of sonic information from a recording, you realize that most recordings aren't even made to sound "live." If Elvis Presley had actually been singing "Fever" in front of me, I would not have been able to hear the jangle of the jewelry on his wrists. If I had seen the Clash at the Palladium in 1980, I wouldn't have been able to hear so clearly both the sound of Paul Simonon's fingers sliding on the bass strings and the growl of Joe Strummer's ragged throat. And I can't imagine a real-world experience sounding anything remotely like the sea of reverb in which Roy Orbison was fighting to stay afloat, and which was faithfully reproduced by the Caliburn.

What really struck me about the Caliburn is how closely it made me listen. I couldn't think about anything else but the music. For comparison, Fremer played some Super Audio CDs on a high-end CD player, and although they sounded great, my mind wandered. Wordsworth famously described poetry as "the spontaneous overflow of powerful feelings: it takes its origin from emotion recollected in tranquillity," and that's what this felt like. The sound of reality comes at you all at once, but records organize the sound into something more ideal, and the Caliburn knew how to make those sounds really sing. What came out of the speakers was an ideal world. This was the way life could sound. This was the way life did sound.

I wish I could listen to it right now.

———————

Still, I would be remiss if I didn't admit that a spectral $90,000 seemed to float above the room the whole time I was listening to the Caliburn. I couldn't help wondering whether I was cowed by that figure; it's hard to argue with that much capital. Like Verdi Fuller ninety years earlier, the Caliburn, by virtue of its cost and the huge brain trust behind it, practically "told" me that the sound would be amazing. As I'm guessing was the case with many in the tone-test audiences, I *wanted* to have a transcendent experience, and if I didn't have one, didn't that reflect badly on me? I wonder if this feeling on a large scale helped the tone tests work. Because let's face it—it's difficult to conceive how so many people could have been tricked by music that sounds, to our ears, like a scratchy, faint version of live sound.

That they could and we can't says as much about the sound of our world as it does about theirs. We have an ingrained awareness of recorded music that people didn't have in 1915. The world is saturated with recordings. If you live in a society that is even semi-industrialized, recordings define the sound of your musical world. As the planet's population becomes more urban and less rural, the recorded world will only get louder. The recording is the closest thing we have to a universal musical condition.

Glenn Gould articulated this state of affairs in "The Prospects of Recording," a remarkably prescient manifesto published in 1966, in which he mocked the posturing of symphonic albums that "eschew . . . splices and other mechanical adventures, and hence are decidedly moral," that flaunt their "live-ness and confirm the faith of the heroically unautomated." He declared the LP to be the modern embodiment of music, announced the imminent death of "the habit of concert-going and concert-giving, both as a social institution and a chief symbol of musical mercantilism," and predicted that tomorrow's children would ridicule the idea that "the concert is the axis upon which the world of music revolves."

He was right. Forty years later, there is still plenty of live music, but whereas that audience in Montclair nearly a century ago collectively perceived recordings as *representations* of music, for their descendants the representation *is* music. A child in Montclair may consume hundreds of hours of mediated music—via stereos, iPods, the radio, MTV, and the many public places where music is broadcast—before ever witnessing a live music event. To a Montclair baby, "live" music is heard through the prism of the recorded.

In this environment, why should anyone but audiophiles strive to make a recording sound like real life? For genres like hip-hop and techno that arose in the years since Gould's prediction, "live" is a meaningless concept; what's contained on the record is not a document of a real-time event because there never *was* a real-time event. An average radio pop song may have the structure of a self-contained performance, of musicians playing off one another, but there is a good chance that none of these musicians were ever in the same room at the same time—if the record contains samples, the musicians may be separated by *decades*—so what event, exactly, is the record recording? If you're the sort of purist—musician or listener—who "eschews splices and other mechanical adventures" (and I've been there myself), yours is a lonely musical road.

Recorded music began with a paradox, one that Edison explored and exploited relentlessly: How can a representation of music be as real and authentic as the music it represents? Every recording is an attempt to come to terms with this paradox; even if, like the aforementioned genres, it rejects the idea of recording something real, it still defines itself in relation to that tradition. How you solve that riddle represents your ideal of perfect sound. Every record is its own tone test, a challenge that proclaims: *This* is music. If we pretend otherwise, if we think of records as just collections of sounds, inert objects devoid of ideology, then we are as clueless as Edison's crowds. It's easy enough to laugh at the tin ears of rubes in 1915, but try a little experiment of your own.

Turn on the radio and listen to the first singer you hear. Really listen to the voice. Try to edit out the sound of the other instruments and concentrate on how the voice sounds. Now turn down the volume and imagine what it would sound like if the same person was standing in front of you singing an a cappella version of the same song. Think about the grain and texture of this naked voice as it plays in your head. Now turn the volume back up. You'll probably be amazed at how inhuman the voice sounds coming out of the speakers. If you're listening to a song on a station that plays new or fairly recent rock, pop, or R&B, it will likely sound even weirder because there is a very strong chance that the vocals were processed during the recording or mixing process with Auto-Tune, a software program that automatically corrects a singer's pitch, which can create a very inhuman droning effect. All this time, you've been listening to distinctly inhuman voices and thinking of them as human.

How do we do this? How do we will ourselves to flunk a tone test that never ends? In 1985, the critic Edward Rothstein listened to a high-end stereo system, marveled at the impressive sound, and puzzled over how Edison could work his tone-test tricks with a system that to our ears would sound scratchy and hollow. He concluded that we all learn a "language of recording," so that when a recording is played, "the listener translates, mapping the heard sounds into a real world, placing the distorted frequencies into a mouth or instrument, and reconstructing sound and its intention." A few years earlier, H. Stith Bennett, a sociologist, had given a name to this phenomenon: "recording consciousness," which he defined as a sense of how to tune our ears in a "society that is literally wired for sound."

Maybe that explains how the tone tests could work. Those audiences had not yet developed a recording consciousness and were thus highly suggestible. But one could just as easily argue the opposite: Without a recording consciousness, wouldn't the sounds coming from the phonograph seem so odd and alien that the audiences could never believe they sounded lifelike?

Since there's no way to know what cognitive experience those audiences were having, let's modify the inquiry. Rather than wondering how audiences could be fooled, let's ask why Edison wanted to fool them. The question isn't as obvious as it might seem. Rather than convince them that the Diamond Disc sounded exactly like life, Edison could have touted his machine's ability to provide a completely unique musical experience, a machine that allowed listeners to experience music in a way that "reality" could never provide. Why didn't he?

A clue lies in the tone-test-like events that came after Edison, and the people who initiated them. Bell Telephone Laboratories tricked audiences with electrically recorded music in the thirties. Ampex engineers did the same thing with magnetic tape twenty years later. In the early eighties, one of the first people to sell compact discs in this country did the trick in a Denver theater with a digital recording standing in for the band onstage. Notice the pattern here: these are all people involved in the audio-industrial complex, people whose jobs involve thinking of new ways to organize and package sound—processing it electrically, affixing it to magnetic tape, or putting it into a jewel case. Les Paul, the first musician to fully embrace the possibilities of magnetic tape, liked the way it could layer sounds; his early records, although they benefit from tape's improved fidelity, are more notable for how otherworldly they sound. Digital editing, the legacy of the CD, is now so advanced that it can make a completely constructed studio recording masquerade as virtually live-in-the-studio, but the most innovative uses of digital audio in the music-making process have been in the service of making sounds that don't sound "natural" at all.

It is the technicians and businesspeople, rather than the artists, who have perpetuated the tone-test tradition. This is not to their discredit. Recorded music is as much science as art, and a successful tone test provides the sort of empirically verifiable results that science demands. But it's worth asking why it is the nonmusicians who have tended to treat recorded music as something that could sound like what your ear considers "real." Why is the challenge always "live" or "Memorex," "real" or "constructed"? And why is the ultimate goal to trick you into hearing the two as the same?

The answer might be in our heads.

At root, every sound is evidence of work: something exerts energy, and the fruit of that labor is a vibration that we call a sound wave. Vibrations can occur in any environment where there is mass and elasticity; the mass is displaced by a force and is motivated by elasticity to return to its original position. But the mass itself does not move with the wave. (Imagine a stadium full of fans doing "the wave," creating an illusion of a flowing wave simply by standing up and sitting down.)

When a sound wave is generated, the mass is the air itself—or rather, the billions of particles that comprise the air—and the elasticity is the natural tendency of the particles to return to a stable position. These are the characteristics of any sound wave, whether caused by the big bang or by John Bonham's drum intro to Led Zeppelin's version of Memphis Minnie's "When the Levee Breaks." Those two particular sounds are alike in other ways: they are both epic and epochal, and each has been cited as evidence of the hand of God (and in Bonham's case, also His right foot). The latter is easier for us to conceive (though nearly as unlikely to ever be repeated), so let's examine the work performed by Bonham, and its effect on us.

You are very lucky. It is sometime in the early seventies, and you are at a mansion in the English village of Headley. The members of Led Zeppelin are here to make their fourth album, and they have invited you along to watch. Today they will record Bonham's drum part for "When the Levee

Breaks." The band wants Bonham's drums to have a booming, reverb-heavy sound. (This is an unusual choice for the time, since the trend in records is toward drums that sound dry, with little resonance.) To achieve the desired effect, they place the drums at the bottom of a stairwell, with the microphone hanging three stories up. You are in the stairwell, a few feet away from the drums. The only person who will be closer to the sound is Bonham.

The engineer announces that the tape is rolling. Bonham counts off the rhythm and then slams his foot down on his kick drum's pedal to begin the beat. Let's freeze time at this exact moment and analyze the next 1/30,000th of a second, roughly the amount of time that elapses each time our hearing system takes a reading. What exactly is happening?

The pedal causes the mallet to strike the kick drum with a force that only Bonham, it would seem, can generate. The skin of the drum impacts the air particles around it. There are a lot of them—400 billion billion just in the cubic inch around the area where the mallet has hit. Like any other sonic source, Bonham's drum has caused a disturbance in the air. The particles are very disturbed. They're rocking—literally. Imagine each attached to its own spring mechanism. The first particle to be impacted is knocked off its unique and stable position in the universe. It swings forward, and then is pulled back by its spring. It overshoots its original position on the way back, is pulled back again by the spring, and attempts to find its original spot. Its initial surge forward has thrown it up against the particle next to it, and that particle begins the same process. There's real slapstick comedy here—particles all knocking one another out of place like circus clowns.

We'll follow the wave into one of your ears.

The wave travels a little more than two centimeters through the ear canal and arrives at your tympanic membrane, otherwise known as the eardrum. The wave vibrates the eardrum, which transfers the vibration to a tiny bone attached to it on the other side. This bone is connected to two others; the three are known informally (and, for our example, appropriately) as the hammer, anvil, and stirrup. The hammer transfers the vibrations to the anvil, which sends them to the stirrup. The stirrup covers the entrance to the inner ear. It is in the inner ear that these vibrations begin to become information. (The inner ear also regulates your sense of balance, an important task at this moment, since Bonham's drumming is about to give you simulated whiplash.)

To understand what happens next, we need an understanding of some of the properties of waves. Every wave has an amplitude and a frequency. The amplitude is a measure of the power of the wave, the degree to which it disturbs the medium in which it propagates. For sound waves, that medium is air, so amplitude corresponds to the pressure changes the wave causes in the air. We perceive amplitude as volume. The relationship isn't linear—that is, we can't simply say the greater the amplitude, the louder the sound—but for now, just think of the amplitude of a sound wave as an expression of soft and loud, usually expressed in a unit called the decibel (dB).

A wave's frequency describes the time it takes to complete one cycle of vibration before beginning to vibrate again. The frequency of a sound wave corresponds to its pitch. A low frequency sounds like bass, a high frequency sounds like treble. Frequency is denoted in cycles per second, or hertz (Hz). (Groupings of a thousand cycles per second are often expressed in kilohertz, or kHz.) Thus the lowest sound human beings can hear, 20 Hz, is caused by a wave that vibrates back and forth 20 times in one second. The upper limit of human hearing is 20 kHz (though for most people it is much lower), caused by a wave that vibrates 20,000 times in one second.

For the purposes of this book, think of the amplitude as the "height" of the wave, a measure of its power, which we perceive as volume; and think of frequency as the wave's "width," the distance it travels back and forth when it vibrates, which we perceive as pitch.

The inner ear is barely the size of a grape. Within it lies a snail-shell-shaped organ called the cochlea, filled with fluid and bisected by a membrane that varies in length from half a millimeter on one end to 1/25th of a millimeter on the other. The vibrations from the stirrup displace the fluid. The way this fluid is displaced allows your auditory system to determine loudness and pitch. Bonham's vibrations begin to become something we can understand, thanks to thousands of hair cells in the cochlea that make synaptic connections with the auditory nerve. As far as you are concerned, Bonham's blast is no longer a wave. It is now a series of electrical impulses.

The nerve endings of the auditory nerve interface with various cells, which eventually connect to a part of your brain called the medial geniculate body. From there, nerve fibers carry the signal to the auditory region of your cerebral cortex. It is here, after this arduous journey of vibrations begetting more vibrations and then finally electrical signals, that the sound

of Bonham's kick drum finally becomes "real" to you. When his stick slams
down on the snare, and his foot makes the kick drum thunder once more,
and his other foot and other stick work the hi-hat cymbal to tie it all
together, your brain starts to hear that distinctive rhythm that changed
music forever. Soon, your brain will send an urgent message that says:
You've never heard a human being make a sound like this before.

You're probably itching to speed up time and let that happen, but before
you do, consider what it would mean for an Edison tone test to set this
process in motion. Like all sounds, the blast that Bonham has generated is
evidence of work, but Bonham is not the only relevant laborer. Without the
work that you have done with your ears, all Bonham has done is make the
air vibrate. For the tone tests to succeed, Edison would have to "own" your
labor, the work you do to turn that vibration into something meaningful. He
would need to convince you that the Diamond Disc Phonograph was as sensitive as your ear. He would have to say, in essence, "The work that your
ear does to process the complex vibrations we call 'music'—this machine
can do that just as well."

This would be a great accomplishment. The human ear, as yours has
amply demonstrated in this one microsecond, is an enormously complex
apparatus. Two ways to describe the power of a sound wave are by intensity,
the amount of power (watts) generated over a fixed distance, and by sound
pressure level (SPL), the amount of force (dynes) exerted on the air molecules. Someone with normal hearing can detect a sound so soft that its
intensity is a mere 1/10,000th of a millionth of a millionth watts per square
centimeter. That sound has an SPL of just .0002 dynes, 140 million times
smaller than the force needed to support an object weighing one ounce
against the force of gravity. An audible sound at 3,000 Hz, the frequency at
which our ears are most sensitive, can move the eardrum as little as 1/10th
of the diameter of a hydrogen molecule.

So the human ear is no joke. If Edison could create something as sensitive as your ear, that would really be something. But it would not be
enough. For the tone test to work, he also needs to "own" your brain. And
therein lies the real challenge.

Scientists have a decent understanding of how the ear handles vibrations, how those vibrations are translated into electrical pulses, and where
those pulses go, but there is still much they don't know about how those
pulses are processed. How is it that you, down in the stairwell, will process

Bonham's thunderous blasts and recognize them as forming a backbeat? How will you compare that backbeat with your memories of other backbeats and conclude that this is something very different, very *heavy*? And how exactly do you even know what heavy feels like? How will your brain pick up on the way Bonham is dragging the beats out until he is almost—but not quite—behind the beat? And most important: Why will this make your body move, your head bob up and down? Why will "When the Levee Breaks" make you feel good?

We enter this world with a remarkably sophisticated grasp of music. Tests have shown that a baby's nervous system arrives pre-equipped to form a musical grammar. Babies can recognize and remember tunes, display a preference for consonance over dissonance, and even identify individual scales and chords. These results suggest to scientists that the perception of music is an evolutionarily ancient neural skill, not some by-product of more recent cognitive processes. Music, and our sense of what it sounds like, begins for us as a way to comprehend the world around us—to recognize patterns and make accurate predictions about what comes next, for example—and survives as something we can enjoy for its own sake. Music is first a means to form a worldview, to represent the world, to ponder and study it—to "record" it. Only later does music become "music."

The discovery that music appreciation is a naturally selected trait buried deep in our lizard brain would not surprise many of the key players in the history of recorded sound, particularly those whose work has involved Edisonian attempts to mechanically (or computationally) create sounds that perfectly mimic organic sounds. The Synclavier, developed in the seventies, was the first fully digital synthesizer, and an early incarnation of today's ubiquitous digital audio workstations, such as Pro Tools. One goal of the Synclavier's developers was to synthesize credible versions of acoustic instruments. Sydney Alonso, who designed the Synclavier's hardware, recalled that after one or two years of perpetual exposure to synthetic violin attempts, which he felt were steadily approaching the real thing, it hit him: "Jesus, this doesn't sound anything like a violin!" Why had the sound seemed perfect—or at least passable—for so long? He decided that it was because we are hardwired to identify sounds quickly and slot them into familiar categories. "It's a psychoacoustic fact that we process the first few milliseconds of a sound, and then relax after that," he says today. "You can imagine the people in the jungle who could avoid tigers were the ones who quickly [hear a sound], decide it's a tiger, and jump. The others wouldn't make it."

"It all goes back to evolution," says Cameron Jones, the mastermind behind the Synclavier's software. "Do I hear a tiger breathing up in that tree and am I about to be someone's lunch, or is that a bird rustling? Human beings evolved with a great capacity to differentiate sounds extremely quickly. Sound sums up the whole human condition, really."

In fact, the sound of music may be an essential element of the human condition. Scientists have recently studied the pleasurable chills-down-the-spine feeling that occurs when you hear a piece of music you love. Using brain imaging, researchers at the Montreal Neurological Institute demonstrated that when this sensation occurs, the parts of the brain that are active include those that process reward and motivation—including biologically motivated rewards such as sexual stimulation and food. This startling discovery has launched the search for a connection between music and brain processes that ensure reproduction of the species and nourishment of the body. The emerging theory suggests that listening to music involves a complex interaction between two types of neural systems: those that analyze patterns and help us form representations of the world; and more primal systems, from earlier stages of evolution, that assess what any given stimulus means for the organism's survival, and what action should be taken.

If this is correct, it means that the music we like helps us articulate, on the most basic human level, what we think the world around us *is*, and also what it *means*. Your auditory cortex tells you that the noise bombarding you at Headley Grange is a rhythm, while something buried deep within your brain, something almost reptilian, tells you that the shit is heavy.

This is what Edison needed to capture to make the tone tests work—not just the ears of his audiences but their brains as well.

In the one second that has elapsed since Bonham began playing, your brain has done as much work as Bonham to make the sound "real." Without your brain, all he has done is create pressure changes in the air of that stairwell. Standing nearby, you get to experience this event directly. For the rest of us, there is an added level of abstraction; devoid of the context you experience in front of the drums, we will still make the sound "real." We'll buy the fourth Led Zeppelin album, or we'll hear "When the Levee Breaks" on the radio. The sound will travel through our ears and brains, and then it will filter through our recording consciousness, the set of beliefs we have developed about what sounds good. Years later, we'll hear that same rhythm recycled as digital samples. Faced with yet another abstraction, we'll still recognize it, and decide how much of whatever it was that you heard when you stood in front of Bonham still exists.

Layers upon layers of cognition, each one a provocation, an opportunity to use our ears, those constantly reappraising organs, to decide if the music sounds "real" to us. For you, communing with Led Zeppelin at Headley Grange, the music is overwhelmingly real. For me, hearing the record or the digital sample, I have to decide: Are those sounds still "music" or are they now just recordings? We begin at a young age to form strong identities around music—in a way that feels so much more personal than books or movies—because the records we like say so much about our ideas of where we fit in the world. Those records help us define what we want life to sound like.

That is what Edison wanted to own, and why he wanted to trick audiences. If Edison could convince you that a Diamond Disc sounds like the way you have decided life sounds, he would own your worldview. He would own you.

There's this great word, *hysteresis*, that refers to the lag a system exhibits when a force acts upon it. If you bend back the tines of a fork, and then remove your hand, the tines spring back a little. The position of the tines is determined not just by where they are at the moment you let them go but also by where they were a moment before. The tines *remember*. That's hysteresis.

Hysteresis is particularly useful for understanding problems in ferromagnetic systems such as magnetic tape recording, the most popular method for recording music in the last half of the twentieth century. Magnetic recording works by passing magnetized particles on tape through a fluctuating electromagnetic field. The goal is for those particles to form a tidy analog of the waveform being recorded. The problem is that, thanks to hysteresis, those particles don't want to move. We're good at motivating them, and we can get them almost where we want them, but no matter what we do, the relationship between the original waveform and its analog is never quite linear. Hysteresis stands between us and our ideal copy.

Although the word sounds like *history* (it's pronounced "his-ter-EE-sis") and looks like *hysteria*, hysteresis has no etymological connection to either word. Its roots are in Greek and refer to a "shortcoming" or "to come late." But I like to think the word, when applied to recordings, encompasses all of these concepts. We want those magnetic particles to line up exactly right because we want a part of ourselves to last forever. But we can never quite create something exactly in our image—which is to say, we never get the sound exactly perfect. The world rebels, exercising its right to hysteresis. But we never stop trying. It's maddening, when you think about it.

And making a recording is just half the battle. A record is absolutely meaningless unless it is played. As an object, it signifies nothing. If you don't play a CD, it's nothing but a coaster. A record is a text that cannot be "read." It must be decoded.

This decoding is directly related to the technologies we use to do it, from tinfoil to $90,000 turntables. The goal of the decoding is always a conflation of the real and the represented, a condition that sets recorded music apart from photography and motion pictures, two other art forms that arose to question what it meant to capture reality. The movie audiences who famously jumped out of the way of the on-screen train barreling toward them quickly wised up. Today, special effects dazzle us, but they don't *really* fool us; we may not know exactly what makes the Death Star blow up, but we know there is no Death Star. Recordings, on the other hand, must trick us to work, and always ask that we suspend our disbelief. We are supposed to hear the sound of Led Zeppelin jamming together in real time. The narrative of a film might jump around in time, but a song is always linear. We're not supposed to hear the sutures. A recording is nothing until it is decoded, and what it decodes is always an illusion.

It is their ability to maintain this illusion that makes recordings unique among cultural artifacts. No other object is such an intractable combination of the subjective and the objective, the irreducible and the economically rationalized, art and science. If recordings are considered to be primarily works of art, they can signify as such only by using the prevailing technological tools of their age. If recordings are considered primarily as products of technology, science, and industry, they can be evaluated only subjectively—that is, as artworks—because what they produce is so abstract and illusory, mere pressure changes in the air. Glenn Gould said it best: "I can think of few areas of contemporary endeavor that better display the confusion with which technological man evaluates the implications of his own achievements than the great debate over music and its recorded future. Recordings deal with concepts through which the past is reevaluated, and they concern notions about the future that will ultimately question even the validity of evaluation." The train barreling toward us is us.

The hum left over from the big bang continues to pump through the speakers of space-time. Edison's phonograph, with its ability to freeze sound indefinitely, was the closest the universe had ever come to replicating that extended celestial dance mix. You had only a moment to capture the sound, but once you did you had it forever. We've been tweaking the process ever since.

The unanswered question is why the phonograph took so long to happen. Walter Murch, the great film editor and sound mixer, once remarked that all you need to record sound is some sort of lathe, a waxy surface, a sharp point for a stylus, and a resonating surface, tools available during the Renaissance, and perhaps as far back as the ancient Greeks or Egyptians. The crucial missing component was an idea that recording sound was even possible. "What held them back was a kind of mental inertia and a poetic license, because sound was the definition of that which cannot be trapped," he said. "Poetically, the beauty of music and the human voice was used as the symbol of all that's evanescent. So the idea that you could trap it in any physical medium never occurred to people until the middle of the nineteenth century."

Edison wasn't the only one to whom it occurred during the millennium's penultimate century. In 1857, Edouard-Léon Scott de Martinville, a French printer and inventor, built something he called the phonautograph. It used a stylus attached to a vibrating diaphragm to etch patterns on a rotating glass cylinder covered in carbon. The result was a "record," in that it provided a visual representation of sound, but not one that could be played.* Twenty years would pass before Edison took the next step with his phonograph, and he was almost beaten to it. Earlier in 1877, Charles Cros, another Frenchman, had described plans for a device very similar to Edi-

---

*In 2008, scientists at the Lawrence Livermore Labs devised a way to play some of Scott's phonautograms. Scott thus posthumously becomes the first person ever to make a potentially reproducible recording, while Edison remains the first person to record and reproduce a sound.

son's, also called a phonograph, but he lacked the funds to build it. There is no evidence to suggest that either Cros or Edison knew what the other was up to. Soon after Edison unveiled his phonograph, it was all but forgotten, by him and the public, for another eleven years. And even *then*, several years passed before the phonograph was considered primarily a musical device rather than a dictation tool.

It's a curious historical arc. Hundreds of years after someone could have invented recorded music, somebody sort of does. Two decades pass before two people have the same idea, almost simultaneously, for something called a "phonograph." Even after one of them builds an actual phonograph, it is almost as though it isn't *really* invented for another decade. After that, it still takes a few years for it to find its place as a recorder and reproducer of music.

It's a stretch, I know, but I can't help wondering if another "big bang" provides a clue for the phonograph's slow development. Archaeologists talk about the artistic "big bang" that happened in western Eurasia at the beginning of the Upper Paleolithic, 40,000 years ago, when Cro-Magnons, the first *Homo sapiens*, began to replace Neanderthals. After 2.5 million years of humans and their ancestors producing objects that were almost always purely utilitarian, such as stone tools, there was an explosion in symbolic representation—that is, "art": paintings, sculptures, engravings, body ornamentation, and musical instruments—seemingly overnight, archaeologically speaking.

The reasons for this spontaneous florescence of art are still debated, but one leading theory is that humans had developed the neurological capacity for symbolic expression during their more than 100,000 years in Africa, but that the ability was never put into practice until they began to migrate around 50,000 years ago. During their travels they encountered both harsh glacial conditions, for which they were not biologically adapted, and Neanderthals, who had survived in these conditions for 300,000 years. Despite these enormous disadvantages, modern humans dislodged the Neanderthals within 10,000 years, largely because their ability to manipulate symbols provided a huge competitive advantage. Body art, for example, could help foster complex social relations, even across large geographic spaces. Images and music helped people create shared histories and beliefs. Once this dormant capacity for symbolic thought was awakened by necessity, its creative possibilities could be explored.

Perhaps something similar happened with the phonograph. Maybe the phonograph, something we had been capable of creating for centuries, came to us when we needed it most, arising so "naturally" that we at first did not grasp the full possibilities of what we'd created. Like art for the Cro-Magnons, what started as utility grew into something uniquely capable of expressing music, just as music itself began as an adaptive trait that remained with us as "music." Of course, this begs the question of why we needed the phonograph. Maybe our mastery over the world had reached a point where we had godlike ambitions and decided to create something in our own image, not only capturing sound, "the symbol of all that's evanescent," but labeling that evanescence as something lifelike, something real.

In *Sound and Sentiment*, Steven Feld's classic ethnographic study of the Kaluli of Papua New Guinea, he describes how birds are a "metaphoric human society" for the Kaluli. For example, birdsongs are believed to be communications from the dead. This belief system is possible because the Kaluli have a general agreement about what each sound means. For us, recordings are the ways we keep in touch with ghosts—by preserving not just the voices of the dead but also the discarded and lingering ideas of who we are and what we want. But our society is messier than the Kalulis'. We never fully agree on what perfect sound is, so we keep trying, defining our sonic ideals against those of others, playing the game to the best of our abilities, in whatever position we occupy on the field. We add more reverb, we pump up the bass, we boost the treble, we compress dynamic range, we send the band back into the studio because we don't hear a single—and we then remix that single, we press the song on vinyl, on disc, as a ghostly collection of ones and zeros that we send around the world. We do what we can to make it sound right and then we hear the sound flow from the speakers and we call it perfect.

Acoustic/Electrical

1

The Point of Commencement

The chain reaction began in the White House.

Shortly before noon on February 20, 1915, Franklin K. Lane, the secretary of the interior, was concluding his remarks in praise of the pioneer spirit, in front of 50,000 people who had gathered at the Tower of Jewels in San Francisco to wait for the start of the Panama-Pacific International Exposition. "The waste places of the Earth have been found and filled, but adventure is not at an end," Lane said. "Here will be taught the gospel of an advancing democracy—strong, valiant, confident, conquering—upborne and typified by the important spirit of the American pioneer."

When he finished, a telegram was sent to President Woodrow Wilson. This was Wilson's cue to press a key covered with gold nuggets, which completed an electrical circuit over a telegraph line with a navy radio telegraphy station in Tuckerton, New Jersey. A relay key was automatically activated, causing powerful electrical waves to emanate from an 835-foot tower. They traveled across the continent and were received by two antennas 400 feet above the ground, on top of the Tower of Jewels. From there, the current traveled through insulated wires to a delicate receiver in the grandstand, near the speaker's platform. The receiver activated another electrical signal that traveled through the expo grounds. It opened the door of Machinery Hall, made water flow from the Fountain of Energy, and triggered several explosions.

Back at the White House, Wilson's guests, who included the California congressional delegation and several members of his cabinet, burst into applause. Wilson himself was more reflective. He said, "This appeals to the imagination, rather than to the eye."

The Tower of Jewels was the centerpiece of San Francisco's new walled city, carved out of 635 acres and 76 square blocks, for which 200 buildings had been demolished. The irony of this urban clear-cutting was that although the expo officially commemorated the opening of the Panama Canal, everyone knew its real purpose was to celebrate the rebirth of San Francisco from the ashes of the devastating 1906 earthquake. To do so, the city had effaced itself once more, beating nature at its own game, just as surely as the Panama project had laughed at geography.

The expo's city was right on the bay, a setting that had been carefully chosen for its symbolism. "It will be set actually beside salt water," William D'Arcy Ryan, one of the fair's planners, had declared in 1913, "on the ultimate frontier of the race's march eastward from its cradle in Asia, on the final coast where only the sea intervenes between it and what the surveyors call 'the point of commencement.' " Uniting the oceans in Panama, building a city on a restless fault line—progress obeyed no frontiers. One local reporter called the expo nothing less than "the height of the tide of modern civilization," like the canal itself "an idea that was really a product of the consciousness of the whole West."

The Palace of Machinery and the Palace of Fine Arts occupied opposite edges of the grounds, symbolizing the expo's exhaustive celebration of science and industry, art and culture. Measuring 1,000 feet long and 136 feet high, and containing a fully functioning industrial plant, the Palace of Machinery was the world's largest building forged from wood and steel. The expo's largest exhibit, built by U.S. Steel, followed the path of iron ore as it was wrested from the mines and forged into steel. When fairgoers grew tired of the relentless march of progress, they could retire to the Joy Zone, site of all manner of amusements, including the Bowls of Joy, a terrifying attraction that launched riders around the inner surface of two enormous cones. The Joy Zone also pointedly contained many of the exhibits devoted to non-Western cultures, such as the Mysterious Orient.

The expo felt global in scope during the day, but thanks to Ryan, the director of General Electric's illumination lab, it was otherworldly at night. Angled lights concealed in foliage threw beams off the palaces at skewed angles. Submerged lights made the pools on the Court of the Universe glow an eerie green, while statues of the "rising sun" and the "setting sun" were lit on top of sixty-foot poles. The fountains of the Court of the Ages were adorned with serpents that appeared to spit green steam. Out in the bay, a battalion of U.S. Marines operated the Scintillator: forty-eight searchlights in seven different colors that shone through a veil of steam created by an actual locomotive, imitating the aurora borealis in the sky above the city.

The real center of light was the Tower of Jewels, hung with 102,000 actual jewels, barely visible during the day but breathtaking at night. These Novagems—cut glass in ruby, emerald, white, pink, purple, and aquamarine—swung in the breeze from the bay, refracting the beams of strategically placed lights. Each night, crowds gathered to witness "the burning of the Tower." Red lights mixed with fires lit along the colonnades to make the metal structure look like it was melting, a graphic reminder of the city that burned in 1906.

The Panama-Pacific Expo took over San Francisco for ten months in 1915, and then simply vanished. Every structure was razed, except for the Palace of Fine Arts and its weird staircases to nowhere. The demolition was the expo's final symbolic act, the planners' ultimate demonstration that the fair was barely corporeal, more like the hallucinatory product of a collective dream. (William Saroyan, who visited the fair as a child, remembered it as "a place that could not possibly be real.")

During those ten months, 18 million people visited the expo. They came not just to see palaces and exhibits but also to catch appearances by famous Americans. William Howard Taft, Teddy Roosevelt, and George Washington Goethals—the famous "canal genius" who oversaw the work in Panama—attracted huge crowds, but one man outdrew them all. He was the man without whom those Novagems might have twisted in a dark night, "a white-haired man of peace," in the gushing words of the *San Francisco Chronicle*, "epitomizing more in industrial achievement than any other in the world's history."

It was billed as Edison Day—Thursday, October 21—a celebration of the thirty-sixth anniversary of Thomas Alva Edison's invention of the incandescent lamp. By 1:30 in the afternoon, ninety minutes before Edison was to be honored in Festival Hall (home of the world's second-largest pipe organ), its 4,000 seats were filled, leaving 10,000 people stranded in the streets outside.

"From the day that he first made an incandescent lamp glow," Charles Moore announced from the stage, "his name has been stamped on history's pages in a plane by himself. It is fitting that he should come here and we should burn incense to him." As Moore read a series of telegrammed tributes, Edison, by this point in his life nearly completely deaf, whispered to his wife, "I'm glad I can't hear him. I'd feel so foolish."

When Moore finished speaking, it was time for Edison to receive an honorary medal. As his wife attempted to pull stray threads off his coat, Edison rose and walked slowly to the stage, trailed by Thomas Insull, his secretary. The crowd was surprised to discover that Edison had nothing to say to them. That had been one of his conditions for participating in this tribute, that he not have to say a word. Instead, he let Insull do the talking. As Insull delivered a speech praising his boss, Edison sat with his head down, occasionally cracking a small smile.

When it was over, as he left the hall, a riot nearly broke out, as people jumped over barricades and sprinted past guards to try to shake the old man's hand. (In the confusion, Edison somehow lost his hat.) He was driven to the Court of the Universe, where he was named Man of the Century. Then it was on to the AT&T exhibit at the Palace of Liberal Arts.

Back in West Orange, New Jersey, where it was already evening, 162 of Edison's friends and family were gathered at his home, waiting for a connection to San Francisco to be made over the recently completed transcontinental telephone line. Outside, 5,000 tiny lights were strung along the street, and spotlights swept the sky.

Edison perked up a little. He'd been looking forward to this part of the day, ever since Miller Reese Hutchinson, the chief engineer at Edison Laboratories, had come up with a novel way to show off the Edison Diamond Disc Phonograph.

At 5:15 on the West Coast, 8:15 in the East, the chief engineer of Edison Labs announced from West Orange, "Mr. Edison is on the wire." The guests in West Orange picked up telephone receivers fastened to their chairs and heard Edison confirm the connection. Hutchinson delivered a speech without opening his mouth or tapping a telegraph. He'd prerecorded it onto a Diamond Disc, which he now placed on a phonograph next to his phone. The disc spun and Hutchinson's voice was heard:

We are all distinctly Edison. This address, for instance, is being made to you by your greatest favorite, the Edison Diamond Disc Phonograph. An Edison Granular Carbon Telephone Transmitter is transforming the sound waves into electrical impulses which, after following the tortuous paths of copper beneath rivers and bays, over valleys, deserts, plains and mountains, are being reproduced in San Francisco as articulate speech . . . By the invention of your friend, Dr. Alexander Graham Bell, speech may now be transmitted all over the world, and through the intermediary of your invention, the Edison Diamond Disc, permanent records are being made of the voices of great statesmen, wonderful human songbirds and the renditions of famous musicians, all of which will be transmitted down the ages to future generations of men and women whose great-grandsires have not, as yet, been born.

As Edison's engineer in West Orange monitored the transmission of his own voice, after every few lines he would announce to the guests, "Mr. Edison is hearing it perfectly." When it was over, for the first time in two days, Edison had words for those who honored him. He leaned over the phone, and spoke loud and clear:

It may seem strange to those who know my work on the telephone carbon transmitter that this is the first time I have ever carried on a conversation over the telephone. Trying to talk 3,400 miles on my first attempt at conversation seems to be a pretty big undertaking, but the engineers of the Bell System have made it easier to talk 3,400 miles than it used to be to talk 34 miles. In my research work I have spent a great many years listening to the phonograph, but it gives me a singular sensation to sit here in California and hear the new Diamond Disc Phonograph over the telephone all the way from Orange, New Jersey. I heard the record of Hutch's talk very plainly. I should now like to hear a musical record. If you have one handy, I wish you would play Anna Case's bird song.

Hutchinson did happen to have a record handy. He had been told by Edison to be prepared to play some music by Case. After removing the disc with his speech from the phonograph, Hutchinson put on a Case record. Case's voice traveled that tortuous path of copper beneath the rivers and the bays, over the valleys and deserts and plains and mountains, through the phone, and into Edison's crippled ear. As the music played, word went back to West Orange, this time in the ghost language of the telegraph's dots and dashes, so as not to interrupt the music: "Mr. Edison is hearing it perfectly."

Edison looked like he was enjoying himself for the first time in days. All the paeans to progress that surrounded him, all the Novagems and the lights that made them shine, and all Thomas Alva Edison wanted to do was listen to a record.

"The phonograph knows more about us than we know ourselves," Edison had declared back in 1888. For someone who had a preternatural ability to give the world what it needed, this was a striking admission. The phonograph was a puzzle. Unlike the telegraph or the incandescent lamp, it solved no apparent problem, fulfilled no apparent need. It was a blank slate awaiting a use and an ideology—"an invention, pure and simple," Edison said. The first of Edison's creations to work in its first incarnation, the phonograph entered the world nearly fully formed, waiting for its secrets to be unlocked. "This is my baby," Edison announced, "and I expect it to grow up to be a big feller in my old age."

But doing what, exactly? Not necessarily recording and playing music. Edison, who designed the phonograph to record as well as reproduce sounds, assumed the natural purpose of the machine would be as a dictation aid. What ideas Edison did have regarding the phonograph's musical applications had little or nothing to do with music as a prerecorded commercial object. Most of his proposed uses—recording the voices of loved ones and famous people, teaching elocution, early versions of answering machines and books on tape—emphasized the act of preserving information, with little regard to how that information actually sounded. Fidelity wasn't the goal; permanence was. In the courtroom, the phonograph would bear witness to someone's *exact* testimony. A document would remain forever unaltered: "As it may be filed away as other letters, and at any subsequent time reproduced, it is a perfect *record*."

For a brief moment, Edison's phonograph was a sensation, the invention that made Edison a real celebrity outside of the scientific community. Unlike his other creations, Edison liked to demonstrate the phonograph himself in public, in front of audiences that included Congress and President Rutherford B. Hayes. But the fledgling Edison Speaking Phonograph

Company did poor business. Stenographers and secretaries found the phonograph unwieldy, tinfoil was a flimsy recording medium, and the sound of recordings, shaky to begin with, quickly decayed with subsequent uses. Once the initial hoopla had died, the phonograph was still a novelty, a "pure invention." Edison put it on the shelf, where it sat for the next ten years.

He never forgot about it, though. Although he put most of his energy toward developing the electric light, Edison continued to brainstorm ideas for developing the phonograph. Meanwhile, Alexander Graham Bell took up some of the slack, conducting phonographic experiments of his own, which culminated with his invention, in 1886, of the suspiciously titled Graphophone. Feeling territorial, Edison resumed work on his phonograph, insisting that Bell's work had nothing to with his renewed interest.

In 1888, Edison emerged with an improved phonograph. Edison still thought the phonograph's primary function would be preservation of sounds, but he was beginning to consider the possibility that many of these preserved sounds would be music. He imagined that "in the far-off future, when our descendants wish to conjure our simple little Wagner operas with the complex productions of their days, requiring, perhaps, a dozen orchestras playing in half-a-dozen keys at once, they will have an accurate phonographic record of our harmonic simplicity."

A memo sent by Edison's aide William H. Meadowcroft reveals the company's evolving conception of what the machine could do: "It seems to me that your Phonograph ought to be absolutely invaluable to professional singers, for the reason they can study the effect of their own singing. Of course I do not mean to assert that a singer cannot hear his or her own voice, but it is a fact that they cannot understand and study their own defects as thoroughly as they could by the use of the Phonograph." A subtle shift was occurring in the Edisonian conception of the phonograph: the machine was now good enough to preserve the complexity of music for all eternity, and could even reveal some of music's defects.

Edison was beginning to suspect that the phonograph was an even more complex "truth-teller" than he had imagined eleven years earlier. The more Edison thought about it, the more he decided that the phonograph was revealing the auditory logic of the natural world, the science that we ourselves were not equipped to perceive on our own. Put a handful of sand on a piano and play a piece of music, he said—doesn't the sand organize itself

into a pattern based on the vibrations? Well, look at the surface of a recording, etched with impressions that appear "with a nicety equal to that of the
tide in recording its flow on a beach." The indentations were science we
could see, transformed by the phonograph into science we could hear: "In
the phonograph we find an illustration of the truth that human speech is
governed by the laws of number, harmony, and rhythm. And by means of
these laws, we are now able to register all sorts of sound and all articulate
utterance . . . in lines or dots which are an *absolute equivalent* for the emis-
sions of sound by the lips . . ." (Emphasis added.)

The phonograph's intelligence was beginning to reveal itself. And it was
already clear to Edison and his team that even if they didn't know exactly
what the machine knew about us that we didn't know, it was obviously
smarter than most of the public. William Lynd, representing Edison's company, toured the new phonograph around Great Britain and was amazed at
the morons he encountered. There was the old woman in Worthing who
insisted there must be a band playing behind the curtain, and the "fos-
silized specimen of humanity" in Lincolnshire whose questions about the
phonograph did not reveal the requisite awe: "If he had referred to a patent
boot-tip or an American potato peeler," Lynd wrote, "I should not have felt
inclined to kick him; but the man who, after hearing for the first time a
machine talk like a living human being, and repeat a full orchestra without
experiencing a feeling of admiration for the instrument and its inventor,
ought to be preserved in a glass bottle as a specimen of nature's imitations
of humanity."

For Lynd, there was no limit to these people's cluelessness. "I have met
with many stupid persons," he declared, "but the man who, when asked to
speak before the Phonograph, turned round to me and . . . said, 'What must
I do? Shall I blow into it?' certainly 'took the cake.' "

There was a more ominous threat to Edison's phonograph than the public's
tin ear and vacuous imagination, one that would take a few years to gestate.
In 1888, the same year Edison's machine reemerged on the world scene,
Emile Berliner, a telephone technician from Washington, D.C., invented a
talking machine of his own, which he called a gramophone. The phonograph and the gramophone worked on the same general principle: during
recording sound entered a horn and impacted a diaphragm attached to a

stylus, which etched an analog of the vibrations onto a soft surface; during playback, the stylus retraced those grooves, caused the diaphragm to vibrate, and the sound was amplified naturally by the horn.

But while the principles were the same, the technologies were quite different. Edison's phonograph used cylinders. The stylus etched its pattern according to a hill-and-dale method, meaning the stylus moved up and down as the cylinder revolved. The groove maintained a fairly constant width, but a variable depth. The gramophone used flat discs. As it spun, the stylus vibrated from side to side, within a groove that maintained a fairly constant depth with a variable width.

Initially, the gramophone didn't seem like much of a challenge to the phonograph. Edison's early plans for the phonograph had called for discs, but he had concluded that vertically etched cylinders offered superior sound reproduction. His thinking was that the hill-and-dale method gave the stylus more freedom of movement, allowing it to trace a more faithful analog. Why would anyone want anything but the most perfect sound? He had reason to be confident. The Berliner Gramophone Company was short-lived, while the phonograph's popularity as a musical device grew, as coin-operated phonographs, proto-jukeboxes, began to appear. Total phonograph sales increased tenfold between 1890 and 1900, spurred by a rapidly growing urban population in the United States. It looked like Edison would own the new century.

During the next decade phonographs moved from arcades into homes. The first commercially available recordings appeared in 1901, also the year a new version of Berliner's gramophone appeared, marketed by the Victor Talking Machine Company. This time the gramophone was a much more viable alternative to Edison's phonograph. Inferior sound quality notwithstanding, there were plenty of reasons for the public to prefer discs. They were easier to mass-produce, and thus cheaper, and they were more durable, more user-friendly, and could hold four minutes of music, twice as much as an Edison cylinder.

Victor benefited from a synergistic relationship between its hardware and software. One of the artists signed to Victor's record division was Enrico Caruso, the Italian tenor whose phenomenally popular recordings, beginning in 1902, made him recorded music's first global megastar.

Around the same time, Victor introduced the Victrola, a gramophone with its horn inside the cabinet rather than thrusting into the air, which gave it an air of elegance and class. The Victrola became the first talking machine to really capture the fancy of the public. Soon enough, "Victrola" became a colloquial term for talking machines, including Edison's phonograph, a development he found profoundly irritating. During the bank panic of 1907 and 1908, sales of talking machines declined by 50 percent. When the economy improved, Victor's sales picked up while Edison's remained flat. Victor, the more urbane company, was becoming more popular in cities, while Edison remained popular in rural areas, perhaps because he himself was so beloved by Middle Americans. They would prove to be Edison's last stronghold in the coming years.

Edison believed his phonograph and the cylinders it played were *objectively* better and refused to concede defeat. It was only a matter of time before the public wised up. To streamline his business, he reorganized all his companies under the rubric Thomas Alva Edison, Inc. (TAE), a name that suggested that the man himself was now a corporation, and that the corporation's main product was the man himself. (In a sense it was: his name often appeared on his cylinders more prominently than the artists'.) TAE introduced the Amberol cylinder. It was made out of a stronger wax and had twice the number of threads as the old cylinder, so that the Amberol held as much music as a gramophone disc. Edison was convinced the cylinder would rise again, but the executives at TAE weren't so sure about that. Unbeknownst to Edison, Frank Lewis Dyer, TAE's president, was overseeing secret experiments in disc technology, but it wasn't until 1909 that Edison was finally persuaded to take the disc threat seriously. He organized a research group within the company that was charged with developing a superior disc.

Although Edison was willing to forgo his beloved cylinders, he insisted that his discs work on the vertical hill-and-dale method. Edison's group concentrated on perfecting every facet of the phonograph. Edison, like future generations of audiophiles, believed that the key to perfect sound was to simplify the process, on the theory that any step that could be simplified or eliminated was one less chance for the original sound to be corrupted. The Victrola's stylus was attached to the diaphragm by a long fulcrumed lever, a fatal flaw, in Edison's view: if the lever were too light, it would flex and bend rather than transmit all the vibrations; if it were too thick it would damp down the vibrations. Better to get rid of it altogether. In Edison's machine, the stylus would connect directly to the diaphragm.

The first version of the Edison Diamond Disc Phonograph was unveiled in 1912, and the consensus among those who were familiar with the mechanics and physics of recording technology was that he'd nailed it. But Edison wasn't convinced. He threw himself into the work of perfecting the new machine over the next three years, becoming so obsessed that he experimented with 2,300 different styli.

Edison began taking a much more active role in the music his company released. He personally selected the artists and even oversaw the songs they released. "Press notices and the reputation of the artists has nothing to do with his decision," one writer noted, "for Mr. Edison weighs only the pureness of voice and the correctness of the interpretation or the musical ability." Edison was a harsh critic, filling his notebooks with brutal assessments of the music he reviewed:

> What a pity it is that a woman with a voice like this should be educated by so brainless a teacher . . .

> If anything would make the Germans quit their trenches, it is this . . .

Yet he could also bestow high praise:

> This is the only clear-cut flute I ever heard—it is perfect in every note and has fine qualities all the way through . . .

Don't get the TAE music staff started on Edison and flutes. There was the time Edison dropped by to tell them there was something wrong with the sound of the orchestra on a record TAE was releasing. He played it for several people in the office, all of whom confessed they couldn't hear a problem. "It's spoiling the music," Edison insisted. Everyone stood there awkwardly as the music played, straining to hear what it was their boss heard. Edison leaned over, sunk his teeth directly into the soft wood of the phonograph—the great inventor, one of the geniuses of his day, prostrate in front of his invention, actually bowing to it! As Edison's hearing had gotten worse, this is how he compensated. His teeth became a de facto stylus, letting him feel the vibrations with his body. He soon deduced the problem. "The keys on that fellow's flute squeak."

Edison's wood-biting routine was more than a gag. His research had convinced him that the three small bones in the ear that convey sound waves from the middle ear to the inner ear were strikingly inefficient. "There is a good deal of lost motion in those bones," he said. "Part of every sound wave that enters the ear is lost before it reaches the inner ear. For that reason, no one who has a normal ear can hear as well as I can . . . The sound-waves then come almost direct to my brain. They pass only through my inner ear. And I have a wonderfully sensitive inner ear. I do not know that, in the beginning, it was any more sensitive than anybody else's, but for more than 50 years it has been wrapped in almost complete silence. It has been protected from the millions of noises that dim the hearing of ears that hear everything. And as a result, when sound waves are projected into my inner ears, either through the skull or the teeth, the waves strike inner ears that are abnormally sensitive."

This wasn't a deaf man claiming that his weak ears had sharpened his other senses. This was a deaf man saying his deafness had made his *hearing better*. And why? Because his hearing apparatus was simplified, as sound took a shortcut, an end run around his outer ear and straight into his mind. The rest of us, we were all Berliners, with our needlessly complicated ears analogous to those pointless levers that connected the gramophone's diaphragm to its stylus.

Edison and his phonograph both knew what music sounded like because they heard its pure essence, unencumbered by the clutter of the world. "Nobody realizes how much music is spoiled by little sounds that do not belong in it," he insisted. "The average person—the person with a normal ear—is not conscious that he hears sounds. That is to say, he cannot call attention to any particular sounds that do not belong in the music. All he knows is that the music does not sound good to him." Edison's phonograph would save music by editing out the natural world that corrupted it. "Forty percent of the sounds that come from an ordinary disk phonograph do not belong in the music. I have invented a new kind of disk machine which, with a clean record, absolutely eliminates all these unnecessary noises . . . I shall put before the world a phonograph that will render whole operas better than the singers themselves could sing in a theater. I shall do this by virtue of the fact that with a phonograph I can record voices better than any person in a theater can hear them. The acoustics of no opera house are perfect. Something is always lost between the singer and the auditor. I shall record the voices of singers in such a manner that nothing will be lost."

The rhetorical gymnastics are extraordinary, the ideas rendered in a language that would belong only to a huckster if the artistic ideas contained therein weren't so revolutionary. A Diamond Disc was not a representation of music, a documentation of a sonic event; a Diamond Disc *was* music, more real and authentic than the music it recorded. "Nothing will be lost"—and, in fact, something will be gained: music as it was meant to sound. Edison claimed the Diamond Disc Phonograph was a "musical instrument." Yet it also "had no tone of its own"—that is, it was completely flat, neutral, transparent, and not attuned to any particular frequencies.

Taking their cues from the old man, the TAE marketing staff began to spread the word that the Diamond Disc did not do something so gauche as "reproduce" music. What the Diamond Disc did was "re-create" music. The Diamond Disc would usher in a new era of artistic production. After more than a quarter of a century, Edison understood the secret knowledge possessed by the phonograph. This is why the phonograph knew more about you than you did. It knew what your world actually sounded like.

Edison knew the musicians would laugh at him—he was counting on it—but he knew in his skull and teeth and inner ear that music was in the same "backward state" in 1913 as electricity had been at the time he invented the phonograph. Electricity and light had changed the way the world looked and the way we saw the world. Now it was the turn of the auditory realm. "If music is worth anything—and in my opinion it is worth much—it is worth rendering perfectly," Edison said. "I am going to do for music exactly what I did for electricity when I invented machines to measure it. When I have accomplished my purpose, I shall be in a position to make a phonograph that will take the lead over all other musical instruments."

While passing through Des Moines sometime early in 1914, Anna Case decided to pay a visit to Harger & Bliss, the local Edison phonograph dealer. There were a few customers in the store, and one of them asked if she'd sing for them. William Maxwell, a TAE executive, would later relate the story as he heard it: "Miss Case sang with one of her Diamond Disc records, then she sang again and paused—resumed and paused again. Her hearers, when they closed their eyes, could not tell when she was singing and when she was not. While our distributors had all known that the tone of the Edison Diamond Disc was wonderfully true, none of them had realized that it was absolutely identical."

What happened to Case in Iowa wasn't totally unprecedented. Ads for Enrico Caruso records often played up the "can you tell the difference" angle, and as early as 1908, Victor was staging concerts at the Waldorf-Astoria Hotel in New York, during which live orchestras would accompany recordings of opera singers. But Case's impromptu performance was something else altogether: proof that even under spontaneous, uncontrolled conditions, everything that Edison said about the Diamond Disc was true. That is, if you believed absolutely that what happened to Case in Iowa actually happened; the story did carry a whiff of the apocryphal. At some point between the Diamond Disc's invention and her visit to Des Moines, Case was said to have participated in low-key "recitals" at the library of Edison's lab in Orange, singing along with her records for small groups of invited guests, who proclaimed themselves unable to tell the difference between the real Case and the recorded one. And wasn't she rumored to be Edison's mistress? Maybe Edison—who believed so steadfastly that "press reports" could negatively affect one's ability to hear the "truth" just as surely as those tyrannical bones in the ears of the nondeaf—was conducting his own experiment in the powers of auditory suggestion.

Contrived or not, Case's gig was the beginning of a grand experiment and huge gamble by Edison. In the summer of 1914, Maxwell and other high-level TAE employees opened a phonograph shop that served as a "retail sales laboratory" at 589 Main Street in East Orange, New Jersey. The location was conveniently near TAE's West Orange headquarters, but it was also optimal because East Orange was "a broad-lawned flower-scented bedroom and boudoir," as Maxwell put it, "about the last place in which you would be inclined to start an exclusive phonograph store." East Orange was a perfect laboratory, a stand-in for the vast expanse of sleepy America that would have to be sold on the Diamond Disc.

Maxwell's crew made the store look and feel "classy," with tea tables, a makeshift ballroom dance floor, and tiger-striped velour divans in front of the record racks. They compiled a list of East Orange's two hundred most prominent citizens, and in September sent out invitations to the store's first "musicale," a demonstration of the Diamond Disc, "wherein Mr. Edison has overcome the limitations and eccentricities peculiar to all familiar types of talking machines." The seventy-four people who showed up heard eight songs; tea was served and dancing was encouraged.

The store started holding musicales twice a week, and high school stu-

dents were hired for the home demonstrations. As the town's elites and aris-
tocrats spread the word, the mailing list expanded. "The invitations to the
earlier musicales were confined to so-called fashionable people," Maxwell
recalled, "but, as soon as the store had attained the desired reputation of
enjoying the patronage of the leading people in town, the management com-
menced to make its appeal to the public at large."

In February 1915, TAE put on the first highly publicized attempt to
stage an event similar to Case's thriller in Des Moines, featuring the opera
singer Christine Miller. "We know this is a daring experiment," the ads proclaimed, "but it proves better than anything our complete confidence in the
purity and fidelity of tone in the New Edison." Other tone tests were held
around New York, and one in Brooklyn reportedly drew 1,800 people.

The East Orange store began adding live musicians to the musicales to
create smaller-scale tone tests, and the response rate to the mailed invitations shot up. The first tests usually featured a cellist, a flutist, or a violinist, but when the store held a test with all three, 343 people showed up and
50 were turned away. Maxwell briefly considered buying streetcar ads but
realized the viral approach had the advantage of making the tests seem
exclusive even though now they were not; the list of those who'd seen one
had grown to 2,000. It was time to expand the tests' scope.

It was one thing to hold a big test in New York, the capital of high culture, and quite another to try it in sleepy East Orange. Many of the town's
citizens found in their mail an invitation to a gala event on June 21: "The
Civic Committee of The Woman's Club of the Oranges takes pleasure in
inviting you to attend a Concert," featuring "Miss Christine Miller, The
Celebrated Concert Contralto and Mr. Isidore Moskowitz, Solo Violinist of
Edison Orchestra." "In addition to the program rendered by these living
artists," read the fine print at the bottom, "several numbers will be played
by Mr. Edison's new sound-reproducing instrument and, through the courtesy of the Edison Laboratories, Mr. Verdi E. B. Fuller will conduct a novel
tone test by comparing the artists' rendition with the reproduction thereof of
Mr. Edison's instrument."

The East Orange tone test was a smashing success, except for one small
detail that would soon become a key part of all future tone tests. Maxwell
noted later, "It was intended to try at this recital an experiment that had
been successfully practiced at the experimental store at evening performances—that is, the darkening of the room when the tone tests were in

progress." Alas, "the lighting facilities of the hall did not lend themselves to this experiment."

After trying the tests in New York and sleepy suburban New Jersey, among tastemakers and the general public alike, it was time to let the sound reverberate across the land. Edison was ready to teach the world how to listen to music.

First he had to enlist some allies, the foot soldiers who would do the selling. Early in the morning on August 9, 1915, three hundred Edison phonograph dealers from around the country descended on West Orange for the first Edison Dealers Convention. For two days, they endured excruciating lectures on such topics as "The Right of a Manufacturer to Control the Retail Price at Which His Product Shall Be Sold" and why Victor's machines were jokes. After lunch on the second day, they sat through a sketch set in a phonograph store ("A lady enters requesting to hear a certain well-advertised artist, and intending to purchase a Talking Machine. She is finally won over to buy an Edison Diamond Disc"), and afterward Verdi Fuller walked to the front of the room. He told the dealers to imagine that they were an audience in a concert hall, assembled to hear some music. He introduced the soprano Alice Verlet and the violinist Arthur Walsh. Bored beyond belief at this point, the dealers certainly weren't looking forward to hearing some opera.

Verlet stood silently beside the phonograph as it played the introduction to *Caro Nome*. A minute into the aria, she began to accompany the record. When she was finished with her final selection, Verlet bowed, walked off the platform, and got a standing ovation. After Walsh did his demonstration, Fuller spoke again. He explained that tone tests were to be an important facet of the Diamond Disc's PR campaign. Fuller had already begun laying the groundwork for the first large-scale tone-test tour.

Think of it as the Monsters of Tone tour. As summer turned to fall, tone tests moved out from the Oranges and New York to the world at large. Most of these featured Christine Miller and usually local musicians. First up was Wilkes-Barre, Pennsylvania, in front of a standing-room-only crowd of 1,400, for a concert that the local paper described as "perfect, it being almost an impossibility to decide the difference without watching the lips of the singer." Then it was on to Philadelphia; Montclair, New Jersey; and Newburgh, New York.

As word got around, the tour picked up speed. The day after Newburgh, 1,800 people sat and 200 people stood (250 were turned away) in the Cambria Theatre in Johnstown, Pennsylvania. ("It seemed almost unnatural to applaud a *machine*," the next day's *Johnstown Democrat* reported, "but so splendid were many of the records which were played that spontaneous applause followed their rendition.") A thousand people showed up in Oil City, Pennsylvania; 1,600 in Ithaca, New York; and 700 in Trenton, New Jersey, where the paper raved about the "perfection" of "Edison's latest wonder machine."

And so it went that fall, as Christine Miller and others moved westward "re-creating" music to rave reviews—in Detroit, Milwaukee, Omaha, Denver, San Diego, and Los Angeles. The tour headed up the Pacific Coast toward San Francisco. On October 21, Edison Day, Miller sang with the Diamond Disc Phonograph at the Panama-Pacific Expo, convincing an awed audience of fairgoers, expo officials, and music critics from several countries that the barrier between the voice and its representation had been broken, as surely as the Panama Canal united the oceans and unified the West.

For the next ten years, Edison tone tests continued around the country and around the world. By the time the last tests were held in 1925, Edison had proven his point about the Diamond Disc. Or had he? As his machine was wowing audiences, the music division at TAE was falling apart.

Even before the tone tests reached the Pacific Coast Edison had become somewhat bored with the Diamond Disc. Two months after he returned from San Francisco, *The Edison Phonograph Monthly*, the communiqué that gave merchants advice and marching orders, announced that it would no longer promote it: "A new baby in a household sometimes results in the elder child being neglected for a time, until the new baby is able to take care of itself. Our new baby—the Diamond Disc—has developed rapidly and no longer monopolizes our attention." The new child was Edison's old love, the cylinder. At the same time he gave the world the Diamond Disc, Edison, much to his executives' chagrin, had invented yet another permutation of that format. A bright-blue celluloid surface wrapped around plaster of paris, it was given the tantalizing name the Blue Amberol.

Although the Diamond Disc was just beginning its ten-year journey into the hearts, minds, and ears of America, for Edison, it was "Cylinder Exclu-

sively Hereafter," as the *Monthly* put it. But Edison was so perversely protective of his new baby that he actually discouraged his dealers from
carrying it unless they could honestly say they'd be perfect parents: "We
are trying to reduce our list of dealers handling the cylinder line. We want
only dealers who will give the Diamond Amberola the representation it
deserves . . . We should rather have one live progressive dealer than half a
dozen indifferent ones. We want a loyal legion of Edison Diamond
Amberola enthusiasts."

The TAE could briefly afford this rejection of its own merchants. Sales
of all phonographs peaked in 1915; between 1909 and 1919, overall production increased 520 percent over the previous ten years. In 1920, the
apex of the tone tests, TAE's sales were strong, as the end of World War I
allowed factories to return to peacetime levels of production. But cylinder
sales never picked up, and in the twenties overall phonograph sales
declined 45 percent. Because Edison held on to the vertical-cut hill-and-
dale method, the company couldn't develop a "universal reproducer,"
which meant that Edison cylinders could play only on Edison machines,
and Edison machines could play only Edison cylinders.

Everyone assumed Edison would discontinue the cylinder line, but he
only grew more attached to the Blue Amberol (and the Blue Amberola phonograph). As the Diamond Disc tone tests swept the country, Edison began
encouraging and publicizing comparison tests between Blue Amberol and
other talking machines. "Score: Amberola 12; Talking Machine 1" blared
one typical *Monthly* headline. Another issue ran a cartoon of two phonographs in a boxing ring, the Blue Amberol kicking the other machine's ass.
And still, Edison kept separating the true believers from the fakers among
his dealers. By the start of 1917, the message was clear: nice dealership,
it'd be a shame if something happened to it. "There Is Going to Be a
Housecleaning!" the *Monthly* announced at the start of 1917. "We are looking into each and every dealer's activities. Those who are not carrying rep-
resentative stocks will be 'put on the carpet' . . . Undoubtedly some dealers
are going to lose their licenses." The missive's ominous sign-off was "A
word to the wise—"

You really couldn't blame the dealers. Their customers weren't interested in the Amberola. It wasn't that they thought the disc sounded better
than the cylinder; they just didn't care one way or the other. Setting an
example that would be repeated by future generations of audio consumers,

the typical music buyer was willing to forgo some elusive sonic pedigree for the convenience and lower cost of discs.

As Edison grew older, his belief in music and the powers of sonic communication only grew, merging with his interest in spiritualism and the paranormal. In 1920, he announced he was working on a machine to communicate with the dead. Not that he was necessarily endorsing the idea of a spirit world, he emphasized. It was logical to assume, however, that if one existed, we would need an exceedingly sensitive instrument to communicate with it, and Edison intended to build that instrument. The phonograph had unlocked the secrets of music; an even more sensitive phonograph might unlock the secret of life.

Edison gave thousands of dollars to psychology professors to study the "emotional effects" of the tone tests, and in 1921 awarded $500 to a Vassar professor for the Thomas A. Edison Prize, a contest for the best essay on "The Effects of Music." A psychologist at the Carnegie Institute of Technology developed a Mood Change Chart that Edison dealers were encouraged to use at Mood Change Parties, to show their "Analysis of Mental Reactions to Music, as Re-Created by the New Edison, the Phonograph with a Soul." Given various dichotomous emotions—"serious or gay," "depressed or exhilarated," "worried or carefree," "sad or joyful"—listeners were asked to chart how their mood changed as they listened to the re-creations.

Through the twenties, Edison continued to believe that what the world always needed was a better machine, that his relentless pursuit of audio perfection would put TAE back on top. He began paying even less heed to signing artists the public actually wanted to hear. "Last year, when you were the only picker of tunes, you refused to let us record the four biggest successes of the year," Walter Miller, Edison's business manager, complained to his boss in 1921. Punning, intentionally or not, he added, "I am convinced that this policy is not sound." By 1927, TAE's sales accounted for just 2 percent of the industry total.

The growing popularity of radio was proving to be a threat to the entire phonograph industry. Radio wasn't just competing with the phonograph industry for listeners; it was also affecting what people wanted music to sound like. Because radio required a microphone, the sound of music on the radio accentuated the role of electric amplification, and phonograph listeners began to want their records to have a louder, fuller sound. Edison, meanwhile, dismissed this desire as the "volume fad" and continued to fine-tune the sound of his records without regard to their ability to amplify sounds. "I don't think the radio will ever replace the phonograph," Edison said on the occasion of the phonograph's forty-fifth birthday in 1922. "I tried it for recording and found there was too much mutilation of sounds . . . I believe I have the phonograph close to perfection." He mentioned that he'd nearly succeeded in recording pianos perfectly and was working on recording Beethoven's Ninth Symphony.

In 1924, Western Electric technicians came up with the first workable electrical recording system. Electrical recording was based on the same principles as acoustic recording, with an added layer of mediation. In acoustic recording, the mechanical energy of sound waves is inscribed on a recording medium. Electrical recording processes first convert that energy into electrical impulses.

Victor and other companies embraced—or at least accepted—the new technology, but as Edison saw it, this was just the Victrola's useless lever all over again, an unnecessary middleman that imposed a barrier between the real-world sound event and its inscription. Why would anyone want that, when the acoustic recording process, the direct impression of the world onto a record, still held such promise? He was proud to say that TAE was now the only "straight phono company."

When Edison finally decided that he needed to take the radio threat seriously, his solution was to begin marketing 12-inch 78 rpm records, which could hold forty-five minutes on each side. Unfortunately, the records sounded too faint for many people's ears and were too fragile to withstand repeated playing. As for innovating the phonograph itself, Edison's son Charles had to gently explain to his dad that the word *phonograph* itself was increasingly passé, and that whatever the company's next machine looked or sounded like, it better have a name that ended with "phonic." In 1928, Edison swallowed his pride and released the short-lived Edisonic machine, with an electrical pickup and a built-in radio. In October 1929, the month the stock market took its fatal dive, TAE released its last records.

On Edison Day at the Panama-Pacific Expo in San Francisco, after the old man had listened to Anna Case's voice coming to him from his home in New Jersey, he did something odd. As the *Monthly* later described it, "Mr.

Edison put the same selection on *his* Diamond Disc at San Francisco, in order that guests at the Laboratory might hear as he had heard. The tones were sweet and clear and perfectly audible, without any strain to hear them; the high notes and trills being exactly as clear as if heard over a short distance 'phone, although not quite so loud." Even if the people at the AT&T booth in San Francisco and Edison's engineer in West Orange knew that Edison planned to do that, the crowd at the lab was surely mystified. But they sat and gamely listened as Edison force-fed them music over the wire.

Edison then endured a telephone conversation with well-wishers at the lab, but after getting off the phone with the chief engineer of AT&T, he decided he'd had enough, leaving his wife to talk with their sons Charles and Theodore in Orange. While the guests in New Jersey adjourned to the TAE executive building to watch a film about the making of the transcontinental phone line, Edison got ready for the last of the tributes to him. That night, 50,000 people came down to the Marina to watch a fireworks display over the bay in his honor. Edison sat patiently with Henry Ford and watched the sky light up from the north steps of the expo's Transportation Building. Every few minutes, the crowd would turn and wave at him up on the stairs, and they wouldn't stop cheering until Edison doffed his hat, like a guy reemerging from the dugout after hitting a grand slam.

On Saturday, two days after Edison Day and two days before 50,000 children were let out of school to see Edison before he left town, a tone test was held at San Francisco's Scottish Rite Hall. "Very successful," Verdi Fuller wrote in his notebook. "Attendance 944. Most appreciative audience yet. Acoustics and presentation perfect."

2

From the New World

Frank B. Jewett, the president of Bell Laboratories, walked onstage at Carnegie Hall and looked out at a capacity crowd of 2,000 people there to see nothing and hear everything. You couldn't buy your way into this concert. Actually, it wasn't so much a concert as a colossal record-release party. Laurance Rockefeller, New Jersey governor A. Harry Moore, Arturo Toscanini, the pianist and composer Sergei Rachmaninoff, and everyone else there that Tuesday night—April 9, 1940—had been invited by Bell Labs to sit in the hall and listen to some records with the volume turned up way past eleven.

Three huge loudspeakers covered in sheer fabric were hung above the stage—one at each end and one in the middle. What everyone was about to hear, Jewett explained, was something that Bell called "enhanced" music. Performances by Paul Robeson, the Philadelphia Orchestra under the direction of Leopold Stokowski, and the Mormon Tabernacle Choir had been recorded on motion-picture film stock using three microphones, each of which embossed a separate track onto the film. Three large amplifiers in the hall's basement would carry each track to one of the loudspeakers, creating a "stereophonic" effect and immersing the listeners in a sort of musical "third dimension" that would allow them to hear the spatial relations of the various musicians at the time the recordings were made. The recorded music would be rendered absolutely lifelike.

But that wasn't all, Jewett promised. This enhanced music would actually be louder—and in some cases softer—than life. That was because Stokowski had rerecorded the original recordings, using a new process developed by Bell engineers. The new recording system compressed a huge dynamic range of sound onto the film. In the postproduction process, the compressed music could be "expanded" for playback, restoring the dynamic range. Moreover, the music could be dramatically altered. If Stokowski thought a certain passage should sound more pianissimo than what the musicians had played, he could soften that music. And if he decided that a certain passage should really rattle the rafters . . . well, the audience was about to hear for themselves.

Harvey Fletcher, the director of Bell Labs, manned the equipment. The program began with four recordings of Stokowski conducting the Philadelphia Orchestra. As colored lighting effects danced across the speaker fabric, the audience heard Mussorgsky's *St. John's Night on the Bare Mountain* and *Pictures at an Exhibition*, Debussy's "Clair de Lune," and Johann Strauss's "Tales from the Vienna Woods." Then it was Robeson doing a scene from Eugene O'Neill's *The Emperor Jones* against a steadily building backdrop of drums that caused several members of the audience to put their hands over their ears in shock.

Next up was the Mormon Tabernacle Choir singing hymns. Let history record that it was the Mormons, disciples of America's homegrown religion, who were the first emissaries of the sonic roar that America bequeathed to the world. The choir's Harold Bennett sang a solo during *Elijah*, Mendelssohn's oratorio about the loner prophet who prophesized doom for pagans, helped the needy, left this world in a flaming chariot, and was due to return to Earth as an opening act for the Messiah. Bennett as Elijah appealed to the Lord. What came next pinned the crowd to their seats.

While selecting music for this demo, Stokowski and the Bell engineers had listened for tonal variety. To demonstrate that the system covered—no, *exceeded*—the range of human hearing, Stokowski had made certain parts barely audible, and others loud enough to blow the roof off. The inventors realized that with great enhancement came great responsibility. Experiments taught them that 120 decibels was the most people could comfortably handle. To be safe, it had been decided that the loudest parts of the demo would not exceed 100 dB, which the engineers estimated to be the sound of 2,000 musicians playing at once. The engineers knew they had done their job when a woman at Monday's dress rehearsal had doubled over during *Elijah*, as though she'd been kicked by a horse.

Now, as the choir took on the voice of a crowd hearing Elijah's appeal answered by God, the evening reached its loudest point so far, shooting toward that 100 dB threshold. Many in the audience were genuinely terrified. One observer heard the sound of "a million Banshees wailing at once."

The night ended with the enhanced recording of the Philadelphia Orchestra playing the explosive *Götterdämmerung* from Wagner's *Der Ring des Nibelungen*. At the climax of the piece, Brünnhilde (voiced by Hazel Hayes) threw herself into the fire; Valhalla was destroyed and the Rhine washed away her ashes, signaling the start of a new era. The 100 dB threshold was reached. It felt, some said, as though the rear of the auditorium was about to tumble into 57th Street. For Arthur C. Keller, a Bell engineer, the lasting image would be of people being blown out of the place.

Many audience members agreed that the stereophonic aspect rendered the recordings—at least those that weren't so "enhanced"—indistinguishable from the real thing. And yet that enhancement caused a disconnect, for these people had made the recordings sound like nothing heard in our natural, unenhanced world. How disorienting was the concert? Enough that Rachmaninoff had a hard time recognizing the sounds as music. "Take that 'Pictures at an Exhibition,' " he said. "Why, I didn't know what it was until they got well into the piece. Too much 'enhancing,' too much Stokowski. I would like to hear more music without enhancement, perhaps some things I know well. Then I might be able to say something."

The next day's headlines told the story. The *New York Herald Tribune* went with SUPER-VOLUME CONCERT RECORDS SCARE AUDIENCE. *The New York Times* put a somewhat more positive spin on the evening: SOUND WAVES "ROCK" CARNEGIE HALL.

The Carnegie Hall blowout of 1940 was the culmination of fifteen years of the electrical recording era, the amplified sequel to the acoustic recording era that Edison had launched with his first phonograph. The electrical era represented huge advances in recording technology, but the real break that distinguished the era was as much conceptual as technological.

Acoustic recording and electrical recording share the same basic analog concept. With each technology, sound waves cause a resonating surface to vibrate, and some sort of inscription technology creates an analog of these waves. With acoustic recording, the analogous pattern is caused by the mechanical energy of the sound wave. Like a footprint preserved in cement, the sound wave impacts the medium directly: the phonograph's diaphragm vibrates, the stylus attached to it etches a pattern, and during playback the process is reversed.

When sound is recorded electrically, the resonating surface is in a microphone. The microphone converts the vibrations into a stream of positive and negative voltages. It is the voltage stream, not the original mechanical energy of the sound waves, that impacts the system. When sound is played back electrically, this voltage stream is re-created—by a stylus vibrating as it traces a record's grooves, for example—and turned back into mechanical energy by an amplifier. Speaker cones vibrate, re-creating the original pressure changes in the air caused by the original sound event.

The distinction between acoustic and electrical recording can be confusing in the context of early phonograph technology. First, because most acoustic phonographs were powered by an electric motor, although the actual technology used to inscribe and reproduce sound was acoustic. Second, because acoustic phonographs could play electrically recorded discs, and the reverse was also true. Third, the machine that really launched the electrical era, the Victor Orthophonic, was an acoustic phonograph.

The obvious appeal of electrical recording is that a microphone can capture a wider range of sounds than an acoustic recording horn. Victor's scientists had mathematically calculated that an acoustic phonograph's horn should measure nine feet long to reproduce electrical recordings in all their glory, and they had devised the optimal way to cram all nine feet, intestine-like, into the phonograph's cabinetry, so that the Orthophonic looked sharp in the living room, without a freakishly protruding horn. The result was hailed as the ultimate conveyor of perfect sound. "Every tone is preserved," *The Musician* raved, under the banner SCIENCE AGAIN COMES TO THE AID OF MUSIC. "[T]he very lowest and very highest tones capable of being heard by the human ear can come through the horn unimpeded by the limitations that have previously restricted the talking machine."

The Orthophonic came out the same year that Edison's ten-year run of Diamond Disc tone tests was coming to an end, when he was involved in his quixotic quest to foist cylinders on a disc-crazy market, and he was just a few years away from leaving the talking-machine business for good. In seventeen years, Edison had sold 48 million Diamond Discs, 7 million fewer records than Victor sold in 1922 alone. Although his customer base was increasingly limited to rural areas, there were a few committed Edisonian audiophiles who, even if they didn't share the old man's fondness for cylinders, were right there with him when it came to rejecting the electrical future—not just electrically recorded discs but the microphone-driven medium of radio that some thought could run the commercial recording industry out of business.

The germ of their discontent is contained in that *Musician* headline about science coming to the aid of music. That was the problem right there, the idea that science could augment and improve music. The goal of recording was not to improve upon music—the goal was to capture it, absolutely, in all its essence. From our vantage point at the end of the first century of the electrical era, it's hard to imagine how anyone could argue that the microphone did not do this better than an acoustic recording horn, or that amplification somehow corrupts the playback process. But that was the Edisonian mind-set. "I wonder if pure tone will disappear from the earth sometimes," one British critic wrote in 1928, explaining his "cringing fear" of radio's influence. "It is a grave danger, for the man-in-the-drawing-room is a careless good-natured devil willing to swallow all sorts of hokum and to be told he has perfect reproduction . . ."

In a rundown of the shortcomings of the new wave of phonographs, Walter L. Welch, an audio archivist, writer, and committed Edison enthusiast, articulated this anxiety over the loss of pure tone. He slammed recording engineers and their "improper conception of what constitutes [a] proper recording." The microphone made it possible to record music in a cavernous concert hall, rather than the small "dead" rooms that were used in the fading acoustic era, which meant that engineers now thought you could reproduce the sound of the music *as heard in that room*. By recording the room as much as the music, you could, in effect, give the listener at home a vivid re-creation of the concert-going experience. What a "fallacy," Welch argued, "because what you're doing is superimposing the acoustical qualities of one room onto another. This only happens in radio, talkies [motion pictures], and gramophones—never in original performances." In other words, why would anyone think it possible to re-create Carnegie Hall in the living room?

These recording practices even influenced people's expectations of live performances. Welch described seeing the Mills Brothers perform, although "I did not actually hear them, as it was necessary for them to have their microphone coddling act amplified ten times through a loudspeaker system or else they could not have been heard beyond the tenth row." The microphone did not clarify sound. It corrupted it.

"Whatever may have been the limitations of the acoustic method," Welch continued, "the drawbacks consisted largely of what was left out of the recording process, instead of the present defects, which are added, namely excess resonance, distortion, over-amplification, and extraneous noises. What proper recordings should do is maintain definition, instead of blending and modulating overtones, harmonics, etc." Welch then played the tone-test trump card. He reminded all the microphone fiends that Edison's Diamond Disc was the only record that had been publicly subjected to a reality challenge, let alone passed one on hundreds of occasions. "And these were acoustic records. That's because Edison was striving to maintain and recreate the human voice. The gramophone, which has supplanted Edison, has overcome Edison's chief limitation, which was the ability to record large orchestras, [but] can't duplicate Edison's feat."

In thirty years, the next generations of Walter Welches, the "high fidelity" audiophiles, would build a sonic worldview around the opposite ideal, that a well-placed microphone and a well-built hi-fi could indeed make the living room a tone-test arena. But we're getting ahead of ourselves. At the start of the electrical era, a few Edisonians drew a line in the sand—one that was scarcely noted and quickly effaced by the rising tide of electrical recording, but a line nonetheless. They turned the limitations of acoustic recording into a worldview. Edison wanted to capture just the music and edit out the world around it, but capturing the music was about all you could hope for in acoustic recording, anyway.

In acoustic recording, you crowd musicians around a recording horn and hope that you generate enough mechanical energy to leave its mark on the wax. You respect the world of sound, approach it on its own terms. Acoustic recording was about just capturing some mysterious entity called "music." Electrical recording implied capturing a whole lot more. And that was the "cringing fear" of the Edisonians. Even more than cylinder versus disc, acoustic versus electrical laid the dialectical groundwork for all future debates about recording.

Of course, you had to be pretty deep in the weeds to notice this at the time. "As the Great War completely disrupted our everyday lives, so has electrical recording caused a prodigious upheaval in our gramophonic existences," *The Gramophone* declared, portentous and self-parodying even by its own nerd-boy, leisure-class standards. "Its advent has resulted in an amiable battlefield with discarded gramophones, records and accessories, which have been gathered up and disposed of as 'surplus,' as relentlessly as was the debris of the late world cataclysm."

"Electrical recording was the biggest revolution in recorded sound since its invention," Michael Devecka, a collector of vintage phonographs, says today. "It overshadows the invention of the LP, tape, or digital."

Devecka lives in Montclair, New Jersey, the site of the tone test of September 17, 1915. I had asked if I could hear some of his collection, because I was curious if, at this late date, the birth of the electrical era, the downfall of Edison and the rise of Victor, was an audible phenomenon. I met him at his home on one of the first stiflingly hot days of summer— "a perfect phonograph day," Devecka explained, because the humidity in the air was an excellent conductor of sound.

"I think it's safe to say that Edison was the 'techie,' and the people at Victor were the businessmen," he said. "Technologically, Edison was right on the edge of the envelope. The deficiencies weren't in the acoustic recording process. It was materials. A lot of what was working against Edison was material science."

Devecka had searched his collection for recordings of songs that the same artist had made for both Edison and Victor. The first was a Diamond Disc recording of the comic duo Collins and Harland doing "Bake Dat Chicken Pie," an example of the "coon song" genre, popular in the late nineteenth and early twentieth century, which featured white musicians doing grossly caricatured imitations of African-American performances.

I could hear startling dynamic shifts, but there was something about the sound that was pleasant and not jarring. "Exactly," Devecka said. "There's a detail and a roundness. With a vertical system"—the hill-and-dale method Edison followed, as opposed to Victor's later side-to-side system— "it's riding a very bumpy road, so you're pushing up and something has to pull back. The diaphragm has to have enough spring to pull back quick enough. It has to have a sweet spot. It has to be able to move up and down. It's gonna be pulled, and it's gotta pull back."

The song ended, and Devecka cued up the version that the duo recorded for Victor, on one of his pre-Orthophonic Victrolas. The sound was somehow harsher, with a brightness that almost sounded like the radio. "The Edison has some air and detail, a little bit more roundness," Devecka said. "The Victor is a little bit more like cardboard cutouts. It's like a photograph that doesn't have quite the right contrast range." I was taping all this on a cheap old-school tape recorder, and even on the tape you can hear phrases jump out, as though the wave emerging from the horn was powerful enough to really scramble the magnetic particles on the tape. The Victor's sound was impressive, but there was something ultimately more pleasant about the Edison sound.

"Victor records have a certain richness," Devecka said. "Victor tried to record the overtones, the noise of the room. The idea was to give it a little more warmth, a little more resonance, kind of that singing-in-the-shower effect. Edison, on the other hand, wanted to record in a deader studio. He wanted accuracy. He didn't want a lot of extra stuff going on."

Next was a recording of Edison's Atlantic Dance Orchestra performing "California, Here I Come," released in 1924, a year before the Orthophonic. "This is kind of moving up the food chain in terms of recording quality, and it's at the point where Edison wasn't pushing the tone tests as much," Devecka said. Again, the Edison had a dry sound that emphasized the clarity and separation of the instruments, rather than the sound of the room.

"The Victor tracks better, and it has a bite and a crispness, but the Edison system was more responsive," he continued. "Victor never really talked about their sound being the 'real' sound. They talked about 'the Victor sound.' They pushed the concept of hearing 'the real Caruso,' but I think it was less about sound quality and more about the fact that it was Caruso and not some wannabe. In other words, 'Only we record Caruso, and nobody else does.' And if you wanted Caruso bellowing out of a horn, Victor did a damn good job of it."

Next, Devecka played an Edison recording of Wagner's "Ride of the Valkyries," but this time he put a Victor reproducer on the Edison machine. Even with the Victor reproducer, the Edison recording still had a certain pleasant quality that made me want to keep listening. "It's musical," he said. "The Victor is like a Ferrari that can go from zero to sixty-nine in a second. It's impressive, but you wouldn't want to drive it on the Belt Parkway much." Or, it occurred to me, listening to the Victor was like listening to a CD, with its high-definition sound that begins to grate, as opposed to the Edison-like experience of listening to a vinyl record.

Devecka played an Edison recording of the "Charleston," recorded right before the start of the electrical era. The sound was incredible—full and pristine. "There's a relaxed quality to it," Devecka said. "It doesn't scream. The acoustic Victors always felt like they were straining a bit."

But having arrived at the electrical era, suddenly things sounded different. Devecka played Edison and Victor recordings of Billy Jones and Ernest Hare doing their ode to the Ford Model A, "Henry's Made a Lady Out of Lizzie." These were both electrical recordings, and I swear you could hear Edison losing the battle. The Victor record just sounded bolder, more at ease with the technology, more cognizant of the future.

Devecka had an interesting way to conceive of the advent of electrical amplification. "People think that what an amplifier does is take a tiny signal and make it big," he said. "What it's really doing is 'borrowing' electrons from somewhere else. Electrons are the carrier of energy. You're adding more of them to perfectly mimic the pattern of the originating electrons." This is why a microphone can "hear" better than an acoustic horn. It doesn't rely solely on the energy of the sound waves. It borrows electrons from out there in the world, from the wall socket and the power grid beyond it. The relationship between a record and what it records was now more complex. The walls of the room in which a sound is recorded don't merely denote a "quiet" space in which to capture sound. They now let in the messy world outside. Suddenly "recording" a sound doesn't seem like such a simple proposition. Tapping into what lay behind those walls meant you could bring electrons in, or send the sound out. Sound was now flexible, elastic. That is the legacy of the electrical era.

In the early 1920s, Bell Telephone Laboratories, the research wing of AT&T, began an extensive study of speech and hearing. Although their goal was to improve the sound quality of telephone transmissions, the research also led to prodigious innovations in recording, including the first workable process to make electrical disc recordings. The Bell engineers discovered that their electrical process expanded the range of recordable sound by 2.5 octaves, made it possible to record music in large rooms, and produced the loudest recordings in history. Bell assumed that the most successful talking-machine company in the world would jump at the chance to license the new technology.

Emile Berliner, the godfather of Victor's gramophone technology, had grasped the musical possibilities of the talking machine before Edison did. His first idea for a "practical application" was a public kiosk where people could record themselves talking or playing music, an even more prescient prediction: "A singer unable to appear at a concert may send her voice and be represented per programme." But Eldridge Johnson, who purchased Berliner's patents and founded the Victor Talking Machine Company with a $50,000 investment, wasn't as forward-thinking. Like Edison, he was no fan of electrical recording, though for reasons that were less philosophical: Johnson saw no reason to tinker with the already successful acoustic Victrola.

He did, however, share with Edison a similar disdain for the effect radio was having on people's sonic expectations. When Western Electric, AT&T's licensing and manufacturing arm, approached Victor with the new electrical recording system, Johnson declined. He reconsidered in 1924, after the Columbia Phonograph Company, Victor's only real competition, licensed the system. By February 1925, Victor's Camden, New Jersey, labs were outfitted with electrical equipment. On March 11, the University of Pennsylvania's Mask and Wig Club arrived in Camden for the world's first electrical recording session. That winter, the Orthophonic Victrola was in stores.

With the Orthophonic a smashing success, Victor made its peace with radio in a big way. Early in 1929, the company merged with the Radio Corporation of America (RCA), creating a new corporation whose total stock was worth more than $626 million. David Sarnoff, RCA's executive vice president, took the long view regarding the synergy between the two industries. "It is clear that in the new era of electrical entertainment now expressed in broadcasting, in talking motion pictures, and in theatre installations, radio and the phonograph play distinct but complementary roles," he said. "The present unification will greatly improve both services by making the inventions and developments of both industries interchangeable." Even more prescient was Sarnoff's understanding of the conceptual shift prefigured by the ongoing electrical revolution. "Every dramatic performance is an act of communication," he wrote in a *New York Times* op-ed headlined WHERE OPPORTUNITY BECKONS. "The phonograph, the player piano, the radio set, all are instruments of musical speech and communication." Recorded sound was no longer a fragile, almost mythical entity. It was now "information," to be amplified and broadcast at will.

RCA Victor was an industrial giant, an all-purpose producer of global sound, generating records, phonographs, and radios. A year after the merger, the company employed 10,000 people, and the Camden complex included thirty-one buildings and 2.5 million square feet of office space, spread over fifty-eight acres, tied together by a private railroad system. Each day, the factories consumed 200 tons of coal and 17 million gallons of water pumped from a private waterworks. The RCA Victor lumberyard was the world's biggest processor of African mahogany and other cabinet woods.

Bell Labs provided the technology for electrical recording, and RCA Victor supplied the industrial base, but the person who united the two by grasping the artistic and economic possibilities of the electrical era was the conductor Leopold Stokowski. As Glenn Gould put it, "no musician of our time has given so much thought to the prospects of recording, or has better exemplified, through his major career decisions, the practical and philosophical consequences of recording." Stokowski loved the idea of amplification because it made music bigger, and he loved radio because it brought music to more people. He put an artist's spin on the communication-based flexible sonic future that Sarnoff described. "Physicists, engineers, and musicians will combine to improve constantly the recording of music," he predicted in his book *Music for All of Us.* "The first step is to make music exactly like the original. The next step is to surpass the original and, through future possibilities of recording, to achieve the dreams of musicians—of making music still more beautiful and eloquent—music they heard within themselves but which was unattainable in the past."

Stokowski championed electrical recording, but he also had an Edisonian's disdain for the idea that any recording could replicate the concertgoing experience by re-creating the sound of a live performance for the home listener. "This is a completely meaningless criterion for music," he said. "A concert hall has thousands of cubic feet of interior space. A living room has only a few hundred. They can never sound the same . . . I am not even certain that the way we hear in a concert hall is the best and only way to listen."

Six feet tall, with a shock of hair that remained long even after it turned from blond to gray, Stokowski was a celebrity to an extent that's almost impossible to imagine for a maestro today. His third wife, Greta Garbo, was forty years his junior. He liked to meditate before concerts and often performed wearing midnight blue rather than the traditional black.

Among musicians, critics, and serious classical music fans, Stokowski's reputation was mixed. His penchant for radically reinterpreting scores, even integrating exotic instruments like tam-tams and theremins, was celebrated by some and criticized as gimmickry by others. "Sometimes, after a searing contact with a new, brilliant and fundamentally pointless recording by him," the critic Irving Kolodin wrote, "I tend to be of the opinion that music per se means little to him, that all he cares about is the effect he can make with a composition." Indeed, Stokowski took the concept of "effect" far beyond just altering scores. For a performance of Saint-Saëns's *Carnival of the Animals* in front of a young crowd, he arranged for an elephant and other zoo animals to parade across the stage. When the Philadelphia Orchestra performed in Guatemala, Stokowski arranged for soldiers to fire cannons during the *1812 Overture*. (The cues got mixed up, so the music was lost in an anarchic fusillade.)

Glenn Gould recalled that when he was a student, the prevailing view of Stokowski was that he was a sellout, although "for some mysterious reason, his innumerable recordings tended to sound better than those of his colleagues—no one denied it, but, at the same time, no one was much interested in thinking about why this might be, either." One reason his records sounded so good is that Stokowski recognized that the electrical world, where recording was no longer limited to a neutral capturing of a performance, exploded all the old categories of what "sounding good" meant. "What, then is the 'natural' sound of an orchestra?" he asked. "Some years ago there would have been many waiting to answer the question in terms quite definite, but the enlarging conception of sound, and new possibilities of controlling and modifying it, inevitably lead us to distrust the certainties of years not long past. The whole sphere of sound has become vastly freer."

The only American conductor whose fame rivaled Stokowski's was Arturo Toscanini, the conductor of the NBC Orchestra. Toscanini once said that when he first moved to the United States from Italy, he found the noise of American cities unbearable, but that over time he was able to tune it out. Stokowski didn't even try. "Don't be shocked at what I'm going to say," he once told Gould, "but I like the sound of street noises. Taxicabs are blowing their horns and all kinds of sounds are going on—they have a rhythm, they have a blending of life in the streets, and it is a kind of music. Some people would say that it is a horrible noise. To my ears, it is interesting because it is life."

Born in England in 1882 to a Polish cabinetmaker father and an Irish mother, Stokowski was a musical prodigy who by the age of thirty was conducting the Philadelphia Orchestra. Stokowski steadily built this provincial orchestra into one of the world's greatest (Rachmaninoff called it "the Stradivarius of orchestras"), famous for its "Philadelphia sound," a sonic richness he attained through such innovations as "free-bowing": instead of bowing in unison, the string players bowed at their own pace, creating different combinations of overtones. (An official with another orchestra called free-bowing "the juiciest sound in the world.") At a time when it was still assumed that the best musicians came from Europe, Stokowski hired Americans, including those who were not male or white. "The rhythm of our life is different from that of any other country," he wrote. "Not only are we building up a distinctive American way of presenting music, but we are also developing distinctly American ways of representing it."

Stokowski was involved in some very early experiments in electrical recording, and hated the results. But he was intrigued by the recording system that Victor, just across the Delaware River in Camden, had licensed from Western Electric. In April 1925, he crossed the river with forty of his musicians to make an electrical recording of Saint-Saëns's *Danse Macabre*. The softly muted one-note piano figure that begins the piece showed off the increased dynamic range and decreased surface noise of the new system. The Victor record became the world's first commercially available electrically recorded symphonic disc. *The Gramophone* raved: "Here is yet another piece of evidence that the gramophone is challenging reality at last."

Stokowski still wasn't completely satisfied. He came closer to the sound he had in mind with the orchestra's recording of Antonín Dvořák's Symphony No. 9, "From the New World," the first electrically recorded complete symphonic work, released by Victor on five discs. If *Danse Macabre* was the death knell of the acoustic era, "From the New World" was the emissary to the electrical world—"the most ambitious electrical recording so far," one reviewer raved. "From the New World" was an interesting choice for such a milestone, given Stokowski's infatuation with America.

Like Stokowski, the Czech-born Dvořák had been inspired by the musical possibilities of this new world, proclaiming that "the future music of this country must be founded on what are called Negro melodies." Those who heard "From the New World" detected strains of everything from "Swing Low, Sweet Chariot" to Native American music to "Three Blind Mice." Stokowski obviously heard all this and more.

In 1927, Stokowski had the Philadelphia Orchestra make another recording of the piece, this time at the orchestra's home base, the Academy of Music, where all of its subsequent recordings would be made. Compared with the 1925 recording, it's striking to hear how much electrical recording techniques had improved in just two years, and how the large room's acoustics improved the sound. The last part of the recording is Stokowski playing piano as he describes the piece we've just heard, noting how one section evokes "the vast and lonely Indian plains" and another suggests "a wild and rhapsodic Negro lullaby."

Two years later, a few months after RCA acquired Victor, Stokowski was part of another first. On October 6, 1929, the Philadelphia Orchestra traveled to New York to play the first radio program broadcast over a network. The more Stokowski dealt with radio, the more he grew dissatisfied with the sound quality. He decided he wanted to do more than merely conduct these broadcasts. When he discovered that the show's engineer controlled the sound levels and mix as it went over the air, the maestro announced, "No one controls Stokowski's sound but Stokowski." He insisted that NBC rig up a portable mixing board that could be placed next to him while he conducted. If Stokowski thought the orchestra sounded too loud or too soft, he'd reach over and adjust the levels. Of course, Stokowski couldn't actually hear what the broadcast level was, and so the engineers frantically tried to control huge shifts in volume. Eventually, they resorted to disconnecting Stokowski's board without telling him.

Meanwhile, the orchestra continued to make records for Victor, and Stokowski grew more immersed in the finer points of recording. Given how intimately music is connected to technology today, it's easy to miss the significance of what Stokowski was doing, how far he was going into uncharted territory. At a time when music at a session was recorded directly onto a disc-cutting machine, before postproduction sound mixing was a realistic possibility, Stokowski learned to "mix" musicians. He worked closely with Charles O'Connell, RCA Victor's artistic director, who would move a roving microphone around during sessions, so that a piece with multiple soloists and large changes in dynamics could be recorded without the engineers having to adjust their equipment. As with radio, however, Stokowski's insistence on complete control had its drawbacks. Not only did he require that the recording engineers consult him before moving any microphones, but he insisted that a panel that controlled the microphones be installed next to him at the podium so he could tweak the sound as he conducted. As with his radio work, this multitasking tormented the engineers.

Besides the technical knowledge he was gaining, Stokowski was beginning to conceptualize what it meant symbolically to record music electrically. In the early days of electrical recording, the conventional wisdom was that you placed the microphone at about the same distance from the musical source as a spectator watching that performance would stand—the implication being that the microphone is a synthetic stand-in for the human ear. What Stokowski came to realize was that the ear is "smarter" than the microphone because our auditory systems make adjustments in perspective that a microphone cannot. When we hear a soloist, we move that sound to the forefront of our consciousness; a microphone just reads it as another sound—more distinct than the others, perhaps, but still part of a two-dimensional picture. The microphone passively receives sound, but we use it to create a multifaceted tonal picture.

In the acoustic era, the musicians gathered around the phonograph's horn like supplicants at an altar, offering the machine the sacrifice of their sounds and hoping to be blessed with an audible record. The microphone changes everything. Those microphones are working for *us*. We'll spread ourselves out in a big room, make the microphone do our bidding, tilt it away from what we want it to suppress and point it toward what we want it to enable. Stokowski was discovering something profoundly simple and massive in its musical implications: if you want to hear more French horn, shove a microphone right inside its bell.

Bell Labs continued its sound research throughout the twenties. A Bell engineer named Irad S. "Ray" Rafuse built a cramped makeshift recording studio high above the top balcony of New York's cavernous Roxy, a theater that hosted a wide variety of entertainment. Cables snaked down from the balcony and connected to microphones in the orchestra pit. After recording a show, Rafuse would take the wax cuttings and head downtown to Bell's office on West Street in Greenwich Village, where he would process the wax into copper masters and then a vinyl record.

Rafuse's experiments yielded interesting results, but Arthur Keller decided that the lab should study the contours of sound in a more organized, quantifiable way. What they needed to do was record some great musicians playing complex music under controlled conditions. Bell approached Toscanini and the conductor of the Boston Symphony, neither of whom were interested, and Stokowski, who definitely was.

Stokowski invited the Bell engineers to come to the Academy of Music and hang their microphone wherever they wanted. In 1931, they transformed a basement room into a studio and sound lab, and began to assemble the world's most fearsome sound system. They built sensitive amplifiers and loudspeakers that were taller than the men themselves. During the Philadelphia Orchestra's 1931–32 season, the Bell engineers recorded nearly every practice and concert. They conducted several simultaneous recording experiments, studying such variables as frequency response, dynamic range, and signal-to-noise ratio. In a posthumous vindication of Edison, Bell's Halsey A. Frederick discovered that vertically cut records, using Edison's beloved hill-and-dale method, offered superior sound.

Sometimes people who came to the orchestra's concerts became part of what were called "frequency tests." Stokowski would ask the audience to be patient while the engineers played various amplified sounds, and noted when they decayed to the point of inaudibility. These sounds, as *The Philadelphia Inquirer* reported after one such concert, included "the bellow of a bull in pain," "the prima donna pipings of an apoplectic but addled contralto," and something that sounded like "the plaintive yowl of a dinosaur calling its mate."

Keller remembered that Bell's prior research had demonstrated that words spoken over a telephone were more intelligible when heard over two channels. He reasoned that dual channels would have the same effect on music. The engineers experimented with separating high and low frequencies into two channels, which they discovered cut down on distortion. "Listening monaurally gives me the sensation of the music being choked and crushed together," Stokowski said. "Binaurally, the music sounds free." The engineers made some records with the high and low frequencies separated into two grooves. It was the earliest example of stereophonic sound, and for Stokowski it was a revelation. "The microphone is a kind of electric ear," he later wrote in *The Atlantic Monthly*. "But the microphone is a *single* circuit or means of carrying the sound to us. To convey music with full and true auditory perspective, we should have, in my opinion, double circuits which could be made to correspond to our method of hearing with two ears and which would give us the tonal spaciousness and beauty of sound that make music so satisfying in a large and well-planned auditorium."

The group further discovered that the binaural effect could be augmented by what Fletcher called "auditory perspective." If two microphones were set up on either side of the stage, with the channels balanced, the recording, when heard through two speakers, sounded as though the instruments were in their positions onstage. If a third microphone was placed in the middle of the stage, the music fused into sound that did not seem to be emanating from any one speaker. The music was everywhere and nowhere.

One day, Fletcher posed a question with massive implications for the coming years of multitrack recorded sound. "Why do you have twenty-five or forty violins?" he asked Stokowski. "Why don't you just have one and reproduce it and magnify it?"

Stokowski allowed that Fletcher might be onto something: Could one violin be amplified to sound like forty?

Through experimentation they discovered that no, it couldn't—not without distorting or sounding fake. Six, on the other hand . . . "Six violins in the orchestra—you can't tell the difference," Fletcher marveled, as he and Stokowski stared at the meters in the basement lab. "You can make an orchestra with about one-third or one-fourth of the number of people you have in it."

Stokowski laughed. "You couldn't do it. The union wouldn't let you."

Besides the frequency tests, the first time the world outside the Academy of Music heard an inkling of what was going on in that basement came during the final days of 1931, when Stokowski and Frederick played some of the new recordings for a joint meeting of the Institute of Radio Engineers and the Society of Motion Picture Engineers at a theater in midtown Manhattan. After they had heard a few selections, Stokowski took the stage. "You have heard these records," he said. "They speak for themselves, especially from the standpoint of recording. You have seen, I am sure, the great advance in the three main things that are essential: frequency range, volume range, and reducing foreign extraneous noises. That is to say, when you heard the great volume of tone coming out from that organ, it thrilled you. It uplifted you. It excited you. I am sure you would find if you analyzed it that your heart was beating quicker, that your blood was flowing quicker, that your nervous system was tremendously stimulated."

Western Electric trumpeted the tone-test angle, reporting that "for the first time" people were able to hear the "true reproduced" sound of every key on a piano. The composer Deems Taylor, who was in the audience, concurred. "You would have to hear it to know," he said, grappling for the words to explain what he heard. "One can only say, rather lamely, that the voices became real. The difference between what we usually hear and what I heard was, roughly, the difference between looking at a photograph of somebody and looking at the person himself."

A similar demo was held five months later for members of the Acoustical Society of America. Decades before Milli Vanilli or Ashley Simpson, Stokowski had a modest proposal, using Wagner's *Tannhäuser* as an example: "Opera today, while pleasing to the ear, is often a sore trial for the eye. Take *Tannhäuser*, for example. Venus, the most beautiful woman in the world, is using her charms to tempt Tannhäuser from the narrow path of virtue. But, unfortunately, the lady who plays the part . . . may sing like a nightingale, but she looks like an elephant. By no stretch of the imagination could one believe for a minute that she is Venus. . . . Electricity will change her. We can take her voice and record it on a disk. Then we can select a beautiful young lady who really may be accepted by the audience for a Venus. Then we can synchronize voice and action and create a perfect illusion . . . Modern advances in sound recording now make it possible, we hope, and this is one of the many horizons now being opened up in music."

A year later, on April 12, 1933, the group finally demonstrated its sonic breakthroughs for a nontechnical audience. The three hundred invited guests who arrived at the Academy of Music were greeted by a completely darkened stage. When the house lights went down, the Philadelphia Orchestra began to play *Götterdämmerung*. After the Rhine washed away Brünnhilde's ashes, the lights came up to reveal . . . an empty stage, as though the musicians themselves had perished with Valhalla. Fletcher stood in the wings and let the crowd murmur its confusion for a few seconds before he walked onstage. The orchestra's musicians, he explained to the shocked audience, were actually in a soundproof room in the basement. That room was wired with microphones that carried the music to amplifiers, and then upstairs to loudspeakers onstage. "What you've just witnessed is an illusion," he said. "An actual presence has been created by placing the sounds of the orchestra into their proper positions in space, just as a stereoscope seems to make images come forward or recede." As Fletcher spoke, other sounds were coming from somewhere, or nowhere, and then they were everywhere. The bewildered audience heard a phantom carpenter walk onstage and begin to saw wood and hammer nails. A phone rang off to one side. The carpenter stopped, picked up the receiver and said hello. The eyes of the audience followed his every move.

Two weeks later, the ante was upped further in an event organized by the Academy of Natural Sciences. Fletcher originally wanted an expanded version of the April 12 show, to demonstrate that it was "impossible for one listening with his eyes blindfolded to know that the actual orchestra was not onstage before him." This demo wouldn't involve recording per se, but it would show how much progress had been made in transmitting disembodied sounds—and what were recordings if not the ultimate example of sound disembodied? Stokowski wanted the musicians separated from the audience. As in, by hundreds of miles.

Radio had already demonstrated that sound could be sent over long distances. But in the days before FM and other modifications, music could not be heard over the radio with anything approaching high fidelity. So why not send it over the phone? The Philadelphia Orchestra was at its home base in Philadelphia; the audience was in Constitution Hall in Washington, D.C. Stokowski's assistant conductor led the musicians in Philadelphia. The orchestra played Bach's Toccata and Fugue in D Minor, Beethoven's Fifth, Debussy's *Prélude à l'après-midi d'un faune*, and, of course, closed with *Götterdämmerung*. The music was carried over specially dedicated phone lines to Constitution Hall, where Stokowski, in the back of the room, sat in front of a board, able to adjust the volume, tone, and balance of the music before it went to the speakers.

Stokowski and the Bell engineers did everything they could to dazzle the audience that night. To demonstrate the "three-dimensional" capabilities of their system, sounds in Philadelphia were broadcast from different heights and depths of the stage; the spatial arrangements were audible in

Washington. To show off volume, the orchestra played at a normal level while Stokowski turned the knob up to "a loudness almost great enough to be painful," in the words of Bell's newsletter. To show off the range of the music, Stokowski switched on various filters, removing one octave at a time from the mix, to demonstrate all that the audience wasn't missing. The fanciest trick of the night was a duet between two trumpeters, one standing on the left side of the stage in Philadelphia, the other standing on the right side of the darkened stage in D.C. When the lights went up, the audience was shocked to discover only one musician onstage.

The program also included a talk by Fletcher, who explained the technology that allowed the audience to hear music coming from hundreds of miles away with such clarity. Again, there seemed to be some construction going on in Philly. The D.C. audience listened as a workman built a box with a hammer and saw, while another worker stood off to the side and offered advice. A soprano in Philadelphia walked around the stage as she sang "Coming Through the Rye," while her chimera mirrored her movements in Constitution Hall.

The Philadelphia–Washington experiment was particularly important to Stokowski because of what it heralded. It was the precursor to what he called—with his typically prescient sense of future nomenclature—"wired transmission." The idea was that music could be transmitted over telephone lines rather than the airwaves, solving the problem of fidelity in the pre-FM era, and that such a transmission would also allow for music to be tweaked as it came off the wire, providing a form of sound mixing in an era when recorded music still had to be cut directly to disc.

But on a larger level, wired transmission was the ultimate expression of an electrical democratizing ethic, forecasting a future in which music was beamed far and wide, and when musical expression was unlimited. "If a gold mine of great capacity were found, or a subterranean sea of petroleum were discovered, it would be quickly developed," he wrote. "But a means whereby Everyman can hear music with overwhelming beauty and eloquence in any part of our vast country, no matter how remote, is neglected and left unused in a laboratory."

Even as Stokowski and Bell continued to redefine what amplified sound could do for recording and transmission throughout the thirties, Stokowski was never quite satisfied. He wanted music to be even more flexible, and he wanted it louder. Especially the latter. "We must enlarge the volume range," he wrote in a letter to Bell in 1932. "I believe that eventually music by radio will have more appeal instead of less appeal than music heard in concert because we can lift the top edge of the volume range far above what it is in the concert hall and stretch the bottom edge down to a point just above the threshold which will increase the eloquence of music to a degree unimaginable at present."

He soon got his wish. The Bell engineers had continued their research into stereophonic recordings, but they weren't convinced there was a commercial market for stereophonic discs. They did, however, think the technology would be useful to the movie industry, so they developed a way to record onto film. The problem with film as a sound-recording medium was that compared with discs, the dynamic range of film (the difference between the softest and loudest sounds it was capable of recording) was limited. Bell's solution was a system that measured the level of the music as it was being recorded. To achieve the stereophonic effect, three microphones were used, all running to their own soundtrack on the film. If the music exceeded a certain volume, the system adjusted it down to the limit while an alternating current alongside the soundtracks expressed how much the sound had been compressed. During playback, each soundtrack passed through a photoelectric cell, which caused an electric current to travel to the amplifier and then the speakers. As it did so, the "control current" told the system how much to amplify the sound currents so that the sound regained its original volume. The system also allowed for the flexible control of each track, so that the music could be "enhanced" as it was transferred to disc—parts could be made louder or softer, depending on the whim of the enhancer.

With Fletcher's assistance, Stokowski used this method to make several Philadelphia Orchestra recordings, as well as some by Paul Robeson and the Mormon Tabernacle Choir. Bell's overpowering amplifiers and loudspeakers, its reality-challenging stereophonic recording techniques, and now the missing link: music that sounded more live than life. In March 1940, Bell announced that a "specially invited audience" would converge on Carnegie Hall to hear records "enhanced in the fortissimo passages to a sound equivalent to 2,000 musicians without altering the tonal quality." At the 1933 demo in Philadelphia, the musicians had been in the basement. At the Washington demo, the musicians had been in Philadelphia. And now they would be nowhere at all, sounding like there were 2,000 of them. Who needed warm bodies? It was the triumph of the recorded artifact, the ultimate rebuke to the Edisonians.

"Every sound that the ear could hear live will be heard in performance," the announcement promised. "The listener in Carnegie Hall will have the same spatial sense as to the source of the sounds as if he were sitting in the original hall, and in addition he will hear the music enhanced by variations of loudness and tone quality according to the interpretation of the original director . . . Stereophonic reproduction . . . has supplied the equipment and technique for the recording without loss of the original music, and with an actual enhancement of original feeling."

The blowout at Carnegie Hall marked the apotheosis of the Stokowski-Bell collaboration, but Stokowski himself wasn't there for the explosion. He had left the Philadelphia Orchestra and moved to Hollywood in 1936 to capitalize on his celebrity. He had appeared in a few films, but his one great cinematic achievement was about to be unleashed on the world.

The *Fantasia* story began with a chance encounter between two living legends. Walt Disney walked into a Beverly Hills restaurant and recognized the famous maestro. Disney introduced himself to Stokowski and asked if he could join him. Disney mentioned that he was interested in creating an animated film around Paul Dukas's *The Sorcerer's Apprentice* and asked if Stokowski would conduct the music for the film. Stokowski loved the idea, and he later persuaded Disney to make a full-length animated feature film based on several classical pieces. Deems Taylor was brought on board to introduce the pieces in the film. Disney, Taylor, Stokowski, and several directors and writers began holding weekly meetings ("sweat-box sessions," they called them) to tackle the daunting task of choosing music for a film that was about nothing other than music, and to work on visual ideas that would complement the music.

The *Fantasia* recording sessions got under way in the spring of 1939, with Stokowski leading his old crew, the Philadelphia Orchestra, at his old haunt and recording clubhouse, the Academy of Music. The music was recorded onto film with a setup that was basically an extreme version of Bell's three-channel stereophonic method, which Stokowski dubbed "Fantasound." The orchestra was divided into eight groups, with a sound camera trained on each, and a ninth camera recording the total sonic blend. A total of thirty-three microphones recorded the music onto the channels. The sessions lasted two months, after which the music was mixed down onto fewer tracks for the finished product.

A few months after the elites were pinned to the wall in Carnegie Hall, *Fantasia* opened in theaters to a much broader audience. *Fantasia* marked the first time that music was a motion picture's primary art. Images illustrated sounds, yet another way Stokowski was ahead of his time. Carnegie Hall had shown the might and power that girded music's marriage with science and industry, but Stokowski had located the real art. Seeing the film was perhaps a less overpowering experience than the enhanced music demo, but it was still a heady sonic experience. When animated musical instruments climbed a staircase of notes, the music seemed to move across the screen. In the film's most famous scene, with Mickey Mouse as the overwhelmed apprentice who unleashes a flood, the music poured out of one corner of the room until it felt like it was flooding the theater.

Stokowski never stopped being a contrarian. As 1940 drew to a close, he conducted a radio broadcast of the Philadelphia Orchestra performing the debut of Arnold Schoenberg's Violin Concerto, proudly described by the composer—like Stokowski, a European transplant to America—as "another unplayable work." How the piece was received by those tuned in at home is anyone's guess, but the studio audience was, on the whole, less than impressed by Schoenberg's twelve-tone excursions. Most didn't applaud, a few walked out, and some even booed. "Why don't you give the piece a chance?" Stokowski demanded. "It's the American way."

His relationship with recording engineers remained stormy. Tom Shepherd, an engineer who worked on some Stokowski recordings in the early sixties, recalled that Stokowski would often tell a musician to play louder, and then also tell the recording engineer to raise the instrumentalist's microphone, and then later on remind the postproduction mixer to make the instrumentalist louder. "You had to know when to listen to him once and ignore him twice," Shepherd said. "What Stokowski was doing defied physical law. He kept making things louder, louder, louder . . . He would not understand that once you reached a certain saturation of loudness everything else had to be softer as a result. There were certain things he wasn't willing to conceptualize." When Stokowski was shown how the needles were pinned in the red, he'd just say, "It doesn't matter, this is art."

Right up to the end of his life, Stokowski remained interested in the musically transformative powers of wired transmission in all its forms. "The contributions of electronics to music is so great that we cannot fully measure its extent and effect on our cultural lives," he wrote in 1958, "because through electronics, time and space have been conquered, so that we can see and hear at any distance and any interval of time . . . Unless all civilization and all inherited and newly created cultural values are destroyed by the madness of war, the contribution of electricity to music will always continue, but in new forms undreamed of at present, always leading to higher forms of musical creation, performance, and inspirational listening made available to Everyman."

Stokowski, born just a few years after Edison's phonograph, died in 1977, its centennial year. Paul Myers, who supervised Stokowski's final recordings, remembered the last recording session, held two months before his death: "He was so frail. Often he would just sit with his eyes closed. But then he'd come alive with interest, inspecting our 16-channel control board and the tape machines." One of the most memorable performances to come out of the session was Wagner's *Götterdämmerung*, the piece that had blown the doors off Carnegie Hall nearly thirty-seven years earlier. Barry Tuckwell, the first-chair French horn player, later said he felt like he'd never played that well before, that Stokowski had "mesmerized" him.

Really, that's all Stokowski ever wanted music to do. His ideal of the perfect world, of sound unbound, was like the Panama-Pacific Expo recast as one giant Joy Zone. He described "great recreation centers . . . like large parks, with music emanating from towers decorated with colored lights that shined at night . . . The music could be sent out by wired transmission . . . The orchestra or other musicians would be in a large hall, so that those who like to see as well as hear music being made could be in this hall instead of in the gardens. The tower would be so high, and the loudness of the music so adjusted, that thousands could hear it in the gardens, either walking about or sitting. The music would be clear and full, but not obtrusive. It could be directed to certain parts of the gardens, but be practically inaudible in others. This could all be done because there is practically no limit, in wired transmission, to the control of loudness, tone-color, and the direction in which the music is sent."

Of course, the centers could not make a profit. They should take in only enough money necessary "to supply us with the various kinds of amusement and recreation of mind and body which we all need, and which would give us all our share of the joy and poetry of life."

Analog

3

Aluminum Cowboys: A Pretape Parable

It is always a dramatic moment for anyone when his own voice comes back to
him undistorted from the black mouth of a loud-speaker. He seems to feel the
intense and absorbing pleasure that a child experiences when he first recog-
nizes himself in a mirror.   —John Lomax and Alan Lomax

> My father told me when I was a child
> "Son, the world is gettin' mighty wise"
>   —Lead Belly, "Turn Yo' Radio On"

Alan Lomax became a man, professionally speaking, during the summer of
1933, when his father, the folklorist John Lomax, took him on a song-
hunting expedition through the American South. A precocious kid and a
prodigious intellect, Alan had enrolled at the University of Texas at age fifteen, spent the following year at Harvard, and then returned for another
year at UT. He had already been praised by Carl Sandburg (a friend of
John's) as "intensely American and flagrantly and vagrantly modern."
When John picked him up at school, armed with an Edison cylinder
machine, donated by Edison's widow, with which the Lomaxes hoped to
record "the secular songs of the Negroes" for the Library of Congress, Alan
was all of eighteen.

The course of his young life was set a few days into the trip, when the
Lomaxes found themselves on the Smithers plantation in Huntsville, Texas.

That night, they entered a small schoolhouse, lit by a kerosene lamp, filled with black plantation residents and the white manager. Feeling all eyes on him, Alan walked to the front of the room with the phonograph and asked if anyone in the room could sing the famous ballad of "Stagolee" into the machine's horn.

A murmur went through the crowd and soon became a unanimous chorus.

"Send Blue!"

"Blue knows more about Stagolee than ol' Stag himself!"

"Blue, white man ain't gonna hurt you! What you scared of? That horn too little for you to fall into it—too little for you to sing at with your big mouth!"

The man named Blue stood up. He certainly deserves the name, Alan thought as Blue walked toward him. The man's skin was so dark it looked blue-back. "Can you sing Stagolee?" Alan asked.

"Yessuh," Blue replied. "I knows ol' 'Stagolee,' and I'll sing it for you." He paused. "If you allow me to sing another song first."

"Well," Alan stammered, "we would like to hear it first, because we don't have very many unused cylinders . . ."

"No, sir," Blue said, picking up and adjusting the recording horn. "I won't sing my song but once. You've gotta catch it the first time I sing it."

Alan relented, and switched on the machine. Blue began to sing:

> Poor farmer, poor farmer, poor farmer
> They get all the farmer makes
> His clothes is full of patches, his hat is full of holes
> Stoopin' down, pickin' cotton, from off the cotton bolls . . .

As he sang, he looked at the plantation manager. The crowd's nervous laughter grew to a roar as Blue continued:

> Poor farmer, poor farmer, poor farmer
> They get all the farmer makes,
> At the commissary, his money in their bags
> His poor little wife and children, sit at home in rags . . .

When he was done, Blue received a standing ovation. But he wasn't finished yet. He motioned to Alan to keep the machine running, looked straight at the horn, and delivered a spoken coda. "Now, Mr. President," he said, "you just don't know how bad they're treating us folks down here. I'm singing to you, and I'm talking to you, so I hope you will come down here and do something for us poor folks down here in Texas."

As the crowd cheered, Alan adjusted the machine to play back the recording. People shushed each other as Blue's scratchy voice emerged from the horn. "That thing sure talks sense!" someone yelled. "Blue, you done it this time!" Alan scanned the audience and noticed that the manager had tiptoed out of the room.

"I realized then what my career was going to be," he wrote years later, once he had supplanted his father as America's preeminent song collector. "As Blue and his friends saw, the recording machine can be a voice for the voiceless, for the millions in the world who have no access to the main channels of communication, and whose cultures are being talked to death by all sorts of well-intentioned people—teachers, missionaries, etc.—and who are being shouted into silence by our commercially bought-and-paid for loudspeakers."

Alan retold this story several times throughout his life. Though the details could change (the schoolhouse was sometimes a church), the conclusion never varied. Alan's epiphany was a key moment in recording history because it neatly summarized the implications of hitting the Record button and making a record of somebody else's music. The key word is "loudspeakers"—its literal definition (boxes that broadcast sounds) and the punning "loud speakers" (the people who are privileged enough to be heard above the fray). It reflects Alan's understanding that sound technology is always ideological, because whoever has access to it gets to have—and be—the loudest speaker.

In that moment, as Alan and Blue faced each other, Alan became a "producer" in the modern recording sense: the person who stands between the musician and the listening world, controlling access to the technology and serving as a mediating check on the music. Blue wanted artistic freedom, but Alan was worried about going over budget (the dwindling cylinder supply). Alan wanted an authentic document of American folk song to give to his corporate and government backers, while Blue wanted something that would appeal to his own demographic. But Blue also wanted to reach a crossover audience, hoping that he'd catch the ear of President Roosevelt himself.

A few weeks later, Alan found a human face for his new life's project. In their search for "secular" songs that were, in John's words, "most unlike those of the white race" and "the least contaminated by Negro jazz," the Lomaxes were coming up short. "So it was that we decided to visit the Negro prison farms of the South," Alan wrote. "There, we thought we should find that the Negro away from the pressure of the church and community, ignorant of the uplifting educational movement, having none but official contact with white men, dependent on the resources of his own group for amusement, and hearing no canned music, would have preserved and increased his heritage of secular folk-music. And we were right."

John was less enthused. He was particularly disappointed that many prisons prohibited convicts from singing while they worked, which made it harder to record material.

But there was one particular inmate who even John had to admit "almost supplied the deficiency." They met him on a rainy Sunday at the infamous Louisiana State Penitentiary at Angola. His name was Huddie (rhymes with "Judy") Ledbetter, but everyone called him Lead Belly. He called himself "the king of the 12-string guitar," and his repertoire was huge. The Lomaxes recorded Lead Belly performing seven different songs that day, including three takes of "Irene," a song in waltz time with lyrics that veered from sweet to mean.

The following summer, the Lomaxes returned to Angola and recorded fifteen more Lead Belly songs—including two versions of "Irene"—with an aluminum-disc machine that provided improved sound. Nearly sixty years later, as Alan reflected on the thousands of musicians he recorded, he would say that being a "sensitive audience for Lead Belly" was his proudest achievement.

Born in 1888, the same year Edison's phonograph made its return to public life, Lead Belly was the first American professional musician to be marketed aggressively as an authentic primitive, as the "other" in the flesh. Although Lead Belly was presented as the embodiment of American folk music, very few of his recordings were released in his lifetime. As a recording artist, Lead Belly is an almost entirely posthumous creation. His music is part of the collections of the Smithsonian and the Library of Congress, two of the most venerable American institutions. With the possible exception of Woody Guthrie, Lead Belly is the closest we have to an "official" national musician, a musically signifying bald eagle.

Lead Belly is "ours," but we are working from a blueprint left to us by those who recorded him while he was alive. There were many, but those who had the biggest effect on our understanding of him were the Lomaxes, who recorded him for the Library of Congress, and Moses Asch, who recorded him for his label, Folkways Records (now administered by the Smithsonian). Each of these men heard in Lead Belly a different combination of artist and artifact, and each treated him as a different combination of commercial property to exploit and authentic Americana to preserve. The Lomaxes mostly recorded Lead Belly for the Library of Congress, yet they also claimed co-writing credit on some of his songs, and for a while each claimed one-third of Lead Belly's income as his "managers." Asch recorded Lead Belly for commercial purposes, yet one of his rules for Folkways releases was that they have limited commercial appeal, and he packaged them to look like anthropological monographs.

If Lead Belly was the first so-called American primitive musician to be shaped and packaged for mass consumption, that would make him the first musician to be "produced." Which means that John, Alan, and Moses—the people who had the power and privilege to shape that raw material—were the first producers. Indeed, for most of America, the Lomaxes literally *produced* Lead Belly, plucking him from the bush and taking him to the big city.

"He really understood what he was," Asch once said of Lead Belly, "in terms of America, in terms of music, and everything else." What Asch meant, of course, was that *he* understood America, in terms of Lead Belly's music. And our understanding of America is shaped by Asch's and the Lomaxes' understanding of Lead Belly, and the steps they took to document him for the ages.

Lead Belly's work with the Lomaxes and Asch took place against the backdrop of the pre-tape era—when for the first time semiportable disc-recording equipment made it possible to capture sound anywhere in the world. This is the story of how Lead Belly's producers used the evolving power of sound recording to preserve—or create—what they saw as the real Lead Belly. It's also the story of how, late in his life, Lead Belly caught the cusp of an emerging technology that allowed him to produce himself.

Perhaps the best way to illustrate the difference between John Lomax and his youngest son is to note that during the summer that Alan's muse was Blue, John's was Black.

At the Tennessee State Penitentiary, father and son met Black Sampson, a convict with a huge selection of work songs. The problem was that Black, a God-fearing man, was reluctant to sing these songs he now considered "sinful," especially for a machine that would bear witness for all eternity. So John summoned the warden, who told Black he'd better start singing. Black began to pray aloud, asking God to forgive him for what he was about to do. Like any good producer, John recognized the power of the first take and managed to record the prayer as well as the songs. "I call this my prize record," he crowed.

As different as John was from his son, he and Lead Belly were more alike than you might imagine. There was a star-crossed quality to their lives. In the years before they met, each circled around the other, often just a few miles apart, each worried that time was passing him by, until they finally joined forces and became producer and produced.

John was born twenty-one years before Lead Belly, in Mississippi, the sixth of ten children, and grew up in Meridian, Texas. A bright, uptight kid, John began doing menial work on the family's hardscrabble farm from the time he was six. Huddie Ledbetter grew up in Louisiana, about three hundred miles from the Lomaxes, in the Caddo Lake area of the Red River Valley, where Louisiana, Arkansas, and Texas meet, a region then considered to be one of America's last unconquered frontiers. Wes Ledbetter, the son of slaves, had managed to save enough money to buy seventy acres for $150. Like John, Huddie worked the fields from a young age, but the Ledbetters doted on Huddie, their only son, making sure he got an education—he was a star student and managed to attend classes through the eighth grade— and encouraging his aptitude for music. By the time he hit his teens, he had taught himself to play accordion, piano, Jew's harp, and guitar.

The Lomax farm was near a spur of the Chisholm Trail, the route that carried huge cattle drives from Texas, across large swaths of the Indian Nations (soon to become Oklahoma), to stockyards in Kansas. John claimed that one of his most formative experiences was lying in bed at the age of four, listening to the distant strains of a cowboy on the trail singing "Git Along Little Dogies." Huddie was also enamored of the cowboy mystique. When he turned sixteen, his parents presented him with his own horse, a nice saddle, and a pistol. John also had his own pony, which he was forced to sell to pay for his education when he was twenty, a heartbreaking experience that made him weep.

Determined to rise above his station, John enrolled at the University of Texas while in his late twenties. Huddie wound up getting a more unorthodox education. At the age of eighteen, he was already playing guitar at the Saturday night parties known as "sukey jumps." After a brush with the law, he lit out for central Texas, mostly supporting himself by picking cotton, and perhaps even taking classes at a black college. He spent a lot of time in New Orleans, soaking up music, everything from jazz to Jelly Roll Morton (whose boogie-woogie piano would have a profound effect on Huddie's music). He eventually moved to Dallas, where he worked in the nearby oil fields and began performing with a sightless guitarist named Blind Lemon Jefferson. It was around this time that Huddie picked up a Stella 12-string guitar with steel strings, which became his signature instrument.

After earning a degree in English at UT, John took a teaching position in the English department at Texas A&M. In 1906, when he was nearly forty, John took a leave from A&M to do graduate work at Harvard, which included enrolling in an American literature class taught by Professor Barrett Wendell. When Wendell had begun teaching this class a decade earlier, it had been the nation's first American literature class. John asked Wendell if he could write about cowboy songs. Wendell loved the idea and introduced his student to George Lyman Kittredge, a Harvard professor who taught a class on English and Scottish folk ballads. Toward the end of the spring semester, John and Kittredge sent one thousand copies of a form letter to newspaper editors throughout the western United States. The letter explained that John was compiling a complete collection of native ballads and songs of the West and asked each newspaper to encourage its readers to send John whatever they had.

The general methodology of academic "song collectors"—such as Kittredge's mentor, Francis Child, whose book, *The English and Scottish Popular Ballads*, was the first serious attempt to examine Western popular songs as cultural artifacts—was to treat folk songs as "literature," rather than sounds. Because the emphasis was on textual analysis, people like Child spent more time in libraries than out in the field, and they weren't typically interested in making recordings. John had other ideas. He started taking small trips to different locations throughout the West—farms, ranches, cattlemen conventions—and asking people to sing their songs for him.

For Child, American folk songs were of scholarly interest only because they preserved English and Scottish musical traditions; any "original" attributes were merely impurities imposed by the New World, not evidence of a thriving indigenous folk tradition. By hitting the road and writing down lyrics of the songs people sang, John was essentially arguing against Child. He strayed even further from Child by attempting to make actual records on a clunky Edison cylinder machine he occasionally dragged along with him. This wasn't wholly unprecedented in the world of song collecting, but it was very rare. Of the few song collectors who had tried making wax recordings in the field, many were so wed to the idea that songs were best preserved on paper that they had simply used the records to help them make musical notations, then shaved the wax so that the cylinder could be reused. John got uneven results with the cylinder machine. He discovered that unless he used earphones to hear what he recorded, "the squeaky, mouse-like sounds bore little resemblance to music."

Two summers later, he set off on a longer song-collecting trip, poking around ranches by day and sleeping under the stars at night. By the end of the year, Lomax's *Cowboy Songs and Other Frontier Ballads* (with a preface written by Theodore Roosevelt, who had taken an interest in John's project) was on bookshelves. It was the means through which most Americans learned of now-standards like "Git Along Little Dogies" and "Home on the Range." To write the book, John had become not merely a collector but also an interpreter. He'd discovered multiple versions of several songs; rather than print every variation, he combined them to create one song for the book. He wondered if he was violating some sort of folk credo. "I have preserved the original sheet on which I jotted down words taken from several sources," he wrote of "Home on the Range" years later. "Yes, I know I did wrong, but I rephrased some unmetrical lines."

He had barely turned on a recording machine, but he was already producing.

In 1915, the year Edison's tone tests debuted, John's wife gave birth to their third child and second son, Alan; a boat carrying ten-year-old Moses Asch and his family docked at Ellis Island on the Fourth of July; and Huddie Ledbetter got himself into trouble.

Huddie's exact crime is lost to history—perhaps a fight over (or even with) a woman. Three days into a thirty-day chain-gang sentence, he picked up his chain and ran into the woods, dodging bullets. After two years of living with his wife under assumed names, he was arrested for shooting and killing his cousin during an argument. One year into a thirty-year sentence, he broke out again. When he was captured, he was sent to the Central State Farm, better known as "Sugarland," outside of Houston, Texas.

Word of his musical talents spread through the prison, and he was eventually allowed to travel unguarded on Sundays to perform for inmates on the farm's various camps. In 1924, Governor Pat M. Neff decided to tour the state's prison system. On the day he arrived at Sugarland, Lead Belly played some songs, including one asking the governor to grant him clemency: "If I had you like you had me / I'd wake up in the morning and set you free." Neff was impressed. He told Lead Belly that he would eventually commute his sentence, but for now Neff wanted Lead Belly to stay at Sugarland so that he could periodically entertain him.

Neff returned to the prison to see Lead Belly several times that year. As he was about to leave office in January 1925, he kept his promise. He woke up and set Huddie free.

It was the spring of 1925, and Moses Asch was a long way from home. Wherever home was, exactly. He'd never quite figured that one out. He was born in a Polish village and left with his family at the age of seven. His father, Sholem Asch, a budding left-leaning novelist, playwright, and essayist on his way to becoming one of the twentieth century's most popular Yiddish writers, moved the family to Paris and then to New York. While living in Brooklyn, Asch became friends with a boy next door who introduced him to ham radio. "Immediately my imagination started to work," Asch remembered. "I saw the possibility, coming from Europe, where there were only boundaries, that this was a medium that overcame boundaries, overcame customs. The air was free."

When Asch was in his last year of high school, his parents moved back to France. Sholem, noting the economic chaos of Weimar Germany, offered Moses a proposition. His son could study radio engineering at Elektronische-Hochschule in Bingen. Sholem would send him a dollar each day from his American royalties; converted into increasingly worthless German marks, the money could easily pay for tuition and living expenses.

Asch arrived at school in 1922 and discovered that the students, who came from all over the world, liked to swap songs from their countries. Asch didn't really know what America's folk songs were, and his fellow students informed him that there weren't any. This struck Asch as ridiculous—America had to have its own songs. While visiting his family in Paris during spring break in 1925, Asch found an original 1910 edition of John Lomax's *Cowboy Songs and Other Frontier Ballads*. "And when I got back," he recalled years later, "I was able to show the kids at school that there was a uniqueness in our culture."

After graduating with an engineering degree, Asch moved back to New York, worked at RCA for a while, and then opened a small radio repair shop in the Williamsburg section of Brooklyn. During the thirties, he specialized in building massive public address systems. As Asch became active in progressive politics, his love of loud sound took on an implied political facet. A booming system meant that sound was reaching more people, who could then be organized more effectively.

He did a lot of work for the International Ladies' Garment Workers' Union, including building a huge PA for their May Day rally. He devised a mobile PA system that ran off a car battery and built sound trucks for campaigning politicians, including Asch's idol, President Roosevelt. He built a huge system for the speech FDR delivered at Madison Square Garden in 1936, at the end of his second campaign. "We even kicked out Madison Square Garden's amplifier and put our own in," Asch recalled.

Asch installed speakers outside the Garden so that FDR's speech would reach the throngs in the street who couldn't get inside. "For twelve years this Nation was afflicted with hear-nothing, see-nothing, do-nothing government," the president announced, his voice bouncing off the midtown buildings. It was the days of hear-everything.

Soon after Huddie left prison in 1925, his old Dallas partner, Blind Lemon Jefferson, made his first recordings in Chicago, and over the next few years became America's first country-blues star on the strength of songs like "Matchbox Blues" (later covered by the Beatles) and "Black Snake Moan." For Huddie, stardom proved elusive. He returned to Louisiana, worked various jobs, ran bootleg liquor, and continued to play music, now often going by "Lead Belly," a nickname he'd picked up at Sugarland. He was soon back in jail, serving a six-to-ten-year sentence at Angola, where the Lomaxes discovered him three years later.

The Lomaxes' road to Angola was also paved with a certain amount of turmoil. In the years since the publication of *Cowboy Songs and Other Frontier Ballads*, John's song-collecting career had largely stalled. When Lead Belly was sent to Angola, John was working as a bond salesman. He had been forced out of his University of Texas job following a complicated chain of events that began when he opposed efforts to appoint Pat Neff to the UT board when Neff's second term as governor expired. (Neff, who had been Lead Belly's savior, was John's undoing.) John had a vague idea for a project collecting African American folk songs, but nothing came of it.

His creeping feeling of regret over letting his life's passion slip away became a full-blown personal crisis when in 1931 his wife died following a long illness. To rescue John from his deepening depression, his oldest son, John Jr., convinced his dad, who was now sixty-four, to become an itinerant folk-song lecturer. In early 1932, the two embarked on a tour in an old Ford sedan, speaking to what were sometimes minuscule audiences and selling copies of *Cowboy Songs and Other Frontier Ballads* from the trunk. They covered 2,000 miles in three weeks, took a break, and began a second leg, pausing to pick up Alan at Harvard. The Lomax men cooked by the side of the road and camped in cornfields. Alan let his hair grow and argued politics with his dad.

The next year, John was named honorary consultant to the Library of Congress's nascent Archive of American Folk Song, for which he would receive an annual salary of one dollar, plus expenses. He wanted to do the project in African American music he'd been considering for so many years, to present the vanishing songs of the American Negro in their proper "context." To do so, he wanted a portable machine that could record sound with decent fidelity onto durable discs that could be played back immediately—not onto fragile wax discs that became "permanent" only after a trip to the factory.

John eventually found a company willing to build the portable machine that he wanted, but it wasn't ready in time for the start of the 1933 trip (hence Lead Belly and others were recorded on cylinders); when John finally received the machine, he discovered that it was barely portable. It weighed three hundred pounds, required two seventy-five-pound batteries, and recorded onto twelve-inch discs made of aluminum and celluloid, each of which held only a few minutes of music. The machine was temperamental, but by the end of the summer, the Lomaxes deposited at the Library of Congress one hundred songs recorded onto twenty-five discs.

By the time they returned the following summer, they had gotten the kinks out of the machine and, through experimentation with microphone placement, had figured out how to get the optimum sound. The songs they recorded with Lead Belly that July sounded remarkably better than the cylinder recordings from the previous year. "Governor Pat Neff" had been a smash for Lead Belly, a song good enough to get him sprung from prison, and now it was time for the always difficult sophomore follow-up. "Governor O. K. Allen," a message to the current resident of the Louisiana statehouse, was more subdued than its predecessor, but the message was the same. Lead Belly begged the Lomaxes to get the record into Allen's hands, so they drove to Baton Rouge and dropped off a disc with Allen's secretary. Miraculously, by the end of the month, Lead Belly was a free man. Though the record probably had little to do with Lead Belly's freedom—he was eligible for release—the Lomaxes were happy to take the credit.

When Lead Belly was sprung, John and his second wife were on their honeymoon. Lead Belly recalled a vague conversation he and John had had about working together someday, and wrote to him about it. John had misgivings. He had images of Lead Belly killing him in his sleep somewhere in the wilds of Louisiana or Mississippi. Still, Alan was going back to school, and John did hate to drive.

"Come prepared to travel," he wrote back. "Bring guitar."

A few weeks later, they were on the road, acting out one of the all-time strangest buddy-movie scenarios: the stodgy white near-septuagenarian and the black fifty-something ex-jailbird songster on the road in the Deep South. Lead Belly did all the driving and cooking, and was basically John's manservant, but the records they made on this trip really were co-productions. When they pulled into a town, Lead Belly would often go off on his own to round up musicians to bring back to John. Lead Belly liked to adjust the recording settings and microphone placement—"over my protests," John grumbled, convinced that Lead Belly was merely showing off for his own kind. Still, the partnership mostly worked. At one prison in Little Rock, the duo discovered that the execution room was soundproof, and therefore sheltered from the echoes that bounced around the concrete prison and played havoc with their recordings, so they turned it into a makeshift recording studio, placing a white sheet over the electric chair, to put the singers more at ease.

Alan joined the tour, and John floated the idea of getting Lead Belly to sing at the upcoming Modern Language Association convention at Swarthmore. Townsend Scudder III, chair of the MLA planning committee, wrote to John to say he "welcomed your generous suggestion that your talented aborigine 'nigger' sing for the guests." Lead Belly was indeed a hit at the MLA. He sang at the convention's smoker, was presented by John during the Popular Literature symposium, and played a private party that night. John was amused to see that "Bryn Mawr intellectuals in evening dress listened curiously to 'Dicklicker's Holler' and 'Whoa, Back, Buck!' "

A buzz began to build around Lead Belly. On New Year's Day, he performed at a Greenwich Village apartment shared by a New York University folklore professor and someone who worked for John's publisher. The guests included several journalists and literary types, who had heard about the MLA performances. The next day, the *New York Herald Tribune* called Lead Belly "a powerful knife-toting Negro, a Saturnine singer from the swamplands." Two days later, he made his first public appearance at the Hotel Montclair on Lexington Avenue. "Northern people hear Negroes playing and singing beautiful spirituals, which are too refined and unlike true Southern spirituals," John said during his introduction. "Or else they hear men and women on the stage and radio, burlesquing their own songs. Lead Belly doesn't burlesque . . . To me, his music is real music."

Over the next few weeks, John arranged for private Lead Belly performances for people from *Time*, the Rockefeller Foundation, and the Bookseller's League. *The New Yorker* published "Ballad of a Ballad-Hunter," a long poem by William Rose Benét about John and Lead Belly ("He was big and he was black / And wondrous were his wrongs / But he had a memory that traveled back / Through at least 500 songs"). John began to worry about the effect the excitement was having on his charge: "I am distressed at his beginning tendency to show off in his songs and talk when his money value is to be natural and sincere, as he was while in prison . . . as this tendency grows, he will lose his charm and become only an ordinary, low ordinary Harlem nigger."

The solution: get Lead Belly out of the city. The three men relocated to a cottage fifty miles away in sleepy Wilton, Connecticut, and were soon joined by Lead Belly's fiancée, Martha Promise (the paparazzi recorded the couple's reunion at Penn Station). In addition to cooking and doing the laundry, Lead Belly commuted back to the city to record material for the American Record Company. At the same time, Alan conducted extensive sessions with Lead Belly at the Wilton house. Although blues songs were just part of Lead Belly's repertoire, they were what ARC wanted most, and Lead Belly was discouraged from recording his more "hillbilly" material, like "Frankie and Albert" and "The Western Cowboy." Meanwhile, Alan tried to steer Lead Belly away from the pop songs he was picking up and toward more traditional material. He also wanted to record Lead Belly telling stories about his life, hoping to preserve on record as much of the "real" Lead Belly as he could before the North swallowed him forever.

In February, Lead Belly and John played themselves in a March of Time newsreel that ended with Lead Belly's songs arriving at the Library of Congress and fading out on a shot of the original Declaration of Independence. In real life, Lead Belly's relationship with John was growing strained. A two-week college tour quickly turned sour. What really irked Lead Belly—aside from John's habit of staying onstage to "explain" the songs, his forbidding Lead Belly to play material deemed inauthentic, and the curfew he imposed—was John's insistence that Lead Belly perform in his prison clothes, rather than wearing the sharp suits that Lead Belly preferred.

After the last show, John announced he was sending Lead Belly and Martha back to Louisiana. John was despondent: the producer had lost control of his artist. "I suffered intense mortification and humiliation at my failure to influence Lead Belly," he wrote. "He had been changed by a little prosperity, and possibly through our own mistakes, into an arrogant person."

Alan checked to make sure the recorder was rolling. "Huddie, can you play 'Green Corn' on the 12-string guitar?"

"I think I can . . ."

Lead Belly didn't stay away from New York for long. He returned in 1936, intent on picking up where he left off, but soon discovered that he was no longer the swampland sensation. To the press he wasn't even an interesting novelty, though what coverage he did get was invariably sensationalistic.

("Bad Nigger Makes Good Minstrel," the title of a short *Life* magazine piece in 1937, pretty much sums it up.) He found it difficult to get gigs. He and Martha were broke.

In Louisiana, Lead Belly had initiated legal action against John, claiming that John never fully explained the terms of his contract. A settlement was reached—Lead Belly received $250—but his relationship with John was over. Although Alan was partially complicit in his father's business dealings—the settlement gave the Lomaxes some royalties, and they retained the right to publish a book of Lead Belly's songs, many of which credited the Lomaxes alongside Lead Belly—he and Lead Belly remained on good terms. The younger Lomax helped Lead Belly get gigs and radio appearances. For the rest of the thirties, a period when Lead Belly made no commercial recordings, Alan continued to record him for the Library of Congress.

Alan also introduced Lead Belly to the people who would form the core of his audience for the rest of his life: mostly white liberals, progressives, leftists, and radicals. For them, Lead Belly was a symbol of noble resistance, with John inevitably cast as the villain. The novelist Richard Wright described the Lead Belly story in *The Daily Worker* as "one of the most amazing cultural swindles in American history." It didn't help that John Lomax's book *Negro Folk Songs as Sung by Lead Belly* included such Lead Belly "quotes" as "Lawd God, I was cuttin' niggers. . . . Putty soon they six ob 'em runnin' down the street with the blood just gushin' out!" The guitarist Brownie McGhee supposedly hated the book so much that he took a hacksaw to his copy.

Alan was an avowed progressive, but he was also John's son. Some of John's beliefs regarding the importance of keeping white and black cultures separate so that the former would not dilute the latter were transmuted to Alan, who gave them a more politicized spin. Alan considered himself a product of the New Deal years, when America's post–Civil War attempt to define a national culture independent of Europe (he surely considered his father's work to be a prime example) meshed with an FDR-inspired sense of civic duty. "The developing concern about what our own American culture was like, about who we were as people, peaked at this time," he wrote. "And the search for American folk roots was part of this." But he also retained some of his father's concern that the real Americana was premodern, and behaved as though the search for America's roots could actually corrupt those roots in the process.

Alan felt that Lead Belly never sang more beautifully than during that fateful summer of 1933, and he always lamented that he and his father hadn't had equipment that could do the music justice. But now that he did have the equipment to record Lead Belly well, the problem was how to mitigate the negative effects of the world that equipment represented—and get the *real* music recorded forever.

Lead Belly became a focal point for Alan's emerging artistic quandary. Alan eventually became an accomplished folk musician himself (he once performed for FDR at the White House) and sometimes even performed concerts with Lead Belly that were billed as "Battle of the Ballad Singers"—Alan was the opening act for Lead Belly. Someone who remembered seeing such a show at Cornell recalled that Alan was "trying to pull Lead Belly off the stage to prevent him from playing the crowd-pleasing, more popular, and less folkie songs."

At some of the commercial sessions Alan set up for Lead Belly, he made it clear that he wanted the material rough and not too perfect. Lead Belly, who by this time was an accomplished and agile musician, and something of a perfectionist, sometimes struggled with this quest for rawness. In a letter to Alan in 1940, he asked if John would perhaps bury the hatchet and come to hear him sing, so that Lead Belly could get John's opinion as to whether his music had changed. In June of that year, Alan helped Lead Belly do some sessions for RCA Victor, some of which teamed Lead Belly with the Golden Gate Quartet, four black singers who had already achieved fame for their smooth, slick harmonies. "The idea was, I don't think Lomax wanted too much harmony, too much precision," Willie Johnson, a member of the group, said. "We did what we were supposed to do. But [we didn't] perfect it, because that is what Lomax did not want. He wanted it rough, you know, and that's what he got."

Two months later, Alan brought Lead Belly to Washington for a one-day marathon recording session—about fifty songs, probably the most productive of any of the sessions Alan did with Lead Belly. Among those numbers was "Green Corn," an upbeat song popular at the local sukey jumps during Lead Belly's youth, and the first tune he learned how to play on guitar. It was a song he kept returning to, recording at least six different versions over the years. The consensus opinion on the song has always been that its title refers to moonshine. John wrote in *Negro Folk Songs as Sung by Lead Belly*, "Lead Belly always sings this old-fashioned air tenderly and joyfully, as if pleasantly drunk on green-corn whisky." But on this day, Lead Belly wasn't inclined to sing it "tenderly," and Alan's request that he do so may have led him to deny that the song was about moonshine at all.

Before the song began that day, it was preceded by a pleasant exchange that Alan recorded. He asked if Lead Belly could perform "Green Corn," and Lead Belly, in an agreeable tone, said he thought he could. Musician and producer were on the same page.

This is what the rest of the recording sounds like:

"Well, let's hear a little 'Green Corn,' " Alan says, and before he even finishes those words, Lead Belly is off and running. He plays less than a full measure before Alan cuts in: "Slow and easy and sweet, Huddie." It sounds like a mild admonition. Lead Belly dutifully slows down, but before he begins singing, Alan speaks up again. "What is 'green corn,' anyway? Tell us as you sing the song."

"This is a fast sukey-jump tune," Lead Belly says, still playing the opening chords. "But the boys take it easy sometimes, when they're on the sukey jump. Keep 'em dancin' so hard, they shuffle around with their partner!" Finally, he begins to sing: "Green corn, come along, Charley / Green Corn, go and tell Polly." He makes it through the first verse and chorus, and moves into the second, picking up speed. It's no longer slow and easy and sweet.

In the middle of the third verse, Alan cuts in again: "What is 'green corn'?"

Lead Belly either doesn't hear or chooses to ignore him, and continues singing. "Stand around, stand around the jimmy john . . ." Perhaps thinking he should cooperate a little, Lead Belly keeps playing, but explains that a jimmy john is a jug for liquor. Back to singing: "Stand around, stand around the jimmy john . . . green corn . . ."

"What is 'green corn'?"

"Green corn . . ." The song comes to an abrupt halt. "What is 'green corn,' Huddie?" The last notes of Lead Belly's guitar fade away.

"Green corn is yellow corn," Huddie replies. "When it's green." They're just words in the song, he continues—most people who sing it probably don't even think about the words. But that's what it means, green corn—corn that's ready to be picked.

Alan says, "I thought you meant green-corn whiskey."

"No, not no green-corn whiskey. They didn't know nothing about no corn liquor at that time. They had old-time liquor, you know, just real good liquor. Wasn't no bootleggers then. Couldn't make no liquor. How're they gonna make liquor if they're all slaves?" He chuckles. "They'd get no liquor until the boss would give it to them!"

That 1940 session was the last time Alan recorded Lead Belly for the Library of Congress. Perhaps he felt that he'd gotten as close as he ever would to recapturing the spirit of 1933, when Lead Belly, cloistered away from the world in prison, sang like an angel.

Alan was born a few months before the opening of the Panama-Pacific International Exposition, timing that is an apt metaphor for his life. As the historian Gray Brechin has pointed out, the Panama-Pacific Expo was in many respects the last of the nineteenth-century World's Fairs, a final flowering of their idealism in the face of the horrors unfolding at the beginning of World War I. Alan was born in the last throes of this old world, enough a part of it to believe, like his father, in the nobility of "pure" cultures. Yet he was also aware that in the New World, the order typified by the Panama-Pacific Expo, with its tributes to the historical determinism of the West and its shunting of non-Western cultures into the Joy Zone, was breaking down. The dilemma that Alan grappled with his whole life was basically that the same technological products of the West that could empower the voiceless—the epiphany he'd had that day with Blue—could also lead to their cultural marginalization. Put a different way: If we're going to affirm the existence of other cultures by exhibiting them in our expo, but put them in the Joy Zone with the arcades and amusements, is it perhaps better just to leave them alone?

Soon after his final Library of Congress session with Lead Belly, Alan visited the Mississippi Delta. In Clarksdale, Mississippi, he was eager to record the choir at the First African Baptist Church. "In the past I had tried to capture the lambent song of Black congregational singing and had always failed," he wrote. "The earlier portable equipment simply could not cope with a church full of Black Baptists singing their hearts out, improvising harmonies, and swinging round a perfect beat better than the best New Orleans marching band . . . You couldn't get the sound or the fervor into a studio or onto an aluminum disc. Now I was ready with good microphones, good acetate, and a professional recorder. I switched on the amplifier and lowered the needle onto the spinning acetate blank."

But once he got to the church, it was clear something was wrong. He wasn't hearing what he expected. Women were wailing, a piano was vamping . . . This was a Southern Baptist church? "My astonishment and chagrin grew by the moment," he wrote. "Where, I wondered, was the fluid and spontaneous harmonizing of the past?"

Alan's research assistant, standing next to him, explained that it was called "gospel." When the music was over, Alan shut off his machine and walked outside, shaken. A reverend was in front of the church, selling gospel songbooks and sheet music. Alan asked him about what he'd just heard. The man told him that the modern Baptist church was moving beyond the old spirituals, toward a more "progressive" music, taught by people who had formal training in music. But what could be more progressive than the beautiful old harmonies? Alan asked.

It's a new day, the reverend said. He pointed to Alan's gear. "Take your own case. You're not here taking notes with a paper and pencil—you have the latest thing in recording equipment. The old must give way to the new."

During the same visit, Alan's decision to turn on his machine changed the course of American music in ways that are simply seismic. At a plantation a few miles outside of Clarksdale, he met and recorded a twenty-six-year-old singer and guitarist who went by the name Muddy Waters. Muddy knew he was a skilled guitar player, but when Lomax played back the song they recorded, Muddy couldn't believe how good it sounded. I can *do* it, he thought. A year later, he moved to Chicago, and a few years after that, he switched to electric guitar and changed music forever.

Also just outside Clarksdale is the famous "crossroads" where Tommy Johnson—and later Robert Johnson—met the Devil, who gave the gift of guitar mastery in exchange for a man's soul. By recording Muddy playing the blues, Alan, as much as any nonmusician, can take credit for setting in motion the development of rock and roll. But you have to wonder if Alan ever thought of himself as the Devil, bearing the gift of recording in exchange for the music's soul. The same technology that taught Muddy how kick-ass he was—that literally gave him the gift of his own voice—also taught other people, far removed from the plantation, how kick-ass he was, which made them think *they* could be kick-ass. And then that music, ripped out of its context, would enter the messy urban world of commercial objects, and the sound would be distorted until it bore no relation to the pure tones Alan heard.

As Alan grew older, his anxiety on this subject grew deeper. It reached its public apotheosis at the 1965 Newport Folk Festival in Rhode Island. On the Saturday afternoon of the festival, a thousand people showed up for a blues workshop that featured some black musicians that Alan had imported from the South and the all-white Paul Butterfield Blues Band. After the first group, Alan introduced the "group of young boys from Chicago" and wondered aloud if "they can play this hardware at all." Albert Grossman, Butterfield's manager, didn't like Alan's condescending attitude. When Alan came down from the stage, Grossman got in his face, and insults were traded. Things escalated, and suddenly the two of them were wrestling on the floor and had to be separated by onlookers.

That dustup was overshadowed by the festival's more famous event. Bob Dylan was in the crowd at that blues workshop. Impressed by Butterfield and his band, he invited them to sit in with him during his performance the next day. That was when Dylan "went electric," enraging folk purists. As the boos rained down on Dylan from the crowd, Alan stood with Pete Seeger backstage, both of them fuming. Seeger, hands over his ears, jumped in a car and drove away. Alan just stood there, yelling at the stage that this was a folk festival—amplification had no place here!

Moses Asch recorded Bob Dylan a few years before the scandalous Newport show, but it's safe to say he would have had no problem with an electric Dylan. What he objected to was anyone who tried to sound like Dylan in lieu of developing a singular musical identity. When he was asked how he chose the artists for Folkways Records, Asch was evasive. "As time goes on, you get to know what is truth and what is falsehood," he said. "For instance, you know the way so many folk singers developed a twang in their voice like Bob Dylan? This is false. It's not common to the man. With Dylan, of course, it was the poetry that counted more than the rendition . . . He stated it as he felt it. That is my main criterion."

During Asch's lifetime, Folkways released an astounding 2,000 albums, ranging from indigenous music recorded in the field by ethnomusicologists, to the debut albums of the Fugs and Lucinda Williams, recordings of animal sounds, and Harry Smith's enormously influential *Anthology of American Folk Music*. But before he founded Folkways, Asch was just trying to get in on the market for Jewish music. Sometime after he built his mammoth sound system for FDR's speech at Madison Square Garden, the New

York radio station WEVD, which featured Yiddish programming and leftist politics (EVD were Eugene Debs's initials), hired Asch's company to rebuild the station's transmitters. The job was so large that Asch relocated his whole operation to the station's offices at 117 West 46th Street, near Times Square.

As it happened, WEVD needed more Jewish music to play on the air, everything from religious recordings to Yiddish theater music, so Asch built a small studio, only ten feet square, in a corner of the office. He began to record musicians for the Jewish market—folk songs, music for religious services—and released records on his own label, Asch Records. He started to develop what can only be called a reverence for the process of making records. For Asch, the recording studio was sacrosanct, a metaphorical safe space where artistic expression could thrive apart from the cruel world outside. He had none of John Lomax's fetish for the spontaneity of music performed in its natural environment. In fact, Asch mostly hated live music, and especially hated coffeehouses, those temples of the folk revival. ("You never see me in those damn places," he explained, "because the guy down there is singing to the audience for the purpose that they paid money like a prostitute.") And unlike Alan, Asch didn't think of recording as a double-edged sword. He didn't worry that the city and all it represented would corrode the authentic expression he wanted to get on record.

Yet he had definite ideas about how records should sound. "My practice has always been to record things *as they are*, with the simplest means of reproduction," he explained. All focus should be on the musical moment, and all attempts should be made to capture it as accurately as possible, while effacing the audible effects of production. "My philosophy was to make a 'flat' record," he said in 1990, looking back on his career. "This means that the frequency used was as flat as possible to the sound that it produced. All the other record companies went with the high boost. I knew that I was documenting these sounds and that a hundred years from now somebody could reconstruct what it sounded like by having a flat curve. For [other companies'] records, they would have had to know how the boost worked and reversed it."

There was a practical as well as a political component to this aesthetic. From the moment the microphone was turned on, it was the musicians' opportunity to be the center of the universe, to preserve their voice for eternity. It was as though by doing as little as possible to his recordings, Asch was simplifying the effects of historical memory. One microphone was enough for Asch. Even in later years, when multitrack recording became the common purview of producers, he resisted, explaining that "the producer reconstructs what happened in the studio to fit somebody's idea of what it should be, but that is not what actually happened."

Asch's idea of authenticity in recordings was significantly different from John Lomax's (and somewhat closer to Alan's). It was, in its way, Edisonian: capture only "the music," this ineffable thing that existed apart from the effects of recording, such as the record companies' predilection for the high boost. John wanted authenticity, but he was not above engineering it, so to speak. If he wanted the convicts he recorded singing work songs inside prisons to sound like they were outside cutting down trees, he would make them breathe heavily as though exerting themselves. John did not mind the idea of mediation in recording, as long as he was the one doing the mediating. He would make the inside of a prison sound like a forest, if that's what it took to communicate the "reality" of African American folk songs. Asch did not venture out of his studio (though he did release recordings of environmental sounds made by others). The studio was sacred for Asch. It shut out all parts of the outside world—symbolized by the invisible hand of the marketplace, changing the music's context as surely as John did when he made trapped convicts sound like they were free outdoors—and allowed in only "the music."

When the studio environment was just right, Asch heard a worker's paradise. Consider his description of a session he recorded in 1944 with the jazz pianist Mary Lou Williams: "We had ten people with one mike, and the sound was perfect. No headphones. Each of these musicians knew what it was about and didn't try to override the other guys. Today they blow wild and expect the mike to adjust. That's why you have to have 48 musicians; each one had headphones and a microphone, and the engineer is supposed to be the musician. We didn't have that."

Lead Belly was Asch Records' first foray beyond Jewish music. He and Asch probably met in the spring of 1941, but Asch knew of the Lead Belly mystique and was of course well versed in the many sins of Lead Belly's first benefactor. "John Lomax—I hated his guts but he was a terrific guy," Asch recalled. "He dressed [Lead Belly] up as a convict, and he would drag him around to show what a great guy John Lomax was." Where John saw Lead Belly as a creature from a different world, Asch saw a kindred spirit. "Immediately, Lead Belly and I were brothers," he said. "I understood him, he understood me, and he utilized me. And I was willing to be used because he knew that through me, through my medium, he was able to express what he wanted."

The Lomaxes (or at least John) looked at Lead Belly and saw—as their own book described him—a "knife-toting nigger." Asch looked at Lead Belly and saw every kid's favorite uncle. Children were mesmerized by Lead Belly, and he loved performing for them, so Asch decided to give them their own Lead Belly album. *Play Parties in Song and Dance, as Sung by Lead Belly* became the first release for Asch's company.

For the rest of Lead Belly's life, Asch was his main producer. Lead Belly recorded about two hundred songs with Asch, more material than he'd ever recorded with anyone else. There were no stories told or interviews conducted on record; Asch would never have dreamed of inserting his voice into the recording process. In general, there's a looseness to those records. A mélange of music and politics coalesced around Asch's studio, and Lead Belly was in the thick of it. Asch often had an open-door policy for the artists who recorded for him. Whenever the muse struck them, they could head over to 46th Street and cut some sides. Woody Guthrie, Lead Belly, Pete Seeger, Sonny Terry, and others all dropped by to play on one another's songs. During his Asch years, Lead Belly recorded what was arguably his most infectious song, a bouncy version of "Pick a Bale of Cotton" with the Golden Gate Quartet, those golden voices that Alan had thought too slick for Lead Belly's brand of rawness. And Lead Belly cut a few versions of "Green Corn," one of which flies by at Minor Threat speed.

Lead Belly didn't find fame and fortune with Asch. In fact, he and Martha were still scraping by. But for the first time in all the hundreds of hours Lead Belly had recorded for various people, he was granted something like artistic freedom. With the help of another member of Asch's coterie, he was about to get even more.

Throughout the FDR years, John remained semifamous as America's supreme song collector—a 1945 profile of him in *Reader's Digest* generated thousands of letters to the Library of Congress from people who wanted information on the Lomax archives—but time was passing him by. He criticized Alan for booking modern black acts like the Golden Gate Quartet on the radio shows Alan hosted, and was annoyed that Alan often hung out with Lead Belly. He was furious when he discovered that his daughter Bess, who had joined the Almanac Singers after college, was sharing a town house in Greenwich Village with members of the group, including Woody Guthrie (whom John considered a vulgar hack) and Pete Seeger. To make matters worse, Lead Belly was a frequent guest.

On January 23, 1948, Lomax arrived in Greenville, Mississippi, where the mayor had organized a John Lomax Day in honor of John's eightieth birthday. As John was holding court with well-wishers at a press conference, he broke into a song called "Big Leg Rose." After he sang the last line—"The only thing I ever done wrong / Stayed in Mississippi one day too long"—he collapsed. The heart attack was massive, and he never regained consciousness.

Lead Belly, meanwhile, was very much alive, but death was on his mind. "I'm scared of dying," he had told a radio interviewer a month after John's death. "I want to live. I want to live as long as I can to see more in the world." This was the year that Asch, after several years of putting out music under a few imprints, launched Folkways Records. The label's first releases were a series of 10-inch Lead Belly records.

A few years earlier, Lead Belly had moved to California in a last-ditch attempt to be a star. There was talk of film projects, including an adaptation of John's autobiography, *Adventures of a Ballad Hunter*, in which Lead Belly would play himself. None of it happened, and the whole experience was an often humiliating lesson in institutional racism, so he returned to New York, as broke as ever, living with Martha at 414 East 10th Street, on the Lower East Side. In the fall of '48, he received an interesting proposition from Frederic Ramsey Jr.

Ramsey, a music critic who had written extensively on the early roots of jazz, was an odd figure in Lead Belly's life. He befriended Lead Belly and Martha, and even briefly lived with them. Ramsey could be as guilty as anyone of perpetuating the Lead Belly myth ("He smiles, and his face shines, bronze-to-copper-to-brown, as the light picks up the rich, beautiful pigment of his skin"), but he mostly saw in Lead Belly an extremely observant and inventive artist, not somebody's idea of authenticity. Ramsey was duly critical of John Lomax and felt that had Lead Belly been allowed to unfold as an artist who was equally at home singing both Gene Autry songs and field hollers, rather than as Lomax's specimen, he might have become a star like his old partner Blind Lemon Jefferson, and would certainly have won more of the black audience. But he also thought John deserved credit for recognizing Lead Belly's genius and helping the world hear it. Ramsey was just as critical of Lead Belly's supporters on the left, "who regarded Lead Belly as their tool and tried to make him a spokesman for their political ends. I thought this was crap."

Ramsey admired the way Lead Belly could adapt his music to any context, from sukey jumps to the big city. "He gives it to you as he sees it," Ramsey wrote, "tough and unedited." So why edit him?

Asch and Ramsey were friends, and Ramsey thought Asch had done right by Lead Belly. But there was still something that even Asch hadn't managed to get on record. For the past few years, Ramsey had thought about recording Lead Belly in a way that somehow did justice to his music, both thematically and sonically. Ramsey managed to procure a Magnecord tape recorder, one of the first generation of magnetic tape machines in the United States. A reel of tape could last half an hour, several times longer than a disc, and the sound of tape was a huge improvement over acetate and aluminum. Ramsey realized tape was exactly what Lead Belly's music needed.

He invited Lead Belly and Martha to dinner at his apartment to talk about the new recording idea. At one point Lead Belly began harmonizing along with a Bessie Smith record as she sang "Nobody Knows You When You're Down and Out." Ramsey decided to start the machine. "You want to sing along with Bessie?" he asked.

"That's a good number," Lead Belly said, as the record ended. "I sure like that." He continued singing softly.

Lead Belly hadn't brought his guitar, assuming that recording would begin another night. But once the tape was rolling, he didn't stop. He recorded thirty-four a cappella songs that night, one after another, with Martha occasionally joining in. After a few takes, Lead Belly asked to hear the playback. "Man, you got something there," he said. "You can just let that thing run. Now let's try some more." Like Muddy Waters a few years earlier, Lead Belly was finally learning, from a record, what he sounded like and what he was capable of. He was hearing what others heard in him, but he was producing himself.

Lead Belly sang songs as they occurred to him, and told stories when he felt like it. Highlights were the holler "Black Betty," an extended version of the work song "Go Down, Ol' Hannah," a quickie "Rock Island Line," a fragile duet with Martha on "Stewball," and Martha singing a solo, "I'm Thinking of a Friend" (Lead Belly kept admonishing her to "let loose," until she told him to knock it off). The last song of the evening was "I Want to Go Home." It ended with him singing those words three times, and then stopping to announce: "That's all—I want to go home."

Lead Belly came back two more nights, this time with his guitar. Other guests dropped by to watch. Listening to those tapes today, you can hear him, along with Ramsey, grasping what this new machine could do. Compared with everything Lead Belly did with the Lomaxes, Asch, and others who recorded him on disc, the sound explodes out of the speakers. You get the jarring brightness of the steel strings Lead Belly used, but there's a warmth to the sound that complements the almost voyeuristic feel of these recordings. You really can hear Lead Belly making a mix tape of his life, including songs that nobody ever seemed to want him to record, like Autry's "Springtime in the Rockies" and the novelty tune "The Hawaiian Song." He talks about his life in greater detail than he'd ever done on any Lomax recording, including his travels with Blind Lemon Jefferson and a story from his youth that cracks up the audience, about surreptitiously sugaring his beer so that the ladies wouldn't realize what a lightweight drinker he was.

As the sessions went on, Lead Belly began to figure out tape's future capabilities. "I'm gonna play my last number," he said, "and I'll tell you what I want you to do for me. I'm gonna end up with 'Irene,' and I want to sing back with myself. Can you do that?"

"No, we can't do that," Ramsey says, than reconsiders. "Yeah, all right, we'll do a very tricky deal. We'll have to superimpose to do that . . ."

"Well, just think it over . . ."

"No, you can't," Ramsey finally says. "If we had a record of you, we could do it easily." They'd have to wait for multitrack recording to be invented.

Taken together, the sessions sound like a summation. "It just flowed out of that guy and he was in the mood for it," Ramsey said years later. "The music was more than just music—it was a whole emotional feeling. He would just sit and listen and he would say, 'Now you do it this way'; it was like an informal but very significant way of passing on a tradition." For the last song of the third session, Lead Belly chose "Leaving Blues," ending on the line "I'm leaving you and I won't come back no more."

Lead Belly and Ramsey never saw each other again. On a tour of Europe the following summer, Lead Belly experienced severe muscle problems. A doctor in Paris told him he was in the late stages of Lou Gehrig's disease. He died in Bellevue Hospital in New York on December 6, 1949.

Lead Belly and John Lomax each dreamed of getting rich off Lead Belly's music, but neither lived long enough to see it happen. In 1950, the Weavers released their version of Lead Belly's "Irene"—now called "Good Night, Irene"—the song that had caught John's ear during that first trip with Alan. It became the biggest song of the year.

Ramsey hung on to the tapes of those last Lead Belly sessions for a few years. Several record companies were interested in releasing them, but none would agree to Ramsey's condition that the sessions be put out in their entirety, unedited, with the songs in the same order, and with the between-song talking included. Asch liked Ramsey's idea, and in 1953, the two began preparing the tapes for a Folkways release.

That same year, Ramsey got a Guggenheim Fellowship to study the history of African American music from the end of the Civil War to the beginning of the twentieth century. He planned to drive around the South with recording equipment, searching for musicians in areas remote enough to have shielded their music from any modern influences, just as John Lomax had done nearly forty years earlier. But once Ramsey started he couldn't believe what he found out there—song collectors everywhere! It seemed like anyplace he went, men with portable tape recorders were shoving microphones in people's faces—"like librarians on an outing," he complained in a letter to Asch. "It is all very pat and not at all reliable. I am avoiding these boys like the plague."

4

Pink Pseudo-Realism

Bing Crosby's first *Philco Radio Time* of the 1947 season began and ended with a lie.

The first thing listeners heard was two jokers playing janitors.

"Hey, Jerry, what are we sweeping the floor for?"

"Bing Crosby is coming back on the air tonight!"

"Since when do we have to clean up the studio for him? With them baggy pants of his, he sweeps his own studio!"

"What's the matter with you? Ain't you heard? Things are gonna be different this year. He bought a belt!"

"That'll probably drag, too!"

When the show was over, after half an hour of singing and goofing around with Peggy Lee and Gary Cooper, Crosby said, "Well, that about wraps up the first Philco follies for the season." Then he threw in one last joke: "I want to thank all the Crosbys, and anyone else in the country who may have tuned in."

None of this had happened—at least not the way the audience thought it did. Bing Crosby had not returned to the air that night for his usual live broadcast. Nobody had tuned in, and Crosby knew it. In fact, when he'd said, earlier in the show, "Ladies and gentlemen, please turn up the speakers of your radios just a little, because here comes a low-voiced gentleman, the pride of Helena, Montana, Gary Cooper"—that, too, was a big fat lie.

A few people in the studio audience may have known Crosby was lying, but even fewer who heard him on the radio were aware of it. By the time they heard the janitors say that Crosby was coming back on the air "tonight," it was weeks later. By the time they'd twisted their volume knobs because Gary Cooper was in the house, he'd already ridden off into the sunset.

The show had been recorded onto magnetic tape six weeks earlier. The tape sounded so good that even the most attentive listener would never have guessed that the show was not live. What virtually nobody in the studio audience knew was that what they were watching was not what the radio audience would hear. What virtually nobody at home knew was that what went out over the air was pieced together from various takes, including dress rehearsals; that mistakes were edited out; that dead air might have been excised to quicken the show's flow. Entire songs may have been constructed from several versions. Listening at home, it was impossible to tell truths from lies. Did Gary Cooper really walk in at that moment? Did the audience really laugh that hard at the janitors' lackluster jokes?

The only people who knew for sure what went on the air the night of October 1, 1947, were Crosby; Murdo MacKenzie, the show's producer; and Jack Mullin, an ex-GI who manned the tape machine and wielded the editing scissors. Mullin had recently returned from the war with the secret of magnetic tape, and he was the first true artist of tape's ingenious duplicity.

Even the show's staff did not immediately grasp how powerful tape was—how much tape could tell its own story, not just the story of the sound it recorded. After one early show that season MacKenzie announced that they'd have to rerecord a commercial for Philco, the show's sponsor, because the announcer, Ken Carpenter, had flubbed a line, saying something like "The new Philcos gives" when the verb should be "give." Hold on, Mullin said, don't bother. He took out his scissors, cued up the bad line, isolated the offending s, snipped it off, and spliced the tape together.

"It was perfect," he later remembered. He called that moment "the great revelation," when it dawned on everyone that you didn't have to redo reality—you had the power to fake it.

Carpenter was so impressed that he asked Crosby for the tiny piece of tape that had been cut out. He put it in his wallet, and for the next few years it was always with him, a preserved forgotten moment that nobody knew existed.

From the time of Edison until World War II, the phonograph symbolized the promise of sound recording. From the acoustic era and into the electric, it was the technical and conceptual model of what recording could and should do. The recording technology evolved but the goal remained the same: to capture and store a sound and re-create it faithfully at some point in the future.

In the background, however, a shadow history was unfolding. In this alternate universe, people were working toward the day when recordings could play tricks with time. In this world, fidelity was just the beginning. The goal was to record sound not merely accurately but also flexibly. Whereas Edison's phonograph was an American actualization of a concept that had been imagined but never realized in Europe, this history began in a fledgling form in America but was soon forgotten as it flourished in Europe. Once magnetic recording reached a certain level of perfection, it reemerged in the United States as a spoil of war, a symbol of the sprawling and multifarious postwar economy, and nothing less than the foundation of twentieth-century recorded music.

The first step of any electrical recording process is converting a sound wave into an electrical current. That's the easy part. More difficult than generating the current is the problem of how to *represent* it on a storage medium so that it can be re-created later. With disc recording—or mastering, since vinyl discs continue to be made today, although disc recording is a thing of the past—the current causes a stylus to etch grooves in the disc. The process has two obvious limitations. First, every recording is final. Once the disc is inscribed, there's no going back. Disc recording suggests the idea of permanence, a trait that fit symbolically with what the Lomaxes thought they were doing when they lugged a disc machine around the South in search of "authentic" sounds. The second drawback is the physical contact between the playback stylus and the disc. Those acetate discs the Lomaxes used were fragile—much more so than today's vinyl records—and every time they were played, they came one step closer to the grave. So although the idea of permanence was etched into every disc, it was undermined by the disc's eventual disintegration.

With tape recording, which works on the principle of electromagnetism, there is no physical contact between the inscriber (the recording head) and the medium (the tape). Instead, the current flows past a highly magnetic material, creating patterns of varying magnetic polarity on the tape. As with disc recording, playback means reversing the process. The magnetized tape is passed over a coil, creating changes in magnetic flux. The changes in flux create the electric current that an amplifier converts into watts.

Because the current can be represented without physical contact, a tape recording is remarkably durable. Those magnetized patterns will last virtually forever. The main challenge of preserving magnetic tape is not the problem of information loss but rather the breakdown of the tape's substrate, the actual material it is made of.

There is something dark and shadowy about magnetism itself. Marvin Camras, one of the American pioneers of magnetic recording, once described magnetism as "a mysterious force that can attract or repel matter, even through a perfect vacuum," and noted that the concept "has been a source of wonder to the best minds of the past centuries, including Newton and Einstein, but has not been explained further and is accepted as a given property of our universe." The concept gets slippier when we consider that a "magnet" is defined as any source of magnetism and that every substance is either attracted to or repelled by a magnet, though usually only to a very small degree. Substances commonly referred to as "magnetic"—such as iron, nickel, and cobalt—exhibit a very strong magnetic attraction called ferromagnetism.

Besides the durability of the recording, tape offered other obvious advantages over discs. As Lead Belly's last sessions make clear, the sound quality is much better. A disc recording held only a few minutes of sound, whereas the reels Frederic Ramsey used to record Lead Belly could hold half an hour. When you listen to those recordings today, the feeling of freedom Lead Belly was discovering is palpable. In his between-song assurances to Lead Belly that he has all the time he needs, Ramsey was clearly captivated by the opportunity to let the tape roll. In this sense, magnetic tape made sound recording more true to life because in the real world, sound events don't just happen in four-minute bursts. Ramsey's insistence that the recordings be released unedited shows how aware he was of this quality. To him, he had a real document, Lead Belly's sonic autobiography. To chop it up would defeat the purpose.

It was natural, given what recording could do at the time, for Ramsey to fixate on the length of the recording and insist it not be compromised. What he missed was the ability to edit. This was another huge advantage tape had over discs, which could not be broken up at all. Ramsey wanted to preserve Lead Belly's uninterrupted moment in real time, but part of tape's promise was that "real time" no longer mattered. Eventually, breakthroughs in technology meant that tape expanded recorded music not only temporally but also *spatially* via multitracking, a concept that Lead Belly and Ramsey grasped in a fleeting moment before realizing it was impossible with the Magnecord.

Tape reshaped the contours of recorded music, first by linking sounds that had not been linked in their original incarnation, and eventually by allowing sounds that had occurred at different times to be experienced simultaneously. You could stack sounds on top of sounds on top of sounds. A disc recording lasted only as long as it took to record. With tape, you were limited only by the time you have on this Earth. You could conceivably spend your entire life just making one record, endlessly splicing, rearranging, or adding sounds. You could make a record that was not in fact a "record": it didn't document and preserve something that had happened. As a child of the phonographic age, Ramsey heard in magnetic recording a way to get closer to the truth. It also promised something quite different. Magnetism itself may be a universal truth, but magnetic recording taught music how to lie.

In 1878, a mechanical engineer named Oberlin Smith visited Edison's lab and asked to hear the phonograph. Although fascinated by the machine, Smith decided its fundamental flaw was the direct contact between the stylus and the record. He reasoned that if there were a way to decode a recording without actually touching the recording's surface, it might yield a more perfect sound.

Smith pondered the question over the next ten years, the period when Edison himself was rethinking the phonograph. In 1888, the year Edison unveiled his improved phonograph, Smith offered a blueprint for an alternative. In "Some Possible Forms of the Phonograph," an article that appeared in the magazine *Electrical World*, Smith described a method of recording sound using magnetic impressions. He theorized that a thread of cotton or silk could be covered by a substance—steel dust or tiny pieces of wire—that could be magnetized by the current of a telephone moved across the thread. The article received little notice, and Smith never attempted to build this machine.

Valdemar Poulsen is sometimes referred to today as the "Danish Edison." But in 1888 he was just a teenager from a prominent family—his father was a high court judge—and something of a disappointment to his parents. A mediocre student whose only interests were physics and art,

Poulsen tried to become a doctor, but in 1893, at the age of twenty-four, dropped out of medical school and took a job with the Copenhagen Telephone Company. During his downtime, Poulsen liked to ponder the mysteries of electromagnetism. He eventually began to think about what it could do for recorded sound.

Poulsen had probably never heard of Oberlin Smith, but he managed to solve a problem that had stumped the early magnetic recording theorist. Smith's model called for discrete bits of steel dust or wire to be magnetized, rather than a whole steel wire. Smith had considered the possibility of using a whole wire but concluded that it would not naturally divide into patches of varying magnetism, and thus could not process a microphone's changing current. Poulsen proved otherwise. In the summer of 1896, he attached a steel wire, slanted at an angle, to two opposite walls of his office. He hung a small magnet, connected to a battery and a transmitter, on a trolley-like device. He placed the trolley at the high end of the wire and let go. As it descended, he ran alongside, shouting into the transmitter. When it reached the bottom, he disconnected the battery and transmitter and placed a telephone receiver in the trolley with the magnet. He let the trolley descend again, and the faint sound of his voice emerged from the receiver.

Poulsen built a prototype machine that used steel piano wire wound around a brass drum and called his invention the *telegrafon*. Like Edison and his phonograph, Poulsen did not immediately think of the telegraphone as a way to record music; the German patent issued in 1898 described a "method for the reception and temporary storage of news, signals, and the like," and Poulsen imagined it would be very useful to record telephone calls. His completed telegraphone was a big hit at the Paris Exposition of 1900. People heard its tinny, fragile sounds, and remarked on how natural they were.

When the hype subsided, Poulsen had a difficult time raising venture capital in Europe, but the formation of the American Telegraphone Company in 1903 heralded a bright future back in the States. The company's president predicted that one day "everywhere in the field of human endeavor, where an accurate record of the spoken word is required or desired, the machine will be . . . doing its work, leaving nothing to the imagination, nothing to chance." The American Telegraphone Company mostly failed, however, in its quest to universalize the machine. It didn't help that Charles Dexter Rood, the industrialist who took over the company in 1908, was later accused of discouraging the sale of telegraphones to the U.S. armed forces—or even selling them defective machines—while selling perfectly fine machines to the Germans, who used them to code messages sent to receiving stations throughout Germany via a transmitter on Long Island.

The real flaw of the telegraphone was that it arrived years before effective electrical amplification. There was simply no good way of enhancing the tinny sounds once they were reconverted from electrical impulses. Other technological dots also went unconnected. Shortly after the Germans allegedly used American telegraphone technology to sink an American ship, the United States began extensive research into the telegraphone's military applications and concluded there were none. This work, which continued throughout the twenties, actually resulted in improved fidelity, but because the naval research focused on recording data rather than on sound, the researchers never bothered to hook up a telephone to the telegraphone. Had they done so, the combination of the amazing fidelity and then-available electrical amplification would have made magnetic recording the far superior method of making commercial recordings, and the history of recording would have accelerated by about two decades.

And so the center of telegraphone activity remained in Europe. In the thirties, companies in Britain and Germany made magnetic recorders that used two-inch steel tape. The Steelton was used by German radio stations, while a British version called the Blattnerphone became a fixture at the BBC.

Magnetic recording was steadily evolving, but working with steel tape was no easy matter. A reel of tape that could hold fifty minutes measured two feet in diameter and weighed close to forty pounds. One minute of recording required about a dollar's worth of tape. The steel was sharp and moved at a crisp 1.5 meters per second, making it akin to a running band saw. BBC engineers operated their machine from a cage to guard against wayward pieces of metal severing their fingers. While the tape allowed for the novel possibility of editing (editing on wire was technically feasible by cutting and tying the wire, but it was all but impossible in practice), cutting and splicing required a soldering tool and a welding torch.

———

If he hadn't been something of an audiophile, Fritz Pfleumer would be best remembered for inventing the plastic drinking straw. Instead, he will always be known as the man who invented the first modern tape recorder.

One day in 1928, Pfleumer, an Austrian living in Dresden, was sitting in a Paris café. An expert on industrial uses of paper, he had just been hired by a company that made machinery for cigarette factories. The company wanted him to devise a cheaper (yet classy) alternative to the thin strip of real gold wrapped around the tips of cigarettes. His solution was a bronze powder mixed with lacquer and spread on paper. He was thinking about this in the café, and it suddenly hit him that he had invented something with larger implications. Pfleumer was aware of the problems and expense of steel recording tape. Why not use a strip of paper instead? All you had to do was find a magnetic substance that would adhere to the paper. Instead of bronze, he would use fine granules of iron powder.

The following year, he completed a working prototype of what he called a "sound paper machine" (*tönendes papier*). It used a strip of paper moving at .5 meters per second. The sound was pretty bad, but Allgemeine Electrizitäts-Gesellschaft (AEG) was impressed enough to purchase Pfleumer's patent in 1932. AEG began a collaboration with Badische Anilin und Soda Fabrik (BASF), a subsidiary of the German chemical company Interessen-Gemeinschaft Farbenindustrie (I.G. Farben). The plan was for AEG to build the perfect magnetic tape recorder while BASF searched for a better alternative to Pfleumer's paper tape.

A few years later, AEG unveiled its machine, which it called the Magnetophon. The tape BASF came up with was a cellulose acetate overlain with a combination of lacquer and pure powdered carbonyl iron. (The carbonyl iron was soon replaced by iron oxide.) It worked great and was cheap: one minute of recording cost just fifteen cents.

The Magnetophon, which made its public debut in 1935 at a radio fair in Berlin, was a landmark device. All tape machines that came after it followed its basic design; all future forms of magnetic tape were remarkably similar to what BASF came up with in 1935. There was only one problem: it sounded really bad, even by the standards of the time. In fact, if you had an ear for how good recorded music could sound, it was pretty clear that this was not a machine made for music. That was the verdict of the General Electric executives who heard the machine in 1937 when AEG officials made a clandestine visit to GE corporate headquarters in Schenectady,

New York. The Americans thought the Magnetophon was an interesting curiosity with no practical commercial value.

American radio was likewise uninterested in magnetic recording, but its German counterpart took a more enlightened approach. The state-sponsored Reichs-Rundfunk-Gesellschaft (RRG) network had been using magnetic recording from the time of the first quality wire recorders. H. J. von Braunmuhl, RRG's chief engineer, didn't think the Magnetophon's sound was broadcast quality, but he sensed that it was one tweak away from greatness. He called in his best man, Walter Weber, and told him to figure out what that tweak was. In April 1940, Germany invaded Denmark, birthplace of the telegraphone, and Weber figured out how to make the German Magnetophon perfect.

On June 10, 1940, AEG and RRG held a public demonstration in Berlin to show off the new and improved Magnetophon. A German press account described it as "a total revolution in sound recording."

Magnetic recording had always worked with a direct current (DC). The secret that Weber discovered was that injecting an alternating current (AC) of inaudible ultrahigh frequencies onto the tape dramatically improved the sound of the audible material. In simple terms, the high frequencies shake up the magnetized particles on the tape. The process was known as AC bias, and it completely transformed the possibilities for making high-quality magnetic recordings. This is what the naval researchers had discovered and then ignored back in the twenties. AC bias had also been discovered by Kenzo Nagai, a Japanese engineer, a few years before Weber. Around the same time as Weber's breakthrough, Marvin Camras, an American as unaware of these early pioneers as they were of each other, also made the same discovery.

Camras was born and bred on the northwest side of Chicago, the son of an often unemployed bookbinder. He had a cousin, William Korzon, who was an aspiring opera singer, convinced by reverb-heavy bathroom acoustics that he was good enough to go pro.

What Korzon needed was proof, so he asked his tech-savvy cousin, who was attending the Armour Institute of Technology (now known as the Illinois Institute of Technology), to help him buy a disc recording machine. Every model they looked at was out of their budget; the discs themselves were also prohibitively expensive. Camras was unaware of the magnetic tape breakthroughs happening in Germany, but he did know something about the work of Clarence Hickman, a Bell engineer who had developed a magnetic recorder that used metal tape, a machine that Bell had declared had no future. Camras soon discovered that metal tape was also out of his budget, so he decided to try to build a superior wire recorder. The major sonic drawback of machines like the telegraphone was that the wire naturally rotated, which caused problems with the magnetic field and led to persistent distortion. During breaks in his studies, Camras worked on a wire recorder that used a specially designed head that recorded symmetrically around the wire, eliminating the problem of wire rotation. When he demonstrated his recorder for his professors, they were amazed at the fidelity.

After graduating in 1940, Camras took his machine to the Armour Research Foundation, which the school had recently established to support its faculty's research. Armour was already involved with military contracts, and the military soon became interested in Camras's wire recorder. Like their German counterparts, the American armed forces were intrigued by the machine's portability, which would allow it to be used in the field to measure and record sonar, a technology still being perfected. But Camras believed his recorder had a future in the home, where people could record themselves or transfer their music from disc to wire, so that their records would not be worn out from overplaying. His specialized recording head was a step in the right direction, and yet Camras dreamed of something else: "recreating natural sound," as he put it. While looking for ways to record high frequencies, he discovered the magic of AC bias. In 1942, five years after GE rejected the DC-bias Magnetophon, Camras brought his AC-bias wire recorder to the same folks in Schenectady. This time, the sound was so good that GE heard the future. The company signed on to make Camras's recorder.

Even more than Camras and Weber, Jack Mullin's life was changed by the wondrous effect AC bias had on magnetic recording. Mullin was a sharp kid from Larkspur, California, a town in Marin County, across the bay from San Francisco. From an early age, he had a passion for classical music and electronics. While studying electrical engineering at Santa Clara University, Mullin befriended Bill Palmer, a Stanford student and film buff who was as laid-back as Mullin was intense. Palmer's father owned a company that assisted with the dredging of San Francisco Bay, and the Palmers were wealthy enough that Bill, after graduating in 1933, could indulge his passion for filmmaking. He formed W. A. Palmer and Company, which gradually evolved into W. A. Palmer Films, a business that specialized in industrial films. Palmer was probably the first person to integrate sound into industrials, and he also pioneered the use of 16-millimeter film.

Mullin also loved filmmaking, and though he wasn't as wealthy as Palmer, his father, a hardware-store manager, supplied him with film from his store. After graduation, Mullin worked as a technician for Pacific Bell Telephone Company. He spent much of his time hanging out with Palmer, and the two began to collaborate. Palmer's skill with mechanics meshed with Mullin's mind for electronics. Between the two of them, they figured out how to add optical sound capabilities to a silent-film camera. Together, they made a historic documentary about the building of the Bay Bridge.

While in his late twenties, Mullin was drafted by the army. Palmer remained a civilian but made army training films while making contacts in Hollywood. Mullin was assigned to a post in Alaska, but during the journey by sea up north, he received word that he had been promoted to lieutenant and was to report to Fort Monmouth, New Jersey. From there, he was sent to a Royal Air Force facility at Farnborough, in the south of England, to investigate why some British radar stations were picking up severe interference. It was at Farnborough that Mullin began to hear things.

Mullin liked to listen to the radio as he worked long into the night. After the BBC shut down at midnight, the only thing on the air was German radio, broadcast far and wide thanks to the Reich's network of strong transmitters. As Mullin sat by himself working on the Allies' communications difficulties, a question began to dawn on him: Was Hitler crazy enough to compel the Berlin Philharmonic to play graveyard-shift concerts for the radio every night? Because that was the only rational explanation for what he was hearing, which was the clear, crisp sound of live music. Mullin knew that American radio, when it wasn't live, was broadcast on transcription discs, and he knew that the sound of those discs was riddled with telltale pops and clicks. He also knew that those discs could hold only a few minutes of music on each side, but these nighttime sounds were seamless, whole movements of symphonies coming through in one transmission. Either Hitler was a fanatic for live symphonic music, or he possessed some sort of top-secret radio technology.

The Magnetophon was hardly top secret. The Germans had shown off the AC-bias Magnetophon in June 1941, articles about it had appeared in general-interest magazines (some sold outside of Germany), and yet somehow the Americans knew nothing about it. Considering that the RRG was playing about 5,000 kilometers of tape every month, this has to constitute one of the oddest intelligence failures of modern warfare. As far as Mullin knew, he was the only one attuned to the mystery of these spooky late-night broadcasts.

As it turned out, a few others had their ears pricked. Back in the States, Les Paul was doing his part for the war effort by working at Armed Forces Radio in California. By the start of the war, Paul was mainly known as a prolific and virtuoso jazz guitarist with a string of instrumental hits, but he was also a voracious and intuitive student of musical technology. His love of guitar and disdain for its passive role in most bands led him to rethink the electric guitar and eventually invent one of the first solid-body electrics.

At a very young age he had been fascinated by the science and mechanics of recording. Paul loved to play his mother's phonograph and when he saw a cutting lathe he figured out how a phonograph worked. If it'll play the record back, he thought, why can't I just reverse the process and make a record myself? He built a microphone out of telephone parts and fashioned a stylus out of steel. He needed a dynamically balanced wheel for the turntable, and a mechanic friend of his father's suggested he use a flywheel, which Paul scavenged from a junk-bound Cadillac. Paul had been jamming with adult musicians since he was nine, and a drummer, who was a dentist, suggested that Paul use a belt from a dental drill to drive the machine. An old Sears-Roebuck lathe that Paul found in his dad's garage provided the machine's lead screw. And so, in 1928, at the age of thirteen, Les Paul, budding bedroom recording artist, embossed onto aluminum the sound of his voice singing "She'll Be Comin' Round the Mountain." The next step was to take his homemade pickup and attach it to his guitar.

While Paul was working for Armed Forces Radio, one of his duties was to assemble edited versions of speeches by Roosevelt, Hitler, Churchill, and other luminaries using a process known as "slip disc." Three people controlled three turntables, each holding a 16-inch disc recording of the unedited speech. A piece of paper was slid under each turntable to hold it in place; letting go of the paper allowed the turntable to spin. One would start the first turntable, playing a recording of the speech up to the point where material would be edited out. When the point was reached, an operator would stop turntable one and start turntable two at the end of the part that was to be edited out. Turntable three would stand by for the next editing point, and so on. All the while, a cutting lathe would make a master of the edited recording.

Like Mullin, Paul knew that pops and clicks were unavoidable with these discs. He also knew that the sound quality deteriorated as the stylus moved toward the center of the disc. So how was it possible that when Paul heard broadcasts of edited versions of the same speeches prepared by the Germans, there was no noise and no gradual degradation of the sound? And he was pretty sure that he and the other slip-disc operators were turning out the final versions as quickly as possible. So how did the Germans always manage to get their speeches on the air first?

In August 1944, two months after D-day, Mullin, now a major, was sent to newly liberated Paris as a major in the Signal Corps. His unit moved into a maharajah's palace and set up an electronics lab. Their job was to investigate any technological advances that the Germans had made during the war. Mullin and his men took several trips to Germany and discovered that the country was crawling with Magnetophons. They were everywhere, in barracks, abandoned bunkers, pretty much anywhere there had been any military activity. The Signal Corps men didn't think much of these machines, and soon a huge pile of German magnetic tape recorders stood rusting in the palace courtyard. Mullin had no problem with that. The sound of the machines was mediocre, certainly nothing like what he'd heard those nights in England.

A year later, the war in Europe was over but Mullin's unit was still in Paris pursuing its assignment. The Signal Corps and U.S. Army Intelligence wanted Mullin to investigate another mystery involving the Germans' use of radio. Throughout the war, Allied pilots had complained that their engines often cut out during bombing runs over Germany. The rumor was that the Nazis were able to use high-frequency radio transmissions to disrupt airplane engines. A tower on top of Feldberg mountain, north of Frankfurt, was the suspected transmission site. But when Mullin and a lieutenant got there, all they found was a cavernous basement room filled with huge generators and diesel engines—nothing that suggested any secret German high-frequency radio weapon.

What they did discover was the Germans' ability to use high frequencies for a more benign purpose. While Mullin was walking around the site, puzzling over its purpose, he met a British officer who was there for the same reason. Like Mullin, the man had an ear for music. Mullin mentioned the symphonies he'd heard late at night, and the officer asked him if he'd been to Radio Frankfurt in Bad Nauheim, a resort town about an hour's drive from Feldberg. They had a tape machine there that had tremendous sound quality—something called a Magnetophon. Mullin was skeptical. No way—there were dozens of those rusting away back in Paris. But the man was adamant: Do yourself a favor and go to Bad Nauheim.

Mullin set off on the drive back to Paris. Years later, he still recalled vividly what happened next: "On the way back to my unit, we came to the proverbial fork in the road. I could turn right and drive back to Paris, or turn left to Frankfurt. I chose to turn left. It was the greatest decision of my life."

The Reichs-Rundfunk-Gesellschaft (RRG) took its operation very seriously. The German radio network was off the air for all of two minutes during the entire war. As protection against Allied bombing, Radio Frankfurt had been run out of a fortified palace in Bad Nauheim. By the time Mullin got there, the station had been taken over by Armed Forces Radio, but it was still staffed by Germans. The Americans had no idea how unique the station's equipment was, and the Germans took it for granted, so when the sergeant on duty was asked by Mullin for a demonstration of the station's Magnetophon, and when the sergeant then ordered his German assistant to fetch a roll of tape for the machine, neither of them shared Mullin's elated reaction.

Suddenly, it all made sense. "It was the answer to my question about where all of that beautiful night music had come from," Mullin said. Except that on another level, it made no sense at all: "I couldn't tell from the sound whether it was live or playback. There simply was no background noise."

Mullin was a quick study. He took one look at the machine's schematics and realized what made it different from the machines collected back in Paris: it was wired for AC bias. The machine was a Magnetophon K-4, the fourth-generation model, and it was one of two K-4s that had been modified for AC bias and were now owned by the German postal service, which administered RRG's transmitters and sophisticated line distribution network. Those two machines were the only officially sanctioned AC-bias Magnetophons in existence. Except for that one modification, that crucial missing link, any Magnetophon rusting in the palace courtyard in Paris was just like the one at the radio station. Any of them could be modified to sound perfect.

Mullin received permission from the army to procure two K-4s, some spare heads, and fifty reels of BASF magnetic tape. He took the machines apart, packed the pieces in thirty-five separate wooden boxes, and mailed them to his mother's house in America. He knew that the heads, which were one of the most impressively designed aspects of the Magnetophon, would be very difficult for him to duplicate, but he was confident he could use the schematics and American parts to rebuild the electronics. So he sent home only the machine's tape transports.

Mullin finally made it back to the Bay Area in January of 1946. All thirty-five boxes were waiting at his mom's house. He reconnected with Palmer and told him about the Magnetophons. Palmer asked his friend to join W. A. Palmer and Company as a full-time employee. Mullin accepted, thinking that he and Palmer could work with the two German Magnetophons, using Palmer's rapidly growing list of Hollywood contacts to promote the use of the German recorders in films.

Mullin and Palmer spent the next few months rebuilding and tinkering with their two Magnetophons. To add AC bias to the recording unit, Mullin read articles that Marvin Camras had written about his Armour research. The Allied Control Commission had nullified all patents held by the Axis powers, so although Weber and Nagai had gotten there first, the perfect sound of AC bias was now officially all-American.

In the spring of 1946, the San Francisco chapter of the Institute of Radio Engineers sent out invitations for the Magnetophon's coming-out party. Mullin, identified as the chief sound engineer at W. A. Palmer and Company, would be giving a presentation on "The Magnetophon, German Sound Recorder, and Its Applications to Film Recording and Other Uses," including an "Actual Demonstration and Recording." This machine was the real deal, with a frequency response beyond 15 kHz. "It is the standard recorder of Rundfunk and was used by the German *Wehrmacht*," read the invitation. "This is without doubt the outstanding recorder for sound."

On May 16 at 7:30 p.m., about a hundred people made it to the NBC building at 420 Taylor Street in downtown San Francisco to hear the sound of the postwar future. In the cavernous Studio A, Mullin and Palmer were dwarfed by a huge speaker onstage as they demonstrated the sound of their refurbished Magnetophon. The crowd was floored. At the end of the night, people swore they couldn't tell the difference between "live" and "Magnetophon."

In March 1945, a few months before Mullin encountered the Magnetophon at Radio Frankfurt and launched its journey across the waters, Theodor Adorno gave a talk at Columbia University called "What National Socialism Has Done to the Arts." Adorno was a recent German émigré and a leading light of the Frankfurt School, a group of neo-Marxist philosophers, critics, and social scientists that had formed around the University of Frankfurt's Institute of Social Research. Adorno had seen the Nazi horrors up close and managed to flee to America, and now he had a message for his new homeland: Don't get too comfortable. The Nazis may be on their last legs, he said, but fascism was far from permanently vanquished. It could reemerge at any time, even in the United States. Sinclair Lewis had said that when fascism arrived in America it would be wrapped in the flag and carrying a cross. Adorno thought it would come wrapped in a paper sleeve and carrying a running time of three minutes.

The goal of the Frankfurt School was to formulate a Marxist critical theory that was more nuanced than so-called "vulgar" Marxism. As Adorno put it, "It is not ideology which is untrue but rather its pretension to correspond with reality." In other words, the true critic was one who could detect when ideology passed itself off as common sense, when the ideological pretended to be the world as it is. The equation can be restated in artistic terms: It is not representations that are untrue but rather their pretension to capture exactly that which they represent.

For Adorno, great art rejected this pretension. A great artist was one whose art depicted the reality of the human condition, while offering a glimpse of something that was perhaps unattainable: a better, more humane, more beautiful world. Adorno heard this ideal in Beethoven, but in more recent trends in German music he detected a corruption that he associated with fascism. Such music no longer attempted to suggest something greater than itself; it was content to be a utilitarian product—a diversion, a hummable tune. "It is this lack of experience of the imagery of real art," Adorno told the crowd that night, "which is at least one of the formative elements of the cynicism that has finally transformed the Germans, Beethoven's people, into Hitler's people."

Adorno feared that a world reeling from the horrors of the past few years might embrace music that made the listener merely feel good, without inspiring any sort of critical impulse. It would be music that erased history. Music that tried to make sense of the unthinkable—music that looked back even as it looked forward, music that was truly dialectical—would have no place in such a world, and *this* is how fascism would once again take root in the body politic. "It is just this taboo of expressing the essence, the depth of things, the compulsion of keeping visible the fact, the datum, and accepting it unquestioningly, which has survived as one of the most sinister cultural heritages of the Fascist era," Adorno said that night. Cryptically, he warned of "a kind of pink pseudo-realism sweeping the world after the war, which may be more efficient but which is certainly not fundamentally superior to the art exhibitions commandeered by the Nazis."

Pink pseudo-realism. The term must have made many wonder what exactly Adorno was talking about. It's almost as if he's sounding a note of whimsy. What could he have meant?

Adorno's dim view of popular music was rooted in a belief that the only reason people liked such music was because it was cynically tailored to mirror their world. In a capitalist society, both they and the music were "kneaded by the same modes of production." (We can assume that, for Adorno, "it's got a good beat and you can dance to it" was the ultimate expression of this false consciousness.) He talked about music mostly as an abstract entity, rather than as a material object, like a record, so he never quite figured out how to apply his critical theory to recordings per se. At two different points in "The Curve of the Needle," an oddly disjointed essay that he started in 1927, at the dawn of the electrical recording era, and revised in 1965, four years before his death, he declares, "The relevance of the talking machine is debatable"—the repetition and the span of decades suggesting that he never did find a side to take in that debate. He was pretty sure he didn't like what the phonograph represented ("stems from an era that cynically acknowledges the dominance of things over people"), but mostly reserved judgment for another day: "For the time being, Beethoven defies the gramophone."

As Adorno stood in front of that audience at Columbia, warning that the Top 40 could provide fascism with an expressway to our skulls, did he know about the Magnetophon that was at that moment on its journey from Radio Frankfurt to the San Francisco Bay? Not likely. But if he did know, we can guess what he'd think of it. However much magnetic tape was an efficient carrier of propaganda broadcast by RRG, Adorno would be more alarmed by the German engineer H. J. von Braunmuhl's boast that in a comparison between a live transmission and one on magnetic tape, "a practiced ear can detect no difference in quality." In other words, it would be tape's "pretension to correspond to reality" that would unnerve him. All the more so when he learned how flexible tape was: whatever you don't want, whatever sticks out, whatever doesn't conform to the smooth flow of the music, you can just cut out with a razor blade. You can take that little strip of dissent, and throw it down the memory hole. The tape will splice back together, the world will fold back in on itself, as though this tiny speck of wrongness, this fly in the ointment, never existed. *Pseudo-realism.*

That still leaves the mystery of "pink." As unlikely as it was that Adorno knew about the Magnetophon, it's even less likely that he knew much about audio engineering terms. But it's worth noting that for audio professionals, "pink noise" is a variation of "white noise." We often think of the latter as a high-pitched sound, but it's really a sound that contains every frequency audible to human beings; it sounds high to us because every octave contains twice as many frequencies as the one below it. Pink noise is a version of white noise that compensates for this imbalance by dropping the volume of each successive octave, so that each has the same energy. If white noise is the whole world of audio perception experienced as a totality, pink noise is an artificial flattening, a sound that applies a contrived logic to this totality.

Soon after his talk at Columbia, Adorno relocated to Los Angeles. At the same time, Mullin and Palmer were traveling around California, spreading the word about the amazing machine they'd plundered from Germany and revamped on American soil.

Since we're entertaining unlikely Adorno scenarios, let's indulge in one more. Let's say he did know about the Magnetophon and was intrigued enough to head north and drop in at the offices of Palmer and Company on Howard Street. He might arrive on the same day that a singer—someone whom Mullin would later recall only as "the fat kid with a really nice voice"—arrived with his manager, who asked if they could use the Magnetophon to record some songs. And what if, soon after he returned to L.A., Adorno received in the mail a complimentary copy of the album the fat kid recorded that day? He would put the record on the phonograph he grudgingly owned, sit back, and listen to the first commercial album in history to be recorded on magnetic tape and mastered onto vinyl, the first of millions more that would be created in the following decades.

What would he have made of *Songs by Merv Griffin*? Would he hear pink? Would he think, *I tried to warn them*?

By the early forties, Bing Crosby was one of the biggest celebrities in America, a huge recording artist, movie star, and radio personality. But there was a bit of trouble in that last department. He was sick of doing his show, *Kraft Music Hall*. Not sick of the show, exactly, just bored with the conventions of radio, particularly the industry's insistence that quality radio was always done live. Live radio not only meant that he couldn't fix mistakes or take a break if he didn't feel like performing that day—it also meant that he couldn't knock off a few shows at once if he felt inspired. Or wanted more time on the golf course.

Crosby had informed NBC that he would continue with his show for the 1944–45 season only if he could record it on disc. Even for a huge star like Crosby, this was a lot to ask. NBC said no, and the show went off the air. The following year, a court order forced NBC to split into two independent networks, NBC and ABC. Eager to establish itself, ABC offered Crosby a show, sponsored by the radio manufacturer Philco, and agreed to broadcast it prerecorded, provided the ratings stayed high.

Beginning in the fall of 1946, Crosby's show was recorded onto 16-inch transcription discs. Editing was technically possible but involved a laborious process similar to the slip-disc method Les Paul and his colleagues at Armed Forces Radio had used. The process always resulted in at least one generation's loss of fidelity, and each disc could hold only four minutes of material, which disrupted the show's flow. And, of course, there were those damn pops and clicks. Crosby's ratings steadily declined that season, and ABC was convinced the discs were to blame.

Four people at the May 1946 demo—Harold Lindsay, Walter Selsted, Frank Lennert, and Charlie Ginsburg—were present or future employees of a small company called Ampex, located in Redwood City, a town in the future Silicon Valley. Ampex had made parts for airplane engines during the war and was now searching for some entrée into the postwar economy. Alexander M. Poniatoff, a Russian émigré who founded the company, had a vague notion that Ampex could enter the professional audio technology

market, despite having no experience with audio technology or the entertainment field. Selsted and Lennert, barely out of college, were particularly
excited by what they heard, so when Palmer, through his Hollywood contacts, set up another demo, they urged their boss to go. Poniatoff was sold
and gave his employees the go-ahead. The mission, as Lindsay would later
record in his notes, was "to produce a magnetic recorder equal to or better
in performance than the German Magnetophon as reconstructed by Mr.
Jack Mullin of the W. A. Palmer Co., San Francisco." By March 1947,
Ampex had built the tape reels and the heads. In May, they tested the
heads at Palmer and Company, and everyone there agreed they sounded as
good as the Magnetophon's.

Mullin and Palmer met Murdo MacKenzie, technical producer for
Crosby's radio show. MacKenzie wanted to hear for himself what magnetic
tape could do. In June, he listened to one of Mullin and Palmer's demos
and was duly impressed. He invited Mullin to use his Magnetophon to
record the first show of *Philco Radio Time*'s 1947–48 season, to be taped in
August and broadcast in October.

MacKenzie offered Mullin the job of engineering and recording the
show. Mullin moved his two Magnetophons into a small room at the building on Hollywood and Vine. He edited every show that season, sometimes
taking as much as a week for each one. Since nobody else in America was
working with tape, he had single-handedly invented the craft of tape editing, using the film editing skills he'd picked up from Palmer. There was no
such thing as splicing tape, so Mullin first tried a cement similar to what
film editors used, but discovered it caused an audible thump when the
playback head passed over the edits. He switched to regular Scotch tape,
but the adhesive often bled out, ensnaring other parts of the recording tape
and turning the reel into a big mess. Rubbing talcum powder on the edit
points helped a bit.

Whatever Mullin did, he had to be extremely careful to save every piece
of tape for reuse because those fifty reels of BASF taken from Radio Frankfurt were all he had. The scarce resources also dictated that actual shows
went out over the air on disc rather than tape. Because each reel could hold
twenty-two minutes of sound, two decks would be required for each show,
one starting as soon as the first reel ran out. Therefore, to broadcast the
show on tape would have required the use of the only two German Magnetophons in America. If one were to malfunction on the air, or if one of

those fragile splices were to come off during broadcast, the show would unravel. So *Philco* went over the air on disc, maintaining a flimsy connection to the old world of radio.

Besides the ability to correct mistakes and to take material from different performances, tape changed the show in subtle ways. As Mullin became a more skilled editor, he could make very small edits, omitting blank space to give the shows a quicker pace than live radio was capable of. And once you started using tape to "lie"—taking snippets from the dress rehearsals, editing out mistakes—it was only a matter of time before somebody thought of more creative lies for sound to tell. During one show, "hillbilly comic" Bob Burns ad-libbed a few farm jokes that got big laughs but were too risqué to air. Bill Morrow, Crosby's writer, asked Mullin to excise the jokes while hanging on to the scraps of tape with the audience's reaction. At a taping a few weeks later, a few jokes bombed. Morrow convinced Mullin to add some laughs to the jokes. It was the earliest form of the laugh track.

At that fateful first Crosby taping in August 1947, Ampex officials showed off the prototype of their Model 200, the American version of the Magnetophon. Crosby and his producers immediately asked Ampex to supply the show with equipment. The deal was simple: Ampex would make the machines and Palmer and Company would sell them.

ABC was wary. It was all well and good that their man Crosby loved tape, but the company wasn't betting on the sound it owned being stored and broadcast on machines made by a bunch of unknowns. ABC pointed out to Crosby that his contract stipulated state-of-the-art recording devices, and that the many recording lathes in NBC's basement did, in fact, represent the industry's cutting-edge machines. Crosby replied that if tape were off the table, then the deal was off. Nervous ABC executives paid a visit to Palmer and Company and weren't impressed with the ragtag operation. Then they paid a visit to Ampex's ramshackle offices and were shocked to discover that Poniatoff's operation had a mere six employees, including one—Myron Stolaroff—who had just graduated from Stanford. This was who they were trusting with their star investment? They told Crosby they couldn't go through with the deal.

As it happened, they had some reason for concern. Ampex was running on fumes: banks were turning down Poniatoff's loan requests, and employees often frantically pooled change to accept packages that arrived COD. Crosby, in an impressive leap of faith, told ABC that he personally would make sure the Ampex machine was built. ABC backed down. Soon, a personal check from Crosby for $50,000 arrived unannounced at Ampex, with no cover letter and no loan terms. Magnetic tape in America lived to see another day, and ABC eventually ordered twenty Ampex machines at $5,000 each.

Crosby's financial backing and promise to ABC made him Ampex's de facto distributor. Ampex would now deal directly with Crosby's company, making Palmer and Company an unnecessary middleman. Palmer protested to Poniatoff that he and Ampex had an agreement; he had a letter from Poniatoff that proved it. Poniatoff, either because he had forgotten about ever signing such a letter or because he was calling Palmer's bluff, told Palmer to show him this letter. Chronically disorganized, Palmer searched through his files but could not locate the letter. And so Palmer went down in history as an unsung but integral part of magnetic tape recording's journey to American shores.

In the spring of 1948, the first Ampex Model 200s hit the streets and immediately became the broadcast standard. (Mullin and Palmer were each presented with a machine.) Almost overnight, other companies followed Ampex's lead. The most immediately successful was Magnecord, launched by employees at Armour Research in Chicago (and having no involvement with Camras). It was hailed as a much cheaper yet still high-quality consumer alternative to Ampex. It was the machine that Ramsey used to record Lead Belly's final sessions.

Even before Les Paul heard about magnetic tape, he had been thinking like a tapehead. Those childhood experiments with phonographs had led to Paul building his own lathe as an adult and putting it to staggeringly inventive use. After his mother claimed she could not tell his guitar playing apart from others, Paul vowed to find a signature style. "I experimented with the sound, came up with lots of ideas," Paul says. Paul called his new method of making music "sound on sound." It was a painstaking process. He would record a track onto an aluminum disc, and then record a second track on another machine, while the first machine played back his first track. The second machine would thus capture Paul's live second performance as well as his recorded first performance. Then he'd begin the process again with a third performance. In this way, he would layer part upon part until he had a finished piece.

Paul had been experimenting with the process since the thirties, obsessively tinkering with it and perfecting microphone placement and sound effects like delay and reverb. He kept this work secret, even from his wife and musical collaborator, the singer Mary Ford. Finally, in late 1947, he was ready to show the world what he'd been up to. He took an acetate to a party thrown by Jim Moran, a Hollywood publicist known for stunts like selling a GE refrigerator to an Eskimo. (Moran is the man who, when police showed up to shut down his boldest PR move yet, famously said, "It's a sad day for American capitalism when a man can't fly a midget on a kite over Central Park.") At Moran's home, a garage on Sunset and Fairfax, the stars were out that night, including the bandleader Artie Shaw and the legendary tough-guy actor Lawrence Tierney.

Music was playing on the hi-fi, and just to see what would happen, Paul surreptitiously put on his disc, an instrumental called "Lover." "Well, you'd think somebody doused the thing with kerosene," Paul said. "It hit the turntable like an explosion." His accounts of his musical exploits sometimes border on the hyperbolic, but it's not hard to see why this song would floor a party filled with stoners. Nobody had heard anything like it. You didn't have to know that Paul had played all the instruments, including the drums. Even today, accustomed as we are to multitracked sound, there's a disquieting unity to the piece, with all the tracks fitting together in a lockstep. From its delicate waltz beginning to its speed-freak ending, the song clocks in at under three minutes. But it actually feels longer, because what you're hearing sounds like several three-minute blasts from different points in time that, through some time-warp trickery, can be experienced all at once.

"Lover" became the first commercially released multitrack recording, beginning a string of sound-on-sound hits by the Paul/Ford duo. Paul's recording methodology soon underwent a crucial shift. As a gift, Crosby presented him with a two-track Ampex Model 300, the second generation of the company's signature machine. Paul modified it to suit his sound-on-sound method. He could record a part on the first track, and then dub it on the second track while simultaneously recording another part on top of it. He could add a third by switching back to the first track and repeating the process. And so on.

Whenever the duo went on tour, Paul would pack his modified Model 300. He would record wherever the mood hit him—hotel rooms, backstage, even at train stations on occasion. The process required a great deal of skill because any mistake meant the whole recording had to be scrapped, since parts were always being recorded onto the master tape. "You don't make mistakes," Paul says today. "We got to the point where when we laid the part down I knew just how loud to make each track. And we recorded backwards so that we did the least important parts first and the most important parts last, so that the fidelity would be the clearest." He laughs. "So the last thing that would be on the record was me."

The first product of the multitrack tape process to reach the public was "How High the Moon," released in 1951. According to Paul, he sketched out the entire arrangement on a coaster while eating White Castle sliders at a bar near the couple's home in Jackson Heights, Queens. The finished song, which even today sounds appropriately lunar, contained a staggering twenty-four stacked parts, half of which were devoted to Ford's vocals. After "How High the Moon," the pair's hit songs kept getting thicker, reaching a high of thirty-seven tracks on "Night and Day." Ford's stacked vocals really pushed some of their efforts over the top. Her voice had a remarkable clarity, enhanced by the new technique that Paul had devised of close miking her voice so that her vocals sound kaleidoscopic—the same voice somehow harmonizing with itself. On "Tiger Rag," Ford repeats "here kitty-kitty-kitty-kitty" and "here puss-puss-puss" as fast as a cheetah, in perfect who-knows-how-many-part harmony.

Ross Snyder, a special products manager at Ampex, began his contribution to the great lie of magnetic tape in a familiar Edisonian way. One day in 1955, he and Walter Selsted were thinking about the Ampex Model 300, the company's next-generation magnetic tape recorder, and how good it sounded. But how good did it really sound to the public? They hatched a plan to find out.

For $5,000, they booked the San Francisco Symphony, and worked out a repertoire with the conductor, Enrique Jordá, who also agreed to let them record some of the rehearsals at the War Memorial Opera House. Snyder measured the dimensions of the hall, while Selsted set up the equipment. To make the recordings sound flat and dry, they close-miked the instruments. Their goal was to record the origination of the sound, while omitting most of its reverberation. When played back, they wanted the room to receive as pure a tone as possible, and let the space's acoustics take care of the rest.

Tickets were sold for the concert. As far as the audience knew, the only unusual thing about that night's performance was that it was a benefit for the symphony's retirement fund. Once the music began, things got weird very quickly.

The symphony opened with Mozart's *The Marriage of Figaro*. If you had exceptional eyesight, and it had ever crossed your mind that a group of highbrow professional musicians would engage in a parlor trick onstage, you might have noticed that the string instruments were wrapped in cellophane, rendering all bowing ineffective. The brass and woodwinds were easier to fake; the players just pretended to blow. Not one note issued forth from a vibrating string or the bell of a horn. During the overture, some of the musicians set down their instruments and walked offstage. Then some more followed. And then more. Some of the audience began to laugh. Others rolled their eyes when they realized it was a stunt. There was applause when it was over, much of it appreciative, some of it no doubt sarcastic.

Snyder watched the show from the side of the stage. When the piece was over, he addressed the audience: Could anyone tell when the musicians stopped playing? Many hands shot confidently up. Okay, Snyder said, how many of you thought it was at this point during the overture? How about this other point? Or maybe here? There were takers for each choice. Snyder smiled and proudly informed the audience that the musicians never stopped because they had never started.

That was the only openly deceptive part of the evening. For the rest of the concert, Jordá intermittently paused the musicians. Snyder would drop his hand to inform the audience that the tape was now playing and the human players were resting. To underscore that tonight was about more than a parlor trick—that it heralded an era when the division between live sound and its representation would be conceptually and practically blurred—one of the pieces performed was a concerto for tape recorder and orchestra by Vladimir Ussachevsky, who was onstage that night operating the tape recorder during the piece.

"I never had more fun in my life than doing that concert," Snyder recalled fifty years later. "I learned what a good actor feels like." But he wanted to make one thing clear: "The deception was convincing, but certainly not final. By no means had we discovered a way to duplicate life."

5

Presence

The first to discover [Enoch] Light's records were, as might be expected, audiophiles. Next came a group Light identifies as "people in general." "Now the kids are picking them up," he continued . . . "We're pulling them away from rock-and-roll . . ."
                                                    —*The New York Times*, 1960

We developed a small following of weirdoes. Then we got the intellectuals. Now the kids are coming.   —Tommy Ramone, 1976

        Everything's ending here.   —Pavement, "Here," 1992

When British pop-metal kings Def Leppard set out to make a follow-up to their phenomenally successful 1983 *Pyromania* album, they didn't think they were making a record that would be the apotheosis of the analog era. They just wanted it to be even more popular than *Pyromania*, which is why they were keen to collaborate again with that album's producer, Robert John "Mutt" Lange. "If it doesn't sell, what's the point in making it?" the singer Joe Elliott would recall years later. "That's what any producer will tell you: 'You're an artist, fine, but I'm employed by your record company to make this record sell as many copies as possible.' And luckily, [Lange] was working with a band that was thinking the same way."

The earliest incarnations of the songs that would become the *Hysteria* album were recorded in Dublin, where the members of Def Leppard were living as British tax exiles following the completion of the *Pyromania* tour in 1984. The band had two four-track tape machines, which they used to maximum effect. "We thought we were the Beatles," guitarist Phil Collen recalled. "We'd start bouncing the tracks so we could do backup vocals." Bouncing was a way to free up tracks by mixing down two or more onto one track of the other machine. While the Beatles did not invent bouncing, their creative use of the practice inspired generations of studio-savvy musicians.

Lange had done some preproduction on the new album but passed on producing it, citing exhaustion. Def Leppard began recording with the producer Jim Steinman but were dismayed to discover that he favored spontaneity over perfection. He wanted to "record the moment"—the most classic recording aesthetic there is—but the band wanted to craft that moment until it shone.

During one session, Steinman told the band they'd nailed a take and should move on. They replied that they were just tuning up.

"But it sounds honest," Steinman said.

"Yeah, but to a kid in Boise, Idaho, it sounds out of tune," Elliott replied.

Def Leppard decided to buy Steinman out of his contract, which meant the band would need to sell 2 million records just to recoup the fee. .

Lange was coaxed back to the project. In the middle of it, drummer Rick Allen lost an arm in a car accident. Allen's decision to soldier on with a specially designed kit, and the band's unhesitating acceptance of this new tack, besides reflecting admirably on Def Leppard's sense of band solidarity, proved just how comfortable they were with finding new ways to transcend human imperfection. But other examples abounded. Eschewing the Marshall amplifiers they used onstage, the band recorded many guitar parts using a Rockman, a small amp designed by Tom Scholz, the mastermind behind Boston, a band whose studio obsessiveness set the stage for Def Leppard. Rockmans were known for their clean sound, thus making it easier to manipulate the results with surgical precision in the editing process. Instruments were recorded separately. For the song "Hysteria," they spent hours perfecting the guitar on one verse. Rather than risk losing this perfection in the next verse, they "flew in" the same part and used it for the other verses. Such was their desire for separation and intricate malleability that rather than play some chords, they would construct them by recording individual notes singly and then blending them to create the chords.

Much of *Hysteria*'s recording was done in a small, dingy Dublin jingle studio. "You didn't need anything extravagant," Collen explained. "It's not as though we'd all set up and play at the same time." Lange believed that it didn't really matter where the basic tracks were laid down. All he needed was a decently clean signal. The real heavy lifting would be done in the mixing stage, using a sophisticated console made by a company called Solid State Logic. "At the time, the big thing was the SSL desk," Elliott recalled. "It looked like something out of NASA."

After three years of recording, the band was surprised when Lange took the tapes and spent nearly five months mixing the record. "Which was beyond belief, really," Elliott said. "We couldn't understand why it was taking so long." Lange was taking so long because "mixing" only begins to describe what he was doing. He was deciding which of the multitudes of sounds recorded across twenty-four tracks to keep, how much reverb and noise gating to apply to the drums, and how to break down and physically reassemble the songs. In short: he was building the album from the ground up.

So much about the making of *Hysteria* illustrates the journey recorded music took in the years after the introduction of magnetic tape, and the state it was in at the twilight of the analog era. There was the album's humble beginning as four-track experiments in Dublin; the complete jettisoning of the idea that rock bands should make records based on real-time performances; the desire to "fix" everything, down to the individual note; the power of twenty-four-track consoles to allow bands to amass huge collections of parts, then spend years building a sonic edifice; the idea that the sound of a record should be tailored explicitly toward salability, rather than a traditional idea of fidelity; the belief that the recording studio itself would no longer dictate the character of a record's sound; the fact that small studios were springing up everywhere; the creeping insidiousness of the SSL mixing console, that NASA-looking acreage of knobs and faders; and of course the enormous amount of time and money invested in making the record.

But what truly made *Hysteria* an analog-era apotheosis was the album itself and the way it sounded. By the eighties the "dry" sound of records made in the previous decade had largely gone out of fashion in the world of big-budget pop recordings—"corporate rock," in the parlance of the time. In its place, the use of such effects as reverb and noise gating resulted in music that approximated the sound of an arena or similar large expanse.

You can hear that in *Hysteria*'s explosive drums, which suggest a vast space, but not one found on Earth. Elliot's heavily processed and multi-tracked vocals don't center the music so much as send it careening out at strange angles. The guitars are all smooth edges and glinted reflections. There is a bouncy, spacey thrust that makes *Hysteria* a perfect soundtrack for a walk on the moon or a rendezvous on top of a skyscraper in Dubai.

"It's an example of a record that's been picked to the bone," says the recording engineer Andy Wallace, whose work crafting a more organic-feeling version of this sound would help Nirvana move many units a few years after *Hysteria*'s release in 1988. "There's not one hair out of place on that record. It sounds sensational, and sonically, it was a wonder . . . but that's not a record I found myself listening to over and over. It could almost have been any band. The band was almost defined by the style of recording and production, rather than having their own character."

It could almost have been any band. One of the most technologically advanced records of its time—a record whose creation required vast amounts of capital—does not document the singularity of a group of musicians. Sure, multitrack recording had already jettisoned the idea of recordings documenting a band performance, but this is something else entirely. Now there is no band.

The ultimate truth about *Hysteria* is contained in Joe Elliot's simple request that the album be "radio-friendly," and his concurrent belief that "the kid in Boise, Idaho," cared if the guitars weren't in tune. Making nice with the radio, and satisfying that kid, meant making a record that effaced the band. To use an old high-fidelity term quickly losing its relevance in the 1980s, *Hysteria* contains no "presence." And to understand how music lost its presence in the waning days of analog, we must begin with the analog era's grandest format war.

"I promise this is going to be a long story," said a grinning David Sarnoff. "If you want to hear it."

Samuel J. Rosenman did not want to hear it. "All I want you to do is answer the question," he replied.

But Sarnoff was in a storytelling mood. "I am not going to answer it the way you want me to answer it."

"If the Commission wants you to give a long story, that is alright. I have asked a question which calls for a short answer."

Rosenman, a lawyer representing the Columbia Broadcasting System, was questioning the RCA Victor chairman of the board on May 4, 1950, during a hearing in Washington held by the Federal Communications Commission to consider which color-television technology would become the nation's broadcast standard. The choice was between CBS, who had devised the first standard, and RCA, whose technology was more recent.

As today's exchange made clear, there was simmering animosity on both sides, though the current TV skirmish was a minor battle compared with what the two companies had gone through on the audio front over the past two years. Known within the industry as the Battle of the Speeds, it pit the 33⅓ rpm LP developed by the Columbia Recording Corporation, a subsidiary of CBS, against the small 45 rpm disc invented by RCA. Although the growing consensus was that the battle was over and CBS had won, RCA refused to concede.

Rosenman surely knew he was probing a fresh wound with his question. He had prefaced it by suggesting that an analogy could be drawn between the claims RCA had made about its 45 and what the company now said about its color-TV technology. The question he asked was this: Did Sarnoff recall that "for a number of years" RCA had refused to make phonographs that could play LPs?

Rather than answer the question, Sarnoff replied that Rosenman's analogy was "incorrect."

"Will you state in what respect?"

By now many in the crowded room were laughing at this pitched exchange. "Well," Sarnoff said, laughing along with them, "that calls for a long story."

Sarnoff then surprised everyone by giving the first lengthy public insider history of the Battle of the Speeds. It was RCA, Sarnoff said, not CBS, who had given the world its first long-playing disc, in the autumn of 1931. Technically, that wasn't true; experiments with LPs stretched back to the acoustic era. But RCA did offer the first real alternative to the 78 rpm shellac discs that had been the industry standard since the twenties. RCA's Vitaphone disc, which began as a way to record synchronous sound on film and was later used by radio stations, spun at 33⅓ rpm and held 11½ minutes per side—three times as much as a 78. The Vitaphone seemed like a natural choice for a consumer format, but RCA handled the transition ineptly and the discs never caught on.

As Sarnoff told his story, he was thinking of Edward Wallerstein. It was Wallerstein who, shortly after becoming general manager of the Victor division of RCA Victor in 1933, put the Vitaphone out of its misery. A few years after ending Victor's grand experiment in LPs, Wallerstein quit to work for Columbia, the label's biggest rival. And Columbia was now owned by CBS.

Columbia's roots stretched back even farther than Victor's. The Columbia Phonograph Company was the lone surviving offshoot of the North American Phonograph Company, which had cornered the talking-machine market in 1888, before going bankrupt a few years later. The NAPC's bankruptcy coincided with the arrival of the first Berliner discs, sowing the seeds of what would eventually become the RCA Victor behemoth. Unlike Edison, Columbia embraced the disc format and began to sell disc machines. By the early twentieth century, Columbia and Victor controlled every major patent related to disc players, with each company blatantly infringing on the other. Rather than sue themselves into oblivion, they agreed to share patents. For the next few decades, Columbia and Victor dominated the industry, though Columbia always ran a distant second.

In 1937, CBS, originally an offshoot of Columbia but now independent, acquired Columbia. Wallerstein, with hopes of rejuvenating Columbia, had urged William S. Paley, president of CBS, to buy the label. Once he did, Wallerstein left his RCA job to become president of what was now called the Columbia Recording Corporation. Paley told him that he would seriously consider any proposals to make Columbia more competitive. Wallerstein suggested that they develop a long-playing disc—only this time, done right.

In Sarnoff's view, Wallerstein had brought more than just the idea to CBS. Though he did not mention Wallerstein by name during his story, Sarnoff accused him of letting Paley know that RCA was working on a format that would transform the industry. "The man who was at the head of the record business deserted us, went to the Columbia Phonograph Company," Sarnoff said, most likely purposely using Columbia's old name, "and told them all about the developments that we had in our plant. This 33 business was an attempt on the part of Columbia to beat RCA to the punch."

Peter Goldmark was also surely on Sarnoff's mind that day. A brilliant engineer and Hungarian émigré who had fled the Nazis and tried unsuccessfully to get a job with RCA before being hired by Paley, Goldmark had designed CBS's color-television technology. After that, beginning in 1946, he led the team that perfected Columbia's long-playing disc, along with Rene Snepvangers, a Columbia engineer, and William Bachman, the company's research director. The Columbia disc, which the company had named the "LP," had grooves 3/1,000th of an inch wide, spun at 33⅓ rpm, and could hold a maximum of 22½ minutes per side.

In April 1948, Columbia invited Sarnoff to hear its still-secret new disc. What happened at that meeting is clearly in dispute. More than one account (including Bachman's) has Sarnoff praising Columbia's accomplishment, but that's not how Sarnoff remembered it. In his version, which he related from the stand in D.C., he responded by telling Paley that RCA had developed its own microgroove technology, a 7-inch 45 rpm disc, that was superior to the LP. "It's the coming system of recording," he recalled saying.

A few months later, Columbia officially announced that LPs would soon go on sale. The company offered the LP technology royalty-free to any company that wanted to use it. To Columbia's surprise, RCA Victor did not announce plans to release LPs or to make LP-compatible phonographs, something other companies were beginning to do.

RCA finally went public with the 7-inch 45 shortly after the New Year, announcing that 45s would go on sale in the spring. Though the 45 held no more music than a 78, RCA touted it as beating the LP at its own game. RCA had designed a special record changer that could hold eight stacked 45s, with as little as one second elapsing between one disc ending and the needle dropping on the next. That meant 32 minutes of almost uninterrupted music.

Columbia was unimpressed. "We are unable to fathom the purpose of the records revolving at 45 rpm," Wallerstein said. But there was a purpose. The 45 sounded better, in the estimation of RCA. That was debatable, of course, but RCA did have recording science on its side. The faster a disc spins (or a reel of tape turns), the higher the maximum frequency it can reproduce because the system has more room to "draw" each moment of music.

RCA was confident that the public would forsake LPs once they heard the great sound of 45s. That's why RCA was so incensed by Columbia's immediate reaction to RCA's announcement, which was to say that they, too, would soon market 7-inch microgroove discs—except that, oh yeah, they'd spin at 33⅓, not 45. That defeated the whole purpose of the 45! "We told Columbia then, and we have reaffirmed since, and we have demonstrated, that you cannot give the same kind of recording on a small 33, 7-inch record that you can on a 45," Sarnoff said during his story.

Once 45s went on sale in 1949, the Battle of the Speeds was on. It would be "a historic disk battle between the Camden characters and the Columbia gang from Bridgeport," the amusement-industry trade magazine *The Billboard* proclaimed. "In many respects the tussle is likely to turn out as fraught with significance as the old battle between the cylinder and the flat disc."

They got that right. Columbia went on the offensive. Wallerstein slammed RCA for making "no provisions of any kind, either in its equipment or records, for long-playing records," and for issuing its own "unorthodox" record that required its own fancy-ass turntable. Columbia knew, however, that without the support of RCA, the LP would have a difficult time reaching dominance. In the summer of 1949, the two companies—along with Decca Records, the third-largest record label—convened a summit to discuss a peaceful resolution to the speed battle. Talks quickly broke down, with RCA accusing Columbia of conducting a clandestine campaign to sink the 45. "R.P.M. Peace Plan Flops," *The Billboard* announced, "Each Company on Its Own."

Although some labels did announce plans to make 45s, the LP clearly had the momentum. During the last days of 1949, RCA finally announced it would release some titles on LP—but only to satisfy a "vociferous minority" of the label's customers. As for Columbia, "we have no plans for going 45," Rosenman said during the same week he grilled Sarnoff. Sarnoff was undeterred. The 45 was "the greatest development in recording the world has produced so far," he said, adding that it was only a matter of time before Columbia began making 45s.

After Sarnoff's testimony, the panel called a recess. Reporters found Goldmark in the crowd and asked him if Sarnoff's account of his meeting with Paley was accurate. Goldmark, who had been at that meeting, remembered it quite differently. He recalled Sarnoff saying, "You caught me with my pants down."

In many retellings of the Battle of the Speeds, it is RCA and Columbia that are caught with their pants down, all the better to shove their heads up their

asses while their intra-corporate shenanigans nearly bring down an industry. There is some truth to that. Record sales during the third quarter of
1948, when the first LPs hit stores, were down 42 percent from the same
period in 1947. A 1949 survey found that only 15 percent of the nation's
phonograph owners purchased records with any regularity. One retailer
described the mood of his customers, unsure as to which formats and players they were supposed to buy, as "plain disgusted."

On the other hand, the speed war coincided with the country's first postwar recession, and many major industries were experiencing declines. And
although record sales were down, 12 million phonographs were sold
between 1946 and 1949, creating what *The Billboard* called "the biggest
potential disk market in history." The 85 percent of the market that was not
regularly buying records was clearly waiting for a good reason to do so. The
public's disgust notwithstanding, the millions that RCA and Columbia
spent promoting microgroove formats may have piqued its interest. Record
sales were fairly strong during the 1949 holiday season. *The Billboard*
theorized that "the so-called 'battle of the speeds,' accused of causing
industrial chaos, has bred a general public understanding of the developments in the industry."

As *The Billboard* predicted, the speed wars did recall the heady days of
Edison's cylinder versus Berliner's disc. Sarnoff, like Edison, believed the
public would make certain sacrifices for superior sound, choosing a disc
that held just four minutes because it sounded better than the one that held
twenty-two minutes.

On the merits, Sarnoff was probably correct. Even today, a well-made
45 rpm vinyl disc sounds noticeably better than its 33⅓ counterpart. But it
didn't matter. The *New York Times* critic Howard Taubman spoke for many
record buyers in 1950 when he admitted that although many 45s were
aurally superior, he preferred LPs for their "sheer listening comfort and
continuity of performances." Even the fact that the 45 survived gave the lie
to Sarnoff's belief in the ear of the marketplace. His format turned out to be
perfect for the song-driven pop market, whereas the classical audience,
which generally cared much more about quality audio, embraced the LP.

Perhaps the biggest evidence that the speed war ultimately galvanized
consumers is that as soon as it ended, interest in "high fidelity" exploded.
Although the original high-fidelity movement is often remembered today as
primarily the purview of *Playboy*-reading, pipe-smoking, Eames chair–
owning bachelors, it was firmly entrenched in the mainstream. On this

point, both *High Fidelity*, the magazine that chronicled the movement ("a major cultural phenomenon"), and *Life* ("a major American enthusiasm") could agree.

What high fidelity actually meant was unclear. By 1949, it referred generally to high-end audio equipment, usually made (at first) by smaller companies, and sold as individual components. Soon enough, high fidelity meant whatever you wanted it to mean. Predicting that the ranks of the 1 million Americans who had "gone hi-fi" so far were increasing at the rate of 3,000 per week, *The New Yorker* reported, "So assiduously has the term 'high fidelity' been plugged and so widespread has been its acceptance, that it has been appropriated by makers of shirts, lipsticks, perfumes, candy, and other singularly unrelated commodities."

By 1953, high fidelity was everywhere. Annual hi-fi sales topped $70 million, as dealers reported figures that they hadn't thought possible a year earlier. The New York Audio Fair drew 20,000 visitors, nearly seven times the attendance in 1949. *Life* published a glossary of hi-fi terms like "golden ear," and even spoke of Alaskan hi-fi lovers' challenge to find "the favored corner location for speakers in the rounded Quonset huts in which many residents live." The *High Fidelity* editor John Conly discussed psycho-acoustics in the pages of *House Beautiful*.

On the heels of *high fidelity*, the word *audiophile* entered the parlance, describing the men (the "hi-fi widow" was a much-lamented figure) whose obsessive commitment to high fidelity seemed to preclude any possibility of actually enjoying their hi-fis. "It has broken families and led men to ridiculous extremes in their search for perfect sound," Jennis Nunley wrote, accusing the movement of creating "a crop of mental aberrants." In "The Ultimate Fi," a short story published in *The Atlantic Monthly*, a hi-fi obsessive removes everything in the house that could be a potential sound absorbent—which is to say, everything in the house, save for a rug, "the final link with his old way of life, his wife having gone with the last-but-one conversation." Soon that goes, too, and he stands alone in the empty room, letting the sound wash over him, "happy at last."

It could be difficult to separate satire from reality. Two years after Nunley wrote, "I give to psychiatry this useful word: audiophilia," psychiatry accepted. Dr. Henry Angus Bowes, clinical director of psychiatry at Sainte Anne's Hospital in Quebec, diagnosed audiophilia as a neurosis, characterized by a "tendency to become preoccupied with and dependent upon the

bizarre recorded sound" and "the urgency of the need and the final insuffi-
ciency of all attempts to satisfy it." "One addict told me he would not be
satisfied until he could hear the drop of saliva from French horns," Bowes
said. He noted a sexual component to audiophilia, a desire for "sterile
reproduction without biological bother; in severe cases, the audiophile's
record collection becomes a symbolic harem." As for the typical woman's
hatred of high fidelity, "perhaps in the man's interest in hi-fi she senses a
rival as shrill and discordant as herself."

If the audiophiles had a conceptual hook on which they hung their obsession, it was the search for "presence," often described in terms of the liv-
ing- room-versus-concert-hall dialectic. John Urban defined presence as
simply "the aural illusion of being in the same room with the performers."
Herbert Brean in *Life* called it a "hard-to-define quality" that could "trans-
port the listener to the concert hall." A recorded sound with presence did
more than just capture the music perfectly. It captured the sound of music
made in a specific space. The audiophile had to feel the sound flowing over
him and bouncing off the walls, as though he were hearing it live. Presence
signaled a return to the Victor/electrical-era ideal—record the room, not
just the music—and a final refutation of the Edisonian belief that recording
should only document the sound of music as heard in a flat, non-
reverberating utopia.

Audiophiles fought passionately over the real parameters of presence.
Some questioned whether complete presence was even possible. "Ever and
always, a loudspeaker will be a loudspeaker," James Hinton Jr. wrote in *The
Nation*. "And Carnegie Hall is Carnegie Hall, not anybody's listening room."

That maxim was put to a public tone test on October 10, 1955, by
Gilbert A. Briggs, a British loudspeaker designer, hi-fi writer, and a model
of the thoughtful audiophile. (He liked to quote Milton and Pope in his
writings.) At an event hosted by Briggs at Carnegie Hall, the audience
heard tapes of music recorded earlier in that room, played back on ultra-hi-
fi equipment. They then compared the tapes to a live performance of the
same music performed in front of them by the same musicians.

This tone test was something of a letdown. The audience "clearly had
expected to hear Carnegie Hall rock with audio," Edward Tatnall Canby
wrote. Many were disappointed by how poor taped music sounded compared

with the live performance, but that may have been Briggs's intention all along. He insisted that the recorded music be played at the exact volume level as the live performance so that the former didn't benefit from sensory-overwhelming volume. If music recorded in Carnegie Hall couldn't compete with live music played in Carnegie Hall—if Carnegie Hall couldn't be sonically rebuilt in Carnegie Hall, in other words—then how could Carnegie Hall be rebuilt in your living room? "A heartening conclusion," Canby wrote, "and the members of Mr. Briggs' audience will think twice, I suspect, before they again demand 'concert hall reproduction' from their home phonographs."

A curious fact about audiophiles is how many of them seldom (if ever) listened to music. Instead, they tested their hi-fis with what were essentially sound-effects records: church bells, thunder, ocean waves, calliopes, foghorns, trains—*especially* trains. They searched for presence not in "concert hall reproduction" so much as real-world reproduction. Conly believed these records were popular because they allowed the large segment of the public who knew little about music to experience high fidelity. He was probably right, but a broader explanation begins with the problem of what makes a shirt or lipstick "high fidelity," and entertains the possibility that the term is no more or less ridiculous when applied to these items than when applied to recorded sound. As a concept, "high-fidelity" suggests quality with an added component of "truth." Hence a high-fidelity shirt is one that aspires to some Platonic ideal of "shirt-ness." A high-fidelity sound is one that sounds like your idea of what the world truly sounds like.

As a concept, high fidelity is aspirational, and it fits well with the post-war sense of possibility and a conquerable frontier. One of Conly's smartest observations about the high-fidelity movement was its connection with the "growing human flood outward from cities and apartments into countless new suburban dwellings . . . each with its TV set in the corner, each situated in the geographic center of a baby-sitter shortage. The living room was establishing (or perhaps re-establishing) itself as the center of American recreational life." Extending Conly's model, we can imagine a map with the concert hall as a central urban hub, and spokes radiating out toward millions of living rooms. Inside each living room is a hi-fi addict searching for that elusive presence—not just in the metaphysical sense of wanting to be transported to a concert hall (being *there*) but also in terms of the word's more literal meaning (being *here*). The living room was the arena where the audiophile assessed his place in a changing world by plotting his connection to the concert hall.

If the audiophiles had a guru, someone who truly understood them, it was Emory Cook, the head of a small independent record label called Cook Laboratories. Conly estimated that most of his magazine's readers would include at least five Cook releases in their top-twenty album lists. Cook knew what they went through. The letters section of *Audio Bucket*, a magazine he published that featured such missives as "High Fidelity Like Love: Words Mean Only What They Choose to Mean, No More, No Less," was called "The Agony Column."

Cook had the classic audiophile backstory. While he was working for Bell, he was assigned to the navy as a civilian engineer specializing in radar after the Pearl Harbor attack. After the war, Cook began building recording equipment in his garage. Thinking he might be able to sell systems to audiophiles, Cook made some demonstration recordings and booked space at the 1949 Audio Fair in New York. His exhibit was a huge hit. But it wasn't his equipment that blew people away, it was his recordings. His space was mobbed by "fevered audiomaniacs," *High Fidelity* reported, "blanching with ecstasy at the tremendous whooshes and roars of Cook's locomotives."

Since Cook had also devised what he believed was a more high-fidelity way to make records, using powdered vinyl in a process he called "microfusion," he decided to start a label. After an album of music-box recordings and one of bagpipes, he struck high-fidelity gold with his third release, *Rail Dynamics*, a sonic document of the New York Central train that ran between Peekskill and New York City. Recording mostly at night to avoid unwanted sounds like car horns, he skulked around the tracks or perched on trestles with his equipment, staying one step ahead of the station agents who thought he was some sort of terrorist or bandit. Sometimes he rode the train and hung mikes out of the window.

Rail Dynamics made Cook a high-fidelity star. He ran his label with thirty employees out of a small house in Stamford, Connecticut, in an unassuming development called Mayflower Gardens, where he'd moved after divorcing his second wife. He soon began taking his recording equipment wherever the spirit moved him. As far as music was concerned, he hated the acoustically flat sound of many recording studios, spaces bereft of presence—"It's like dying, being in a dead room"—and worked hard to include as much presence as possible, as when he recorded an organ concerto at a cathedral in Mexico while also capturing a conversation between two priests and an altar boy who were a hundred feet away. But it was his nonmusical sounds that really solidified Cook's reputation. He wanted to bring much more than the concert hall into the living room. For the *Summer Thunderstorm* record, he climbed Mount Washington in New Hampshire to capture the sound of a violent storm, coming within fifty feet of getting fried by lightning. At the 1954 Audio Fair, the sound of the *Queen Mary*'s horn from his *Voice of the Sea* album was so deafening that fair officials threatened to shut him down.

Sales figures regularly placed Cook Laboratories among the top twenty most-successful record labels, even as they released works like *Ionosphere*. Made with help from scientists at Dartmouth and the Naval Research Laboratory, *Ionosphere* featured twenty-six minutes of clicks and whooshes gathered from the solar-radiated upper atmosphere, punctuated by the ghostly sounds of radio transmissions sky-waving up to the ionosphere and bouncing back to Earth. Some Cook releases were either wry critical interrogations of high fidelity or piss-takes aimed at either his presence-seeking followers or (more likely) major labels, whom he accused of biting his style and diluting the high-fidelity concept.

Cook reached new levels of genius or mockery in 1956 with *The Compleat In Fidelytie*, which "might be the *last* hi fidelity record," the liner notes suggested. "In many cases the user will find it impossible to play—but no matter, that is not necessarily unusual for hi fidelity." One track is just a wobbly recording of two songs taken from Edison cylinders, perhaps a nod to the phonograph genius who, had he lived to hear high fidelity, would have found the whole presence fetish absurd. "Baby, Phone" proves that an infant's cry can be so annoying that a ringing telephone sounds like music to the ears. "Mexican Firecrackers, 1893 Pump, 10,000 Hens, Early American Violinist" sounds like . . . you get the idea.

After the initial period of mass audiophilia, stereophonic sound was high fidelity's second act, although the concept was nothing new. It had been more than twenty years since the first Stokowski/Bell stereo explorations, but by the early fifties stereo was still mostly a curiosity. Bell hadn't done much with its research, largely because there was no easy way to make a stereo disc. There was Stokowski's Fantasound system for *Fantasia*, but most theaters were not equipped to take full advantage of it.*

Now that magnetic tape was available, stereo was a much more realistic possibility. By the end of 1952, it had been a little more than five years since Ampex had built its first Model 200 magnetic tape recorder, based on the Magnetophon Jack Mullin had imported from Germany. The company was still manufacturing only a single-track recorder, but Ampex wanted to make the move to stereo machines. For this to be a realistic commercial prospect, the recording industry would have to be convinced that stereo was the future so that the labels would begin recording their acts in stereo.

Ross Snyder of Ampex had recently sent to Bill Cara, a sales manager at a Los Angeles home audio store and a recording buff, an Ampex Model 400 recorder, modified for three channels. Cara, who chaired the planning for the upcoming Audio Fair in L.A., pitched to Ampex the idea of having a special exhibit to show off the possibility of stereo sound. Ampex loved the idea, so Cara took his Model 400 to a train station in the San Fernando Valley. He connected three microphones, spaced fifty feet apart, along the track, and waited for the next train.

"Far in the distance, when he heard the train approaching, he turned everything on," Snyder recalls. "He got the train going through, stopping, blowing out a lot of steam, even a nearby car starting up. I swear it was a Ford V8, because I knew what a V8 sounded like."

Cara took the finished tape, which ran nearly thirty minutes, back to his home. While he and Snyder watched and made suggestions, Mullin cut and spliced the tape, and added two other recordings Cara had made, of a Wurlitzer organ and of the Santa Monica Symphony.

The finished tape was played every half hour at the Audio Fair in January 1953, through three speakers placed a good distance away from one another for maximum effect. And the effect was maximum. The stories of early motion-picture audiences jumping out of the way of on-screen trains

---

*The word *stereo* has become largely synonymous with *binaural*, but *stereophonic* actually describes any recording or broadcast with two or more independent tracks and channels. Binaural sound—two independent tracks/channels—is the most common form of stereo.

may be largely apocryphal, but people really did jump at the Audio Fair. ("It was really funny to watch them," Snyder says.) The way the three microphones had been spaced far apart, so that as the train moved the signal faded in one channel and grew stronger in the next, created the very real sensation of a train bearing down on the listener.

Despite the effectiveness of these demonstrations, the stereo revolution happened gradually, largely because of the lack of stereo discs. Beginning around 1954, a few stereo releases began to trickle onto the market, but the only way to hear them was on a reel-to-reel tape player like Ampex's "stereophonic tape phonograph," which cost a whopping $700. Tapes cost at least three times as much as LPs. It was because of the large investment required to become a consumer of taped music that Ampex had decided to go with two channels instead of three. "We felt that stereo would fall flat on its face," Snyder says. "So two was the smallest number that could deliver any kind of stereo effect."

Of course, audiophiles were agog. "Stereo tape and the lunatic fringe should get on well together," wrote Roland Gelatt, announcing that "a new phase of the high fidelity boom is in the making." It was a dark time for hi-fi widows. "Wives are like that, I'm afraid," Gelatt wrote of his spouse's less-than-thrilled response to his tape of *Also Sprach Zarathustra* played at maximum volume. "But, to judge from present indications, a good many wives will have to make their peace with stereophonic tapes in the coming year."

Meanwhile, throughout 1957 the record industry scrambled to come up with a way to make stereo discs. Mindful of the chaos caused by the Battle of the Speeds, they proceeded with care, to ensure that whichever method they chose would be adopted uniformly throughout the industry. They wound up choosing a system designed by Westrex, a Western Electric subsidiary.

One of the first people to really put the Westrex cutter to the test was Enoch Light, a former bandleader whose Light Brigade was popular during the big-band era of the thirties, and who now helped run a label called Grand Award Records. Around 1959, he noticed that most people's understanding of what stereo could do was limited to sound-effects records, largely because it was much easier to get an impressive stereo effect with a nonmusical sound. Renditions of table tennis games, with the balls ping-ponging from left to right, were a perennial favorite.

Stereo music recordings were more subtle, owing largely to the fact that musicians don't typically run all over the stage. Recording in stereo meant recording direct to two-track tape (or to three-track tape, and then mixing the three tracks down to two). The kind of stereo effect you got was the same kind Bell and Stokowski had discovered: a geometric sense of where the musicians were in relation to one another onstage. Light realized the public really needed stereo music thrown in their faces (literally) to appreciate its full possibilities. "Stereo wasn't getting across to the average person," Light said. "I figured that separation had to be emphasized to attract their attention—not ping-pong as such, but separation used as part of a musical continuity."

Light's partners weren't interested in his idea, so he formed his own label, Command Records, and put together the Command All-Stars band, built around the percussionist Terry Snyder. Making a record was a slow, tedious process. They needed to be able to record their performance in such a way that the left channel would only pick up, say, one of Snyder's bongos, while the right picked up the other. In the end, the project required about thirty, three- to four-hour recording sessions during the summer of 1959. Then came the fastidious process of mastering the tape to disc, a task that required fifteen or twenty Westrex cutters. All told, what Light had assumed would be an $8,000 to $10,000 investment had ballooned to almost $80,000.

Most of the songs on the album, which Light called *Persuasive Percussion*, were well-known standards like "I'm in the Mood for Love," "My Heart Belongs to Daddy," and "Love Is a Many-Splendored Thing." But the album was recorded and mastered with such care and the stereo effect was so dramatic, that it was unlike anything most people had ever heard. It was presence blown way, way up.

Even the album's packaging made it seem like a special document for those with discerning taste. The cover featured an abstract pattern of black dots designed by the painter Josef Albers. The extensive liner notes (so extensive that the album packaging was perhaps the first use of a gatefold sleeve) featured a track-by-track description of what aspect of your stereo each song was designed to test. *Persuasive Percussion* was like a concept album, with the "concept" being your hi-fi. Listening to it was like taking a space-age tone test, with the liner notes as your guide. Can you hear every bell during Snyder's downward sweep of the Chinese bell tree on "Misirlou," or is it just an undefined "metallic swish"? Does the xylophone lose "identi-fiable timbre" when it appears with the baritone saxophone on "I Surrender, Dear"? Can you hear air around the flute on "Aloha Oe," or is there a buzzing sound? If the answer to any of these questions is the latter, there is something wrong with your cartridge's tracking.

Persuasive Percussion was an enormous hit, a *Sgt. Pepper's* (before there was one) for the hi-fi crowd.* What the Ampex demo had done to jump-start the stereo revolution from the production end, *Persuasive Percussion* did from the consumer end. At the end of September, Light brought 150 copies of the album to a hi-fi show in New York. "The next day, 99 percent of all exhibitors showing off hi-fi stereo equipment used that record from then on," Light said. *Billboard* claimed it was the only album from 1960 that merited any attention. Over the next three years, Light would put seven more similar albums into the Top 10.

Other record companies began releasing records in the same vein, stereo demonstration discs that featured blatant stereo ping-ponging, copy-ing Light right down to the exhaustively technical liner notes. Many of these albums had the word "percussion" in them, whether they were partic-ularly percussive or not. "There are ninety million idiots in this country who will buy anything with the word 'percussion' in it," one producer said, explaining why he shoehorned percussion into the title of a record that was decidely unpercussive.

To understand how enamored the public was with stereo, consider the cele-brated response accorded to the man who created stereo ex post facto.

In 1956, Jack Somer graduated from City College in New York with an engineering degree and took a job with RCA Victor at its main record-pressing plant in Indianapolis. For more than a year, he worked on improv-ing the factory's robotic record presses, until he got a more interesting assignment. Arturo Toscanini, the conductor of the NBC Orchestra, had recently died, leaving behind a catalog that was completely monophonic. He had made a few stereo recordings in his later years, but RCA Victor didn't think they were good enough to release. Such was the demand for

*The design of the *Sgt. Pepper's* album was notable for its early use of the gatefold sleeve, but Light actually got there first.

stereo records that Toscanini's album sales were now slipping. The label called Somer's boss and asked him if there was a way of reprocessing mono records into stereo. Somer's boss wasn't sure, but he knew that Somer was the only person in the lab with a musical background, so he asked his young engineer to look into it.

Somer was thrilled by the sound of stereo and had been impressed with Enoch Light's stereo productions. "I can remember very clearly what it was like to hear my first stereo recording," he says. "It was absolutely shocking." But what RCA wanted him to do to the Toscanini records was in some sense more difficult. These were mono recordings, made by using a single microphone to capture each performance, so there were no discrete sounds that could be separated to create a stereo effect.

Somer began by spending several weeks tinkering with Toscanini's recording of Beethoven's Ninth Symphony. ("You are talking to a person who can almost legitimately claim to have listened to Beethoven's Ninth Symphony more than anyone else on Earth," he says today.) Somer knew of a Swiss conductor who had experimented with using comb filters to split a mono signal into narrow frequency bands, and then fed some bands into one channel and the rest into the other, to create a stereo effect. The problem, Somer discovered when he tried the process, was the static nature of the system. "You got a very boring sound, and sounds wandered across," he says. "As an instrument would shift from low to middle registers, it would go from left to right. So I thought, no, this is going to have to be a dynamic system where you follow a score—which I was able to do because I could read music—and you remix the frequencies to maintain a wall of music between the speakers, while having better control of where things were."

Somer finally perfected a complex system that let him manipulate filters, delays, and other effects as the music played, in a way that created a credible stereo illusion. RCA was impressed enough with some preliminary results to send Somer to the company's studios in New York. Because RCA couldn't devote a dubbing room to his project, Somer worked from midnight to 8:00 a.m., and somehow matriculated full-time at the Manhattan School of Music during the day. "I lived on M&M's and ginger ale for a year," he recalls.

RCA decided that Somer should prepare three Toscanini recordings for release: Respighi's *Fountains of Rome* and *Pines of Rome*, Ravel's orchestration of Mussorgsky's *Pictures at an Exhibition*, and Dvořák's Symphony

No. 9, "From the New World," the piece that Stokowski had used for the first electrical recording of a complete symphonic work. Somer's dynamic system allowed him to continuously adjust the parameters of the filter, to keep the music sounding balanced and pleasantly stereophonic. Every night he and the engineer would record one of the pieces onto two-track tape, with Somer reading the score and "conducting" the engineer. They would listen to the recording, Somer would make notes in his score, and they'd apply the changes the next time. After a year of work, the records were ready for release. RCA called them "enhanced stereo" discs.

When they came out in 1961, there was some of the expected carping. Alan Rich in *The New York Times* blasted the "tomfoolery" of the records and longed for the days when records just captured a performance. William Bachman of archrival Columbia, a grizzled veteran of the Battle of the Speeds who helped invent the LP, sniffed, somewhat predictably, "You have a single signal to start with. We don't think there is any honest way to make two out of it. It's like separating mush and milk; once you get them together, you can't get them apart." To Somer's annoyance, even some admirers of the records were referring to them as "pseudo-stereo."

Most reviews were positive, and the records sold well. Somer, at the age of twenty-six, found himself the center of attention, hailed for working wonders by turning monaural water into stereophonic wine. *Life* called him the "young man with a good ear." For Somer, being feted for reanimating the master at such a young age was overwhelming and left him thinking, what next? "The three albums were released, and I don't know, I think the sales were pretty good, but by that time, after all this incredibly mind-blowing publicity, I went into a state of depression," he says. "I couldn't take it. I'm not joking. I had to start seeing an analyst. I just couldn't handle the—I guess you would call it fame. *Life, Time, Newsweek*, all these people writing my name, my parents were going crazy calling all their friends and stuff."

Somer stayed with RCA and eventually became a staff producer. "After the release of the albums, I was going on with my life," he says. "I was called into the boss's office, and he said, 'You've got to do this magic on a bunch of pop recordings.' And I said I couldn't spend months doing a single pop album. Because I was an elitist. So I said, 'Look, I can do a static system that will kind of create a two-track stereo impression, but it won't be the kind of thing where every single instrument is treated with kid gloves. Impossible.' "

Throughout the fifties, as audiophiles pursued their demented quest, as stereophonic trains mowed people down, and as phantom ping-pong balls bounded across the room, the art and science of recording was steadily migrating to a state of perfection. Most of the major recording studios were owned by the record companies, which themselves were part of larger corporate entities, such as RCA Victor and CBS/Columbia, so they had the resources to achieve the highest quality recordings. Studios were staffed with formally trained engineers who considered themselves technicians, not "artists." Their job was to record a performance as accurately as possible.

Columbia's studios were particularly revered, and still are by engineers today. "Percy Faith, early Marty Robbins, early Andy Williams—if you can get your hands on those records, you'll hear a big difference between what records sounded like then and today," says the recording engineer Tony Bongiovi. "Because technology was actually better, sonically, in the fifties."

The jewel among Columbia's facilities was its 30th Street Studio, which had previously been an Armenian church, in Manhattan's Murray Hill neighborhood. The singularity of the main room—the hundred-foot ceilings, the plaster walls, even the fact that the wood floor was unvarnished—all contributed to its signature sound. Since Mitch Miller, Columbia's head talent scout, was a musician himself, he instantly recognized the unique character of the space and what a perfect canvas it was for recording music. "That was the greatest thing about 30th Street—the acoustics were just beautiful," says Frank Laico, an engineer who spent many years at 30th Street. "When we took it over, Mitch Miller said, 'I want that studio untouched by human hands.'"

Like many engineers of his generation, Laico received some of his training during his time in the service, working on electronics projects for the military at the U.S. Recording Company in Washington, D.C. He felt it was his job as the engineer to keep himself out of the recording and to make the records as "transparent" as possible. Not that there wasn't artistry involved. Even before 30th Street began recording in stereo, Laico and the other engineers crafted records that even today provide a vivid sense of musicians in a room. Records were often cut live, with the musicians in the back and the singer front and center. If the singers wanted to do overdubs, Laico would usually just put a monitor next to them as they sang over the already recorded music. These sorts of practices often caused "leakage," what happens when a microphone designed to pick up one thing, such as a singer's voice, also picks up something else, like the backing track coming out of the monitor. This can be a headache for engineers, since it gives them less control of the signal, but Laico thought it added a note of realism. "I enjoyed the leakage," he says. "It was the leakage that made it more natural."

The Columbia sound was studied by the next generation of engineers—people like Joe Tarsia, who would go on to apply some of the 30th Street techniques when he recorded many of the Philly soul acts of the late sixties and seventies. "I love reverb, and I love a big sound, but I never had a big room to work with, so I was always trying to simulate what they did at Columbia," Tarsia says.

One of rock and roll's most famous origin stories involves the invention of amplifier distortion. The story goes that Jackie Brenston and his band were driving from Clarksdale, Mississippi, to Memphis to record at Sam Phillips's Sun Studio in 1951, when guitarist Ike Turner's amp fell out of the car. When they got to the studio, they discovered the amp was broken, but Phillips liked the grungy sound it made and told Turner to play it as it was. The result was "Rocket 88," considered by many to be the first rock-and-roll song.

Did this actually happen? Phillips maintained it did, and he always seemed to have a pretty good handle on the mythology surrounding Sun. But the relative veracity of the Ike Turner story is beside the point, which is that, at the exact moment that high fidelity was ramping up, a new music was developing around an aesthetic that valued low fidelity. While the world was thrilling to the possibility of a recording that was so "correct" it was indistinguishable from that which it recorded, a new generation, out of either choice or necessity—and usually both—was learning how to record things "wrong."

Just compare what went on at 30th Street Studio with what transpired at Sun. "The nice thing about it is when we had it, we had it," says "Cowboy" Jack Clement, an engineer who came to work at Sun in 1956. "We didn't have to go back and remix it and all that kind of stuff." So far, so hi-fi;

Mitch Miller's boast about 30th Street—"what we were hearing at that moment in the control room is what you hear when you put on the recording today"—is almost identical. Laico loved the sound of leakage, as did Clement. "Sound would leak back into the vocal mike," he recalls, "and for some reason that sounded good." Like Columbia, Sun often cut records completely live.

Even the way Phillips achieved the famous Sun "slap-back" effect (something that others had done, but which Phillips really made distinctive) was not totally dissimilar to the way Columbia sculpted the vocal signal in 30th Street's special echo chamber. Sun used an old RCA radio console. It was mono, but it could take up to six microphone inputs. To get slap-back echo, the signal from the vocal mike was split into two identical parts. One part went straight to the tape. The other took a more circuitous route, traveling to a second tape machine, which then routed the signal to the first machine's tape. There was no tape in the second machine; it was there solely to delay the signal. This added step would make the second signal hit the tape a moment after the first, creating the echo.

Similar goals and somewhat similar methods, and yet a 30th Street record sounds completely different from a Sun record. Part of the reason is simple economics. Columbia had CBS money and a church; Sun had neither. "One reason a place like Columbia sounded more realistic is that they had an echo chamber," Clement says. "Sam knew how to build one, but he didn't own the property, so we never got around to it." In other words, a Columbia record reflects a real space, while a Sun record constructs an imaginary space. And in a way, that space could be vaster. Just listen to "Blue Moon of Kentucky," the B side of Elvis Presley's first Sun single, "That's Alright, Mama." The echo is so extreme that it almost does the opposite of what echo is supposed to accomplish. Instead of blowing up his voice, it cuts into it. But the overall effect is similar to hearing someone singing outside in a heavy wind, with the sound waves being blown all over the place.

The important thing to remember is none of this echo was "happening" in the performance. The musicians weren't hearing it, and, in a sense, they weren't causing it. They were just generating the signal to be processed. Slap-back was the very antithesis of high fidelity—not just because it distorted the signal, but also because it had nothing to do with capturing a performance.

Phillips's use of echo, particularly on the Elvis songs, is what really drew Clement, a musician with limited engineering experience, to Sun. "It was the first thing I wanted Sam to show me when I went to work there," he says. Clement soon pushed the echo even further. On his suggestion, Phillips purchased a small sub-mixer, basically a mike-splitter that made it easier to selectively apply echo to multiple elements in the music, such as turning echo on the snare into a shadow rhythm, something Clement liked to do on Jerry Lee Lewis records. "To me, that board was a musical instrument," he says. "I wasn't trying to deal with reality. I was trying to improve on it."

Sun records are so romanticized for their supposedly authentic simplicity that it's startling to hear Clement talk like a hip-hop DJ, but there you have it. It's telling that while Miller and Laico almost subordinated themselves to the heavenly sonic perfection of that old church, right down to the unvarnished floors, it wasn't until thirty years after Clement left Sun in 1959, when he returned to produce U2's *Rattle and Hum* album, that he even realized Sun *had* a natural sound. "When I first got there, everyone told me what a great sound it had, and I thought they were kind of full of shit," he says of his tenure there. "I kind of figured it out when I was over there with Bono, years later. It had a presence to it."

Whatever it was that Sun Studio had, RCA, for whom Elvis Presley recorded after leaving Sun in 1955, couldn't get it or replicate it, despite all its New York engineers' advanced training. It was the first great example of a band losing some of its sound when it makes the move from an indie to a major label. Not that those RCA records don't sound incredible, even today (*especially* today). Just check out the snare drum sound on "Hound Dog."

The sort of records Elvis made in his first years at RCA—which mostly sounded "correct" in the 30th Street sense—were nowhere near the norm for pop music as the sixties progressed. In broad terms, the World War II generation were audiophiles who longed for hi-fi; their boomer offspring were not and did not. In the new pop world, what mattered was sound that hit you like a train, as opposed to sound that mimicked a train about to hit you.

This template was really set by the first producer-as-auteur, Phil Spector.

Before he constructed his infamous "wall of sound," no other producer had so consciously used the studio to bring to life a specific sound that had no counterpart in reality. Not only did Spector not care about high fidelity, he actively courted high infidelity. One of the guiding principles of his wall of sound was that no individual instrument should be discernible, except for the drums. Sounds were intentionally lost amid oceans of echo and reverb. Spector also preferred to mix to mono rather than stereo, to preserve that feeling of an impenetrable block of audio.

The sense of creating something that had no connection to real-world sound could overwhelm even those involved with making the records. "See, it was not truthful at all," Larry Levine, Spector's engineer at Gold Star Recording Studios, once said about the sound coming into the control room during a Spector session. "What everybody strives for in studio speakers is truth; this didn't in any way duplicate what you heard in the studio; it was just exciting and thrilling and full-bodied. The musicians would come into the control room for the playback and just be blown away. They simply could not believe that what they were hearing was what they'd been playing, and it made them excited."

Joe Meek was Spector's counterpart in Great Britain, legendary there, but known in America mostly for producing "Telstar," an instrumental by the Tornados that topped the American charts in 1962. Like Spector, Meek was the first of a kind—the first British freelance producer/engineer—and his work, though not as commercially successful as Spector's, was arguably even more indicative of changes in the culture. Ten years older than Spector, Meek had a background familiar to the hi-fi generation. When his parents gave him his first real gramophone at age ten, he was delighted to discover that if he shouted into the machine when the needle was on the run-out groove, he could record his voice. "I thought I'd discovered something marvelous," he said in a taped autobiography. "Of course I was really doing what Edison discovered years before." During his two years in the Royal Air Force, he worked as a radar technician and became fascinated with wire recorders and disc cutters.

His journey toward recording mirrored Emory Cook's, but what Meek did after his time in the service placed him squarely in the postwar generation. He eventually built his own studio—unheard of at the time—and began to produce a string of hits. He was fascinated by outer space and recorded a concept album called *I Hear a New World*. Like Spector, the world he heard had no basis in reality. He became famous for using the studio to build that sound from the ground up. In particular, he was a pioneer in the use of dynamic-range compression, traditionally utilized in recording to dampen unwanted peaks in the sound. Meek realized that by applying egregious amounts of compression, he could create effects that seemed like they were jumping out of the speakers.

What Spector and Meek had in common was that their records so aggressively rejected traditional ideas of high fidelity—judged by those standards, their recordings sound terrible—in pursuit of maximum salability. They understood that in the new consumer culture, the postwar generation would not merely tolerate "corrupted" sounds, but also embrace them. Not for nothing did Tom Wolfe dub Spector the "tycoon of teen." Meek bragged that his music was "completely pop minded."

One of the keystones of this new consumer youth culture was the emergence of the portable transistor radio. And Meek and Spector's blatant quest for hits led both of them to make music that sounded like it belonged there. Their music, and indeed most of the pop music of the era, was purposefully produced to sound optimal on an AM station as heard through a tiny speaker. That's why so much of the music sounds excessively tinny to us today. As opposed to the audiophiles' desire for *everything*, the new pop world was interested only in sounds that sold—and the way they sold was by sounding good on the radio. As Tarsia points out, "What was the sense of filling the record with sounds that could not be heard on the air?" Or, in Spector's case, why worry about the sound of individual instruments that will barely make it out of the speakers, when you could pool your resources and build them into a sound that leaps out of them?

The Meek-produced "Telstar"—"the one record that epitomizes the first excitement of the postwar, mass consumer society," in the words of the pop critic Jon Savage—is such a pure, joyous distillation of this new world that it doesn't need words. The first sound is an orgasmic explosion that presumably represents a satellite liftoff, but which may as well be the sound of cash registers mating. Its trippy melody bears an eerie resemblance to Percy Faith's "Theme from *A Summer Place*," a quintessential example of a 30th Street record. Years of rock-critic analogy abuse notwithstanding, nothing has ever sounded like anything else "on acid." But suffice to say: "Telstar" sounds like acid on Percy Faith.

Meek and Spector embraced this new world as individual auteurs, but if there was one label that collectively institutionalized a radio-ready aesthetic, it was Motown. Tony Bongiovi remembers it well. "Understand, it's 1965, and Motown could do no wrong," he says. "They had this acoustic sound that engineers in New York were trying to replicate." You can hear the sound in the Supremes' "Where Did Our Love Go?" For the entire song, quarter-note handclaps keep the rhythm. They begin the song in the right channel, quickly migrate to the left, and remain there until the last few seconds, when they merrily skip across the stereo field and back, as though daring the listener to figure out the secret of their sound.

Bongiovi, a seventeen-year-old in New Jersey who hoped to become a recording engineer, thought he could. Using his high school physics and calculus, knowledge he'd picked up by convincing New York engineers to let him sit in on recording sessions, and *Sam's Audio Encyclopedia*, Bongiovi calculated that it had something to do with a reverb that had a very quick decay. Those handclaps were short and sharp, each one announcing itself and then leaving just a little trail.

Setting up some equipment in his parents' concrete-walled garage, Bongiovi set out to reproduce that decay based on his calculations. When he felt he had it, he called Motown in Detroit and managed to reach one of their staff engineers. Bongiovi explained that he was a high school student who was interested in recording. He told him about the echo he had created in his garage. "Is that how you get that sound?"

Stunned, the engineer asked the kid if he could make it into the city that night. Gladys Knight was playing at the Copacabana, and someone from Motown would be there to record the show. Bongiovi made it to the Copa, and "next thing I knew, the guy was talking to my parents about flying me out to work on some sessions," he says. "On the day I was supposed to take my SATs, I skipped out and I was on a plane to Detroit."

For the next few years, Motown periodically flew Bongiovi to Detroit to assist on sessions. It was an incredible education. "They were light-years ahead of everyone else," he says. Over time, through careful calculation and fortuitous mistakes, they had created Motown's unique radio-friendly sound. Aspects of the sound are easy to identify, such as the foregrounded vocals and the drums placed farther back in the mix, and the odd reverb that Bongiovi had identified. But there's something ineffable about it, a combination of the unique studio and the practices of the engineers. The

echo chamber that produced a sound that nobody in New York could replicate was the result of a mistake in construction that the producers decided
sounded better than what the plans had called for. They were plugging
some instruments directly into the console. They had two eight-track tape
machines, when most studios were using four-tracks.

With his Motown experience, Bongiovi had no problem breaking into
the engineering world. "All these studios were chasing after me," he says.
"So I went from high school to, like, $250 a week. Which was—Jesus, gas
was twenty-three cents a gallon. I was rich."

The story of recorded music in the postwar, predigital era is largely the
story of multitrack tape recording. Contrary to popular belief and many
years of mythmaking, this story does not begin with Les Paul. While the
idea that Paul "invented" the multitrack recorder is practically part of
America's folk heritage, like Ben Franklin flying a kite, the story really
begins back at Ampex, where Ross Snyder was thinking about the kind of
music Paul was making with his sound-on-sound technique.

As Snyder heard it, Paul's ambition far outstripped the technology. As
great as Paul's records sounded, they didn't sound good enough. Paul lost a
generation with every added track, plus there was the fact that one mistake
ruined the whole tape. There had to be an easier way, some method of using
the same tape recorder to record different tracks at different times on the
same piece of tape, so that they played in perfect sync, but without having
to keep dumping tracks. Snyder contacted Paul and asked if he'd be interested in such a system. Paul definitely was.

Snyder decided that what was needed was a recorder with a stack of
heads that could be used for both playback and recording, depending on
what you needed at the moment. That way you could record a track, switch
it to a playback channel, and use its head to play it back so that you could
add another one on top of it. But while the concept was simple, actually
building such a machine presented many problems. You'd need heads that
affected only their allotted part of the tape, with no "cross talk." You'd need
to be able to sync them up by microseconds, so that the sounds on the various tracks would mesh properly. You'd need to switch among the heads in
a way that minimized clicks and other noises. Finally, all those massed
heads increased the possibility of an audible hum on the tape.

Snyder decided that eight tracks was the most that could fit on one-inch tape with an acceptable signal-to-noise ratio. In 1956, Paul paid $10,000 for the first Ampex Model 300 to be modified with the eight-track overdubbing system that Ampex was calling Sel-Sync. The machine, which eventually became known as the Octopus, stood seven feet tall and weighed 250 pounds. It was shipped from Redwood City to Paul's New Jersey estate. Snyder and a few others came out to help Paul set it up. It was the first time the inventor of sound on sound met the man who invented the perfect sound-on-sound machine.

Ampex never sold many Sel-Syncs, partly because they were impractical for commercial recording studios. And Paul, after years of laborious sound-on-sounding, never had another hit once he acquired his Octopus. His star was waning with the ascendancy of rock and roll and other new forms of pop that embraced multitracking to such a degree that it soon became impossible to imagine the craft of record-making without it.

As with so many aspects of their history, the Beatles' evolving use of multitrack technology serves as a primer for how multitracking changed music. When the group first began their recording career, it was still a world where musicians were musicians and technicians were technicians, and the twain didn't meet. Paul McCartney recalled that during the band's early sessions at Abbey Road, the studio that would become their home, the control room seemed "like heaven, where the great gods lived, and we were down below."

Owing to the conservatism of EMI, which owned Abbey Road, the studio's technology often lagged behind other studios'. Abbey Road was still a one-track mono facility in the early sixties, so recording pretty much meant capturing a performance. Early in the Beatles' recording career, the studio upgraded to two-track capability—which allowed the band to record music on one track and vocals on the other—but Abbey Road didn't move to four tracks until 1963.

Like most rock-and-roll bands, the Beatles were not releasing stereo recordings, so four tracks were more a convenience than a creative tool. (The stereo revolution that had captivated audiophiles meant little in the rock-and-roll world.) For "I Want to Hold Your Hand," their first four-track recording, they used the machine to record four separate performances, and chose their favorite for release. "A Hard Day's Night," recorded in April 1964, put the four-track to better use. They recorded bass and drums on track one and John Lennon's vocal on track two. Lennon's second vocal and McCartney's backing vocals went on track three. On track four, they added piano and the jangly guitar at the end of the song. They mixed the four tracks down to one track of another four-track machine to create the mono release. For the stereo release, they mixed the four tracks down to two tracks.

By the time of the *Revolver* sessions in 1966, the band was regularly attending mixing sessions in the control room—an unattainable "heaven" a few years earlier. Now they began to get more creative with the four-track. They began to "bounce." To conceive what bouncing entails, just remember the simple process used to create "A Hard Day's Night." The four tracks from one machine were mixed down to one track (or two for the stereo version) on a second machine. The finished song now resided on the second machine. Think of the bounce from the first machine to the second as analogous to pouring four different types of colored sand through a funnel into a jar. The result would be a jar in which all four colors would be visible, but no longer separable.

Now consider how "Penny Lane" came together. The group recorded a piano part on track one of the four-track recorder, another piano part on track two, a third piano part with a tambourine accompaniment on track three, and a harmonium accompanied by percussion on track four. All four tracks were filled, so they bounced them all to track one of the second four-track machine. Work could now continue using the second machine's three open tracks. They filled these with, respectively, yet another piano part; McCartney singing solo; and McCartney harmonizing with John Lennon. The tracks were once again full. Now they bounced back to the first machine, splitting everything they wanted to keep onto two tracks. On the two open tracks, they added another piano part and scat vocals as a placeholder for the eventual brass and woodwinds part.

With all tracks filled once again, they bounced back to the second machine, splitting onto two tracks everything they wanted to keep. On the two remaining tracks, they overdubbed brass and woodwinds over the scat vocals. Finally, they mixed all four tracks down to one, creating a final ready-to-release mono version of the song.

In a way, all this bouncing wasn't so different from Les Paul's sound on sound. Recording like this took an enormous amount of foresight, because although you can keep bouncing indefinitely, every bounce means the loss of a generation, which degrades the sound. And with just four tracks, you had to know what you were doing. If Lennon or McCartney hit a bum note when harmonizing on a take, the whole take had to be redone because both voices were going onto the same track and were thus inseparable.

By the late sixties, eight-track machines began migrating into studios. The first Beatles song to get the eight-track treatment was George Harrison's "While My Guitar Gently Weeps" in 1968. With the expanded number of tracks, the Beatles once again embraced the future, albeit in an unlikely way. More tracks means more room to experiment, to second-guess, without as much bouncing. Eight tracks, in short, meant that you could overthink, overcorrect, overproduce music, which is exactly what some Beatles fans think happened here.

The first recorded version of the song was just Harrison's voice and acoustic guitar, with an overdubbed organ near the end. The band made a four-track version with bass, drums, guitar, and organ, and these were mixed down to two tracks, then transferred two months later onto an eight-track tape, thus leaving six tracks. Harrison spent an entire evening session by himself trying to record a backward guitar solo on track five, which was eventually discarded. Two days later, still with six open tracks, Harrison recorded two separate lead vocals with maracas; one track was used for drums and one for lead guitar, leaving two unused tracks.

Harrison now decided he didn't like any of it, so the band started over. They taped twenty-eight more takes and decided that the twenty-fifth was the best. Four tracks were filled with drums, acoustic guitar and guide vocal, lead guitar, and keyboards. The next day, guest Eric Clapton recorded a lead guitar on one open track. The three remaining open tracks were filled with fuzz-toned bass, a few organ notes, and the lead vocal with backup harmony.

The recording was complete, but Brian Gibson, an Abbey Road engineer, thought it never got better than Harrison's original solo take. The eight-track "gave them the immediate temptation to put more and more stuff on," he said. "I personally think it was best left uncluttered." Gibson also recalled that the Beatles became so addicted to the choices offered by eight-track that they once overdubbed so many instruments that the drums—presumably one of the first things to be laid down—became all but inaudible, forcing them to record Ringo playing a chair cushion on the downbeat to try to add a little oomph to the buried snare.

By the time the Beatles broke up in 1970, sixteen tracks was becoming the norm and some studios were already making the move to twenty-four. Transistor technology, which had transformed radio in the fifties, now infiltrated the recording studio. Consoles and recorders powered by vacuum tubes were replaced with solid-state models, which used transistors instead of tubes. With the increase in tracks, the change was inevitable. Tubes were too expensive, too noisy, too hot, and too difficult to wire for such large machines. For better or worse, recorded music, to become more flexible, severed the last link with the high-fidelity era. "Once it went to solid-state, it was over," says Bongiovi. "There was a big sound change with the solid-state console and the solid-state tape machine. But we had to do that. Solid-state forced tube technology to retire."

"It's all about harmonics," explains Ron St. Germain, an engineer who began recording in the early 1970s. "Sound is complex, and solid-state resistors don't vibrate. A tube allows the sound in—it bounces around there. There's more body and harmonic resonance, more of the true harmonic fundamental of the instrument. So it basically has more tone."

Solid-state is really where recorded music meets the devil at the crossroads, getting the gift of convenience and flexibility in exchange for . . . it's not exactly clear, but in their darker moments some engineers would say "soul." "To be honest, I think the records made in the fifties and sixties were better-sounding than the ones in the seventies and eighties," St. Germain says. "But there's no way we could accomplish sonically what we did in the seventies and eighties without solid-state electronics." Geoff Emerick, the Beatles' engineer, still thinks *Abbey Road*, the last album they made, suffered for being made on a solid-state machine. "*Abbey Road* was the first album that we recorded through an EMI transistorized deck, and I couldn't get the same sounds at all," Emerick said in 2002. "There was a presence and depth that the transistor just wouldn't give me that the tubes did."

There were other problems associated with the track inflation. One problem was overcrowding. With the move from eight to sixteen tracks, the width of the tape doubled, from one inch to two inches. But tape any wider than two inches was too unwieldy for the machines. So when the tracks increased by one-third, to twenty-four, the tape stayed the same size, so the available bandwidth *decreased* by one-third. "They added eight more lanes to the interstate without widening the roadway," St. Germain says. "Basically, the end product was significantly reduced compared to the sixteen-track format that preceded the twenty-four-track's so-called advancement." The overcrowding caused problems of cross talk, meaning that sound from one track could bleed over to another as far as three tracks away. That could be controlled by good engineers, but a more vexing drawback of the decreased bandwidth—one that actually affected the sound of the finished product—was that the tape wasn't picking up as many "transients," the very high and very low frequencies that fleshed out the sound.

Some engineers resisted the development. At Media Sound Studio in New York, where Bongiovi, St. Germain, and several others who would become elite engineers in the coming decades were working, the staff conducted an A/B test between their sixteen-track console and a new twenty-four-track. It wasn't even close. They called the company that had loaned them the new machine on spec and told them to pick it up. When nobody came, the engineers were so annoyed that they wheeled it out onto 57th Street and called the company again. But musicians didn't share their disgust. In the new world of recording, many were willing to forgo some fidelity if it meant having more tools to construct recordings. "Eventually we had to go to twenty-four tracks to remain competitive," St. Germain says.

As twenty-four-track consoles became the norm throughout the seventies and eighties, some engineers tried to compensate for their decreased fidelity by limiting the number of times they bounced tracks. Their thinking was that they could offset some of the decrease in audio quality caused by the decreased bandwidth, since every bounce degraded the sound a little through the loss of a generation. Hugh Padgham, who produced the Police's *Ghost in the Machine* and *Synchronicity* albums, tried to impose a zero-tolerance plan. "I refused to—or absolutely tried not to—do any bouncing, particularly on the drums, because you would lose that transient response," he says. "So we were left with fewer tracks to start with, because I recorded the bass drum on its own track, the snare on its own track. I used up six to eight tracks for the drums alone. Since I refused to bounce them down, that left fewer tracks for everything else." The perverse upshot of these practices was that for the twenty-four-track dissenters, the new technology actually made the act of recording *less* flexible than it was during the sixteen-track days.

Even if you had twenty-four tracks at your disposal, it was amazing how quickly they filled up. The most common way to do multitrack recording is to record the vocals last. With sixteen tracks, there might be just one track open when it was time for the vocals. If there was a flubbed line or a missed note, you could redo it entirely or you could leave it and try to cut and splice a bit from another performance. With twenty-four tracks, there might be five or six open tracks. You could record a vocal on all of them and construct a final vocal by switching between them while mixing.

And *still*, you could run out of tracks. Making Queen's infamous "Bohemian Rhapsody," still considered a marvel of recording, "was basically one big track bounce," according to the song's producer, Roy Thomas Baker. For the many three-part harmonies, singer Freddie Mercury recorded the same part on three tracks, and then bounced all nine. The song required so much bouncing to fill up tracks that they were down to the eighth generation by the end of the song. According to Baker, you can hear the distortion on Roger Taylor's drums, a sound that people assume was done on purpose, and which many often tried to replicate.

As the number of tracks began to multiply around the start of the seventies, the response from many engineers was to close-mike instruments and to separate the musicians, often into different rooms. They wanted to eliminate leakage, so that every track was a discrete puzzle piece that they could swap in and out of the final mix or run through various processors to shape the sound. This allowed for greater control during the mixing process. You didn't have to make as many decisions while recording. Just lay everything down on tape, and if you decide the guitar solo doesn't work, remove it from the mix. For added control, studios became flatter, deader, less reverberant, and records began to sound drier. "It's like dying, being in a dead room," Emory Cook had said twenty years earlier. Presence died a million deaths in the seventies. In its place was the Edisonian dream: record the music, not the room.

There was a cultural and geographic component to the dry-as-a-bone sound. It was especially prevalent in West Coast studios, and especially audible on the California-centric rock bands of the seventies—put on an Eagles record and you'll hear it. Or better yet, listen to the early Steely Dan records, technological masterpieces made with the engineer Roger Nichols.

But really, it was everywhere—rock, disco, funk—the sound of the age. It wasn't necessarily bad from a listener's perspective. Minimalist seventies classic-rock records—ZZ Top, Bad Company, AC/DC—do sound "live" in an Edison-biting-into-wood sense. The music is intimate, unencumbered, right in front of you. But if you stop and think, they really don't sound the way bands do when you hear them live, when "presence" is blown up to mammoth proportions. Kick drums and snare drums, for example, end up sounding similar. Mike Thorne, part of a younger generation of producers and engineers who would eventually rebel against this aesthetic, compared the drum sound of the era to "a falling ham sandwich."

There were holdouts, of course. It's difficult to imagine how Led Zeppelin records would have sounded if John Bonham's drums had been given the era's typical sonic treatment. (Supposedly, Bonham would hurl his sticks at any hapless engineer who tried to close-mike his kit.) And for engineers weaned on the Columbia sound, these new methods were apostasy. "Ridiculous" is how the producer Joe Tarsia describes the California studio aesthetic that developed in the seventies. "It was the producer not willing to commit. He wanted to be able to take the guitar out later, which you can't do if it's bleeding into five other microphones. So you put him in his own little booth and close the door." Tarsia still managed to record large numbers of musicians in a room, leakage be damned. Listen to the Delfonics' beautiful "Didn't I (Blow Your Mind This Time)" and you're hearing all the musicians playing at once in the same space. Only the vocals were overdubbed.

In the midseventies, Bongiovi, the former Motown wunderkind, began to notice a lot of musicians were complaining about how the new studio practices were affecting their playing. Bongiovi had worked with several disco and R&B bands so he encountered a lot of horn and string players, and they seemed to be having the hardest time. The problem was that without the benefit of echo and reverb, the rooms were so dead that musicians couldn't really hear themselves play. As a result, they tended to overplay to compensate.

Bongiovi started asking musicians their favorite room to play. There were three that kept coming up: the Manhattan School of Music; the Eastman School of Music in Rochester, New York; and the Boston Pops Concert Hall. He went to all three places and measured the reverberation time, the time it would take for a sound to decay. He decided that he would try to build what he called a "reverberation-time-based studio." The room would be constructed such that its acoustics gave sound a quick decay time—three-fourths of a second, like the famous Motown reverb. Also, a sound made at any spot in the room would need to reach any other point in the room in no more than three-quarters of a second. Musicians would get the ambience they lacked in dead rooms and would even be able to record in the same room, with a minimum of the bleeding that drove engineers crazy.

The idea seemed ridiculous to a lot of engineers, and Bongiovi had trouble finding investors. Fortunately, he landed a gig producing Meco's disco version of the *Star Wars* theme, which went to number one in the fall of 1977. He used his first $260,000 royalty check for a down payment on an abandoned building in Manhattan's Hell's Kitchen neighborhood that was once a Con Edison power station.

The key to the Power Station's appeal was the way Bongiovi designed it so that it sounded live, while tightly controlling the decay time. "The Power Station became the most technologically advanced analog studio on the planet, but a lot of what I did there I got from Motown," Bongiovi says. Records that came out of the Power Station had an instantly recognizable Motown-ish ambient sound. Listen to Bruce Springsteen's *The River* and *Born in the U.S.A.*, David Bowie's *Let's Dance*, Chic's *Risqué* and *C'est Chic*, the Rolling Stones' *Tattoo You*, and you'll hear the most signature sound of the era, a transition away from seventies dryness. The staff engineers—people like Bob Clearmountain, Neil Dorfsman, and Jason Corsaro, plus a producer like Nile Rodgers for whom the Power Station was a second home—would go on to define much of the sound of eighties music.

Bongiovi had thought long and hard about the emotional implications of a room's dryness or lack thereof. "When you go into a doctor's office and you're very sick, and the guy tells you that you have cancer and you're gonna die in six months, that's usually a very dead room, with lots of sound absorption. You wouldn't expect the room to be very reverberant, like a bathroom, because the sound would be diffused, and you'd feel cheated. The intimacy is gone, and [at that moment] you want that relationship."

The dry sound of the seventies had foregrounded this intimacy. There is nothing between you and the music coming out of the speakers. What Bongiovi essentially did with the Power Station was sacrifice that intimacy and replace it with something more communal—both in terms of the sound of the records and the interactions that went into making them. He made sure to put carpet on the floor of the lobby and sound absorption material on the ceiling, "so that when you walked into the lobby, it sounded extremely dead," he says. "When you opened the door to the main studio, and heard that three-quarters-of-a-second decay and saw the big high ceilings, psychologically you felt like wow, this is a really live studio. It gave musicians a better orientation."

Nothing announced the arrival of the Power Station quite like its signature ambient drum sound, a real rebuke to the dry percussive sound of the seventies. Bongiovi isn't sure who exactly discovered the drum sound, but he thinks it was Springsteen's drummer, Max Weinberg, playing on someone else's session. Someone had the idea to put the drums in the studio's main room. Bongiovi had already recorded several percussion instruments there, placing mikes ten to fifteen feet away to get room ambience, but nobody had ever tried it with a full kit. They found that same approach worked. They could get the big booming sound of ambient drums, but the acoustic properties of the room meant that other musicians could be miked so that they could play in the space simultaneously without leakage. "The drums were an accident, since the studio had been designed with horn and string players in mind," Bongiovi says. "But that was a nice pleasant by-product of having a reverberation-time-based design."

The effect was achieved using what are called "noise gates," which are programmed to shut a microphone off instantly if it detects a certain level of power. The result of shutting off that reverb-drenched sound so abruptly is a drum that sounds unsettling and larger than life. Gated drums would go on to be one of the most overused trends of the eighties, though technically it's not the drums that are gated—it's the room mike. That's why the effect was so intense at the Power Station, because the ambient mike was picking up such a strong reverberant sound before gating.

Ask any recording engineer today to describe the sound of eighties records and you'll likely hear a discourse on the hapless overuse of gated drums. More broadly speaking, it was the era of the ambient drum sound, kicking into gear just as the creator of the greatest ambient drum sound in history, John Bonham, checked out of this world. Even records that eschewed the headache-inducing percussive brashness of the Power Station clique were liable to have drums that suggested room ambience. And although the Power Station was the epicenter of this sound in America, an even more explosive drum sound was being developed in London.

You know it. You're listening to Phil Collins the singer croon his way through the stark "In the Air Tonight," when suddenly in the middle Phil Collins the drummer improbably produces the hammer of the gods from up his sleeve. That massive drum sound, which defined the eighties as much as the Power Station's did, emerged from a studio that had unique acoustic properties and a mixing console that would revolutionize studios and recording practices in the coming decade and beyond.

The Virgin Records impresario Richard Branson had recently launched the Townhouse, a London counterpart to the Manor, a recording studio he owned in a small village near Oxford. Headed by the chief engineer Mick Glossop, the Townhouse had two recording rooms, one with the traditional soundproofing and bare-bones aesthetic perfect for dry recordings, and one with a more experimental setup. For this second space, which they called the Stone Room, they put stone slabs on the floors and covered one wall with a type of stone found in the Cotswolds section of England.

Like the Power Station, the room represented a radical departure from common studio practices of the era, because of all the reverberant stone surfaces. Glossop and Phillip Newell, the Townhouse's technical director, wondered if they'd gone too far. "I remember standing there with Phil and saying, 'This sounds much too live to me, I think we're going to need to control it with some sort of acoustic treatment,'" Glossop says. "Because we weren't used to it. We were still in the era of [studios with] very controlled, dead sound. Phil said, 'I know what you mean, but we've exceeded the budget. So this is absolutely it. Let's see how it goes, and in six months we can deaden it down a bit.' So that room would never have sounded like that if we'd had another five thousand pounds!"

For the studio's consoles, the Townhouse mavens turned to Solid State Logic (SSL), a small British company owned by Colin Saunders. In the early seventies, Saunders, a home-taping fanatic living in a small village near Oxford, had been doing some location recording of a pipe organ when he thought of a way to eliminate the tangle of wires that connected the keys to the pipes, using a single cable and a serial linkup. Saunders sold the system to people who built and restored pipe organs, and used the proceeds to start a company that would make recording consoles for studios.

At the time, there was no console industry to speak of. Consoles were usually custom built, by people without a lot of hands-on experience in recording. Consequently, the machines had small flaws that were becoming more of a problem as multitracking became more sophisticated. Some were technical, but others were related to ergonomics, because as mixing became a more integral part of the recording process, the layout of a console's knobs and faders could help or hinder an engineer's job.

Saunders's unique insight was in understanding that the new realities of recording in the multitrack world demanded consoles that made the engineer's job easier while fostering maximum flexibility. The Townhouse was one of SSL's first customers. "They were completely off the radar," Glossop says. "We sat down and had a chat, and he went through the layout of the desk and showed us how the channel strip was laid out. And I was really impressed. Everything was in the right place. Apart from the fact that Colin was a very ingenious guy with a lot of imagination, he had a little sixteen-track studio where he recorded stuff, so he'd spent hours sitting behind the desk. He knew what was wrong with other desks and thought, well, how am I going to make it better?"

An SSL console was installed in the Townhouse's Stone Room. The combination of the room's acoustics and the SSL's flexibility accidentally created the room's famous drum sound. One of the SSL's seemingly simple but enormously useful features was something called "reverse talkback," a separate input on the console where you could plug in a studio microphone, hung from the ceiling, that allowed the engineer to hear what the musicians were saying between takes. This input included a very heavy compressor that squashed loud sounds and boosted quiet sounds, so that no matter what other racket was occurring in the studio, the engineer in the control room could converse with a musician in the recording room.

One day Hugh Padgham was engineering a recording session for Peter Gabriel's third solo album, with Phil Collins on drums. Padgham pressed the reverse talkback button at the same moment that Collins started banging his drums. The compressor acted as a supersensitive noise gate, making the drums, which already benefited from the Stone Room's reverberations, sound more gargantuan. Padgham played the sound for Gabriel, who said, "We have to use this!"

One perk of the SSL board was that every channel had its own noise gate and compressor, so Padgham liberally applied gating to the drum microphones. As with the Power Station, the combination of the Stone Room's very live acoustics and the gating effect resulted in a sonic boom with little decay. As Padgham puts it, "We had this enormous sound going from a hundred percent to naught percent."

From the Townhouse Studios, SSL consoles quickly spread throughout the recording world. Part of the reason for their popularity was that Saunders was designing consoles that could easily be tailored to any studio. But there was also the SSL's many technical innovations. There were the noise gates, but even more important was the SSL consoles' automated mixing capability. With it, you could essentially program the console to apply fades and effects at prescribed moments. Instead of you having to dance around this huge console, trying to make the right changes in real time, the console would actually do it for you, moving the knobs and faders based on a time code added to the tape. Other consoles had variations of automated mixing, but the SSL was the first to do it right.

Several other SSL features made the console ideal for the new age of recording. A "total recall" function recorded the static position of every switch on the desk, so that work on a mix could continue at a later time. Every channel could easily be linked to compressors, faders, and other effects, and engineers had the ability to route the signal through dizzying arrays of processing. A monitor allowed engineers to note song cues and link different mixes at those cue points.

The SSL console was the culmination of three decades of analog multi-track recording innovations. Its ability to give engineers heretofore unrealized abilities to move sound around set the stage for the digital recording and editing materials that would appear in the nineties. Thanks largely to the SSL console—as well as the use of outboard gear that could be interfaced with the console to produce even more effects—music could (and did) now sound excessively produced, or overproduced. The SSL is the final gateway that leads to Def Leppard's *Hysteria*. "They were basically a quantum leap from the old manual style of mixing into the space age," Ron St. Germain says of SSL consoles. "They really introduced the foundation for what has become the new age of mixing."

There was a trade-off, of course, the same one that had accompanied the transition from tubes to solid-state technology in the console world in the early seventies. While flexibility increased, the overall fidelity of the music declined. "The equalizers, faders, dynamics processors, and the actual components were not of the audio quality of the majority of the desks that preceded them," St. Germain says of the early SSL consoles. For most engineers, including St. Germain, the newfound flexibility was worth the decline in audio quality. In any case, the question would become moot, because SSLs were soon everywhere. Established studios like Abbey Road added them to stay competitive. "I didn't like the way it sounded, but economics dictated that I either bought one of those things or people would go someplace else," says Tony Bongiovi, who installed an SSL console at the Power Station in 1980. "The studios protested, the producers didn't like it, but if you wanted flexibility, this is what we had."

When the SSL began its ascendancy, the world of recording studios was undergoing a major change. In 1978, the number of twenty-four-track studios in the United States doubled. More producers and engineers were freelancers who moved among studios, as opposed to being on staff at just one studio. With SSLs everywhere, you no longer needed to know the quirks and intricacies of a particular studio in order to use it. "In the early days, if I went to another studio, I was scared because I wouldn't know if I would be able to use their console," Hugh Padgham says. "But suddenly every studio had an SSL, so an engineer could go from one studio to another, because the gear was all the same."

As for how music actually sounded in the eighties, the irony of all this new sonic flexibility is that the dominant sound of the era was more "live" than it had been in a long time. But it was a constructed liveness, just as Motown's studio practices, so huge an influence on Tony Bongiovi, resulted in a sound that suggested a real acoustic space (all that reverb) while sounding utterly unlike music that was actually live. The Power Station and the Townhouse were arguably the two most influential acoustic spaces of the era. Their natural ambience created bright, booming sounds that sought to imitate the immediacy of live music. If Madonna's *Like a Virgin*, produced by Nile Rodgers and recorded at the Power Station, sounds like a bunch of musicians playing together in one room, that's because that's basically what it is. To understand how radical a departure that sound was for groove-oriented R&B-inflected music, just compare it to the clean, precise sound of so many disco records released in the seventies.

Even the big ambient drum sounds begat by the Townhouse and the Power Station, so abused during the eighties, were attempts to engineer a new sort of immediacy—that is, the old sort of "presence"—in music. "At the time, myself and a few other younger engineers were rebelling against that very dry seventies Steely Dan sound," Padgham says. "Because we didn't think it sounded real."

The noise gating that the SSL made so easy to apply to any channel of the board facilitated this return to presence, but the new consoles' flexibility also helped people craft recordings that were paeans to signal processing. The obsessively constructed records that the producer Trevor Horn was overseeing—by bands like ABC and his own Art of Noise—were products of the new SSL era. And of course there was *Hysteria*, with its jackhammer-springy drums suggesting a band playing a hockey arena on Mars, and its slick moneyed production offering a presence too perfect for our material plane.

Certain superstar producers became associated with the new SSL-ed world of recording, people like Trevor Horn and Steve Lillywhite, whom Padgham recalls "playing the SSL board like an instrument, jumping back and forth between channels." The bright, shiny sound of Lillywhite-produced albums by bands like XTC, U2, Big Country, and the Psychedelic Furs is the organic side of the SSL's überproduced aesthetic. But it was Bob Clearmountain, a young engineer whom Bongiovi brought to the Power Station, who truly took the eighties sound to the bank. The big records that Clearmountain produced, engineered, or mixed, including Bruce Springsteen's *The River* and *Born in the U.S.A.*, the Rolling Stones' *Tattoo You*, Bryan Adams's *Reckless*, Hall and Oates's *Big Bam Boom*, and David Bowie's *Let's Dance*, suggest music heard live in cavernous spaces, with an almost heliumlike sense of lightness and bounce counterbalanced by drum sounds that by today's standards sound ludicrously pummeling.

As his success mounted, Clearmountain found himself being hired to mix records he had not produced or engineered, an unusual practice up to that point. It was a natural progression. Just as the SSL console increased the possibility for mixing to transform a recording, it was Clearmountain who paved the way for "mixing engineer" as a specialized job description.

Sometime in the early seventies, Mick Jones and Joe Strummer, the co-leaders of the Clash, traveled to Jamaica, a country that had already given them a wealth of thematic and musical inspiration. Expecting a promised land where Rasta and punk would recognize each other as subcultural brethren, they instead felt preyed upon and hassled, afraid to leave their hotel. The trip inspired "Safe European Home," the first song on the Clash's second album, *Give 'Em Enough Rope*, a hilariously self-aware send-up of the politics of culture. "I went to a place where every white face is an invitation to robbery," Strummer sings. "I don't wanna go back there again."

The song ends with a rush of overlaid lyrics, so it's easy to miss the song's most curious line: "24-track European home." It measures the distance between Europe and the third world in the currency of the multitrack. The Jamaican studios where the reggae Jones and Strummer loved was recorded probably had no more than eight-track capability. Lee "Scratch" Perry, the recording pioneer who produced Junior Murvin's amazing "Police and Thieves"—covered by the Clash on their debut album—had only four tracks in his infamous Black Ark Studio. He routinely bounced tracks so many times that the woozy distortion became part of Perry's aesthetic. Meanwhile, safe European and American studios were at sixteen, going on twenty-four tracks.

As it happened, the Clash themselves were turning their own private Jamaica—the scruffy sound of their debut album—into the complex world of twenty-four tracks. For *Give 'Em Enough Rope*, the band's official American debut, they hired the big-shot producer Sandy Pearlman, expressing admiration for the sound he had achieved on Blue Oyster Cult's records. Pearlman clearly understood that for a band to be taken seriously by the music industry, it had to have a sound that bespoke of access to money and tracks. He told the writer Greil Marcus that there were "more guitars per square inch on this record than in anything in the history of Western civilization."

The awkward transition that the Clash sing about symbolically was being enacted by many bands that grew out of the original punk-rock era. They were forced, to varying degrees, to conform to a new world of high-level production, in order to be taken seriously by the mainstream industry. The ways they adapted their sound to the twenty-four-track world is the flip side to the story of the studios and technologies that transformed recorded music in the seventies and eighties. The irony was that some of the key changes in the recording world, such as the big ambient drum sound, were pioneered by people like Padgham who were inspired by punk to create sounds that ran counter to the prepunk norms.

During the years he was getting the Power Station up and running, Bongiovi produced Talking Heads' debut, *Talking Heads '77*, and the Ramones' second and third albums, *Leave Home* and *Rocket to Russia*. For '77, his work behind the scenes included doing tape edits on every song to make them tighter—taking out a bit of guitar if it came in too early, for example—and he replaced Tina Weymouth's entire bass part on four songs. "Some of the stuff she played were like the wrong notes inside the chords," he recalls, "so I said, 'Tina, can we try another bass part?' She said—and I'll never forget this—'I've been playing these notes for a year, and no one's ever complained about it.' "

Bongiovi went to the band's label and asked for a budget to hire outside musicians. He recruited former Motown house bassist Bob Babbitt and arranger Brad Baker to listen to the songs and decide which parts Weymouth got wrong. The record was being made on sixteen tracks, with Weymouth's bass on track one. Since David Byrne had not yet recorded his vocals, track sixteen was still open, so Bongiovi used that track for Babbitt's bass. After Babbitt recorded his parts, Bongiovi dubbed track sixteen onto track one. "The band didn't even notice that I did that," he says. "No one, to this day, knows what happened."

For "Psycho Killer," the album's signature song, Bongiovi wielded a heavy razor blade, cutting the song into pieces and reassembling it into its finished form. "Of course, they hated that," he recalls. "But you have to package that stuff so you can sell it, and you can't package a rambling group of musical expressions that don't mean anything."

When he produced the Ramones' records, Bongiovi felt that his main job was to convey the sensory overload of a Ramones performance—Johnny Ramone's wall-of-sound guitar, Joey's strikingly odd looks, the overall roar, the visual concept of the Ramones as leather-clad pseudo-greasers—in a way that would compensate for the Ramones' musical shortcomings. It was a very Edisonian view, in a way, this belief that the recording would reveal the unfortunate "truth" about musicians without the distractions of the live event. "I don't mean to cast disparaging comments on the Ramones, but they weren't good musicians, and they could only do one thing," he says. "I needed to fill out the sound a little bit, but I had to do it in such a way that no one would know that was being done."

To beef up Joey Ramone's reedy voice, Bongiovi double-tracked his vocals. To tighten up Johnny's imprecise chord changes, he had him "punch in" several parts, an overdubbing technique in which a musician plays an entire part again, accompanying the previous recording of himself, while an engineer switches over to replace the old performance with the new one at the desired points. Bongiovi added some piano here and there, overdubbed some percussion, and even added a timpani on the chorus of "Sheena Is a Punk Rocker." "If you really, really listen, you can pick those things out," he says.

To my ears, the timpani is completely inaudible on the album mix, and maybe, possibly, sort of conceivably slightly audible on the mix used for the single. But "Sheena" does have a sort of pop sheen to it, and the single did make it to the lower reaches of the pop charts, a real accomplishment for a band as musically and conceptually unorthodox as the Ramones. How much Bongiovi's producing was responsible for the song's success is of course impossible to say. "My guess is that if you could tell there was a timpani on 'Sheena' you wouldn't like it," says Steve Albini. "If he thinks the reason the song is good is that he put a timpani on it, he can kiss my ass. That's a classic example of someone saying that a band's actual reality is not enough. 'What they need is *me* sneaking my magic timpani in there.' What a load of shit."

Albini, an engineer who runs the Electrical Audio recording studio in Chicago, was one of the scores of people who heard those Ramones albums at an impressionable age and were moved to start bands of their own. For Albini, that meant eventually forming the acerbic and enormously influential Big Black while an undergraduate at Northwestern in 1982. By then, bands that were punk or punk-derived and wanted to make and release records found themselves in a very different position than what first-wave bands like the Ramones and Talking Heads had found themselves in during the seventies. Those bands already had to deal with the problems of translating their sound for a recording-studio environment.

Glossop recorded groups like the Ruts and the Lurkers at the Townhouse and recalls dealing with the same issues that Bongiovi had faced with the Ramones and Talking Heads. "A lot of kids bought cheap guitars and amplifiers, because they didn't have any money, and put thin strings on the guitar because it was easy to push down," he says. "But if you used thin strings you had to be accurate with your fingering, which was another thing. It was a constant problem just keeping stuff in tune. But if it sounds a little out of tune, that helps the identity, because it means you're not slick like Steely Dan. So weaving through all these factors was a challenge. There would be a lot of punch-ins. It would be in tune for thirty seconds, and then you'd have to stop the tape, roll back, retune."

By the mideighties, the major music industry had largely concluded that punk was a commercial failure, and signed fewer of these bands. The development during that period of an independent rock infrastructure— indie labels, a network of clubs that hosted small touring bands, college radio, 'zines—was largely a reaction to this freeze-out. Along with this new business model came an alternative conception of what recordings should sound like. The first-wave punk bands were just happy to be able to make records. If they had to have their parts overdubbed by a Motown session musician, well, that was part of the price you paid for access to the hallowed studio.

But at the same time, the idea of making records didn't seem quite so rarified. Portable four-track recorders, which had first become available in the seventies, were now giving musicians an opportunity to experiment with recording themselves. Just as Alan Lomax's disc recorder had convinced Muddy Waters of his own greatness, the existence of four-track machines, even if many bands didn't have them, subtly promoted the idea that a band's natural sound was something worth preserving. "In the past, if a garage band made a recording, if they were lucky it was with a stereo mike in the middle of the room," says Andy Wallace. "But now they could play around with recording themselves. They weren't at the mercy of Atlantic Records telling them Tom Dowd was going to make their record."

Except that, in a way, they still were. Although the number of independent twenty-four-track studios had exploded since the early seventies, most were still staffed by professional engineers who wanted to make professional recordings. They wanted to prove they could compete with the Power Stations of the world, and they weren't very sympathetic to indie bands that wanted their records to sound different. It was difficult to find someone willing to make a simple recording that stood as a cogent snapshot of a band's reality. Albini emerged as one of the more adept practitioners of this lost art. "An awful lot of what I've done as an engineer has been trying to make the experience of listening to a record match up with my sense memory of having been there when something happened," he explains. It was an aesthetic that served as a rebuke to a world in which rock records were increasingly "made" rather than recorded, painstakingly assembled at great expense over long periods of time, with phantom timpani everywhere.

Albini became notorious for his distaste for the word "producer," with its implications that anyone other than the musicians themselves is calling the shots. He prefers the credit "recorded by" to "produced by," but he most prefers not to be credited at all, since he considers his role to be one of facilitating, rather than actively asserting his preferences—much the same way engineers of Frank Laico's generation viewed their jobs in the fifties. The distinction is debatable, of course—one could argue that transparency in engineering is as much of a chimera as objectivity in journalism—but it underlines just how much recording aesthetics had turned around since the original hi-fi era. Think of Elvis moving from Sun to RCA as the archetypical indie artist signing to a major label. Just as William Paley's CBS empire begat the 30th Street Studio and some of the most realistic sounding records ever made, RCA's capital underwrote the finest equipment, a studio environment vast enough to represent a real space, and not least, engineers with formal training who considered themselves technicians rather than artists. At Sun, you had people like Sam Phillips and Jack Clement learning as they went along, playing the mixing board like an instrument and using tools like slap-back echo to jerry-rig a virtual sonic space out of the cramped confines of Sun Studio.

Elvis's move from Sun to RCA resulted in records that were more transparent, less "produced." Jump ahead to the eighties, and the reigning big-ticket studio is the Power Station, started by someone who admired the pure ambience of recording made by Columbia's engineers at 30th Street, as well as the somewhat more constructed ambience of Motown. Although studios like the Power Station facilitated the recording of musicians in a resonant room, the use of high-tech tools such as SSL consoles by engineers like Bob Clearmountain resulted in records with a booming, larger-than-life sound.

The SSL era meant that major-label recording aesthetics were more similar to Sun than Columbia, more Phillips than Laico. As much as he reveres the classic Columbia sound, Bongiovi followed more in the footsteps of Phil Spector or Joe Meek. Whereas Albini goes for "sense memory," Bongiovi claims never to have made a record recorded "correctly," by which he means a pure capturing of sound. "Everything I've ever done has been 'I want a hit,'" he says.

It was the independent artists, led by people like Albini, who wanted presence in the original hi-fi sense. The sound of early rock and roll was a distinct if implicit refutation of the correct high-fidelity recordings of the prerock era. It was the sound of the nascent baby boom inverting the hi-fi fetish that their parents had acquired on the suburban frontier. By the eighties, the pendulum began to swing back, and the American descendants of Sun were making records that strived for the prerock feel that reached its apotheosis with Enoch Light. Not that every Albini-engineered recording sounds like it was made in a church. (Though some do: for an idea of what would have happened if Laico had made rock-and-roll records, check out "Prayer to God," by Albini's own band, Shellac, or Silkworm's "Give Me Some Skin.") But the best of them convey that "sense memory" concept that Albini uses as a guide. You really get the sense of a group of musicians playing together in a defined space.

When indie or punk-inspired bands tried to update the sound of their records to conform to major-label standards, the results were often awkward. According to Albini, the problems were more often procedural than production-driven. "It's not so much that they were subjected to a different technology," he says. "I think the problem was that they were put in a different environment where it was expected of them not to sound like a real band anymore."

These were groups of musicians accustomed to playing live who were entering a twenty-four-track world. "Instead of a band walking into a session and playing the way they did every day," Albini says, "the band would show up at the studio and have a session constructed around them piecemeal in an alien environment. They were doing something different to create a simulacrum of what they did every day. And it should come as no surprise that if a good-looking woman comes into your bedroom and drops her clothes, that's going to be a lot more effective than if someone brings in an arm and a leg and one ass cheek and starts bolting them together."

What was the musical equivalent of fitting together arms and ass cheeks?

"The first thing would be for the drummer to play to a metronome," says Albini. "The correct tempo for the song would be determined by the producer, based on his read of what the groove required. (And I guarantee you he would use a phrase very much like 'what the groove required.') Other instruments would be overdubbed on top of that, normally not even in the arrangement that the band would use if they were playing the song at a gig, but in some superspectacular way that the producer decided on, thereby removing any element of interplay between the live musicians. The guitar player might have an amplifier that is as integrated into his playing style as the instrument he chose, but the producer would choose a different amplifier, or have the bass player plug directly into the console, despite the fact that he has never plugged his bass directly into his earhole."

From a listener's perspective, the change that resulted from a band's indie-to-major transition was sometimes hard to pin down. The Pixies' 1988 Albini-engineered *Surfer Rosa* is still a landmark of indie-rock production, a perfect example of the potential power of a transparent recording aesthetic. To this day, its drum sound is especially sought after by engineers. The Pixies followed it with their major-label debut, *Doolittle*. It's a very good (some would say great) album, and it doesn't sound as though its producer, Gil Norton, has pressured the band to drastically alter its natural sound, but the production lacks the bite and immediacy of *Surfer Rosa*. Listening to *Surfer Rosa* is a much more you-are-there experience. Even if you prefer *Doolittle*'s songs, chances are you'll be more knocked out by its predecessor's sound.

Of all the formerly indie bands to be put through the major-label wringer, it was Nirvana that really cracked the code. *Nevermind*, their 1991 DGC Records major-label debut, integrated the big-bam-boom sound of the eighties while simultaneously wiping the slate clean. It sounded like it belonged on the radio, but it also seemed like a natural extension of the band's Sub Pop Records releases. What happened after *Nevermind* is a classic example of how recording aesthetics had been turned upside down since the start of the rock-and-roll era. Kurt Cobain declared that *Nevermind* sounded too slick and hired Albini to record the follow-up, *In Utero*, hoping for a sound similar to the Pixies' *Surfer Rosa*. In other words, moving up in the music world meant winning the right to abandon a produced sound in favor of a snapshot of a band playing.

Predictably, the result was controversial. Various accounts had some combination of the band, its management, and DGC dissatisfied with the result, which generally sounded more live than its predecessor, with the jagged transient sounds that occur when you're actually hearing live music. *Nevermind*, by contrast, had the oomph and wallop of a band onstage, but the guitars sounded limited, creating a smooth simulacrum of the live experience. Several of the tracks wound up being remixed by R.E.M. producer Scott Litt, and the result was an uneasy compromise—a less restrained sound than *Nevermind* but somehow lacking the punch of *Surfer Rosa*.

Nevermind producer Butch Vig helped repackage Nirvana for mass consumption, but it was Andy Wallace who put a shiny wrapping on the package and tied the bow on top. In terms of influence on commercial rock, Wallace was to the nineties what Bob Clearmountain was to the eighties, the mixing engineer whose work defined the sound of the era. Wallace's mixing credits after *Nevermind* included many of the bands that tried to take some variant of "underground" music into the mainstream—Sonic Youth, the Rollins Band, Rage Against the Machine, White Zombie, Faith No More, Helmet, Soul Asylum, Cracker, and so on—plus a wide swath of big sellers of different sorts, such as Sheryl Crow, Ben Folds 5, Limp Bizkit, and Linkin Park. Clearmountain, at his peak of influence, "probably had 60 or 70 percent of the Top 10 on the radio at one time, but Wallace probably broke his record in the nineties," says Ron St. Germain.

Like Clearmountain, Wallace is modest and doesn't look the part of someone who rewrote the rules of rock mixing; his calm demeanor and trim white beard make him seem more like a pediatrician. They both give the impression of having listened very carefully and thoughtfully to music. Since they also share an understandable reluctance to elucidate a consistent aesthetic, lest they seem to take credit away from the musicians whose records they mix, it's dangerous to draw too many conclusions about why Clearmountain's and Wallace's mixes sound the way they do. Still, it's worth pointing out that Clearmountain, a Bongiovi protégé, came out of the Power Station orbit. Bongiovi's formative experience was at Motown, and he built on that label's studio innovations to create the Power Station, whose ambient sound was a response to musicians' complaints about the hassles of making records in the arid eighteen-going-on-twenty-four-track world.

Wallace, who got his professional start around the same time as Bongiovi, also took inspiration from sixties R&B and soul, though he had a different opinion of Motown and its as-heard-from-across-the-room drum sound. "I think one of the reasons they did that was that it [didn't overwhelm] the vocals," Wallace says about the technique. "But in a lot of cases they were so ambient that, to me, they kind of lacked power." The brightness of the Motown sound, explicitly tailored to AM radio, set it apart from the sounds of most other R&B labels, such as Stax. "I love old R&B records, recorded in a small studio, super-dry, with almost no reverb on anything," he says, pointing in particular to the output of Sue Records, a small New York label best known for releasing Ike and Tina Turner's early records. "They were typically just dry as a bone, right in your face, but they had a warmth. I've always liked things that sounded like excellent demos, and all the old soul records sounded like that, other than Motown." Stevie Wonder famously challenged Motown chief Berry Gordy to let him deviate from the label's recording aesthetic, which Gordy agreed to when Wonder threatened to take his services elsewhere, and the result was *Talking Book*. Compare the sound of Wonder's drums on an earlier song like "Signed, Sealed, Delivered" with "Superstition," and you'll hear the sound Wallace admired.

While Bongiovi was looking for an alternative to that seventies sound, Wallace had his own studio in California, where the dry sound really thrived. He had a drum booth to get the requisite separation, but he made the top part of the walls more reflective, to add a little "liveness" to the cymbals. "Possibly because I came up in that era, I've always leaned toward having drums on the dryer side," he says.

After selling his studio in 1980, Wallace moved back to the East Coast and eventually developed a solid reputation for engineering and mixing funk, dance-pop, and early hip-hop music by the likes of Nu Shooz, Afrika Bambaataa, and Run-D.M.C., including the latter's collaboration with Aerosmith, "Walk This Way." The rap/rock hybrid of that song, as well as another Rick Rubin–produced project that Wallace worked on, the Beastie Boys' *Licensed to Ill*, has become one of the most important sonic templates of the last twenty years. It was Wallace's facility with dance music, as much as his comparatively dry mixes, that set the stage for his role in breaking *Nevermind*. There is a head-bobbing quality to "Smells Like Teen Spirit"— it's no surprise that hip-hop DJs were slipping it into their set at the time— and an awareness of hip-hop is arguably the single most recognizable aspect of alt-rock in the nineties. Break beats were everywhere—just listen to Dave Grohl's drumming on the chorus of "Teen Spirit."

Wallace's work wasn't so much a radical departure from Clearmountain's as it was a subtle redefinition. The typical Wallace mix was rarely as dry as the seventies California ideal. But like Clearmountain, Wallace's methods were informed by the advent of SSL consoles. He typically uses very little outboard gear when mixing, preferring instead to work with the SSL's built-in gating and compression features. And although he contributed heavily to the nineties yen for compression in recordings, he's also known for "riding the room"—he'll bring up the ambient mikes at different parts of the song to flood the mix with a bit of room tone, something you can hear used to good effect on "Smells Like Teen Spirit." The overall sound is a drier alternative to the Clearmountain school. It makes sense that Wallace's less reverb-happy approach would captivate Gen Xers. Many of their earliest childhood musical memories were probably of dry-sounding seventies records, and the sound was a comfortable alternative to the overblown sound of the eighties, when Gen Xers were growing up and life was getting complicated.

In an era when the "live" sound epitomized by the Power Station and Townhouse felt "produced," while indie rockers gravitated toward a sound that was lean and pure but didn't really sound live, it was the postpunk band Mission of Burma, all but ignored in their day, who came up with the most powerful-sounding alternative. *Vs.* rings with a sense of presence that is pure late fifties prerock Columbia.

Capturing the sound of Mission of Burma playing in a room was an obsession of their producer, Rick Harte, who also ran the label that released their records, Ace of Hearts Records. Harte wasn't an engineer, but he had a clear sense of what he wanted. He knew that the conventional wisdom of most recording engineers in the late seventies and early eighties was that you had to put musicians in different rooms, an approach he felt made otherwise fierce punk and postpunk bands sound "like Foreigner." The band had already tried making records the established way. Their first single, "Academy Fight Song," "was supposed to be very gritty and hard," Harte says, "but the band wanted to add all this stuff, so when it came time to mix it, it sounded like a symphony." For the next release, the *Signals, Calls, and Marches* EP, Mission of Burma made a concerted effort to sound stripped-down, but wound up sounding pinched. So for the first LP, Harte decided he needed to capture the band in all its onstage glory. Like Emory Cook thirty years earlier, Harte had had enough of the sound of music in a flat recording studio. Like Laico and the Columbia engineers, he would record the room as much as the band.

To do so would go against not only the grain of mainstream recording techniques but also the aesthetics of punk and postpunk records. Harte was a big fan of the burgeoning indie-rock underground but felt that most of the records shortchanged them. "I thought the bands were incredible, but there was a terrible sameness to their records," he says. Even a touchstone like the Gang of Four's *Entertainment!* didn't move him: "It was so thin, and I wish it had more low end." On the other hand, Harte's model was, of all things, the first album by Generation X, Billy Idol's pop-savvy punk band. "The sound was magical," he recalls.

Normandy Recording Studios, where Mission of Burma decided to record, had a cavernous room that would provide plenty of space-defining reverb. Harte wanted Burma to set up in the same positions they used onstage. "The engineers were horrified and furious," he says. "We had a horrible engineer named Phil Adler, who was just hopeless. He said it would never work, and that the instruments would bleed into each other. But the bleed is music. At a live show, sound bleeds through the mikes and the PA."

In the end, some of Adler's fears were borne out. Drummer Peter Prescott's floor toms needed to be overdubbed because the floor-tom mike had mostly just picked up bleed from other instruments. Mixing was a struggle; Harte described the attempts to balance out the sounds on the various tracks as akin to a chess match. But it worked. There is a dynamism to the record—just listen to the decay of Prescott's crash cymbal as it dissolves into Roger Miller's guitar on "Trem Two"—that most rock albums lack, and a ferocious roar that provides a credible approximation of a Mission of Burma concert.

Most indie bands of the era didn't have Mission of Burma's patience or Harte's stubbornness, so their records tended to sound much drier and flatter. They were lo-fi, in that they lacked a certain dynamic expansiveness when compared with the big ambient sound of the eighties, but at their best they had a clarity that bespoke "reality," at least to my ears. The early output of Pavement is a good example. In 1989, they released *Perfect Sound Forever*, an EP on 10-inch vinyl. Everything about it was a semi-reactionary rebuke of the current state of recording. The 10-inch disc size was an antiquated format that dated back to the days of 78s. That it spun at 45 rpm recalled the confusion of the Battle of the Speeds days. The title of this decidedly analog document is a phrase early advocates of digital audio used to describe compact discs. The high-end crackle (the band called its publishing company Treble Kicker Music) made the record sound like it was engineered to explode out of a transistor radio, like those by Joe Meek, or Phil Spector, or Motown.

The irony (and this band was big on irony) was that the group's would-be Spector felt like his hands were tied. Pavement's early records were made in Stockton, California, in the modest garage studio of Gary Young, the band's drummer. He was also nearly two decades older than the only "real" members of Pavement, Scott Kannberg and Stephen Malkmus. Young found the band's whole recording aesthetic baffling—its love of noise, fuzz, sonic obfuscation. "I never understood it," he told me in 1993, shortly after leaving the group. "I mean, I know how to make a record sound like Def Leppard." What Kannberg and Malkmus were after was the opposite of Def Leppard, and nearly the opposite of the Wallace sound, which by the time Pavement released its masterpiece, *Slanted and Enchanted*, in 1992, was becoming the sound of alternative rock, thanks to Nirvana.

As always, I don't think you can separate the sound of *Slanted and Enchanted* from the songs. Young's production is excellent. As with many great dry recordings, it sounds to me like music heard at night. It perfectly encapsulates a band issuing forth musical missives from nowhere—in this case, California's Central Valley, a stand-in for far-flung sprawling regions nationwide, housing the new middle class, just like the sprawl that John Conly noted was launching a million audiophiles in the fifties.

"Here" was the only song on the album that had any reverb on the drums, Malkmus explained in the liner notes to the tenth-anniversary reissue of *Slanted and Enchanted*. All the other drums were dry. His reason, rendered in exquisite and requisite self-referential pseudo-irony, speaks volumes: "Albini said reverb sucks, remember??"

Digital

6

Perfect Sound? Whatever

Nothing since Edison's and Berliner's inventions has as much revolutionized what can be heard from a record as has the most recent invention, the Compact Disc. Its invention [raises] the old confusion about what a sound recording really shall be. Should it be the ultimate in static, realistic "photography," comparable with a total in holographic still-frame? Or should it better compare with a motion picture; i.e. with an awful, dynamic transition of one situation, the performance in nature, into a completely different situation which exists in the home of the average listener . . . [T]hrough the last two decades, flexible sound processing has apparently been the pipe dream . . . [T]he awareness which recently has been directed towards the phenomena and philosophies of sound may well be worth the attention of all who can do something about it, be they artists, producers, engineers, marketing people, etc.

—Peter K. Burkowitz, Chairman, PolyGram Filmed Entertainment, 1983

From the early 1980s up till now, and probably for another fifteen years to come—this is the darkest time ever for recorded music. We'll come out on the other end, and it'll be okay, but we'll look back and go, "Wow, that was the digital age. I wonder what that music really sounded like. We got so carried away that we never really recorded it. We just made digital records of it."

—Neil Young, 1992

Bruce Springsteen liked to listen to music on a Panasonic boom box while he canoed on a river near his New Jersey home. One summer day in 1981, it fell out of the boat and sank to the muddy bottom. Springsteen managed to retrieve it, hosed it off, set it on his porch, and a few weeks later it somehow came back to life.

In early 1982, Springsteen, with the help of his guitar technician, recorded some songs at home, on a primitive portable studio system that neither man really knew how to use. They didn't realize you were supposed to monitor sound levels, maintain tape speeds, and clean and align the machine's heads. To achieve a slap-back effect, Springsteen ran his guitar through something called a Gibson Echoplex. When it was time to do the final mix down to two tracks, the only thing in the house with a line input was the immortal boom box—not ideal, but it had to do. When he was done, Springsteen shoved the cassette into the pocket of his jeans jacket, where it remained for months. Without a case.

In a proper recording studio a few months later, Springsteen tried to rerecord the songs, but they weren't sounding right. Something about the sterile environment made these songs, explorations of American dread and longing, seem awkward, like hoboes at a dinner party. Frustrated, Springsteen played the original cassette for Toby Scott, the engineer on these sessions. "There's something about the atmosphere on this tape," he said. "I want it to sound like this. Can't we just master off it?"

The answer was no, not really. The riverbed, the hose, the Echoplex, the crazy levels and grimy heads, the weeks spent in sweaty denim—they all added to the recording something that was sonically crucial, but also stubbornly resistant to mastering it for vinyl. Every time a mastering engineer tried to make a lacquer disc of the music, the needle, as if in protest, would literally leap out of the groove. Finally, two mastering engineers, Bob Ludwig and Dennis King, discovered that if the levels were set extremely low, they could just manage to get the thing on disc. The result was *Nebraska*, an album nearly too lo-fi for vinyl.

An opposite fate awaited Springsteen's next album, though it, too, served as a rebuke to the vinyl LP. *Born in the U.S.A.* was released in the spring of 1984 on vinyl and cassette. By the end of the summer a million copies had been sold, and the album was being readied for a second release of sorts. Ludwig, working at his mastering studio in Maine, made a recording of the album from an analog master tape. Rather than traveling to a cutting machine, the output of this analog master tape was routed to a Sony digital recorder. Instead of an acetate lacquer, the sound was encoded onto a three-quarter-inch U-matic tape—a professional-grade videotape format that doubled as a good medium for storing digital audio information—running on a Sony videotape machine. Instead of vibrations etching patterns onto lacquer, the sound was translated into a binary language.

What was stored on the tape was a series of 16-bit binary code. That means 16-digit numbers comprised of just ones and zeros. The moment the digital recorder encountered the music—Danny Federici's piano chord at the start of "Born in the U.S.A."—it analyzed the voltage in both the left and right channels and translated each channel's feed into one of 65,536 possible 16-bit numbers. It did this 44,099 more times before one second had elapsed. (Max Weinberg had just hit his first snare drum downbeat.) By the time the song was over, the system had gone through this process 12.3 million times. By the time the album was over, it had repeated the process more than 100 million times.

When he was done, Ludwig sent the tape to a recently converted cassette factory in Terre Haute, Indiana, owned by the CBS Sony Group of Japan. The tape was brought into a room containing air so pure that no cubic foot had more than 1,000 particles larger than .5 microns (.0005 millimeters), by workers who wore dust-free hooded white suits that made them look like a hazmat crew. The tape was inserted into a rack of components connected to a cutting machine. Because even tiny vibrations could wreck the process, the machine had been built so that it was not mechanically connected to anything else in the building. It was encased in concrete with a perimeter of Styrofoam, and rested on a pad embedded twelve feet into the Earth.

Meanwhile, in another clean room, a spin-coating machine applied a thin layer of photoresist onto a plate of green soda-lime glass. As the solvents in the photoresist evaporated, a worker used an ellipsometer to measure the disc's thickness, down to the nanometer.

The glass plate was brought into the other room and fitted into the cutting machine. As the tape played, the information on the tape directed a laser to turn on and off. Whenever the laser was on, it burned a microscopic pit into the photoresist, exactly .6 microns wide. Every zero told the laser to remain in its present state—either on or off. Every one told the laser to switch to the other state—from on to off, or off to on.

This was a stereo recording, so every sampled moment was actually two 16-bit numbers, a total of 32 bits. The system divided these 32 bits into four sets of 8 bits, and then converted each of these 8-bit numbers into a 14-bit number based on a chart in the system's memory. At the end of every 14-bit number, the system placed three more bits of metadata. One was there to correct a quirky effect low frequencies had on the system. The other two maintained a specific polynomial equation in relation to the values of all preceding bits. If the playback system encountered missing or damaged data, it could figure out the correct values by examining these two bits.

For one more level of error correction, the data was interleaved—that is, jumbled together and laid down by the laser out of chronological order. That way, a big defect on the surface of the disc, such as a scratch, would scatter the "bad" data among different sections of "good" data, making it much easier for the system to figure out what was missing.

The system digitally encoded *Born in the U.S.A.* in real time, so it took about forty minutes altogether. When the disc was ready, workers loaded it onto another machine. A nickel-plating process turned the disc into a glass master. The master was used to create a few metal stampers, from which finished discs would be fabricated.

One of these stampers was loaded into an injection-molding machine. In another room, workers carefully opened a huge bag of polycarbonate pellets. This was a delicate task in itself. Polycarbonate, a high-grade plastic, was used in many industrial processes, but this one required a heretofore unrealized level of purity because one speck of dust could ruin the reflectivity of the finished disc. The bag itself was washed, its long neck was fitted over a shroud connected to a large bin, and a string was pulled to release the pellets. They traveled to the injection-molding machine through special pipes made of a stainless steel alloy strong enough to handle the stress of millions of pellets flying by without any particles breaking off. Even the coupling of the pipes had been fussed over because the tiniest breach, combined with the hot, dry air carrying the pellets, could create a partial vacuum that would suck dirty air into the pipe.

When the pellets reached the molding machine, they were heated. As they became molten, they fused into a disc. The information on the stamper—those billions of pits and spaces—was transferred onto the disc.

The newly minted disc received a coat of aluminum several million times thinner than a sheet of paper. Before the aluminum could oxidize, it was covered with a clear lacquer. Then it was ready, the first compact disc to be made in the U.S.A.

The next day, a crisp autumn morning, the plant's workers, Sony executives from the United States and Japan, reporters, and various dignitaries, including Indiana's governor, gathered in a tent outside the factory. Speeches were given about the role of Sony, CBS, and Terre Haute in building the digital future. Everyone there received a copy of *Born in the U.S.A.*, along with a CD containing old Edison recordings.

At one point, those standing nearest to the street heard a faint rumbling noise. They turned to see a Chevy with a bad muffler cruising down Fruitridge Avenue. As the car got closer, the rumbling got louder, and more heads turned. The driver leaned his head out the window and shouted, "FUUUUCK YOOOU!"

Who was this stranger? Just some random Wabash Valley hesher? Probably. But maybe he knew what he was doing. Maybe he understood what a momentous occasion this was. Maybe he'd been following the development of digital audio. He knew that CDs had been rolling out of overseas factories for the past two years, and he knew what they promised: a final link in the digital audio chain. With a compact disc, a sound could be captured and frozen in pristine digital form, and remain that way right up to when it was "thawed" in the home.

The thing is, this guy didn't want "thawed." He didn't want pristine. I imagine his noisy Chevy having a cheap tape deck with dirty heads. As he cruises down Fruitridge, it's playing "Magic Carpet Ride" or "We're an American Band" or "Rainbow in the Dark" or "Photograph." It sounds grimy, and it sounds good. And now these douches under the tent want to take it away from him. Fuck that!

Compact discs brought the analog versus digital debate down to street level. Those *Born in the U.S.A.* CDs meant the digital forces had established a beachhead in America. Maybe this dude was the first to fire back.

The symbolism could not have been more obvious: *Born in the U.S.A.* chosen as the first compact disc made domestically, handed out with an Edison sampler. It communicated the message that the CD was the latest chapter in the great American story of recorded sound.

The web of symbols gets thicker. The CBS Sony Group's Indiana plant opened two months before Election Day 1984. By then, President Ronald Reagan, attempting to catch some of the *Born in the U.S.A.* fire, had praised Springsteen's "message of hope" at a New Jersey campaign stop. In doing so, he was linking "Born in the U.S.A." to "Morning in America," a slogan used in Reagan campaign ads that summer. Besides their structural and syntactical similarities (the stress on the first syllable, the echo of "born" and "morning," the synonymous last words), the phrases fit together thematically. Springsteen's is about "birth"; Reagan's is about "rebirth," the beginning of a new day. Springsteen invokes pride of place: This is where I am from, this is me. Reagan's promises a clean slate, an erasure of history: The place in which I was born is itself reborn.

Now consider that the official name of the "Morning in America" ad was "Prouder, Stronger, Better," which bears more than a passing resemblance to "Perfect Sound Forever." That was the slogan that Sony and Philips used to promote their joint invention, the compact disc. Or so people think. Actually, that phrase was never used in a promotional capacity—not by Sony, Philips, or any other company. They made claims that were similar, but the exact origins of "Perfect Sound Forever," like "High Fidelity" in the analog era, remain unknown. Something about this evocative phrase caught a mood as surely as its analog counterpart did in the fifties. The message "Perfect Sound Forever" evokes is not far removed from "Born in the U.S.A." and "Morning in America." It marks the end of a historical arc: what Edison tried to do, we've done.

"Born in the U.S.A.," "Morning in America," "Perfect Sound Forever"—and at the point where they intersect, there is the CD: a new morning of perfect sound born in the U.S.A. that will last forever. But as is often the case with symbols, the material reality of the CD blows a fat speck of dust into all this symbolic polycarbonate, starting with the obvious fact that the compact disc was most certainly not born in the U.S.A. It was conceived in the virtual space between Japan and the Netherlands, birthed in Tokyo and Eindhoven, and traveled to these shores in the custody of a Japanese partnership.

As for the CD ushering in a new era of recorded sound, that is definitely true—but the break with audio tradition was so great as to render nearly meaningless the link to Edison implied by the schwag given out in Terre Haute. From every angle the CD player, compared with the phonograph, is a model of precision and complexity. The player's laser beam, which is reflected through lenses similar to those used in electron microscopes, must have a diameter of exactly 1.7 microns when it reaches the disc's surface. When the beam encounters a pit, its wavelength must decrease by exactly half, so that a photodetector can decide if the system should read a 1 or a 0. A CD begins spinning at 458 rpm and gradually decreases to 197 rpm as the beam moves outward. When it was unveiled, the technology could inspire hyperbole even from technicians. Jules Bloomenthal, one of the principals behind Soundstream, the first company devoted to digital audio, recalls some people claiming that fashioning a CD required a level of precision so advanced that only a few spots on Earth would be seismically stable enough for CD manufacture.

"It was the biggest jump in technology that the audio industry had ever seen," says Roger Lagadec, a Swiss engineer whose research into digital signal processing became a key component of the CD system. "The CD was really the big bang," agrees K. A. Schouhamer Immink, a former Philips engineer who was on the team that built the technology, "and then everything changed."

What changed, exactly, was the entire theoretical framework of sound reproduction. An analog recording is an attempt to paint an accurate picture of sound by using a method that accurately replicates the way sound behaves in our world. A sound wave is continuous; it moves through the air as a coherent whole. An analog recording of that sound event is also continuous. The groove of the record is unbroken. If you were to draw a sound wave with a pen the way an analog recorder does with a stylus or recording head, the pen would never leave the paper.

A digital recording is not continuous. It is discrete. The philosopher John Haugeland has defined a digital system as "a set of positive and reliable techniques . . . for producing and reidentifying tokens, or configurations of tokens, from a prescribed set of types, taking into account a margin of error, within which all performances are equal and success is total." In other words, a digital system is amenable to objective analysis. It performs a discrete series of token identifications, and as long as each step has been carried out within a prescribed margin of error, the system has performed successfully.

For a compact disc, the "tokens" are "samples" of an audio signal's power at precise intervals. The system essentially takes measures of the wave's amplitude and connects them. Again, if you imagine yourself drawing a sound wave, this time imitating a digital system, you would do it by plotting points on graph paper. What you would have is a jagged "staircase" line. The goal of a digital system is to make the squares on the graph paper small enough so that to the listener the line seems smooth and continuous.

This commonly used jagged-staircase metaphor, although useful in understanding how digital audio works, is misleading in one important sense. It implies that listening to digital audio is akin to watching a movie, as though our ears were ignoring actual breaks in a sound wave, the way our eyes are tricked into not knowing that they're spending a significant amount of the experience in darkness.

One good way to understand the difference between digital and analog audio is to start with the end product, which is exactly the same in either case: a current that makes your speakers vibrate in a way that re-creates the sound waves captured by the recording. Whether created by analog or digital technology, the sound waves that your speakers emit are continuous, just like natural sound, and indeed there is no objective way to analyze those waves and conclude whether the source is analog or digital. It has to be the same because we need mechanical energy in order to perceive sound. We can't hear digital code or voltage fluctuations.

Working backward from the speakers, we see that what your amplifier processes is also the same in both cases. It translates voltages into a current that makes those speakers vibrate. It's useful to remember that all a digital audio system samples is amplitude, not frequency. If I digitally record myself hitting middle C on a piano, the digital system doesn't "hear" middle C; it registers a series of power fluctuations that, in the end, will make middle C emerge from your speakers.

It is the method by which these power fluctuations are noted that truly differentiates analog and digital. Since sound does not naturally break down, a digital system subdivides it using the smallest possible piece of information there is: the bit. A bit is a unit that describes one of two possible directives. These are typically described as 0 and 1, but any two symbols or terms can be used as long as they represent two—and only two—alternatives. The power of binary code is that by breaking down information into its smallest possible form, it can represent virtually anything using only two elements.

The power of binary code has enormous implications that extend beyond a computer solving problems. In a groundbreaking paper published in 1948, Claude Shannon, a mathematician and engineer, proved that any piece of information can be transmitted over a carrying channel and reconstructed at the other end with very little chance of error, provided the information is transmitted at a rate, in bits per second, smaller than the channel's carrying capacity, also expressed in bits per second. That may seem like an opaque conclusion, but Shannon's "A Mathematical Theory of Communication" practically invented modern information theory. In terms of its effect on how we live our lives, it stands as one of the most important documents of the twentieth century.

Shannon's paper argues for the idea that information exists apart from whatever esoteric meaning it is meant to convey. As he put it, "These semantic aspects of communication are irrelevant to the engineering problem." What is important is that the message be drawn from a set of possible messages, and that the system that processes that message be designed to accommodate any of those possible messages.

At root, the analog versus digital dilemma is about whether or not something so self-contained as a sound wave can be expressed in bits. "Breaking down sound damages it," says Akin Fernandez, a self-described "fine art noise artist" and owner of the British independent record label Irdial Discs. "Sound is contiguous. It is resistant to Shannon's information theory, which is fine for converting text into bits, but which doesn't work well for converting sound. Sound needs to be dealt with on its own terms. If you are going to break it up, it must be broken into such small pieces that the granularity is at a one-to-one ratio with the carrier medium—i.e., air. The human perception of sound is a fundamentally analog affair. Meat is analog."

Breakthroughs that predate Shannon's, however, suggest that digital audio has science on its side. In the twenties, Harry Nyquist, a Bell Labs engineer, concluded that any analog signal can be re-created digitally if it is sampled at precise intervals, at a rate that is at least two times faster than the highest frequency component of the signal. In other words, the system must be fast enough to get at least two good samples of every wave. If a signal tops out at 13 kHz, it must be sampled at a rate of 26 kHz, or 26,000 times a second. This value is known as the Nyquist frequency, or the Nyquist-Shannon sampling theorem. Precision is important. The intervals between samples must be exactly uniform. In 1937, a British engineer named Alec Harley Reeves invented a suitably exact sampling method called pulse code modulation, but it was many years before computers became powerful enough to really explore the possibilities of PCM.

Using PCM, the CD system takes a sample every 1/44,100th of a second and expresses the sample as a 16-bit number. Sixteen zeros means total silence (or sound too faint for the system to register). Sixteen ones is the most powerful sound the system can register without fatal distortion. These values are the tokens in Haugland's definition of a digital system. The number of bits and the sampling rate define the margin of error. Each time the system takes a sample and assigns it a value, it is compromising by rounding a little up or a little down. If the CD sampled at a higher rate, or expressed values using more than 16 bits, the representation would be more accurate. But as long as the CD is working according to its systematic parameters—44,100 16-bit samples every second—it is operating perfectly.

Now we can begin to understand the problem with calling a recording "perfect," and why digital audio represented such a radical departure from the old narrative of progress in the audio world. An analog system begins with the idea that there is an objective world out there—a world that is wholly singular, or perfect—and our job is to approach that singularity, to aim for that perfection. Like the old conundrum about the impossibility of getting from point A to point B—no matter how close you get, the remaining distance can always be halved—we'll never reach the goal, but we'll strive for it like the heroic species we are. That's why the word *fidelity*, with its implication of "truth," resonated so strongly with the first audiophiles.

A digital system is the ultimate negation of this idea. The system begins with an idea of perfection and works backward. The CD system "knows" that the entire world of sound can be accurately depicted using a set of 65,000 building blocks, as long as 44,100 of them are used each second. Moreover, perfection, in the analog sense, is not even a theoretical possibility. You can sample a signal one billion times a second, and you're still breaking up something smooth; no matter how many bits you use to describe the signal, it's still an estimate, a compromise—however tiny— with the sonic world. As Ivan Davis once put it, analog is about "approximating perfection," while digital is about "perfecting approximation."

As a concept, "perfect sound forever" is like "high fidelity" with a sort of ahistorical arrogance. We define the parameters of perfection, pretend these parameters are objective truths, and then congratulate ourselves for satisfying them. We speak of the "digital domain," because digital is a world that we built ourselves. When a senior adviser to George W. Bush told Ron Suskind that people like Suskind were part of the "reality-based community"—those who take part in the "judicious study of discernible reality"—while Bush true believers "create our own reality," what was he saying if not "we're digital and you're analog"?

Critics of digital audio in general, and the CD in particular, have often seized on this arrogance, this presuming to manipulate the natural and call it real. "Listening to a CD is like looking at the world through a screen window," Neil Young, the most famous antidigital voice, wrote in 1992, ten years after the CD's commercial debut. "If you get right up next to a screen window, you can see all kinds of colors through each hole. Well, imagine if all that color had to be reduced to one color per hole. That is what digital recording does to sound. All that gets recorded is what's dominant at the moment. I would like to hear guitars again, with the warmth, the highs, the lows, the electricity, the vibrancy of *something that's real*, instead of just a duplication of the dominant factors. It's an insult to the brain and heart and feelings to have to listen to this and think it's music." (Emphasis added.)

On the most basic level, the analog-versus-digital debate reprises old debates: cylinder versus disc, acoustic versus electrical, 33⅓ versus 45 rpm. These were all debates about "what a recording shall be," as Peter Burkowitz puts it, about situating your preference in terms of that eternal choice between making a recording that documents the objective world or making one that transcends it. But there is something more going on with analog versus digital. If this were just about ears and sound, why does Young mention "the brain and heart and feelings"? Why does Fernandez mention "meat," as though analog represents something fundamental about us as sentient beings?

Talking to people who were on the forefront of the digital audio revolution, it is striking how many recall being driven by the sort of messianic zeal that can be sustained only by youth, an unwavering belief that what they were doing was big enough to change the world. "I was young and naïve," Immink, the CD engineer, says. "It was one of those thoughts you have when you're young, which is basically that this is so good it will obviously succeed." Jules Bloomenthal says, "I can't tell you how intense Soundstream was, in terms of being a small number of people [who felt] they had a mission in the world." Walt Stinson, one of the earliest retailers in America to push the CD aggressively, recalls, "It was the idealism of youth. We were very conscious that we were creating the future."

If all these people were doing was inventing and promoting a new way to listen to music, why was it naïve to believe in its success? Why did what they were doing feel like a "mission"? Why did they feel like they weren't just making audio history, but actually creating the future?

And why did this future make some people so angry?

In a 1995 issue of Peter Bagge's underground comic book *Hate*, the slacker antihero Buddy Bradley is discussing music with Phil, another hipster. Buddy is trying to gauge the quality of Phil's musical taste.

"Tell me," Buddy says, "do you own a CD player?"

"Of course not," Phil replies.

"Hmm," reads the thought bubble over Buddy's head. "Maybe this guy's alright."

Try to imagine any other piece of home electronics—or any other consumer durable, period—that could inspire this sort of exchange. Somehow, ownership of a CD player connotes something important in ways no other object can. We know what Buddy means. Don't we?

Throughout the eighties and early nineties, an explicitly stated anti-CD stance became common among—for a lack of a more precise description—the type of musician who might read *Hate*. A thumbnail sketch reveals the evolution of the argument. In the liner notes to *Songs About Fucking*, Big Black's 1988 swan song, head mouthpiece Steve Albini throws down the gauntlet as he heads out the door: "The future belongs to the analog loyalists. Fuck digital." Three years later, Slint released the moody and cryptic *Spiderland*, an arid dark horse of an album that would quietly grow to legendary status throughout the decade. On the back cover, Albini's dictum is recast as an aesthetic recommendation: "This recording is meant to be listened to on vinyl."

The following year, Big Black posthumously echoed Slint's recommendation with the CD-only retrospective *The Rich Man's Eight Track Tape*. In case the title of the album doesn't clue you in to what Big

Black thinks of you for buying it, Albini's liner notes leave no doubt: "This compact disc, compiled to exploit those of you gullible enough to own the bastardly first-generation digital home music system, contains all-analog masters. Compact discs are quite durable, this being their only advantage over real music media, you should take every opportunity to scratch them, fingerprint them and eat egg and bacon sandwiches off them. Don't worry about their longevity, as Philips will pronounce them obsolete when the next phase of the market-squeezing technology bonanza begins." The taunting continues on the surface of the disc itself: "When, in five years, this remarkable achievement in the advancement of fidelity is obsolete and unplayable on any 'modern' equipment, remember: in 1971, the 8-track tape was the state of the art."

On Urge Overkill's *Stull* EP, released the same year, the argument becomes more personal. "What's This Generation Coming To?" describes a world made possible by the philistines Albini warned us about. The lyrics include "Every time I hear a CD, seems like someone's trying to shoot me with a laser beam," and "Don't take my vinyl away!"

Finally, in 1994 we encounter the strange case of Pearl Jam, and their third album, *Vitalogy*. They've become one of the biggest bands in the world, and they're not sure they like it—especially singer Eddie Vedder, who takes solace by retreating into his room, digging out some vinyl, and having a sort of audio-autoerotic experience, as described on "Spin the Black Circle": "See this needle / See my hand / Drop drop dropping it down oh so gently," "You're so warm / Oh, the ritual / When I lay down your crooked arm," "Pull it out / A paper sleeve / Oh, my joy . . . I'm so big . . ."

I'm so big? Are we still talking about records?

In the eight-year mininarrative described by these five albums, we've gone from "a war is brewing and you better take sides" (Big Black), to "analog is the correct way to experience this piece of art" (Slint), to "digital is the *only* way to experience this piece of art, making it suitable only for morons," to "digital is killing my soul" (Urge Overkill), and ended up with "analog is like fucking" (Pearl Jam). Each time, the message has become more personal, but also more expansive and thematically diffuse. By the nineties, when the alt-rock gold rush hit, it was not uncommon for indie bands making the jump to major labels to make deals that allowed their former labels to release vinyl versions of the band's major-label albums.

Somehow, analog stood for something organic, rooted, and objective, against the unnatural relativist subjectivity of digital.

You could tell by the sheer amount of discourse surrounding it that the analog-versus-digital divide had a significance that extended far beyond music. People weren't using liner notes to take a side during the Battle of the Speeds. I've yet to come across a song whose message was "don't take my Edison cylinder away." But now suddenly you had Young, not the most loquacious fellow, writing op-eds. You had record company executives raising the issue of "what a sound recording shall be." You had articles appearing in sound engineering journals with titles like "What Is Reality?" By the end of the seventies, a doctor—an actual physician—would fret that not only was digitally encoded sound "no longer music" but it was also killing us by degrees.

This was nothing less than a referendum on our relationship with the world—do we make it, or does it make us?—and with the machines we have created to help us understand the world. P. B. Fellgett, a cybernetics professor who often wrote about digital audio issues for the journal *Studio Sound* in the early eighties, urged people to pay attention to the unfolding debate because it revealed how one person's enhancement could be, for someone else, a corruption of something natural and real. "Progress is not always a straight line," he wrote. "Often, we must go backwards."

Predicting that the analog loyalists will inherit the Earth means believing that the future belongs to those who reject the future. So it's appropriate that the first traces of the digital world appeared seven years before *Born in the U.S.A.*, in the year of No Future.

In December 1977, to mark the one hundredth anniversary of Edison changing the world by reciting "Mary Had a Little Lamb" while the tinfoil spun, Brooklyn College hosted a four-day get-together. The Phonograph and Our Musical Life attracted musicians, academics, critics, and music industry executives. An anxious theme emerged, a nagging suspicion that one hundred years of recording progress might have unwanted effects, that progress, as Fellget had said, is not always a straight line, and sometimes we must go back. Conference organizer H. Wiley Hitchcock set the tone in his response to John Cage's opening remarks. "The record industry has been making records so perfect . . . that you lose any sight of the fallibility of humans," he said. "Such recordings are a fiction: they're too perfect, so when you hear a concert you are almost let down by what you hear."

Musing on "what a record records," the composer Roger Reynolds worried that recordings were straying too far from the live experience. "Is this intensification of contrast between the private experience of recordings and the public experience of performance unimportant?" he asked. "How are we to retain the ability to 'hear between the grooves' in the fact of increasing dissemination of recorded materials and of the proliferating equipment that allows ever greater clarity and intensity of sound reproduction? Intuitively, one feels that any practice which results in elevating the image of the real at the expense of the real should be resisted."

William Ivey, a country-music historian who would one day oversee the Library of Congress's National Recording Registry, considered part of the phonograph's legacy to be a flattening out of local musical cultures. "We once had a fairly vigorous assortment of regional musical styles in this country in both popular and folk traditions, but the impact of recordings— setting national standards of what, and how, music should be performed— has pushed us toward a homogenization of these distinctive traditions . . . Recordings have, quite simply, changed the way we hear music. Performances are now joyously diffused through space and preserved through time, but our audience has come to focus extensively upon the recording itself rather than upon the music it contains . . ."

Although Reynolds took a less alarmist stance than Ivey regarding this joyous diffusion, he still noted that modern music was blurring the line between "the unique quality of experience as directly lived" and "packaged experience as editorially contrived." He predicted that the coming age of digital technology would speed this process by offering "an editorial capacity that is scarcely to be imagined."

Something was in the air that year. Alan Lomax, the éminence grise of American song collectors, now thirteen years past his freak-out at Newport, warned that the "oppressive dullness" of the worldwide music industry, combined with the one-way communication model that dominated the mass media, was obliterating local cultures. It was a threat as dire as the world's looming ecological collapse. "A gray-out is in progress," he warned, like a man seeing evil portents in a solar eclipse, "which, if it continues unchecked, will fill our human skies with the smog of the phoney [sic] and cut the families of men off from a vision of their own cultural constellations."

Two books published in 1977—Jacques Attali's *Noise* and R. Murray Schafer's *The Soundscape*—confronted this smog of the phony and tried to make sense of the overall sound of our world. Attali, a French economist and adviser to François Mitterand, and Schafer, a Canadian composer and founder of the World Soundscape Project, both take the position that the control of sound has always been a corollary to political power. They both relate Hitler's famous claim that he could not have conquered Germany without the loudspeaker. Both point to Muzak as a prime example of sound gone wrong (Schafer: "bovine sound slicks . . . the embalming fluid of earthly boredom"; Attali: "akin to castration . . . this music is not innocent"), with Schafer going as far as claiming that America—"with its highly idealistic Constitution and the cruddy realities of its modern lifestyles"—is Muzak's natural habitat. He's that bored with the U.S.A.

Their respective diagnoses of the problem are two sides of the same punk 45. For Attali, changes in music presage similar societal changes. He writes that we are no longer living in the Age of Representation, when musical experience was organized around the model of performance. Ours is the Age of Repetition: music is chiefly defined by recordings and therefore the repetitive industrial processes that create them. This signals the overall dominance of life by the voraciousness of capitalism. In music and life, Attali longs for more "noise" in the Adorno sense: sounds that reflect our reality while also critiquing it.

For Schafer, like Lomax, the problem is too much noise in the global soundscape, so that the sound of the true and real gets obliterated. In our cacophony he hears the sound of domination over nature, of colonialism, of the flight of airplanes drowning out flights of fancy. "Schizophonia" is the name he gives our global malady, "the split between an original sound and its electroacoustical transmission or reproduction." In other words, we have become so skilled at making sound behave unnaturally—unmooring it from its original context, tossing it around the world, storing it later for future use—that sound has lost the power to signify. We're lost in the fog, alienated from our sounds and thus alienated from ourselves.

Schafer and Attali may differ on the exact nature of the disease— schizophonia or flatlined monotony, too much disruption or not enough— but they both agree that the problem began the moment we first learned how to reproduce sound. As Schafer puts it, "At the time hi-fi was being engineered, the world soundscape was slipping into an all-time lo-fi condition."

What was the panic of 1977 really about? It was much more than a lament for a time when records were records and music was music, although that was certainly part of it. The dread was also about a larger loss of control that went beyond a mere nostalgia for the days when there was a clear demarcation between the real and the represented. If we were created in God's image, and if we in turn created the phonograph so that a part of us would last forever—making us God-like—then perhaps we were being punished for our hubris. It was as though Guglielmo Marconi was right all along—sound never truly dies, and all the billions of hours of recorded sound we'd created over the past century was overflowing the sewers and landfills of our minds. The consequences of what Edison had done a century ago were finally catching up with us.

There was a sense that something was on the horizon that would make the issue impossible to ignore. It would be something that would make sound even more flexible. Would it finally persuade us to clear the air? Or would we embrace our fate and breathe deep the smog of the phony?

The most talked-about album of 1977 (at least among people who liked to talk about such things) was *Never Mind the Bollocks . . . Here's the Sex Pistols*, but the most listened to was Fleetwood Mac's *Rumours*, the biggest album of 1977 and now one of the biggest of all time. As someone who thinks both are great, I can confidently say that on that dialectical scale, *Never Mind the Bollocks* is analog and *Rumours* is digital—not so much because of how they were made but because of what they communicated: "No Future" versus "Don't. Stop. Thinkinabouttomorrow."

Something else happened in 1977. As the year wound down and the cognoscenti gathered in Brooklyn to worry over the phonograph's legacy, two guys who ran a fledgling classical music label in Cleveland began placing calls to Salt Lake City in hopes that America's first digital audio company might help them release the world's first commercially available digital recordings. The company said yes to them, and then yes to many others—including Fleetwood Mac, who became the first superstar band to record an album digitally.

Yesterday's gone, yesterday's gone.

Three things you should know about Thomas Stockham: First, he was the father of digital audio. Second, he helped bring down a president. And third, the second thing was not unrelated to the first.

It was Stockham who led the team that examined the mysterious eighteen-and-a-half-minute gap on the Watergate tapes. Using a computer program written by Stockham, they were able to determine—and then represent visually—the frequency response caused by the desk drawer that had contained the hidden microphone. They demonstrated that this energy pattern was missing from the gap, and concluded that the erasure was therefore deliberate and not due to a mistake made by Nixon's secretary while she transcribed it.

The process was called "blind deconvolution," and it was based on a deceptively simple idea that went all the way back to Joseph Fourier, a French mathematician and physicist whose accomplishments included helping Napoleon improve his weaponry. By studying heat flows, Fourier had concluded that waves can be broken down into smaller sine waves. Stockham, an engineer and professor whose background was in waveform processing, used Fourier's theories to investigate the problem of deconvolution in signals. Any signal is actually composed of signals that are convolved—that is, wrapped together like the individual strands of a rope. If a signal is made up of two convolved signals, and you know the value of at least one of them, deconvolution is relatively easy. But if the only data you have is the convolution itself, you are faced with the problem of blind deconvolution.

Using the nascent science of digital technology, Stockham initially examined the visual applications of blind deconvolution. Given a blurry photograph, one could use digital technology to determine the data that was distorting the image, remove it, and be left with a perfectly restored image. But in the early sixties, while a professor at MIT, Stockham had been intrigued by a crude digital audio system—a microphone, speakers, and an analog/digital converter connected to a room-size computer—built by some of his graduate students. He eventually reasoned that blind deconvolution could do for recorded sound what it did for recorded images. If you had an old recording that had been made under less than ideal conditions, you could determine the frequency of the unwanted distorting data and remove it, thus producing a perfect recording out of an imperfect one.

Stockham thought that a recording could be described in mathematical terms. Very simply put, a recorded waveform is produced when a musical input is convolved with the frequency response of the recording mechanism. If I sing into an acoustic phonograph's bell, what gets recorded is the combination of my voice and the acoustic properties of the bell. If the frequency response of the bell could be deconvolved from the recording, only the original waveform would remain. One would have a perfect recording, but more than that, one would have a literal reconstruction of the past by essentially eliminating the very thing that mediated between the past and our present: the original recording device. The true artistic worth of blind deconvolution, Stockham explained, "is not so much on producing a recording of modern quality as it is on having a clear glimpse into past musical events."

As a test case, Stockham decided to restore some old Enrico Caruso records. The challenge in doing so was not merely the inferiority of recording equipment in the early twentieth century. The problem with old acoustic recordings is not that they sound "bad"; engineers were capable of producing fairly linear recording systems, with minimal distortion. The problem was that every recording mechanism from the period had its own unique frequency response, and adjustments could make the same equipment have different responses from session to session. What Stockham would need was the actual machine Caruso sang into when he recorded a song, set up in exactly the same way. But unlike Nixon's desk drawer, he didn't have that machine, so he did the next best thing. For every Caruso record he restored, Stockham found modern recordings of the same material done by other artists. By digitizing them and analyzing the waveforms, he was able to determine what was probably missing from the Caruso recordings, and what was there that did not belong. He could boost some signals and eliminate others.

RCA was impressed enough with the result of Stockham's work to release sixteen of the digitally restored Caruso arias, mastered onto regular analog LPs, in 1976. By that time, Stockham was at the University of Utah and excited enough by the possibility of digital audio to form a company called Soundstream with a few colleagues, with the aim of producing the first perfect digital recording system. Stockham reasoned that a recording should document an event exactly as it occurred. But a recording made on magnetic tape, no matter how well made, was more than just a recording of the music; it was also a recording of the tape itself. The sound of the tape became part of the recording. We don't want a recording of tape plus music, Stockham reasoned, we just want the music.

Now if the tape contained digital data—ones and zeros—the tape would become transparent, merely a conveyor belt. The recorder that Soundstream built used a Honeywell tape deck to record digital data onto one-inch magnetic tape. For editing, the data was dumped onto a hard drive the size of a washing machine. The data could be displayed visually on a computer screen—a common sight today, of course, but incredibly advanced for its time. Using a tablet and a penlike instrument, one could tweak an interval as small as .00002 seconds. By 1977, the Soundstream system had been demonstrated publicly and several experimental recordings had been made, but nothing had been released commercially. Then Telarc Records called.

Telarc was a classical music label formed by Jack Renner and Bob Woods, two musicians in Cleveland who were obsessed with recording. Renner and Woods were trying to answer two age-old questions: First, what does live music, as heard from a great spot in a great room, really sound like? And second, how do we import it into someone's living room? To them this was an obvious goal, one accomplished by capturing the music perfectly and processing it minimally, and they couldn't understand why anyone would think otherwise. But the bloat of record production had infected the classical world as much as the pop world. Labels like CBS and Deutsche Grammophon were releasing symphonic records made by setting up a small army of microphones, and then mixing them down into the final product, a trend Renner and Woods found appalling. "If you want to take a picture of the Grand Canyon," they liked to say, "it's best to get a very large-format camera and take one picture."

Renner and Woods experimented with recording the Cleveland Orchestra direct to lacquer disc, but it was an exceedingly delicate process. Even a great master tape, the gold standard of live recording, contained dreaded tape hiss. When they heard about Soundstream, they felt like they'd discovered kindred spirits. "Telarc said, 'Give us an orchestra and we will produce the best audio signal we can,'" says Jules Bloomenthal, a member of the original Soundstream team. "Tom [Stockham]'s commitment was, 'Give me the audio signal and I will record it and reproduce it as faithfully as humanly possible.' And I think that combination of interests and goals is more responsible for the digital audio revolution than perhaps anything."

Renner and Woods wanted the world's first digitally recorded release to enter the world with a big bang—literally. For two days in April 1978, they recorded the Cleveland Symphonic Winds at Severance Hall, performing pieces by Holst, Bach, and Handel. Woods produced and Renner engineered, using a Soundstream recorder. For Holst's *Suite No. 1 in E-flat*,

Woods and the conductor, Frederick Fennell, talked about getting the biggest drum sound they could. Fennell took a bedpost from his home, wrapped it in leather, and auditioned various drums. Recording bass drums had always been a challenge because they produce a low-frequency whoosh that a microphone often can't handle. To mitigate this effect, a bass drum would usually be recorded with the head facing away from the microphone. As a result, a significant amount of the drum's energy went unrecorded. Woods and Renner had discussed the problem with Stockham, who was confident that the Soundstream recorder could handle the bass drum in all its glory. When the record was released, the sound practically knocked the wind out of listeners. Journalists and audiophiles began referring to "the bass drum heard round the world."

After capturing on record a drum that sounded like a cannon, the next step for the Telarc/Soundstream team was capturing the real thing. This time, Soundstream's ability to handle such an explosive sound posed risks for the listener. The fourth Telarc release, a recording of the *1812 Overture*, came with a sticker on the front that read, "Warning—Digitally Recorded Cannon. Please Ensure a Proper Listening Level Before You Play This Recording or You May Damage Your Loudspeakers." They weren't kidding. "We know you don't believe us, but you're gonna damage your system," Woods told skeptics. "How do we know? Because we found out the hard way. We played it back and ruined our own equipment first!" For some who didn't heed the warning, the destruction was worth it. "We got letters from people saying, 'Wow, that recording was great—it blew out all my speakers!' " Bloomenthal says.

According to Woods, the collaboration with Soundstream even yielded a linguistic breakthrough. "It was Telarc that coined the word 'digital' to be used for PCM recordings," Woods says. "I was thinking that 'digital' was really hot, because I had a digital watch instead of an analog watch. I remember the day I asked Tom Stockham. I said, 'Tom, is there any reason why you couldn't call a recording made from this technology a "digital" recording?' He said, 'No, of course not.' I've asked around if anybody knows anyone else who did this before we did." He's yet to find someone.

Not everyone was willing to bask in the digital glow of the Telarc-Soundstream lovefest. One day in 1979, Bloomenthal was in a Los Angeles studio, assisting with a recording session that used the Soundstream recorder. Someone mentioned that an engineer in another studio in the building had asked to hear the machine. No problem, Bloomenthal said. It wasn't until he had set up the machine in the other studio that he realized where he was: a classical music label and recording company called Sheffield Lab. He felt like he'd walked into a trap, but it was too late to turn back. Bloomenthal shook hands with the man who requested the demo, played him some music, and waited for his opinion. The man politely said he expected the machine to sound bad, but not *this* bad.

That was Doug Sax, Sheffield's president, a notorious antidigital crusader who often wore a T-shirt emblazoned with STOP THE DIGITAL MADNESS. He had played around with a Soundstream machine, as well as a digital recorder made by 3M, and concluded that the prodigital forces' claims of perfect reproduction were completely unfounded. "We used to talk about the three greatest lies ever told," he says. "The first one was 'the check is in the mail.' The third one was something dirty. The second was whatever you wanted it to be, so [for us] that became, 'the copy sounds just like the original.' "

In fact, the very idea drove Sax nuts. "*Nothing* sounds like the source," he says. "I don't know of a system that sounds as good as what comes through live on the console." The question was, if digital wasn't the same, was it still musical? Sax thought not. And Soundstream had the nerve to preach their gospel at professional forums like the Audio Engineering Society conferences! "I lost it one time," Sax says. "I went into their room at the AES. [They were playing] a symphonic recording, which is man's greatest creation, and it was absolutely the worst thing I'd ever heard. It was harsh, unfriendly, 100 percent unnatural. I yelled and screamed and told the lady there that this abomination was the worst thing to ever happen to recorded sound. That lady was Mrs. Tom Stockham."

As for Mr. Tom Stockham, he took these criticisms in stride, figuring science didn't have a chance against arguments that were essentially faith-based. You could look at the waveforms; the evidence was right there that his system reproduced sound with greater accuracy than any analog system. If people still refused to admit it, what could you do?

Woods's response to Sax wasn't so sanguine. "My reaction was, 'Go fuck yourself,' " he says, laughing. "Yes, there were some limitations, but there were also some hellish gains and improvements. We were so thrilled with the benefits that we weren't interested in sitting around crying about things that weren't quite up to snuff."

Sax and his fellow analog loyalists weren't the only ones alarmed by the encroaching digital tide in 1979. On the other side of the country, a psychiatrist in New York had made a startling discovery.

When John Diamond was a child in Australia, his life was saved by a song: Dick "The Canadian Crosby" Todd's version of Gene Autry's "You're the Only Star (In My Blue Heaven)." Diamond was in a hospital, gravely ill, when he slipped on some headphones and heard the song playing through the hospital's internal sound system. Suddenly he felt his strength returning, and soon enough, he made a miraculous recovery.

Diamond could still remember exactly how it felt to hear that song. Now that he was a mental health professional, he believed strongly in the healing power of music. He encouraged all of his patients, no matter what issues they were working through, to make music a regular part of their lives—listening to it, and, if possible, playing it themselves. But recently he had noticed that music did not seem to be doing some of them any good. In fact, it appeared to make their ailments worse. If they were battling anxiety, it made them more anxious. If they were having trouble sleeping, it made their insomnia worse. It even seemed to make someone who was battling a painkiller addiction crave the drug more.

During his youth, Diamond had experimented with building his own hifi components. He still had a passing interest in sound technology, and he was aware of the steady encroachment of digital audio. It didn't take him long to figure out that many of his patients were listening to records manufactured from digital masters. Could that be the problem? When he could find them, Diamond substituted analog versions of the same songs or pieces—sometimes even by the same performer—and the music once again proved therapeutic. He listened closely to some digital recordings and didn't like what he heard. He compared Stockham's deconvoluted Caruso restorations with the original 78s, and the difference was striking. He found every digitally remastered album he could and compared them with the originals. These were identical recordings, but the supposedly lo-fi 78s not only sounded better, they *felt* better.

Although he was an MD, Diamond drew heavily from holistic and alternative medicines, including acupuncture and applied kinesiology, a controversial health system developed in the sixties by a chiropractor. Applied kinesiology adherents believe that many of the body's problems, both physical and mental, arise from an imbalance among chemical, mental, and structural factors, and that these imbalances can be detected by various manual muscle tests. Diamond designed a test in which he pressed down on a subject's outstretched arm while music played, and told the person to try to resist. Diamond found that when an analog recording was played, the subject could almost always resist the push, but when the recording was digital he could easily press the arm all the way down. He concluded that there was something about the digital signal that the ear perceived as alarming or unnatural. This triggered stressful feelings that caused a disturbance in the body's natural acupuncture system, which explained the loss of muscle response.

The more Diamond thought about it, the more he decided that the digital process so disrupted music's essence—its life-affirming quality, perceived throughout history and across cultures—that what came out was no longer music. He was invited to present his findings at an AES conference in Los Angeles in May 1980. He warned his audience about the grave consequences of the coming digital transition. He explained the theory behind the test he had devised, and then said he would demonstrate. He asked if the heads of Sony and Philips were in the house. They were not—or if they were, they wanted nothing to do with this stunt—but he did manage to coax some people onstage.

Sure enough, the tests worked. The audio professionals watching them were, by turns, stunned, intrigued, and very suspicious. Word spread throughout the conference. To Diamond's dismay, many skeptics tried to perform the tests, failed to reproduce Diamond's results, and concluded that Diamond had had some sort of card up his sleeve. The battle played out over the next few years in the letters page of the *Journal of the Audio Engineering Society*, but the debate was moot. The battle Diamond was fighting had already been lost. The regime change, the mass transition to digital, was already in full force, although most people wouldn't realize it for a few years. Two months before Diamond's talk, a team of engineers from Sony and Philips had put the finishing touches on the final link in the digital chain. Bob Woods recalls, "I parked my butt in Japan, on Sony's doorstep, in about 1980, and said, 'Whenever you're ready . . .' "

Upon meeting Stockham, Toshitada Doi, a Sony engineer who worked on digital audio products, is said to have remarked, "Sony may be biggest, but

Soundstream is best." Given the history of the recording industry, it would be more accurate to say, "Soundstream may be best, but Sony is biggest."

It's a familiar story, one that goes all the way back to the Edison cylinder and its losing fight against the Berliner disc. Stockham was a true visionary. His thinking was so advanced that in 1977, two years before Sony released its first Walkman, he already foresaw the iPod ("It is not outrageous to imagine carrying several hours of music in a box the size of a deck of cards"). The Soundstream recorder was lovingly crafted by people obsessed with the idea of fidelity and it showed, most obviously in the Soundstream digital editing system. Other companies had begun building digital recorders in the late seventies, but only Soundstream offered visual computer-based editing.

Every Soundstream recorder cost $50,000 to build, just for the parts. By 1978, the company had built ten, offered at a price of $160,000. It wasn't merely the cost that drove away a lot of potential buyers. Too many audio professionals were intimidated by the complexity of the machine. Not only would they be spending a lot of money to buy it, but they were wary of paying Soundstream more money to service it.

Soundstream soon changed its business model to become a full-service recording company. If you wanted to make a record using the Soundstream recorder, you essentially rented the machine and a Soundstream employee to help run the session. The company kept a recorder in Los Angeles (primarily for mastering), one in New York, one in Europe, and three others that moved from city to city. There was an editing system in Salt Lake City and one in L.A. Soundstream was involved with about eighty commercial releases. Most were classical, but they also included Fleetwood Mac's *Tusk* and *Live* albums. Soundstream offered its services to the Rolling Stones, but the band declined on the grounds that the grittiness of tape was integral to their sound.

Meanwhile, companies like Sony, 3M, and Denon began making digital recorders that were much cheaper and simpler to use. It didn't help Soundstream's prospects that the music industry was mired in one of its worst slumps ever. Even Telarc began using competing machines because Woods and Renner could no longer afford to keep flying to Utah for every editing session.

Stockham knew that the next step would be a digital playback system for the home. He had some ideas of his own—particularly a system for encoding digital information on a sheet photographically, thus eliminating the need for a physical pressing—but by this time, the Sony-Philips juggernaut was in full force. In 1980, Soundstream was sold to people who had no clue what they were getting, and who proceeded to run the company into the ground.

Following the 1964 Olympics in Tokyo, researchers at NHK, the Japanese broadcasting service, began looking at ways to improve analog tape technology. After concluding that there were really no improvements left to make—tape was as perfect as it could get—a team led by Heitaro Nakajima turned their interests to digital technology. The gigantic machine they built had no practical worth, but Nakajima was hooked. When he compared the sound with an analog recorder, "it was [as] if somebody had removed a veil out of the way."

Norio Ohga, a high-ranking Sony executive and classically trained opera singer, had had an uncannily similar reaction to digital audio (for him, it was like "removing a heavy winter coat from the sound"). So when Nakajima went to work for Sony, Ohga wanted him to continue his digital research. Sony cofounder Masaru Ibuka, however, thought it was a dumb idea, so Ohga had Nakajima work on it surreptitiously. Nakajima instructed two of the forty engineers he supervised, Toshitada Doi and Senri Miyaoka, to work on a digital recorder. What they came up with sounded okay, but like Nakajima's original digital recorder, the size of this one—roughly that of a refrigerator—made it an impractical consumer device.

In 1975, Sony released the Betamax videocassette machine, and Nakajima saw a great opportunity. The signal-to-noise ratio of the Betamax made it ideal for digital audio, so without changing the makeup of the machine, Nakajima's team adapted a Betamax to process a digital audio signal. Two years later Sony began selling the PCM-1, a PCM processor that could be used with any Betamax to create a digital audio recorder. Herbert von Karajan, Hitler's favorite conductor and a friend of Sony cofounder Akio Morita, pronounced it the best-sounding audio device he had ever heard.

Ohga decided the next logical step was to replace tape with some sort of digital disc. Led by Doi, a Sony team developed a disc with a thirty-centimeter diameter that could hold a whopping eight hundred minutes of sound. Ohga called Lou Ottens, a colleague at Philips, the Dutch company that had developed the compact audio cassette (what we now call simply the audiocassette) in the sixties. For several years, Philips had been conducting cutting-edge research with optics and lasers, and in 1975 introduced the Laservision video disc, which turned out to be a complete flop. After Laservision's collapse, Ottens decided the optics work should continue in pursuit of an audio disc, reasoning that, unlike video, there was already an existing music consumer base that would embrace a good optical disc.

Philips's working prototype was 11.5 centimeters in diameter, which struck Ohga as a good size. He proposed that Sony and Philips collaborate on inventing the perfect digital audio disc. Sony could bring to the table its expertise with digital audio issues, while Philips could share its work on optics. Beginning in August 1979, a team of engineers from both companies began shuttling between Eindhoven and Tokyo. (As the prototype of the player took shape, it was given its own first-class seat on KLM.) Philips wanted a 14-bit system and a disc that could hold an hour of music, while Sony argued for 16 bits and 74 minutes, supposedly because that was the length of Beethoven's Ninth Symphony. (The Beethoven anecdote, which has become part of CD lore, is most likely a digital audio urban legend.) Sony's specs became the standard, which required making the disc's diameter half a centimeter longer.

Sony's biggest contribution was the CD's sophisticated error correction, of paramount importance in a system that processed billions of bits for each disc. Led by Doi, the Sony engineers adapted the Reed-Solomon code— named after the two MIT researchers who'd developed it—for use in the CD system by adding those extra bits on the end of each sample and then interleaving the samples. The CD was one of the earliest practical applications of the code, which was also utilized to transmit data from the *Voyager 2* space probe.

As impressive as Sony's command of the audio side was, it was the Philips engineers, with their expertise in optics, that really made the CD tick. They had to figure out how to get the data on disc, and make sure there was a robust and sturdy way of processing it.

By the spring of 1980, the team had completed the bulk of its work. One year later, at 10:00 a.m. on May 27, 1981, Akio Morita and Frank L. Randall Jr., the vice-chairman of Philips's North American operations, presided over a press event at New York's Plaza Hotel, just off Central Park and across the street from Sony's offices. "Giant steps are usually taken by giants, nobody else having the requisite stride," Hans Fantel wrote of the event. "Last month the world of audio was treated to the rare spectacle of two giants stepping in tandem, departing boldly for the future."

Everything was going according to plan. Sony and Philips both opened factories devoted to production of CDs and CD players, and the giants began laying the groundwork for global CD domination. In exactly eleven months, Sony and Philips would unveil their baby at *Billboard*'s International Music Industry Conference (ICIM) in Athens, Greece. The Philips contingent would be led by Jan Timmer, who had recently been promoted from the head of Philips's South African office to president of PolyGram, Philips's affiliated record label, with the express command that he convince the other labels to see the digital light. Sony would be chiefly represented by Michael P. Schulhof, the former head of Sony's hi-fi division who had been handpicked by Morita to oversee Sony's business interests in the CD. Schulhof, who had a PhD in particle physics, was an enthusiastic convert. "You could hear a crescendo that blew you away," he marvels. "You could not help but be impressed."

"Look, son, you propose the bullshit!"

That was one of the constructive criticisms that Akira Suzuki, a Japanese Sony executive involved with publicizing the CD, remembered hearing from record-company executives he met in Athens, who had no trouble remaining unimpressed. (Another, which didn't get as lost in the translation, was "fuck you.") This year's ICIM conference theme was "The Challenge of Change," but most of the music-biz people, already dealing with the industry's historic downturn, were not in the mood to be challenged or changed. In his opening remarks, M. Richard Asher, the deputy vice president and chief operating officer of CBS Records, announced that everyone would one day look back and realize that "today, April 27, 1982, was the first time you heard about the miraculous recovery of the record business." Surely, the CD emissaries thought, news of this wondrous new disc will bring glad tidings. "Wow," Suzuki recalled years later, "totally opposite is our big surprise."

The reps from Sony and Philips weren't expecting candy and flowers. They knew they were asking the record labels to invest millions in a new audio format at a time when their industry was mired in perhaps its worst slump ever. But they weren't prepared for the bile that greeted Timmer's presentation, "The New Technology Fueling the Growing Home Entertainment Industry." Depending on whom you asked in the industry, Philips's last bright idea, the compact audiocassette, either had not yet begun to give the industry a needed boost or had already failed outright; either way, why should the labels believe Timmer when he said the CD would be a "big leap forward"? This all smelled like another attempt by Philips to subsidize its hardware with the sweat of record companies, and the crowd let Timmer know it. He may have been running a record label now, but he definitely was not one of them.

"Timmer got soundly trounced," Schulhof says. "Everybody thought they'd gotten beaten up, but Timmer probably took more bashing than anyone." (Timmer later confided that he felt he'd "barely escaped physical violence.")

Schulhof, who was onstage as part of the discussion panel for these opening speeches, ended up doing the CD demo on behalf of both companies. The crisp digital sounds of Herbert von Karajan conducting the Berlin Philharmonic did nothing to calm the beast. An increasingly popular talking point then circulating in the record business was that home taping was "killing" the industry. All the audience heard in the pristine sound of the CD was a better master tape for pirates.

Some of the members of the onstage panel even got into the act. Jerry Moss, the chairman of A&M Records, was running the panel, and he used his bully pulpit to articulate the crowd's discontent. "I fear what the hardware people are going to come up with next, to confuse and confound the consumer," he said, "and I loathe seeing the erosion of sales and excitement in the record business because of that confusion."

Now this was too much. Imagine—you've just been involved in the most thrilling new development in audio technology since Edison, a complex system of data and waveform processing that integrates the same technology that allows *Voyager* to send photos back from *fucking Neptune*, and you're now being lectured on "the erosion of sales and excitement" by the head of a label whose flagship act is Styx! And all of his cronies are staring daggers at you from the audience—hadn't they noticed that the most popular album in America that week (and what would become the most popular album of 1982) was the debut from Asia, a putative British "supergroup" whose vaguely cartographical, implicitly colonialist name, which extended to the album's can't-be-bothered-with-a-title title (*Asia*), merely hinted at the band's mercenary blandness? The best these guys can do to generate sales and excitement is Asia's *Asia*, and consumer apathy is somehow *your* fault?

Yes, totally opposite is your big surprise.

"We're talking real innovation," said Philips's Robert Huber, manager of compact disc operations, fanning the flames. "The compact disc's future is secure. The only question is whether you will join the future." Hans Gout, PolyGram's senior director for the compact disc, tried to play good cop, calling the CD "small and beautiful." But nothing worked. Everyone got shouted down—even Ohga. When the mike was opened to the audience, the hostility grew further. How did they expect the labels to invest so much in manufacturing infrastructure? What about piracy? And what was this about having to pay patent royalties to Sony and Philips? Amid the chaos, some would later swear they heard people transmuting their anti-digital sentiments into a chant: "The truth is in the groove! The truth is in the groove!"

This was not good. Sony and Philips had a lot riding on the compact disc. Each company had experienced a high-profile disappointment in recent years—Sony with Betamax and Philips with Laservision. Both companies had made it clear from the top down that the stakes were high for the CD. (Timmer had confided to at least one Philips engineer on the CD team that he had "invested his last penny" in making the CD work.) Although several companies were beginning to make CD players that retailed for $650 to $950, CBS/Sony and PolyGram were the only record labels that had committed to releasing titles on CD. Yet even with the high cost of players and the low number of discs, Philips was forecasting annual CD sales of 10.6 million by 1985. Sony was predicting nearly twice that amount.

After the debacle at IMIC, Sony and Philips went to work convincing record companies to get on board. Walter Yetnikoff, the fiery head of CBS Records in the United States, smelled desperation. Sure, he told Schulhof, we'll start releasing CDs—if you buy our cassette factory in Terre Haute, Indiana. ("They thought they had found a good sucker to buy it," Schulhof says.) Schulhof soon grew tired of these shenanigans and decided to bypass the labels and talk directly to the artists, reasoning that if he could convince them, they would convince their labels. One of the earliest high-profile stars he sold on CDs was Stevie Wonder.

Meanwhile, in October 1982, a Japanese pressing of Billy Joel's *52nd Street*, on CBS/Sony Records, became the world's first commercial CD release. In a few months, CD players would go on sale in the United States. If Sony and Philips expected millions of people to start buying players and discs, they had to start getting the word out, and not just to record companies.

Grubstake was about the last band you'd imagine being at the forefront of the digital audio future. Or any future. Yet this popular local folk trio was standing onstage at Denver's Rainbow Music Hall, the first act on a night billed as "an introduction to digital sound." The capacity crowd of more than a thousand people who filled the room on this night in March 1983 knew nothing about what was in store for them. The tickets had been free, given away on local radio stations, with no indication of who or what would deliver this introduction. When Walt Stinson, the co-owner of the local hi-fi store ListenUp, had begun the evening by announcing that Grubstake would do a few songs, people figured the act was just an analog warm-up for the digital headliner.

After they'd played a few songs, bandleader Jack Stanesco cued the next song, an a cappella sea chantey, by plucking a low note on his acoustic guitar. Except that he didn't. That sound had been recorded earlier. Between songs, Stinson had turned off the live microphones and patched a tape into the PA. Now he—and Grubstake—hoped for the best.

Before he cofounded ListenUp, Stinson had worked for IBM, so he knew something about the theory of digital audio. He and his business partner, Steve Weiner, had traveled to Japan in 1981 to examine this new invention they'd heard about called the compact disc, and had loved what they'd heard. As soon as players and discs became available in the United States in early 1983, ListenUp became one of only fifty-four stores in the country to carry them. Record stores were still wary of CDs, so if you were a very early adapter, you were probably getting your discs as well as your CD player from a store like ListenUp.

As evangelical as Stinson was about CDs, he knew that the players were expensive, the number of albums available on CD was minuscule, and that hearing was believing. He considered himself a student of the industry, and he'd read a lot of Edison's old promotional material. So he decided to mount a tone test.

Using a digital recorder, Stinson had recorded Grubstake playing songs from the stage. Stinson and the group listened to the tape and decided which two songs sounded the most "real." The first of these was the unaccompanied sea chantey. Grubstake was in the middle of the song when Stinson entered from stage left and tapped Harry Tuft on the shoulder. Tuft stopped "singing," as Stinson, wearing a face of grave concern, appeared to be telling Tuft something. Harry listened, and then made a face like he'd just remembered he's supposed to be singing, and hurried back to the microphone. The audience didn't appear to sense anything amiss.

The song ended and now the band began lip-syncing a raucous sea chantey called "We'll Rant and We'll Roar." As far as the audience could tell, they were ranting and roaring. But now Stinson came out again to talk to Tuft, and this time led him off the stage. When Stinson returned, he walked over to Steve Abbott on the right side of the stage and then led him off, leaving only Stanesco.

Now the audience got it. They'd been fooled. The crowd was on its feet, giving a standing ovation that drowned out the rest of the song.

People like Stinson were the grassroots end of a publicity and marketing juggernaut that, in the space of a few years, transformed the CD from an expensive curiosity into the dominant music media. Stinson made theatricality a key component of his pro-CD campaign. At one event he held at the Gates Planetarium in Denver, he smeared a CD with peanut butter and jelly, dunked it in water to clean it off, and then demonstrated how it still played flawlessly. Using a blade, he made a cut in the disc from center to edge, and it still played with no problem. Unlike the audience, Stinson knew that all he was doing was cutting into the protective acrylic, not the disc itself; he also knew that the interleaved data and error correction meant that as long as he sliced from center to edge, rather than in a spiral pattern, there would be no problem in playback. "There was an element of hucksterism, as I look back on it," he says. "It was very dramatic, got a lot of people's attention, and got a lot of press."

On the other end of the huge industrial apparatus pushing the CD, an unprecedented corporate alliance was forming. The same month Grubstake and Stinson introduced Denver to digital audio, Marc Finer, products communication manager at Sony, coordinated the first meeting of the Compact Disc Group. Led by a PolyGram executive named Emile Petrone, it brought together representatives from the hardware side of the business—the companies that were making players—and the record labels, controllers of the software. The goal was to encourage joint promotional campaigns, compare notes, and foster the notion that everyone was in this together. Each side eyed the other with barely contained distrust. "The first meeting was a joke," remembers Chris Byrne, who was the vice president of marketing at Pioneer. "It was the funniest thing I've ever seen in my life." As they had made very clear in Athens, the record companies felt like they were the ones taking the risk, and they wanted some assurance that players would be plentiful and eventually more affordable. The hardware companies wanted to know why they should make such a commitment without any guarantee that the labels would make CDs a standard format.

The hardware companies in the Compact Disc Group could at least agree that CD players were a good idea. There was nothing close to that unity among the ego-driven record labels. At one meeting, executives from two labels nearly came to blows over a half-inch difference of opinion regarding the proper size for CD packaging. Even within labels there continued to be tension. Jerry Shulman, then a marketing executive for CBS Records, gave monthly presentations to get management to take the issue seriously. "At each company, there was someone like me," he said. "We became a guerrilla task force, not only to the general public but even within our own companies."

As for reaching consumers, everybody in the CD business faced an enormous problem. Product awareness was extremely low—market research by Magnavox, the American wing of Philips, suggested that as little as 1 percent of Americans were familiar with the term "digital audio." In the twenty-five biggest media markets, Sony arranged for one rock station and one classical station to receive a CD player and the label's entire catalog of CDs. In return, the station would agree to note on the air every time a CD was played. Stations were encouraged to mention the format's great sound, its lack of surface noise, and its durability. Clubs and bars around the country hosted Sony Digital Nights, at which players and discs were given away. The Compact Disc Group hired a publicist to work on product placement. CDs began showing up in the background of soap operas. In *Rocky III*, Rocky, now rich and complacent, had a robot with a

CD player. J.R. on *Dallas*, to judge from his digital hi-fi setup, was suddenly an audiophile. In search of a younger demo, Sony and CBS put on CD seminars at colleges. MTV's first-ever spring break coverage was a CD promotion, culminating with a hunt for buried CDs on the beach.

Part of the CD's allure was its combination of two signifiers of the future: computer technology and lasers. During a demonstration of a Sony CD player, Finer surprised executives at one label by placing the disc in the machine's open drawer, walking around the room, and casually pressing the button of a remote he was carrying. "All of a sudden, as if by magic, the drawer closed, and music emanated from the system," he says. "These music industry guys went nuts." Robbin Ahrold, a member of the Compact Disc Group who was a vice president at RCA, remembers public demonstrations that showed off the label's digitally remastered version of Elvis Presley's *Greatest Hits*. After hearing the first words of "Love Me" (*"Treat me like a fool . . ."*) played on a vinyl record, with the attendant needle noise, people would gasp when the CD was played for comparison. "It electrified people," he recalls. "Because there was no sound, and then all of a sudden there was his voice."

Amid all this public demonstrating and guerrilla marketing, there was also traditional Madison Avenue sloganeering, which led to the spontaneous coining of an immortal phrase. One Sony print ad displayed a photo of the inside of Carnegie Hall, with a spotlight on a seat in the middle of the seventh row, and the words "Seventh Row Center Forever." Although the first three words would seem to imply that the experience of hearing music from the best seat in the house could now be re-created in your living room, Finer says that the intended emphasis was on "forever": CDs were so durable that the music they contained was rendered immortal. Around the same time, Magnavox began using the slogan "Perfect Sound" in ads for its CD players, a claim that took Sony by surprise. Somehow, the two phrases were combined in the public imagination, and journalists began referring to the claim that CDs offered "perfect sound forever."

The people who actually built the CD sometimes viewed the circus of promotion in America—the tortured semantics of "perfection" and "forever," the peanut-butter-smeared discs, the *Wizard of Oz*–ish demonstrations of the CD's magic—with a certain amusement. "I remember the first promotional material from Sony and Philips was atrocious," says Lagadec. "There was a famous picture of a very elegant lady's hand holding a CD, and she was touching both sides, so she had a lovely thumbprint on the side that was going to be read by the CD player. And this was stupid. But it certainly carried the message across that it was going to be a very robust system."

Not everyone was convinced of the superiority of the CD, but the promotional bonanza was so effective that detractors were put on the defensive. *"I have not heard a single compact disc that sounds as good as the identical recording,"* Edward Rothstein wrote in an article about audiophiles, the italics suggesting someone shouting to be heard over all the digital huzzahs. A master narrative was being written and agreed upon, and it said that CDs were perfect. But as the CD forces continued to make headway with consumers and eliminate the last vestiges of resistance within record companies, they met considerable resistance from two related constituencies: audiophiles and audio professionals.

For the former, opposition to the CD often made them feel like the people in *Invasion of the Body Snatchers* who know what's going on and watch in horror as their fellow citizens become pod people. Could they really be the only ones who heard what was wrong with the CD? Were they the only ones who recognized the sonic insanity? The journalist Michael Fremer vividly recalls a public demonstration of the CD at an AES conference. "The first disc they used as a demo was Roxy Music's *Avalon*, one of my favorite records," he says. "It sounded horrible but my attitude at that point was, well, it's the early days of this, it won't be good at first, but it'll get better over time. But instead, everyone went, 'Oh, wow!' 'What do you mean, *wow*? This sucks!' "

It was no mystery why the average person, regardless of the marketing, was so taken by CDs. They solved certain problems that afflicted LPs. "Speed control was corrected, noise, pops, clicks, resonance—all the problems of cheap turntables were solved by the CD," Fremer says. "What *wasn't* there was great, but what *was* there was terrible."

This sense that something was going horribly wrong in the global soundscape, and that they were the only ones who had ears sensitive enough to hear the problem, gave some of the anti-CD people a single-minded sense of purpose. "Oh God, they followed us around," Ahrold says. "They would find out we were doing a demo and they'd show up in the audience, and—I won't say they heckled, but it would be, 'How do you answer *this* question: *blah blah blah* . . . ?' It could be at an audiophile store or at Macy's—you'd see them there: 'Oh shit, *he* showed up again?' "

For the audio professionals who were against the CD, part of the problem was that the digital changeover had begun without their input. More than at any other time in the history of sound recording, the technicians' opinions simply did not matter. "They had their egos bruised by having consumer guys deciding what the quality of their sound was going to be," Lagadec says. They could deal with 99 percent of the public not knowing what "digital audio" meant: what galled them was that so many of the people involved in the making and selling of music seemed equally clueless. "A gulf of misunderstanding about just what digital recording is seems to be opening up between artists, producers, and record manufacturers on one side, and the studio business on the other," the Association of Professional Recording Studios, a British organization, wrote in an open letter published a few months after the first CDs went on the market. "In the private opinion of many on the studio side . . . an unhappily large proportion of those on the other side have no idea what they mean when they talk about 'digital records.' "

The CD's skeptics found an unlikely sympathetic audience: some of the people who actually built the CD. They noted that the myth of CD perfection seemed to be an American invention. "In Europe the CD was conceived as a mid-fi product from the beginning," Lagadec wrote in *Stereo Review* in 1985. "I have no argument whatever with people who say that the performance of CD players varies and that the best of CD is lagging behind the best of analog." America was not only where the myth flourished; it was also the site of the loudest backlash. "The most vocal people who made statements against the CD as the proper standard, both for final products and in the studio, were from the United States," Lagadec says. "You had these 'golden ears' all over the place."

"They were right, I think," Immink says of the CD's critics. "Because the quality of the analog-digital converters at the time was not [up] to our standards. Much later, we learned how to do it." Did Immink and the other engineers on the CD team ever consider telling their bosses that the compact disc did not sound as good as it should? "It was not our purpose to discuss that," he says. "It was up to the software makers, to the owners of the content."

Like no other product in the history of audio technology, the separate narratives about the CD as a new technology and a consumer object were completely intertwined—convoluted, even. "The truth is," Ahrold says, "we were learning digital mastering at the same time we were learning [to manufacture] compact discs, at the same time we were learning to market compact discs."

We all know how this story turned out. The CD, despite the dogged efforts of the analog loyalists, took over the world. Five years after entering the market with almost zero name recognition, the CD was the fastest-growing home entertainment product in history. In 1983, 800,000 CDs worth $17.2 million were shipped to retailers. By 1991, the number of CDs shipped topped 333 million, worth $4.3 billion. The number of CD players sold worldwide jumped from 350,000 in 1983 to 836,000 one year later, then increased almost 400 percent to 3 million, and then 9 million. By the early nineties, the annual figure had topped 40 million. More so than record companies had ever hoped, people methodically replaced their vinyl and cassettes with CDs, and that changeover kept the music industry expanding until 1997. Even after that, when the industry began to shrink under the weight of downloads and its own stodgy business model, the manufacture of CDs did not peak until 2000.

Analog loyalists commonly charge that the CD was about the music industry's reliance on innovation, no matter what the musical cost, as a means of economic survival. There is some truth to this, and the more honest among the CD's early architects and proponents have candidly acknowledged it. "The industry was in need of a format change," says Schulhof, noting that there has typically been a new breakthrough in audio technology every fifteen to twenty years, beginning with the move from Edison's cylinder to Berliner's disc. "The CD came along at the right time."

Jan Timmer of Philips considered the industry's slump to be an argument in favor of his company investing so much in developing the CD. There was a similar calculation on the Sony side. In 1981, Alan Kilkenny, Sony's public affairs director, was already describing the CD as not just a key component for the music industry's survival but also nothing less than historical inevitability. "The change from 78 RPM to LPs was nearly as important to the growth and survival of the home entertainment industry then, as the move from analog LP to Compact Discs is for us all now," he wrote. "If we want to ensure a future where the record companies can sell a product up to the standard at least of the domestic equipment which is going to play it in the home, [compact discs] point the way forward."

The music industry benefited from the CD in ways that went beyond just increasing the amount of product sold. When CDs were first introduced, the process of making them was expensive and the error rate was high. Five years later, the manufacturing costs dropped to $1.45 per disc and kept dropping. ("The question of manufacturing costs is really not one we're supposed to discuss," says Mike Mitchell, the executive vice president and general manager of Sony's Terre Haute plant. "It's not very much, though.")

The music industry also profited in a more subtle way. The aesthetic underpinnings of the "perfect sound forever" claim dovetailed nicely with the industry's image of itself in the future. Recall that Stockham launched the digital audio revolution by deciding that the perfect recording was one that captured the music faithfully without leaving any imprint of the recording apparatus. The most "surprising" thing about the concept of digital audio, he wrote, "is that, except for the use of a finite number of digits to represent each sample, the reconstructed audio can in theory be made to be *exactly* the same as the original." This idea was picked up by the developers of the compact disc, who introduced a metaphor familiar to fifties audiophiles. Philips called the CD a " 'transmission system' that brings the sound of an orchestra into the living room." An early commercial for Sony's CD players boasted, "Now Sony turns your living room, car, and backpack into a concert hall."

The idea in turn trickled down into mainstream discourse surrounding the CD. The CD made it possible to "go into a store and walk out with a *perfect duplicate* of original studio recordings," Glenn Kenney wrote in *Stereo Review*. The idea even surfaced in more scholarly places. "Digital recording," Andrew Goodwin, a critic and communications professor, wrote, "now ensures that the electronic encoding and decoding that takes place in capturing and then reproducing sound is such that there is *no discernible difference* between the sound recorded in the studio and the signal reproduced on the consumer's CD system." (All emphasis added.)

What was usually left unexplained was how exactly a CD could transfer the studio to the living room—and why an analog medium could not do the same thing. It would be one thing to believe that concert-hall-in-the-backpack rhetoric for music that had been recorded digitally, such as Telarc's CDs. But the vast majority of commercial records up to that point had been made from analog tape masters. And even if you believed that Stockham's notion of digital perfection was true, it was an undeniable fact that early CDs were hit-or-miss; they weren't made by people who knew or cared about deconvolution. So how was what you heard from a CD "exactly" the same as what the engineer at the original recording session heard in the booth?

There was a better way to argue for the validity of the "perfect sound forever" ethic, which was to note that the old audiophile-driven concert hall–living room dialectic had increasingly less relevance to how modern music was created. For most records, there was no original performance to be copied. As more music came to be recorded digitally, you could argue that the finished product was just a long string of code—not the accurate depiction of real-world sound events. And the reality of a digital system is that as long as the tokens are moved correctly within the margin of error, it is behaving perfectly. Lagadec, who never had a problem with the analog loyalists' criticisms of the CD, argues that the CD best reflects the realities of modern music. "You cannot reproduce what took place in the studio because there was no studio in the first place," he says. "There were many studios and individual sessions, and therefore the only thing you can reproduce is the stuff that has finally been mixed together at the last stage, and given to a very good mastering engineer. This can be reproduced very faithfully by CD, because you do not really try to reproduce an experience that never existed."

This is the true ideal of digital perfection, one that makes Stockham's original goal seem quaintly analog. The goal of perfection now has more to do with moving data around perfectly while maintaining its integrity—it is more about processing than recording in the traditional sense. This ideal naturally followed from the application, by Stockham and others, of Claude Shannon's information theory to the field of sound. Music really is just data.

To the industry, this sound-as-data ethic of perfection foretold a bright future, when entertainment could be sent anywhere and everywhere—a gold mine of a one-way communication model. As PolyGram's Peter Burkowitz observed, "through the last two decades, flexible sound processing apparently has been the pipe dream."

It couldn't last, of course. Even before MP3s began wreaking their havoc, there were cracks in the armor. The fragile alliance forged by the Compact Disc Group fell apart when Sony and Philips tried to follow up the CD with digital audiotape as the new consumer digital format. This time the labels said no way, fearing that DAT would bring copyrighted music to new heights of piracy (little did they know . . .). But for a while, the CD seemed like a beautiful future. Here's Sony's Alan Kilkenny, daring to dream in 1981: "The Compact Digital Audio Disc is another step in an exciting new age of digitized sound, and eventually one can envisage satellite broadcasting of the digital audio bitstream for ultimate conversion in the home . . . [S]ooner or later we can expect the link to the home to be digital as well, bringing live concerts into the home with alarming realism."

To which those of us parked in the twenty-first century, who have now endured a decade of the music industry complaining that it is drowning in the "digital audio bitstream of illicit downloads," might reasonably request of Kilkenny that he be careful what he wishes for in 1981. Soon enough, he and his colleagues would discover just how alarming realism could be.

Looking back, one of the most interesting things about the claims of the CD's "perfect sound" is that the parameters of this perfection were decided almost by default.

When the Sony-Phillips team was designing the CD in the late seventies, they kept putting off making key decisions regarding the quantization and sampling rate. The engineers were finally informed that if they didn't make those decisions soon, managers at the two companies would decide for them. After some debate, they settled on a 16-bit system, and a 44.1 kHz sampling rate. The 44.1 figure was a combination of science, habit, and expediency. Sony's PCM recorders sampled at just slightly over 44 kHz, a figure that corresponded to the maximum amount of two-channel digital audio information that could be stored on one frame of analog videotape. After long deliberations, and with time running out, the team settled on that figure, rounding up to 44.1 because "it was easier to remember," Immink says. "There was no other reason."

"For very practical reasons, it was okay to agree on 16 bits and 44 kHz," says Lagadec. "It was vastly superior to the LP and cassette. It worked well. But at the time there was a sort of tacit understanding that the world would not stop at 44.1."

But the world did stop at 44.1—at least until Sony's introduction in the nineties of the Super Audio CD, which doesn't use any PCM technology and offers superior sound. The compact disc, however, is frozen in time, just the way it was when it was dreamed up in 1980. And nothing reveals the way the analog-versus-digital debate forces hard science to collide with murkier psychoacoustics quite like the issue of 44.1.

Recall that the Nyquist-Shannon sampling theorem states that as long as the sampling rate is at least twice the Nyquist frequency (the highest frequency component of the sound being sampled), which in turn means the system has at least two chances to take a reading of the wave before the cycle ends, there should be enough data to reconstruct the sample perfectly. Since the absolute upper limit of human hearing is 20 kHz—and for most of us it's much lower—44.1 kHz, which requires a Nyquist frequency of 22.05 kHz, should be fine.

But there is another equally important component to the theorem: all frequencies higher than the Nyquist frequency must be eliminated completely. To do so requires something called a "low-pass filter," which every digital system contains. The theorem assumes the presence of a perfect low-pass filter, but in the real world there is no such thing. Some of those higher frequencies always manage to sneak through, and when they do, they introduce distortion into the system in the form of aliasing.

The best way to understand aliasing in the audio world is to consider a common example in the visual world. In old Westerns, the spinning wheels of fast-moving wagons sometimes appear to be going backward. This happens because the frames of the film are not moving fast enough to describe adequately the motion of the wheel's spokes; presented with this incomplete sketch, our eyes interpret the wheel as moving backward. The same principle holds for audio. A frequency above the Nyquist cutoff can "reflect backward." Suppose the sampling rate is 40 kHz. The Nyquist frequency will be 20 kHz. If a frequency of 22 kHz (2 kHz over the limit) gets through the filter, it will reflect back and sound just like an 18 kHz sound (2 kHz under the limit). Distortion has been introduced into the system.

Now consider the 44.1 rate. It should be fine. The Nyquist frequency—22.05 kHz—is well outside the range of human hearing. The presence of any frequencies up around the 22.05 kHz range shouldn't make a Nickelback CD less listenable, just as the billions of microscopic pits on its face don't make it less suitable as a coaster. But factor in the presence of an inevitably imperfect low-pass filter, and the margin for error decreases. If a sound with a frequency of 24 kHz passes through the filter, the aliased result will be indistinguishable from a sound with a frequency of just above 20 kHz. We're suddenly back near the range of human hearing, where this distortion matters.

The 44.1 figure raised some eyebrows. As early as 1971, Stockham had argued that the cutoff frequency should be at least 45 percent of the sampling frequency. That's why the Soundstream recorder sampled at 50 kHz; there was a larger margin for error, as any aliasing was less likely to reflect back into the audible realm. "I think Tom felt that Sony was walking on thin ice with 44.1," says Bloomenthal.

Complicating the issue further is the fact that 20 kHz is really the extreme upper limit of human hearing. A typical twenty-five-year-old cannot hear anything above 13 kHz. This reality would seem to make the possibility of audible aliasing occurring at 44.1 kHz much more remote. However, there are those who argue that by making the cutoff frequency 20 kHz, the music suffers, regardless of what the normal range of human hearing supposedly is. "If you ask a guy with so-called 'golden ears' what will happen if you restrict bandwidth to between 20 and 20,000 Hz," Lagadec says, "his response will be, the proles won't notice, but by God *he* will."

One thing that Telarc's Bob Woods valued about the Soundstream recorder was that the 50 kHz sampling rate meant the cutoff frequency could be 25 kHz. Regardless of whether one could hear these upper frequencies, they were necessary. "Even for people with limited hearing," he says, "my experience is that if something is missing in the reproduction system, you'll hear a change in timbre, color, or other qualities that make an instrument sound like what it sounds like."

"The reductionists will say that the human ear cannot hear beyond a certain range, so there is no point in saving these frequencies," says Akin Fernandez, the musician, label owner, and antidigital activist. "We say that sound is not only heard, it is also *felt*, and that we should be striving to increase the resolution of our recording and playback systems, not trying to constrain them for convenience or to fit inside the constraints of the current technology."

Steve Albini, one of the earliest analog loyalists, has engineered hundreds of albums since his "fuck digital" declaration. He still hates CDs, though he long ago decided not to fall into the trap of trying to explain what exactly made them sound bad. "The only way I can quantify it is to say that I listen to master tapes all day every day for a living," he says. "If there's a master tape that I'm familiar with, and I hear it on a vinyl record and on CD, as long as the vinyl LP is properly manufactured, it always sounds more like I remember the tape sounding . . . The CD doesn't sound as good, and I don't know why that's the case. I want to stay out of the game of guessing what the problem is, expecting that there's one simple solution to this. I think the CD standard is very crude. It was standardized so early that it wasn't possible to standardize it at a high level of resolution. It was the bare minimum they could do to get by. They wanted to get a digital product out as soon as possible."

Even for Albini, a go-to voice for the proanalog view, there are shades of gray. A few years ago, he was doing a mastering session for the Breeders' *Title TK* album at Abbey Road in London. He listened to the original stereo master tapes, a copper reference playback disc made from a test cut, and the high-resolution 24-bit digital made from the output of the mixing board. "All three of those sounded great to me," he says. Then someone played the digital version down-sampled to 16 bits/44.1 kHz, the version that would go on the CD. "I kind of got a lump in my gut, like 'Oh, *this* is what people are gonna listen to?' It was a real bring-down. I guess it does take serious attentive listening and a constant exposure to things to recognize when something shits the bed on you in that way, but I don't think the CD format is capable of exceptional sound."

Of course, some pros will claim the exact opposite. "When people say 'You should hear that record on vinyl, that's how it's supposed to sound,' that's a lot of crap," says Bob Clearmountain. "I suffered through mastering records for years and years, and it was always a huge disappointment. I'd get my reference [disc], and go, 'Jeez, is that it? Is that all I get for all that work?' It was awful. You'd have to make all these compromises with vinyl, just to get the needle to not jump out of the groove. There were all these things you couldn't do, all these rules. And then finally, when digital came along, even the early days with CDs that were harsher, it was like, well, at least I'm not losing everything I lost on a vinyl record."

It is possible to be a digital audio pioneer and still believe that people like Albini and Neil Young have a valid point. "I could probably have run a test that made him look silly," Lagadec says of Young. "But what would I have accomplished? I would have made a technical test that said that according to a very simple criterion, Neil Young could not hear beyond 14 or 15 kHz or so. But he is a genius. He knows everything there is to know about sound, and if I were to compare what he says with the result of a test that I engineered, I would say screw the test, he knows what he's talking about."

Doug Sax, another original analog loyalist, long ago made peace with digital as the technology improved. But he still remembers feeling vindicated as some of the original digital hoopla died down. "I had some of my best customers say, 'Doug, I love your work, but . . .' and they'd go to New York and [make a record] on a digital console," he says. "Well, a couple of them came back in two years. They'd left because I didn't have a digital console, and they *came back* because I didn't have a digital console. One said, 'I don't know what it is, but when I run it through this place [Sheffield's studio] it sounds like a record.' "

That assessment—"it sounds like a record"—may go a long way toward explaining the analog-versus-digital divide. As with most matters relating to analog and digital, it takes us back to Stockham. He had no problem with people preferring analog to digital, as long as they didn't invoke "accuracy" as part of their argument. What these people liked about analog, he maintained, were things added to the record by the system—distortion that was perceived as warmth and so on. Stockham was trying to eliminate the effect of the medium altogether. "This is a matter of 'fidelity' versus 'what you like,' " he said in 1994, commenting on the debate. "I have no feelings of any type that people shouldn't like what they like. But I do get upset when people don't understand that what you like might not be exactly like the original you were trying to put back together in the recording process. There's nothing wrong with not putting it back together the same as it was; it might even be a lot more fun. But if you're talking about fidelity, you shouldn't say that you don't have it when you do."

This ethos was at the heart of the Soundstream mission. On the day Bloomenthal met Sax in L.A., he encountered another engineer who happened to be raving about the sound of a certain mixing board. The problem with the antidigital contingent suddenly made sense. "There shouldn't be a 'sound' to a board," Bloomenthal says. "It's like water or air. There shouldn't be a smell in pure air, there shouldn't be a taste to pure water, and there shouldn't be a sound to the mixing board. It ought to be totally transparent. And that was my first inkling that these people who religiously believed in tubes or vinyl or direct-to-disc, there's a sound there they like, but from Dr. Stockham's point of view, where fidelity is the main thing, that sound is a distortion. They may like the sound of the distortion, but don't tell me that it's a higher-quality recording system."

In the CD era, a Boston-based recording engineer named E. Brad Meyer has done some of the most extensive empirical analysis of the analog/digital debate and reached conclusions that seem to support the Soundstream view. Meyer began with a conundrum: as an engineer he was convinced that the CD was capable of reproducing his master tapes better than an LP. And yet he had to admit that an LP sometimes sounded "smoother, more delicately detailed, rounder, gentler, and more accessible—more musical, if you will," when compared with the same album on CD. He wondered, "Why does the achievement of what appeared to be a long-sought ideal—the delivery to the consumer of the master tape—sometimes fail to satisfy us?"

Meyer concluded that the sonic differences between an LP and a CD was not due to any supposed shortcomings in the way a well-made CD is put together. There is no inherent weakness in the digital process. Rather, the differences arise from "euphonic effects of the analog record/playback chain." For example, a turntable's stylus often has difficulty reproducing upper treble sounds. "These frequency-response errors turn out to be crucial to the LP's 'musicality,'" he argued. "Many links in the recording chain, including the microphones, were designed with LPs in mind, so many master tapes are too bright in the upper midrange and lower treble. The LP system tends to tame that hardness. Otherwise, the sound is always mildly irritating, and the listener is slightly but constantly repelled, making it very hard to relax and enjoy the music."

In other words, if it's accuracy you want, you should go with the CD, assuming it has been made with care. But maybe it's not accuracy you want. "If you could find strange creatures that had never been exposed to music, and you were to make a comparison for them between the best-manufactured LP on the planet and the CD version of the same recording, and then ask which sounds better, they would look at you strangely and ask whether you are out of your mind," Lagadec says. "Because to them, with no musical tradition, the CD would obviously be running circles around the

LP. But these are people without musical experience, without long-term exposure to the sound of analog tapes and the sound of LPs and so on. The people that pass [proanalog] judgments have been—all of them—living in the musical universe for a long time, and what they have become familiar with in their formative years is very naturally what they take as a reference."

"We learned one very clear thing about LPs," Woods says. "All you gotta do is take the blank lacquer, have no signal coming down, cut a series of silent grooves, put it onto a turntable and what do you get? You get"—he makes a soft hissing sound—"a nice, soft, round, pink noise. Everything you're listening to on an LP is being heard through that filter of pink noise. And so it has the tendency to feather the edges of things. It gives the record a sense of a little warmth. Violins sound like *really special* violins. But if you stand in front of a real violin, it's got some grit. It's got a little edge to it."

Maybe Rothstein had it backward when he wrote that CDs "end up sounding not like perfect sound, but like perfectly unreal sound." Maybe our world really does sound like a CD, and what an analog fan wants, like Sax's returning client, is a record that sounds like a record. Maybe the analog impulse isn't so much about absolute truth as it is utopian. The analog fan longs for the days when there was a clear boundary between reality and its representation, because maybe in the sound of their favorite records they hear a better world.

If there's no consensus on the "perfect" issue, can we all at least agree that the sound is "forever"?

No, it turns out, we cannot.

In the northern New Mexico desert, about 125 miles east of Santa Fe, patterns are carved into the desert floor. Viewed from above, they form a linked pattern of circles and diamonds, the logo of the Church of Spiritual Technology, a wing of the Scientologists. They mark the spot of an underground vault built into a mountainside. Inside, steel-lined tunnels—supposedly strong enough to withstand the effects of a nuclear war—hold thousands of titanium records stored in protective metal boxes. The records contain recordings of speeches by Scientology founder L. Ron Hubbard. According to reports, the records can be played on a specially designed solar-powered turntable.

The church won't confirm any details, but the idea behind the turntable is that in the aftermath of a catastrophic global holocaust, our species might have to start over completely. The directions for using the turntable are given in pictograms because who knows what language will be like in the world that rises from the ashes? The turntable is self-powering because who knows how long it will take the new world's denizens to learn the trick of harnessing electricity? There is another argument in favor of building and maintaining this turntable, one that raises the profoundly annoying possibility that the Scientologists may actually be right about something.

The idea of "forever," so important a component of the digital mystique, may turn out to be one of digital's biggest myths. "For me, the overriding problem with digital systems—and this has been their problem since their advent—is that they are impermanent," Albini says. "The reason it's called 'sound recording' is that you are making what is meant to be a permanent record of an event. And there is no digital technology that is capable of making a permanent recording in the sense that an analog technology could, whether that be a wax cylinder or any magnetic analog recording. Those are all effectively permanent. Barring someone going out of his way to physically destroy the medium, it's there for good."

An analog recording on magnetic tape is a continuous pattern of magnetized particles that can be damaged or altered. A digital recording, whether on DAT or some sort of hard drive, is just a string of numbers. But the magnetic tape is remarkably robust; stick it in a food dehydrator every twenty years or so, and there's no reason the tape can't have an indefinite life span. The digital data, however, is a prisoner of its host medium. If something goes wrong with that medium, the data is lost forever. Sax says he often hears engineers complain about the problems caused by old hard drives. "The truth is, when you're remastering albums that are forty years old, the master tapes moan and groan, but they play," he says. "With digital, when the hard drive won't play, they can't retrieve the thing. It's gone."

DAT has proven particularly troublesome. Once DAT failed to become a consumer format in the eighties, DAT machines became a cheap alternative to expensive tape machines in low-budget recording studios. "DAT was never intended to be a master format," Albini says. "Sony and Philips needed to find a way to make their money back on the DAT machine, so they pressed it into service for broadcast audio."

"Consider all the music that was recorded onto DAT and PCM-1630"— Sony's early U-matic digital tape recorder—"as the sole master," Fernandez says. "This was done regularly from the early nineties up to today. All those recordings are unfaithful. Many of the DATs recorded back then will not play cleanly. They drop out and glitch and engineers have to run the tape back and forth to try and get a clean pass on the broken parts so that they can edit together a restored version of the master. The true scale of this disaster has not yet begun to dawn on the people who have these tapes stored."

Albini concurs: "I'd bet my house against a doughnut that for the next hundred years there will be more working analog tape machines than DAT machines."

There is an even more insidious problem with digital systems. As much as binary code might be a universal language, the methods of processing it are always evolving. "There really isn't an archival medium for digital data," Albini explains. "Computer technology has changed so rapidly that drive specifications and media specifications change constantly. That's one of the benefits of the computer paradigm—it changes quickly to adapt to its market. But it also makes formats into orphans. Lets say you discovered a nine-track tape of a digital audio recording. What would you do with it? You wouldn't be able to play it. You wouldn't be able to decipher the audio that's on it. Even if you could find something to play it back to, you'd need to find some way of looking at the file, some way of determining what that data meant. It's a virtually irretrievable recording once the specific system it was recorded on is no longer in use." The mighty compact disc may not be immune to this vicious evolution. "The vinyl record will certainly outlast CDs. I don't think we will see the end of vinyl LP manufacture in my lifetime."

It's too early to know if this dystopia is what's in store for our digital audio world. But if it ever comes, a lot of music will no longer make a sound. Neil Young said we'd wake up one day and wonder what the digital age really sounded like. What an awful question to ask and literally not be able to answer.

There sure are a lot of things to hate about CDs. The flimsy jewel cases, the annoying antitheft bar-code stickers, the shadowy embedded layers of antipiracy code, the death of cover art—they all seem symptomatic of a culture of mediocrity and utility slipping into a surveillance state. As for their sound, the problem for me isn't so much the harshness, a common complaint. It's more the sensation of distance I feel between me and the music. There's a disagreeable, frictionless quality to the sound that may be the downside of substituting a phantom laser for the diamond stylus.

It never occurred to me that my distaste was some sort of pathology. I hadn't entertained the option that CDs made me sick. But I wanted a professional opinion, so I sought out Dr. John Diamond, the man who sounded the alarm about the impending digital apocalypse when the CD was still an optic glimmer in the corporate eye. On a rainy fall night I found his home at the end of a wooded cul-de-sac in a hilly part of Westchester County, New York. Diamond welcomed me into the room at the back of the house where he sees patients. Shelves crammed with records covered the walls, and a drum set sat in the corner.

Diamond, who positively exudes health, served peppermint tea. I asked him about his infamous appearance at the 1979 AES convention. "It has been said that 1,100 people were there, but 50,000 said they were," he said, echoing the famous claim about Dylan at Newport. "After I made that presentation, I got clobbered from on high, especially by Pioneer and various companies. The only people who took me seriously were some TV stations." He wrote up his findings, went back to his practice, and watched the world kill itself by degrees as digital audio swept the planet. "We had this one window of opportunity in all of civilization to use recordings to help people and not stress them," he says. "But nothing happened."

To hear Diamond tell it, many people have quietly admitted to him that he's right. He claims that he tried to contact Stockham prior to the AES conference, and wound up speaking to his wife, Martha, who told Diamond, "I'm so glad you found a problem, because my husband gets a headache every time he listens to his records." (Martha Stockham denies that her husband, who died in 2004, ever experienced any physical ailments caused by listening to Soundstream records, denies ever telling Diamond that he did, and says that Tom was convinced that Diamond was a shill for people pushing direct-to-disc analog recording.) Diamond notes that today there is even a term—"digital fatigue"—to describe the feeling people get from listening to digital audio. "Over the years, I spoke in the wilderness," he said. "I just had to wait twenty or twenty-five years, and it's all coming around. Sales of CDs are going down, and more people are complaining, but they don't really know what they're complaining about. They say it's not warm, it's unfriendly. The point is that people aren't listening to music like they used to. They put it on as background. It's convenient. Well, a prostitute is convenient, but it isn't making love."

Diamond isn't exactly an analog purist. He has no truck for audiophilia of any sort. "Sound quality is such a stupid idea," he said. "To imagine that the Berlin Philharmonic is in your room is a form of psychosis, somehow." He folds his distaste for digital into a larger critique of modern alienation. "The only reason that CDs can exist, that digital can exist, is because we have lost touch with our feelings. We have no feeling anymore. Kentucky Fried Chicken: what a wonderful *feeling*! The latest violent movie: what a wonderful *feeling*!"

I asked him what he believed happens when someone hears digital audio. "Regardless of the musical source, it puts the person into a state of hatred," he said. "That's the word for it: hatred. And this is what is increasingly killing our society. Think about it. Virtually every communication we have—radios, telephones, television programs, everything our exalted president receives—is coming through digital. And this is what, in part, is behind [events like] Columbine."

A digital-free world, he said, would be a less violent world. So listening to digital audio is itself a violent act?

"It is, it is. Because we see it as an act of violence toward us. And so we respond in defense."

But what exactly happens physiologically?

"I'm not telling you. It's not physiological. It affects the acupuncture system."

Diamond explained that he knows the problem, and he has a working prototype of something that would solve it. He implied that this solution might exist in microchip form, but says he doesn't want to go into detail for fear that someone will steal his idea. He has no interest in doing an organized, double-blind study, because he believes that no matter what he did, the industry would still find a way to discredit him.

By now we had been joined by his assistant, Erica, and his wife, Susan, an opera singer who shares her husband's healthy glow. Diamond said he'd use me to demonstrate the pernicious effects of digital audio. I stood up while Erica cued a record, one of the early digital recordings mastered onto vinyl. "This is just a demonstration," Diamond said. "The first negative response occurs instantaneously and lasts for between fifteen seconds and a couple of minutes, depending on how healthy you are. Then it changes and goes to another situation."

Diamond told me to extend my left arm, palm facing up. He pressed down on a point behind my elbow, and told me to resist the pressure by keeping my arm at a right angle. Erica dropped the needle on the record. As the music played, I kept my arm up. After a few seconds, Diamond removed his hand. He repeated the pressing two more times, and I was able to resist with little effort.

The music started again, and Diamond pressed on my arm. "Life is good," he said. "Say that: 'Life is good.' "

"Life is good," I repeated.

"Life is bad." Diamond nodded at me.

"Life is bad." My arm swung toward the ground. His pressing didn't feel any different, but I couldn't keep my arm up.

"Health is good," he said.

"Health is good." My strength returned, although his touch still felt the same.

"Love is good."

"Love is good." Still going strong.

"Hate is good."

"Hate is good," I agreed. My arm swung down again.

Erica stopped the music.

"We will now play the record for a minute or so, and you will now test it with 'hate is good' and 'love is bad,' and 'life is bad' and 'death is good.' That's what digital is doing to the bloody world. It's reversing what I call our inner morality on an unconscious level."

At Susan's suggestion, everyone but me took a few drops of Life Energy Plus, a mostly herbal supplement that Diamond has put together, which he says mitigates some of the negative effects of digital. The music started again. "You're going to test weak, weak, weak, and suddenly you will test strong, because your body now has everything reversed."

And when the music started again, that's what happened. If the message was "love is bad," I had the will to resist, if love was said to be good, my arm gave out. When the choice was between "life" and "death," death gave me strength. It wasn't as though my muscles felt stronger or weaker, and it didn't seem like Diamond was pushing any harder. But judging from my body's reaction, something was making me hate love and love death.

"That's how you've been turned around," Diamond said, removing his hand. "And that's what that fucking stuff is doing all the time all over the fucking world!"

"What happened to me just then?"

"Your brain got fried," Diamond replied. "You got turned around. We have an inner morality that says you don't kill people, you don't do all these negative things. Yet after this you're inclined the other way. It doesn't mean you'll do it, but for example, if you're driving, and you can cut a guy off, you're more likely to cut him off. And so on and so on and so on."

There is much about Diamond's theory and demo to be skeptical of, to say the least. If Diamond knows what the problem is, as a doctor shouldn't he tell the world? Shouldn't somebody be doing trials on the chip or whatever it is that Diamond says can fix the problem? And then there's the matter of the test itself. Diamond's probably right that no amount of "proof" could dislodge the global digital audio infrastructure, but a successful double-blind test would send shock waves through the audio world. As for my experience, assuming that Diamond wasn't subtly changing the force of his pushing, or moving his hand subtly onto or off of an acupuncture pressure point, there's still a chance that I was influenced by what I expected to happen, or even what I hoped would happen. Did I want my antidigital opinions reinforced? Did the test prove that my ears shape my worldview, or that my worldview is a filter for my ears? I'll never know. But *something* happened to me that made my arm go down.

Of course, the persuasion might be the whole point of the exercise, whether Diamond realizes it or not. His reluctance to make it scientific only seems strange if you think of Diamond as a doctor and his muscle test as a health diagnostic. Considered as a tone tester, the methodology makes sense. He's part of a rich Edisonian tradition of people trying to convince the world to hear through their ears. Right or wrong, visionary or quack, Diamond is responding to a world where the phonograph has never stopped playing, to the point where it's playing us.

"Just imagine I'm right," he said as I headed for the door. "I mean, okay, if you want to do proofs, proofs, proofs, you have to pay me for that. But just imagine I'm right!"

7

The Story of the Band That Clipped Itself to Death (and Other Dispatches from the Loudness War)

It had been four years since the last Red Hot Chili Peppers album, and much had changed in the music business. Growth had slowed, the industry was unstable and rife with mergers and firings, the Internet was screwing up the business plan, and the "alternative rock" juggernaut was waning. The Chili Peppers had ridden that wave with their four-times-platinum 1991 album *Blood Sugar Sex Magik*, and then waited four years for the follow-up, *One Hot Minute*, which had gone platinum only once. The band had managed to hang together through fifteen years of drugs, death, and personnel changes, but nobody in this business seemed to have "careers" anymore. For the Chili Peppers to do it again, they'd have to hit the ground running like a breakout act.

The Chili Peppers made *Californication* with longtime producer Rick Rubin and engineer Jim Scott. The finished recording was given to mastering engineer Vlado Meller, whose job was to perform the final steps that would turn it into a CD. The most significant thing he did was to make the music sound big and leap-out-of-your-speakers loud.

"Scar Tissue," the first single from *Californication*, was released to radio a few weeks before the album was available. There were hundreds of radio engineers out there ready and willing to do to their stations' signals what Meller had done to *Californication*. They, too, wanted an explosive, attention-getting sound.

Every station had its own unique way of processing its signal, but typically the first thing the signal would encounter is something called a phase rotator. The sound of the human voice is volatile and often produces an erratic signal that can cause distortion when heard on the air. The phase rotator smooths out this signal. In doing so, it radically changes the shape of the waveform generated by the voice. This didn't present a problem for CDs a few years earlier, before people like Meller started making them sound so loud, but for a song engineered like "Scar Tissue" the phase rotator had unintended consequences. *Californication* had been mastered at such a high level that there were times when the signal was too "hot" for the CD system to handle. At these moments—too brief to hear consciously—the signal ceased to exist. One unintended effect of the phase rotator was that these areas were now distributed randomly throughout the song, dotting it with little bits of missing detail—each one "a bit like a scar from a severe burn," as two radio-processing masterminds put it, giving new meaning to the song's title. "Scar Tissue" had barely begun its processing journey, and it was already damaged goods.

The next step was automatic gain control (AGC). The AGC's most basic function was to regulate levels to compensate for any wide swings caused by the DJ's voice, but it had also come to be an essential tool to deal with the growing disparity of the loudness of current commercial recordings versus those from earlier eras. Without AGC, you'd have to constantly adjust your radio's volume control. A typical rock or pop station, the kind that would play "Scar Tissue," would have already reached the conclusion that sounding less loud than its competitors was commercial death, so AGC was used to keep the signal loud at all times. Any significant differences between soft and loud parts of a song would be much harder to hear on the radio. It was all loud, all the time.

After going through some stereo enhancement and equalization, the next stop was a multiband processor. The processor separated out the music's different frequencies into several groups—low bass, semilow bass, midrange, treble, etc.—and then processed each separately. Any peaks in volume were squashed and the softer parts were moved up, so that there was little difference between the music's average level and its peak level. The problem was that Meller had already done something similar in the mastering process, and these radio processors were designed for records made in a bygone era (just a few years earlier) of not-so-extreme loudness. The processors were programmed to look for peaks in the signal, but "Scar Tissue" didn't really have peaks. It was more like one gigantic peak. Encountering "Scar Tissue," the multiband processor concluded its job was to squash that peak, which is to say, it clamped down on the whole song, not just on isolated points.

The end result was that when the new Red Hot Chili Peppers single—which had been mastered to sound as loud as possible and thus herald the return of this mighty band—came blasting out of the speakers, it actually sounded less loud than records the station was playing that were mastered at much lower levels. To be clear: "Scar Tissue" was made to sound big, broadcast via a process designed to make radio stations sound big, and came out on the other end sounding smaller than it would have, had it not been made to sound big in the first place.

You couldn't ask for a better symbol of the strange state of music in the last moments of the twentieth century. It was a time when the recording industry responded to the increased dynamic range that digital technology offered over analog by making records whose dynamic range was narrower than those of the analog era. When the craft of making records was locked in a death race to see who could use digital audio to its *least* potential. When one of the leading practitioners of that craft, someone who had been involved with the making of *Californication* and was horrified at the way it sounded in the end, found himself unable to listen to virtually any CD made since 1992 straight through in one sitting. When a Chili Peppers fan launched a petition drive to get the band to make records that weren't so loud.

We need to ask ourselves some hard questions. What would make a highly respected mastering engineer—somebody who literally makes records for a living—suddenly unable to listen to any recording for more than a few minutes at a time? What could make fans of the sort of rock band who perform naked except for genital socks want the band to quit making such a racket?

What happened to music in the nineties?

I first heard "Wingwalker," by the Chicago band Shellac, in 1993 or 1994. One of two songs contained on a 45 rpm vinyl record called *Uranus*, "Wingwalker" is ostensibly about a woman who performs acrobatic feats on the wing of an airborne plane. But I like to think that the real subject is the record itself, the singular uniqueness of this material object. (In classic postpunk fashion, the sleeve lists every component used to make and manufacture the disc.) I can't play it for you, so I'll do the next best thing. I'll show it to you.

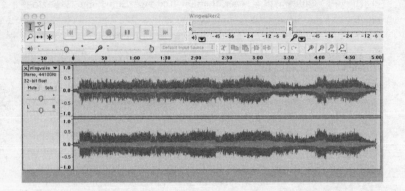

The graph expresses the power of the signal from moment to moment. The farther the dark areas extend on either side of the 0.0 in the middle of each channel, the greater the signal's power.

Those first few seconds, where the signal is small, are Bob Weston's bass line, which he'll play for most of the song. It's the plane's engine revving up and starting down the runway.

Guitarist Steve Albini declares: "Time was, I could move my arms like a bird . . ."

Drummer Todd Trainer comes in with a whiplash fill; the wheels are lifting up . . .

". . . and FLYYYYY . . ." As Albini screams, his guitar issues some feedback that sounds like a siren and somehow evokes a kite whipping in the wind. It feels like those first few moments of flight, when you will yourself to believe that this metallic beast will get off the ground. You can see this all happening with that big spike at around the eight-second mark. Then, all at once, the screaming and guitar drop out. We're at cruising altitude.

"She was a wingwalker, the 'it girl' of the sky . . ."

Albini plays a little melodic line that meshes with the bass and drums. It's the graceful acrobatics. The separation is clear. We're listening to a man narrate a story about a woman on a plane. "And now I got an engine, a big perverted engine, runs on strength of will. Who could deny me the right to fly?" Now Albini *is* the woman on the wings of the plane. "You know it's my art—when I form my body in the shape of a plane . . ." And now the woman is acting like a plane. That spike at around the two-minute mark is the chorus crashing in. Albini's guitar is in lockstep with the rhythm. Man, woman, and plane make a synchronized climb for a higher altitude. The engines are firing; the signal stays strong as the band tumbles over itself throughout the guitar-drenched chorus.

"I'm a plane! I'm a PLAAAAANE!"

It's a violent transformation. The scream continues and the feedback has returned. And then all of a sudden—that drop at 2:20—we're out of the chorus and the guitar is soon doubling the bass exactly. The transformation is now apparently complete. "Now I got an airframe, a big perverted airframe . . . you know, it's my art . . . when I disguise my body in the shape of a plane!" We're back into the chorus—that spike around 2:42.

"I'm a plane!" the wingwalker says.

"I'm *a plane*!" Weston screams.

Albini/wingwalker: "I'm a PLAAAAAANNNE!"

And now everything falls apart. But as the song collapses, the signal initially gets stronger, as you can see at the three-minute mark, before dipping precipitously. The bass drops out completely, the guitar feeds back, Trainer slams his sticks repeatedly against a cymbal so hard it sounds like it's raining in the studio. Has the plane crashed? Albini and Weston sound possessed. "Look at me," they keep saying, "I'm a plane!"

As the rainy wash of the cymbals continues, the wingwalker loses it entirely. All the layers of representation—a crystal-clear recording of a band impersonating a woman impersonating a plane—collapse. Albini's babbling: "And a plane becomes a metaphor for my life . . . and I suffer for it . . . how it shines, and as it shines . . . so she suffers . . . under the weight of my plane . . . you know, it's my art . . . it's my art . . . when I disguise my body in the shape of a plane!" Is he speaking for her? For himself? Is this about his art, making a record? The rain continues, and then the bass begins again. The engine is apparently revving. The rain suddenly stops, Trainer slams into that drum fill, and we're airborne again. That spike at around the four-minute mark is the explosion of feedback and screaming: "PLAAAAAANE!" That drop about nine seconds later marks the end of both. Now it's just the steady rhythm of the engine. And then graceful acrobatics of the guitar. The band starts to wind down around 4:40. Was this all in her head? In our heads? At the end, it's just the guitar playing the bass line and Trainer playing as softly as he can. She's either landed, flown off into the horizon, or ascended to heaven. That final spike at the end is a subdued cymbal crash.

Hearing "Wingwalker" capped a period of about ten years of my life when it seemed like every few months I'd discover a new piece of music that made me think, Wow, I didn't know music could sound like that. (It started with R.E.M.'s *Reckoning* in 1984.) I remember the music as almost having its own autonomy—being almost frightened of the way the Feelies' *Crazy Rhythms*, heard in the dark, seemed to make the air visibly ripple, or wondering how it was that Public Enemy's *It Takes a Nation of Millions to Hold Us Back* seemed to erase the audible world's low frequencies while still somehow offering an enormously powerful version of low end. You can represent any recording with a picture like the one of "Wingwalker," a two-dimensional shape defined by an *x* and *y* axis. The records I discovered during those ten years seemed to add a third dimension, becoming an actual physical presence in the world. And more than that, they were special enough to add the fourth dimension of time, so that the music not only existed as an object, it also *moved* in the world, imprinting itself by the way that its shape—the peaks and valleys that defined the wingwalker's physical and psychological journey—seemed to make the air molecules dance as the shape unraveled.

"Wingwalker" was the apotheosis of that decade because it seemed—to my ears—to be the full realization of that process. It was the product of people who wanted to capture a once-in-a-lifetime sonic event as accurately as possible, done so powerfully that the process of using a record to exploit that possibility of musical shape-shifting was taken to a new level. Listening to "Wingwalker" was like watching a great play from the front row: the actors are close enough to touch, but at the same time a world away. Any recorded sound can be made loud by turning up the volume, but to me "Wingwalker" was itself the loudest thing I'd ever heard because it couldn't be ignored.

My point is this: a great piece of recorded music has its own shape. It sounds great to us because it takes that shape and makes it move. But it begins with the shape. No other song ever made sounds quite like "Wingwalker," just as surely as no other looks like it.

So let's jump ahead another decade or so, and look at another song. This is a picture of the Black Eyed Peas' "Let's Get It Started."

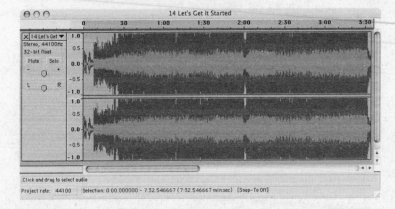

As you can see, it has almost no shape at all. It's just a solid wash of color. Bob Katz has this to say about "Let's Get It Started": "one of the worst-sounding, most distorted, overcompressed, and maybe the hottest pop record ever made." We'll get to what the third criticism has to do with the first two, but for now let's just clarify the fourth—"hottest pop record ever made"—starting with the fact that it's not a compliment. In the recording world, a "hot" record is one that has been recorded to sound very loud. It is a record that is loud even if your volume control is low.

Katz is a mastering engineer who runs Digital Domain, a mastering studio located in a suburb of Orlando, Florida. Back in the eighties, he began to notice that the advent of the compact disc was having a peculiar effect on music. Every year CDs seemed to be getting hotter. When a new loud benchmark was reached, somebody else figured out a way to go even louder. It was nothing less than a loudness war.

There were loudness wars that predated this one, but they were mostly low-key and played out either in the recording or radio world, but not both at once. The one Katz noticed was taking place on both fronts, aided and abetted by the advent of digital audio, and it was being fought with an unprecedented intensity. It was so severe that it deserves its own proper noun nomenclature: the Loudness War.

If Katz wasn't literally the first person to notice the gathering storm clouds of this war, he was definitely the first person to understand its implications for music. "I took notice ten years before," Katz says, "but I had to wait for the world to catch up with me."

The effects of the war are easy to hear. "Today, if you accidentally put

on the current loudest disc after your favorite loudest disc from ten or fifteen years ago, you could damage your ears or the player," Katz says.
You've probably experienced something similar at one time or another: your
CD player switches discs, and the next one sounds either irritatingly loud
or annoyingly soft. If almost all of your shuffled music is loud, soon enough
you'll forget that the not-so-loud ones need to be turned up, and it will seep
into the background. Imagine the nonloud music is your band, or released
on your label, or being broadcast by your radio station, and you understand
the basic impetus for the war.

Katz had singled out the Black Eyed Peas song as one that "really
fucked it up" for anyone hoping for a semblance of sanity in the conduct of
this war. Once I paid attention to how it sounds, Katz promised, "It'll freak
you out." After listening to it, I knew what he meant. The song was firing on
all cylinders all the time. As you can see from the picture, after the song's
intro, the rest of the signal looks like somebody painted the signal onto the
picture with a thick brush.

But you could be forgiven for hearing the song and yet not hearing the
problem. That's because this is the way music sounds today. Consider two
other sonic pictures, which I chose more or less at random, and because I
like the songs. The first is "The Fallen," by Franz Ferdinand, and the second is "The Seed," by the Roots.

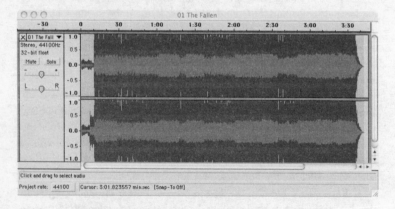

Both songs have that same painted-on look. "The Fallen" begins with a
two-measure guitar riff intro. Midway through the second bar, the drums

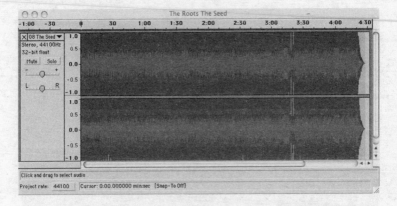

crash in, and the rest of the song is unrelentingly hot. "The Seed" follows a similar trajectory. From this extreme aerial view of the song, you can't even see the brief intro to the Roots song—three beats of ?uestlove's snare drum.

Now look at two songs from older CDs: the title track of Neil Young's 1975 album *Tonight's the Night*, from the original CD release in 1990, and the Pixies' "Where Is My Mind?" from the CD release of their 1988 album *Surfer Rosa*.

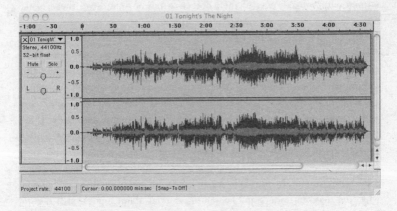

The peaks of both songs don't come anywhere near the top of the picture. In the early days of CDs, mastering engineers were wary of pushing the technology to extreme loudness because of concerns that it would over-

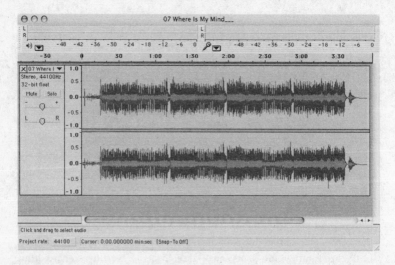

whelm the first generations of CD players. They left it to the consumer to decide how loud the CD should be. Keep in mind that simply by turning up the volume, you can make these songs jump out of the speakers as much as "The Fallen" and "The Seed." Ultimately, the intrinsic power of both songs is not compromised, even if their objective power—the level those peaks reach in the pictures—is less than it could be.

It's easy to see why the newer songs sound louder than the older ones: the new songs slam against that sonic ceiling, and those old songs don't come anywhere near it. This is true, but it's not true enough. Look at this picture of Massive Attack's "Angel," from their 1998 album *Mezzanine*. Each of those spikes is a drum beat, alternating between kick and snare, with the hi-hat and occasional crash cymbal bubbling underneath. Those spikes are hitting the top of the picture, or coming very close, meaning that every second or so the signal is reaching, or nearly reaching, maximum loudness. The signal doesn't have that painted-on look, but it's still spending a lot of time at the top. Yet "Angel" does not sound loud. To understand why, you need to understand something crucial about loudness: It doesn't really exist.

Most likely, you've heard the loudness of sounds described in terms of decibels (dB). Unlike an objective unit of measurement such as a mile or a

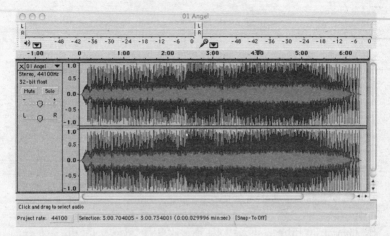

pound, a decibel has no intrinsic value. A mile is a mile no matter where you are; a pound of feathers weighs the same as a pound of lead. But what a decibel is depends on the context, because a decibel is just a way to compare one value with another.

You'll often hear audio people mention "0 dB." The term does not refer to silence. It means "the sound to which all others are compared" ("ground-zero dB," if you will). What it stands for can vary greatly. The decibel level of a sound describes its power, or "intensity," relative to 0 dB, which is a barely audible sound (130 dB is usually the threshold of pain). In digital audio systems, 0 dB refers to 0 dBFS or "full scale"—the most powerful signal the system can handle—with all other values expressed as decibels below full scale. But no matter what 0 dB is, each successive increase in decibels refers to an increase in power of about 26 percent. The decibel scale is, in some important ways, very useful for describing the sounds we hear. At the lower part of the scale, a change of 1 dB is about the minimum necessary for people to perceive a difference in volume.

There are limits to what the decibel scale can tell us about what and how we hear, however. Understanding these limits is crucial to understanding loudness. The intensity of a sound is directly related to the amplitude of the wave—literally, the wave's size. Increase the amplitude, and you'll get a corresponding increase in intensity. The sound's intensity is related to how loud the sound seems to us, but the relationship between the two isn't nearly as tidy. Two sounds with the same intensity won't necessarily sound equally loud to us, because we don't "hear" intensity. Intensity is an objective value that can be measured; loudness is not. Intensity is what makes our eardrums vibrate, but when those vibrations are translated into electrical impulses in the cochlea and sent to the brain, the magic of psychoacoustics takes over. As Llewelyn Lloyd, an early loudness researcher, put it, intensity "is correlated with what happens outside our heads," but loudness "exists only inside our heads."

The first people to provide an organized map of our internal loudness detector were Harvey Fletcher and Wilden Munson of Bell Labs. They conducted a study in which they presented subjects with pairs of tones at different frequencies—one in each ear—and instructed them to tweak the volume of the tones until they sounded like they were at the same level. The data demonstrated that low-frequency sounds must have a greater intensity to sound as loud as high-frequency sounds. For example, a 1,000 Hz tone at 50 dB sounds as loud as a 100 Hz tone at 60 dB. You can demonstrate this phenomenon by slowly turning down the volume of your stereo. Notice that as you approach silence the bass seems to vanish before the treble does. The Fletcher-Munson curves showed that as intensity increases, this discrepancy decreases.

This quirk of hearing has played an important role in enabling the Loudness War. If you play the same piece of music at two different volumes and ask people which sounds better, they will almost always choose the louder, partly because more of the frequencies are audible. A hot signal will provide a little boost so that the music played at a low volume sounds fuller. It can also add heft to mediocre sound systems by giving them a semblance of low end they would otherwise lack.

Another factor affecting how loud something seems, independent of the intensity, is what comes before and after it. We assess loudness based on average levels, not peaks, and we are constantly assessing what the average level is. You've probably had the experience of watching TV and reaching for the remote to turn down the volume when a commercial comes on. You'd swear that the commercial was being broadcast at a much higher level. The truth is that the station you're watching is most likely broadcasting at full power at all times. The sound of whatever you were watching just before the break probably reached the same peak as the commercials—just not as often. Our musical environment works the same way. "If you tune your dial to a classical station and compare it to a hip-hop station, you'll find that although they have the same power, one is substantially louder than the other," says Bob Ludwig, one of the mastering world's most esteemed engineers. "That's because the classical station is reaching the maximum peak once every minute or so, and the hip-hop station is hitting it several times a second."

Waging the Loudness War means finding new and better ways to decrease or "compress" dynamic range, so that a record's average levels are nearly as high as the peaks. Look again at the picture of Massive Attack's "Angel," and compare it with "Let's Get It Started," "The Fallen," and "The Seed." Although "Angel" peaks very high very often, there is a great deal of distance between those peaks and the lowest point of the signal. The dynamic range of the song is very large. The other songs have almost none.

This widespread lack of dynamic range is unprecedented in musical history. Dynamic range is one of the things that makes music a thrilling experience. Again, the visuals tell the story. Just look at the picture of "Angel." Notice that the bulk of the signal is in the middle, but those spikes shoot toward the heavens. Those spikes are known as "transients," the parts of the signal that extend far past the point that most of the signal reaches. Their name makes them sound superfluous—just random signals passing through town—but transients provide a lot of music's crucial detail. It's a little unfair to draw too many conclusions from these images. To fit the whole song into each picture, a great deal of detail has been sacrificed, and if we went in closer we'd be able to see the signals in all their complexity. But looking at these songs from a distance like this is analogous to the overall experience of our current soundscape. We're surrounded by music that does nothing but shout.

All wars have their follies, and the biggest folly of the Loudness War is that winning means degrading the technology that made the war possible.

One advantage that digital had over analog—something even analog loyalists had to concede—was its improved dynamic range. It enabled Telarc's "bass drum heard round the world": never before had a recording system been able to handle the full amplitude of a bass drum without deferring to distortion. And yet, just shy of a quarter of a century later, one of the most widely disseminated tracts of the anti–Loudness War movement was an impassioned screed about how Rush's 2002 album, *Vapor Trails*, sounded "like dogshit," largely because the sound of Neil Peart's bass drum had died an ignoble death in a war it shouldn't have been fighting. "I cannot say this enough," wrote Rip Rowan, editor of the audio engineering

Web site ProRec.com. "It's hands-down the worst sounding CD I own." It was so bad that Rowan, a huge Rush fan, couldn't even listen to the whole thing all the way through. And it wasn't just Rush: "Most of the current crop of rock CDs have been punished by the LOUDER IS BETTER process, and I know I am not alone when I say, once and for all, ENOUGH IS ENOUGH."

How did we reach this dystopia, barely twenty years after a drum sound stoked the nascent digital audio community's revolutionary fervor? It didn't have to be this way. A digital audio system cares only about a wave's amplitude, not its frequency. For every sample period—44,100 each second—the system analyzes the wave and decides what its amplitude is at that moment. By connecting the dots, the system reconstructs the wave's shape, and this shape dictates the frequency. Each bit adds 6 dB to a digital system's dynamic range. The CD uses 16 bits, so it is capable of 96 dB. That's at least 20 dB more than an analog vinyl disc. The dynamic range of our ears is 130 dB, so the CD should have resulted in music that approaches the breadth and complexity of our ears. And yet, it's not unusual today for a pop CD to have a dynamic range as small as 6 dB.

Dynamic-range compression—and its more simple variant, limiting—is the most common weapon in the Loudness War, and the reason why dynamic range has been sacrificed in the name of the Loud. I'll demonstrate. Here, once again, is the picture of "Angel."

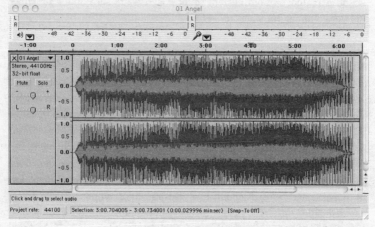

Let's say I want to make "Angel" sound louder. If I could, I'd just move the whole signal up, but that's impossible. The uppermost point on the vertical axis corresponds with 0 dBFS (full scale), and there is nothing beyond it. There should be a sign on it saying HERE BE DRAGONS, like those old maps of a flat Earth. The system has no way of representing anything over that value. So we need a plan B, some way to reduce the song's dynamic range, to impart that sensation of loudness.

The problem is those damn hippie transients. Look at them there, squatting on all that prime upper-level real estate, stretching out and making themselves comfortable, while the taxpayers (the bulk of the song) are stuck there in the middle. It's not fair, I tell you! So let's draw a line in the sand, beyond which no transient can trespass.

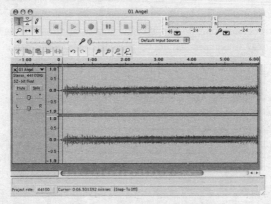

There, that's better. We've cut those transients down to size. Now that we have all that open space, let's build us a subdivision and move out to the suburbs. We'll just apply an algorithm to amplify the entire signal, like so—

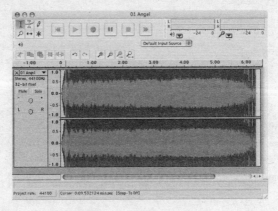

and everyone's moved into the gated community. I have now created a signal in which there is little variation between the peak and the average, which will give me a much louder "Angel."

The art of compression is about learning how to massage the process of maintaining a limited dynamic range. There is nothing inherently wrong with compression as a tool in recorded music. Engineers use compression for a variety of reasons, including getting specific sounds, giving the music added heft, and increasing separation among instruments. Compression doesn't kill music; people who wield compression like a cudgel kill music. The real problems begin when our quest for loudness makes us greedy, when people decide that compression is something we'll have to pry out of their cold, dead hands. Let's take a closer look at "Angel" in its original uncompressed form. This is a close-up of one of those spikes.

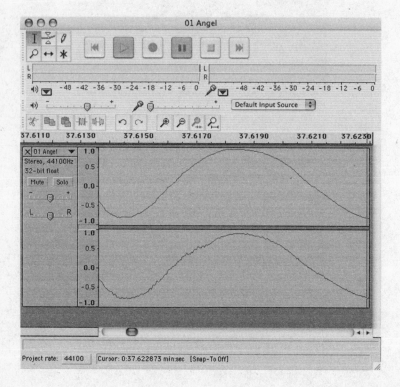

Notice that it just barely grazes the top before beginning its journey downward. Now let's look closer at "Let's Get It Started." This is a picture of about .02 seconds.

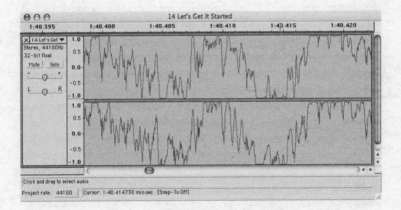

Notice that the wave seems to be slamming against the 0 dBFS ceiling. Compression has been applied to limit the dynamic range, but somewhere along the line—in the recording, mixing, or mastering process—somebody decided to take it a step further. Let's go in as tight as we can on one of those peaking areas.

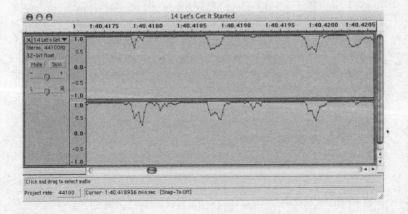

That's roughly .003 seconds. Each dot represents one sampling period, 1/44,100th of a second. The dot marks the value of the wave's amplitude at that precise moment. For several consecutive sampling periods at this point in the song, the system was presented with a value too high for it to read. So the system just sliced off the top of the wave, a phenomenon known as "clipping." The result—a wave that looks like a plateau instead of a mountain peak—is called a "square wave," and it's something that never occurs with sound waves in the natural world. For the duration of those flat-topped samples, "Let's Get It Started" was just a blast of noise and distortion. The song is full of such moments.

Even some of the harshest critics of the Loudness War defend the use of clipping in moderation. Others take a harder line on clipping. To them, clipping is to the Loudness War as torture is to the so-called War on Terror, which is to say they think the fact that clipping is now part of the respectable discourse is evidence that a state of permanent war has driven us all a bit mad. "Distortion is part of rock and roll, but it's been taken to an extreme that I'd love to see us get away from," says Kevin Gray, an engineer at AcousTech Mastering in Los Angeles who specializes in audiophile vinyl releases. Gray thinks that the practice of clipping is being driven by the big New York mastering houses. "Everything I've seen coming out of New York—they're doing this now," he says. "It's an East Coast thing. I guess they just want that extra little bit of loudness for some reason."

A lot of hip-hop, contemporary R&B, and dance music uses clipped percussion as a conscious aesthetic choice. The big distorted blasts of synthetic snare drum suit the music. Even plain old regular snare drums can be clipped and maintain a modicum of their full-bodied selves because the snare sound is not totally dissimilar to the distortion that clipping causes. It's the low-end percussion that has suffered the most in this war. For people like Rowan, who was appalled to discover "thousands of ruined kick drum transients" when he examined the signal for *Vapor Trails*, the journey from the bass drum heard round the world to the Neil Peart bass drum you can hardly hear has been particularly tragic. "What a shame," Rowan wrote. "What a crying shame."

Rowan wasn't the only one who felt that something was desperately wrong with music around the turn of the twenty-first century. Something was going around, some sort of a malaise. Music just wasn't doing it for people who had depended on it their entire lives. Something was eating away at it, and many of these people were reaching the same conclusion.

In an extraordinary essay that appeared in the online magazine *Stylus* in 2006, Nick Southall wrote that although the Flaming Lips' new album, *At War with the Mystics*, wasn't a bad record, it was "an incredibly LOUD record. So it might as well be bad because I simply cannot stand to hear it." And the Flaming Lips weren't isolated offenders. All music seemed to have its dynamic range crushed like grapes before it reached the public. "It's this flatness, this clipping, this unwavering attack, that wears and tires and means you won't listen to your favourite records, if they're from the last few years, as often as you might want to, because they are intrinsically unmusical and unpleasant," he wrote. He described a musical climate that made him feel "like Alex at the end of *A Clockwork Orange*—battered, fatigued by, and disgusted with the music you love . . . I very much doubt this is just me."

It wasn't. Similar cries weren't necessarily emanating from musicians, but engineers—particularly mastering engineers, the people who were actually making the CDs and dealing with the industry's increasing demand for loudness—were sounding the alarm. "The music we listen to today is nothing more than distortion with a beat," mastering engineer Bob Speer declared. "It's anti-music, because the life of it is being squashed out of it through over-compression." Kevin Gray says, "I can't stand to listen past track three on most albums done since 1992. By the time you get to track three, you're like, 'This is just irritating me,' no matter what volume it's playing at. I usually start out playing it loud, but by the time I get to track two, I've turned it down 3 or 4 dB, and then by the time I get to track three, I'm done. It shouldn't be that way. It's not musical."

In December 2001, a group of engineers and producers met to decide which album would win the Grammy for the Best Engineered Album, Non-Classical. They considered 267 albums and hated them all. Even the ones that had clearly been recorded well sounded to Roger Nichols, the architect of that classic seventies Steely Dan dry sound, like they had been mastered to compete for the "loudest when played on the radio or boom-box in a trunk-rattling Toyota" Grammy. "Every single CD was squashed to death, had no dynamic range, and sounded like crap," he later wrote on his Web site. "Instead of listening to find the best CDs entered, we had to change the criteria and listen for the least offensive entries."

A skeptic might decide that the wonkish opinion of audio technicians has no bearing on the way most people hear music. But you could also consider these people the archetypical coal-mine-dwelling canaries, defining a problem that most of us could only feel intuitively and emotionally. Because whether or not you thought loudness and compression were a problem, it was clear that the Loudness War was changing the way people heard music. In an article in *Stereophile* in 2003, John Atkinson described his experience of seeing the Weary Boys play bluegrass at the annual South by Southwest music convention. He left after a few songs, when he realized he wasn't enjoying it. The mostly acoustic instruments, as heard through the PA, sounded "relentlessly loud, compressed, clipped, and distorted to the point where any light and shade in the music had been obliterated." Walking through the crowd toward the exit, it struck him that nobody else seemed bothered by the sound. Maybe, he wrote, "they were all so accustomed to it—this is what music is *supposed* to sound like—that their expectations had been diminished."

Even some of the most enthusiastic combatants in the Loudness War agree that a loud sound achieved through compression involves a Faustian deal with the psychoacoustic devil. The belief is that a compressed sound will always be ear-catching but that too much compression will lead to a sort of listener fatigue. So the further you're willing to go with compression, the more you risk the listener just tuning out. The idea that this fatigue is a by-product of digital compression "is almost universally held," says mastering engineer Greg Calbi. "I never heard the word 'fatigue' once when I was cutting vinyl."

In fact, it's so universal that the radio industry has made it part of its business model, with stations weighing the relative merits of a compressed signal. The theory is that a heavily compressed signal will snare listeners as they scan the dial because the station will sound exciting and crystal clear. But if the signal is too compressed, that excitement will quickly wear off and listeners will switch off their radios or change stations. "People will turn away if they think there's too much compression," says Frank Foti, president of Omnia, one of the leading manufacturers of audio processing equipment for radio. "They don't know why, but they'll change the station, and it could be because the way the radio is being adjusted goes against what sounds good to a person's ear."

Stations tweak their processing based on the type of ratings they're after. Pop, hip-hop, and R&B formats live or die by their cumulative (cume) ratings. Advertisers are mainly interested in the aggregate number of listeners, so these stations usually employ heavy processing to achieve what radio engineers call a "hype" sound. "The conventional wisdom says that cume is bolstered by loudness processing, which lets the station stand out when people are pushing their buttons or scanning across the radio dial," says Robert Orban, one of the early pioneers in the science of radio processing. A station that plays smooth jazz, on the other hand, is assumed to have listeners who keep the radio on for extended periods, such as in the background at work. These stations are judged by time spent listening (TSL) ratings, and are therefore less likely to employ heavy compression, lest they drive away listeners.

Even gender is said to play a role in loudness fatigue. If stations are gunning for a female demographic, they'll often go easy on the processing. Foti says, "Twenty or thirty years ago, when I was a baby engineer, I remember being told there was psychoacoustic research that said women were much more sensitive to extreme amounts of density or heavy compression, especially high-frequency distortion. I don't know if it's the mechanics of their inner ear, or the chemical differences that exist between men and women, but certain things are supposed to sound much more annoying to women than to men."

I had heard so many references to studies that were said to document the link between compression and fatigue, especially from adamant anti-compression advocates, that I started to wonder why I couldn't locate any. It turns out the evidence might be strictly anecdotal. "I am unaware of any studies on this phenomenon," says Stephen McAdams, the head of McGill University's Centre for Interdisciplinary Research in Music Media and Technology, who studies the psychoacoustics of music cognition. "It may be an urban myth." McAdams thinks that if compression has a fatiguing effect, it's most likely a cognitive fatigue brought on by decreased dynamic range. You get tired of constantly hearing high levels with little variation, sort of like the way eating your favorite food three times a day for a month will make you sick of it. Marc Ballora, a Penn State music technology professor who has written about loudness, argues that the fatigue caused by compression is more of a physical phenomenon. Decreased dynamic range means an increase in the average amplitude of the waves striking the eardrum and moving it back and forth. "When you've got this part of your body that's being exerted like that it's going to bring about fatigue," he says.

The radio industry may have introduced a note of economic rationality into the issue of compression fatigue, but it's more difficult to codify the problem in the recording world. If you are a radio station's program director who ups the compression and ratings improve favorably, you've done your job. With records, the goals are murkier. To begin to understand why, consider again the relationship between intensity and loudness. They are linked but not identical, because the former is an objective measure of sound and the latter is purely subjective. What links intensity and loudness is that they are both an expression of power. Intensity is about power in the literal sense, of the impact that a sound has on the world by the force it exerts on air molecules. Loudness, since it exists wholly in our brain, is about symbolic power.

Simply put, a loud record, executed effectively, is a powerful record in both senses of the word. It has the power to imprint itself on the world, while proving its power through high sales. I can remember that when Dr. Dre's *The Chronic* first came out in 1992 it was almost eerily ubiquitous. It was more than just very popular. It seemed to take over the environment. For a few months, the soundtrack of human life was a constant Doppleresque loop of "Nuthin' But a 'G' Thang" playing out of a passing car. That's how life sounded to me, anyway. Something I discovered much later was that Dr. Dre was notorious in the recording world for pushing his engineers to find ways to make his records louder. For a record that really captures its moment, which I think *The Chronic* did, loudness can be the tweak that lodges an album irrevocably in the human consciousness.

But the wages of loudness may also mean music that doesn't so much own its moment as rent it. In his *Stylus* manifesto, Southall argued that Oasis's 1997 album *(What's the Story) Morning Glory?*—which, as well as being a hit in America, had an epoch-defining status in the United Kingdom similar to what *The Chronic* had achieved in the United States—was so successful "precisely because it was loud; its excessive volume and lack of dynamics meant it worked incredibly well in noisy environments and crowded pubs, meaning it very easily became a ubiquitous and noticeable record in cultural terms." From 1995 to 1997, Oasis was the biggest band in the United Kingdom, one of the biggest bands in the world, and very big in the United States, where they had a gold album (sales of 500,000) for their debut set, *Definitely Maybe*; followed by the four-times-platinum (4,000,000) *Morning Glory*; and then *Be Here Now*, which was certified platinum once. That's a lot of momentum on which to build a career, but Oasis couldn't sustain it, although they remained prolific. Over the next eight years, they released four more albums, none of which even went gold. But what's even more curious is that they didn't move many more units with their first three smashes. *Definitely Maybe* finally hit platinum status in 2001, but as of 2006, the other two have yet to move up another platinum notch. This is especially surprising for *Morning Glory*, which had all the earmarks—in terms of sales, press, and general cultural cachet—of one of those classic albums that continue to sell moderately but steadily in perpetuity.

The story of Oasis is really the story of music in the nineties. Everybody seemed like a one-hit wonder. The reasons for this development are complex, but though the connection is impossible to prove, it's interesting to point out that this change corresponded with the intensification of the Loudness War. And it seems reasonable to speculate that the war's escalation was itself a response to this change. Labels began to devote enormous amounts of resources toward making an album a success. Part of pushing product down the public's throat naturally continued: the louder things got, the louder they needed to get, like a gambling addict forced to bet increasingly reckless sums to repay his mounting debt.

Some mastering engineers maintain that this vicious cycle of loudness is a root cause of the music industry's troubles. "The record labels blame Napster, MP3s, CD burners, and a host of others for the lack of CD sales," Speer noted. "While there is some truth to their constant whining, they only have themselves to blame." According to this belief, the public, without realizing it, is repelled by the sound of music today. If true, this would suggest that loudness fatigue is not only real but a mass phenomenon. We're seduced into buying loud records in droves, but we eventually discard the music when we realize what it's doing to us.

Chris Johnson, an engineer who runs a small mastering studio in Vermont, had a hunch about what happened to music in the nineties that made longevity so rare. He compiled a list of the all-time best-selling albums and assigned each a score by multiplying the number of platinum certifications the album received by the number of years the album has been available. He called this modified list the most "commercially important" albums. The ranking method favored older albums, but that was the point. These were the albums that had proved to be the most commercially durable, still selling year after year.

He analyzed the songs visually and discovered that they shared a common trait. All of them, no matter the genre, have incredible, breathtaking dynamics. They are the kind of productions that are spacious enough to exhibit huge dynamic range and thus provide a sense of "high contrast" among the various parts of the song. "The more strongly they sell, the more likely it is that they will have high-contrast characteristics," Johnson wrote on his Web site. "There is a common factor shared among even very dissimilar multiplatinum hit records, having to do with peak amplitudes, and this is exactly what is destroyed by current high-level mastering practices."

In other words, the records that people keep coming back to are those that breathe, something that hypercompression prevents music from doing. Johnson's theory is that the Loudness War coincided with changes in the music business in the nineties. In a jittery, unstable industry, more emphasis was placed on working a few titles hard to guarantee megasales. Loudness is a way to make sure these recordings have maximum impact. And it works—for a while. But when the marketing dies down, this isn't a sound that keeps people coming back. The result is a seeming nonstop parade of brief careers and one-hit wonders. The industry grows more nervous, the marketing grows more intense, the records get louder, forever and ever amen. "It's simple," Johnson writes. "Return to High Contrast—or DIE."

One of Johnson's discoveries was what he calls "the hit record bass drum" that appears in many of the albums, characterized by transients that are given the room to trail off below 30 Hz and above 90 Hz. To have a bass drum sound like this, you need to have room for peaks that are as much as 24 dB hotter than the body of the music; it's common on rock CDs today to have bass drums that crest at a mere 9 dB. Pink Floyd's *The Wall*, a prime example of an album with the classic drum sound Johnson describes, came out less than two years after Telarc's momentous digitized bass drum, yet this bass drum—recorded on tape and mastered to vinyl—occurs courtesy of a dynamic range that digital today doesn't bother with.

"The only possible way to get THIS sound is through high-contrast sound engineering," Johnson writes. "[Y]ou can never, ever, EVER get this sound in its full scale and drama and glory while still even pretending to put out 'competitively loud' mastering jobs. If you crank this up, it's among the most glorious feats of sound engineering out there—it reeks of high-budget, high-gloss luxury. But if you put it on after *Californication*, it will sound like you unplugged the damn CD player."

Perhaps it's not fair to look at these and draw too many conclusions about what doesn't work, and what people don't want. The problem with Johnson's theory is that albums like *Californication* haven't been out long enough to even approach the sales of an album like *The Wall*. But it is fair to draw conclusions about what people *do* want, or what they've wanted in the past and continue to want today. If Johnson is right, then maybe the records on his "commercially important" list hold some sort of key to what we—as a society—want from music.

I wonder, myself. The first rock album I ever owned was the Eagles' *Their Greatest Hits 1971–1975*, which I received as a gift seven years before I heard R.E.M. I liked it a lot. As it turns out, I was one among very many. It is now the biggest-selling album of all time, twenty-nine times platinum, and also tops Johnson's "commercially important" list with a score of 675, beating *Led Zeppelin IV* (23 million, 660). This isn't the appropriate forum to discuss what our extreme Eagles fandom says about us as a society, but it's worth speculating about why we keep coming back to them over and over again. Johnson thinks it's the dynamics. Analyzing "Witchy Woman," a seemingly typical-but-innocuous bit of me-decade misogyny (c.f. "Evil Woman," "Devil Woman," etc.), he found a recipe for musical bliss on a mass scale.

"It's gratifying, but unsurprising, to discover that the single most commercially important album in [Recording Industry Association of America] history contains some of the most striking dynamic contrasts pop music's ever seen," he writes.

Who knows—maybe we've all discovered that the Eagles are the most potent analgesic for our hypercompressed world, like taking hits of pure oxygen after coming in from the smog. To paraphrase my man Glenn Frey (channeling Jackson Browne), maybe the sound of our own wheels is making us crazy.

Why do we fight this war we cannot win? Sax, the original analog warrior, thinks the car CD player launched the war because people now expected their music to be audible above the engine and environmental noise—even the quietest parts. Tardon Feathered, the nom de guerre of a San Francisco–based mastering engineer who has monitored the war, blames the CD jukebox for similar reasons. Calbi mentions the rise of the iPod; with the next song just a click away, the music has to grab your attention. Katz describes "sociological factors": fewer people sit and listen critically to music, preferring to use it as sonic wallpaper, so music must be loud enough to compete with everything around it.

"But there's another factor," Katz says, "a technical factor." It begins with the fact that the compact disc offered at least 20 dB more dynamic range than LPs. It was a vast sonic space waiting to be colonized. The future turned on who would fill this space, and how. The identity of the first person to fire the first shot in an analog-era loudness war is lost to history, but there are educated guesses. "The story I heard, and it could be apocryphal, is that Phil Spector started it," Gray says. "Spector and Motown." Certain producers drove mastering engineers to make their records sound as loud as possible (Gray recalls that Mike Curb, impresario of the Osmonds, liked his stuff way hot), but there were several constraining factors.

First, you really had to know what you were doing. "To get the kind of compression in analog that people are now getting with digital, you had to compress at multiple stages," Gray explains. "You would compress when you recorded, you would compress when you mixed, and you would compress again when you mastered. Sometimes you ran the music through a daisy chain of compressors."

Second, there was a physical limitation. The louder the signal, the wider the grooves of the album need to be, and the shorter the playing time. As LPs increasingly became cohesive works rather than just collections of songs, they got longer, and loudness became less of a priority. "When records were still sixteen to eighteen minutes per side, everyone was fighting for every dB they could get on vinyl," Gray says. "I noticed around 1975—probably because album sides were getting longer—it didn't seem like as much of an issue. I didn't have to cut everything hot-hot-hot-hot."

Any loudness war thus involved finesse as well as hard choices. Today's Loudness War requires neither. Relatively inexpensive devices with names that sound like they were copped from an Amphetamine Reptile Records catalog circa 1990 (for example, Finalizer and Maximizer) allow any jackass to add quick-and-dirty compression. And length is no longer a consideration. The overall number of ones and zeros won't increase when the signal gets louder, only the combinations will be different. You can go all the way up to 0 dBFS, and your signal will be pristine.

Another crucial difference between an analog and digital loudness war is that analog technology, by its very nature, includes a DMZ, whereas digital technology promotes trench warfare. This is a volume unit (VU) meter.

In the analog world, the VU meter is the standard way to measure the strength of a recording's signal. The VU meter measures voltages, which are expressed in a decibel scale called dBm. Notice the zero a little to the right of center. That's a reference point for 0 dBm, the

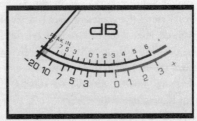

point where a certain signal has a strength of 1 milliwatt. There's no technical reason that requires that this particular spot be the reference. In the thirties, engineers from NBC, CBS, and Bell agreed that it would make a good standard. It represents the point above which sound begins to audibly distort, but the distortion is gradual—unlike in the digital domain, where everything is perfect right up to 0 dBFS, where the signal simply ceases to be—so having the needle go into the red a bit is not a disaster. Depending on the kind of music being recorded, one may even want to push the needle into the red and make the distortion part of the recording aesthetic.

But 0 dBm is just a spot to aim for, not a precise destination—which is good, because the VU meter isn't capable of giving a precise reading anyway. The needle is always a little bit behind the signal because it is displaying an average of the previous fraction of a second. At any given moment, the signal may actually be peaking as much as 14 dB higher than what the VU meter displays. The reading is inexact, but since our ears perceive loudness based on averages rather than peaks, the VU meter "hears" like we do. The signal is represented as an average, in much the same way your brain represents the input it gets from the inner ear as an average.

The digital domain doesn't care about averages. It's all about peaks. So 0 dBm represents what you kinda sorta *should* do; 0 dBFS represents what you *can* do. Neither analog nor digital requires that an average level be agreed upon by everyone, but it's easy to understand why the architects of the digital domain didn't devise one: Why bother if a sound is just as free from distortion a step away from HERE BE DRAGONS as it is a mile away? With that mind-set in place, the Loudness War was all but preordained. It was the lack of any agreed-upon average level that led to, as Katz puts it, "the wild, wild west of average levels going up and up."

The "nearly perfect creation" is a common trope of science fiction and comic books. Someone or something—often a synthetic creation—is introduced into the world nearly perfect, except for one fatal flaw. That's how Katz views the compact disc: "one of the world's great developments" but lacking something that could have forestalled the anarchy and lawlessness of the digital frontier. He wishes they had designed the system with metadata on each disc that would automatically adjust playback so that every CD conformed to an industry standard of average levels. No more jumping up to turn down the volume when your player's carousel switches from an old CD to a new one, and no need for a war. "It's a terrible demonstration of the lack of foresight on the part of the medium's developers," he says.

There actually was an attempt to create such a standard when the CD was introduced. The Audio Engineering Society recommended that all CDs should have a maximum peak no higher than -18 dBFS. In other words, 18 dB below full scale would be similar to 0 dB on a VU meter, and there would be plenty of room for stray transients that rose above -18 dBFS. "The AES said, 'Okay, the digital standard, oh boy, we're gonna leave *tons of headroom*—no clipping issues here!" Feathered, who at the time worked as a recording engineer, recalls. But that consensus began to disintegrate almost immediately. "Pretty rapidly, it became 'Okay, you can go to -14, that's still plenty of headroom.' And then, around the time consumer DATs started coming [the mideighties], it was -12. Sony began placing a dot on their meters at -12."

For a while, this standard held, because 12 dB was still plenty of headroom. "Depending on the recording, some needed another 14 dB of dynamic range," Feathered says. "But most pop mixes coming out of the console could fit on a VU meter, basically riding at 0 dB and peaking up at 2 or 3." That meant that in the digital realm, these CDs were hovering around -12 dBFS and occasionally peaking at -10 and -9. Still plenty of space before the dragons appear.

But it didn't last, due to what might be called the "zoo paradox." The polar bears at the zoo have a deep moat around their enclosure so that they can't escape. A wall separates the public from the moat, but you can't go right up to the wall. The closest you can get is another wall set back from the inner wall. Why does this outer wall exist? Because children and stupid adults might lean too far over the first wall and tumble into the moat. Nobody thinks that outer wall was built with them in mind. The wall is always for "others." And so it was with -18, -14, -12, and any other seemingly arbitrary line drawn in the digital sand. Why should I, a responsible engineer, be held back because the engineer in the other studio can't be trusted? The frontier beckoned, stretching all the way to 0 dBFS.

The makeup of the new technology made settling this frontier seem not just possible but necessary. If you weren't using the upper 12 dB, you were, in effect, leaving 2 whole bits unused. The 16-bit CD system became a de facto 14-bit system. Where was the fun in that? When you thought about it, throwing away those 2 bits was an insult to the fine folks at Sony and Philips who had labored so hard to make the system all it could be. Feathered says, "There were a bunch of people who were very logical and said, 'Well, I realize what the standard is, and I realize why somebody had to pick a standard and tell the rest of us to calibrate our machines [to conform to that standard], but if you're trying to get the best signal you can, you want those extra bits.' So guys like me, when recording, the goal was to not go off the top of the scale, because as long as it's all being captured on there, there's no clipping. If it peaks at the top, you've got a great recording."

While recording engineers began seeing how close to the 0 dB sun they could fly without getting burned, it was the mastering engineers—the people who had to actually make the CDs—who sounded the alarm. "When I moved into mastering," Feathered says, "guys were still insisting that for a mastered record, 'No, no, no, gosh you're running up at -6. That's way too hot.' But there's no clipping. 'Yes, but there's a standard, across the board.' "

And so, with nothing but toothless "suggestions" to hold them back, the adventurous engineers lit out for the prairie and made it all the way to the coast. As with any unrestrained geographical expansion, the problem was the sprawl. If people had agreed to peak at full scale but average somewhere below it, CDs would have realized their full dynamic range potential. But as the uncharted sonic landscape became conquered, everyone wanted to live on the coast. And when that got crowded, the restless among them wanted to expand even further, but of course there was nowhere else to go; the land ended at 0 dBFS. The only thing to do was to compress and, eventually, to clip.

Somewhere in this tale there's an object lesson about how people allocate limited resources in the absence of any regulatory structure, some sort of cautionary fable about unrestrained neoliberalism. Or there would be, if loudness were a limited commodity like oil, water, land, and whatever else drives the real wars of the twenty-first century. But it's not. Loudness is bountiful. Thanks to our volume knobs and the wonders of amplification, we have more loud than we know what to do with. The gobs of dBs at our fingertips are like the empty calories in the processed food that makes us fat.

The Loudness War isn't even like the eighties cola war. Coke or Pepsi is a banal choice, but it is a choice. The Loudness War is all about giving people something they don't need or want, and which in any case they already have plenty of. It's more like a classic arms race, a cold war fought with hot records. And since the destruction of music—the compressing, the clipping, the tiny dynamic range that makes a mockery of the CD's capabilities—is not merely mutually assured but actually happening, there is no rational reason why all forces don't agree to disarm.

So why don't they?

"This is America," Feathered says. "You know, capitalism rules. You're supposed to get the advantage on the other guy. Everybody's trying to make a record that sounds like 'more of' than somebody else's—one that just goes BOOM!—and jumps right out of the speakers."

The two main categories of soldiers in this war—mastering engineers and radio engineers—have a lot in common, starting with the fact that many people don't really understand what they do, even though what they do has an enormous impact on the sound of music.

In the engineering world, an old nickname for mastering is "the black art," because of the mystery and magic that surrounds it. A reel of magnetic tape leaves the studio and is somehow transmuted into a hard disc with grooves on it. Even today, when anyone with a CD burner can "make" a CD, only a good mastering engineer can give it that special sonic veneer that makes it sound like a "real" record by commercial standards.

Radio engineers enjoy a similar air of intrigue and mystery. "One interesting facet of broadcasting is that many engineers and program directors have long thought of audio processing as 'black magic,' using 'black box' technology to accomplish apparently magical things," notes Frank Foti. The program directors dictate how they want their station to sound, and it is the engineers, using processors in the studio and at the base of the transmitter itself, who bring it to life. Like mastering engineers, they take the raw signal and make it "sound like radio."

As similar as their jobs are, mastering engineers and radio engineers tend to have vastly different attitudes regarding their conscription in the Loudness War. In radio, the war tends to be a spirited affair, infused with the sepia tones of a Ken Burns documentary. The enemy, the terms of victory, and even the rules of engagement are clear. A station competes against the other stations in its market. The station wins the war if the engineer can make it sound louder than its competitors, and ideally wins the ratings battle as well. FM stands for "frequency modulation." The bandwidth of the signal remains constant, but the frequency is constantly modulating, drifting a bit off its appointed spot on the dial. The amount of modulation determines how loud the station sounds. The FCC regulates the modulation rate, but it's like a posted speed limit: everybody understands that they can go slightly over the limit without reprisals. Short of overmodulating, a station can apply compression to give the signal the oomph of added loudness.

The mastering engineers' Loudness War is redolent of more recent global conflicts, and they've got the temperament to show for it. Their goal largely goes against their training. Mastering has always involved compression because the dynamic range of magnetic tape is greater than a vinyl record's. But now they're asked to be little more than human compressors, smashing the life out of music. As Gray puts it, echoing the complaints of many of his colleagues, "It's really pathetic." Solidarity is difficult, because the enemy walks among them: the unprincipled mastering hacks who tout their ability to achieve loudness at all costs, forcing everyone else to follow suit if they want to stay in business. "There's a machismo element to the level wars," Calbi says. "That's why most mastering engineers won't really be frank about it."

Radio engineers may gripe about the vague directives of their program directors, but mastering engineers really want to frag the lieutenant. "I don't blame mastering engineers for the level wars," Calbi flatly states. "Clients have pushed us to make it louder." He's not talking about the musicians so much as record company execs. The real culprit is the "good ol' five-CD changer" they use to listen to music, Gray says. "They'll put four CDs in the changer that they all know are loud, and the A&R guy wants to hear their band's latest CD, as it's mastered, up against those. And if it's not as loud, it's sent back to the mastering place for more compression."

The engineers try to explain that their less-hot versions will sound better, and just as fierce, if the consumer only increases the volume. But in an unstable music industry, this is a tough argument to make. "Knowing that the job of turning it up is on the onus of the listener is a hard concept to accept when you're trying to sell records," Katz says. Record companies will sometimes even set up "shoot-outs" among mastering engineers, giving several the same song to master and awarding the job to the loudest one. As Calbi puts it, "When you hear you're involved in a shoot-out, you really want to kill yourself."

But there's a broader historical reason the radio engineers are singing "It's a Long Way to Tipperary," while the mastering engineers may as well be doing their job against a backdrop of thumping copter blades and "The End." The digital-era Loudness War is being fought on radio's terms. The offensive began during the same summer that the compact disc was let loose in America.

"It's eight minutes after 6:00 a.m., August the second, 1983. Ladies and gentlemen at this time radio station WHTZ signs on the air. WHTZ is owned and operated by Malrite Communications, and broadcasts at a frequency of 100.3 megahertz. Signing on the air, this is WHTZ"—cue trippy outer-space noises—*"serving the world from the top of the Empire State Building, Z-100"*—cue the sound of explosions—*"GET OUT OF THE WAYYYY!"*

On August 1, WHTZ had still been WVNJ, a station that alternated between "beautiful music" (an easy-listening format) during the day, and lite jazz at night. The station was in last place; its ratings were, essentially, zero. Still, there had to be *some* people who went to bed on August 1 after setting their clock radios, tuned to WVNJ, to come on at 6:00 a.m. And let's say a few of those people hit the snooze button and woke up, still groggy, five minutes later. They'd probably be too startled by the explosions and the rocking feline-themed song (Survivor's "Eye of the Tiger") that followed to notice that the DJ had a slight nervous tremor in his voice. (He was wondering what he'd gotten himself into.)

If it sounds like the pilot for *WKRP in Cincinnati*, that's no surprise, since the man behind the mike had been the program director at the Atlanta radio station that inspired the show. But to understand the true significance of this moment, you need to know that New York is generally considered to have the loudest, densest, most aggressively processed radio market in the country. Nobody knows exactly why this is. Perhaps it's the proximity of Madison Avenue, its advertising ethos driving up radio's will to impact a message on listeners. Maybe it's just New York's inherent brashness and inflated sense of its own self-worth. And it almost certainly has to do with the fact that every commercial New York radio station bears the legacy of WABC, whose heavily processed signal might be the single most influential sound radio has every produced.

In the early 1960s, WABC became the biggest Top 40 station in the country. Its DJs, such as Dan Ingram and "Cousin Brucie" Morrow (who introduced the Beatles at their famous Shea Stadium concert), turned millions of people on to rock and roll, while the sound of the station had an incalculable effect on how people thought rock and roll could sound. It was called "color radio," a big, reverb-heavy sound that often pervaded even the news, courtesy of a huge echo box (six feet long, four feet high, one foot deep) called an EMT. Color radio was perfect for the era of transistor radios. It didn't actually increase loudness, but it made the tinny sound coming out of those radios seem bigger, more substantial and exciting. An entire generation of future engineers learned from WABC that a signal did not have to be "pure" to sound good, and that a station's sound could be as important as the music it played. "It sounded so much larger than life," Paul Sanchez, an engineer at New York's WBLS, says. "It felt like you were missing something when you weren't listening."

During WABC's early years, Mike Dorrough was working as an engineer at a small recording studio owned by Casey Kasem (who would later become famous as the host of the *American Top 40* radio show) and Bob Hudson. Dorrough was obsessed with a particular problem that plagued both radio and records. When records were being cut, it was common to use a very simple limiter to ensure that the dynamic range was kept in check, because if it got too loud the needle would jump out of the groove. Similarly, AM radio stations employed limiters to prevent their signals from overmodulating. The problem with such simple limiting was that it treated the signal as a cohesive whole. If a bass drum was being struck at the same moment a singer was hitting a high note, the limiter would clamp down on everything, even though it was just the low frequencies (the bass drum) that were spiking too high, a phenomenon called "pumping."

Pumping shortchanged the music, but it also revealed how our ears worked. As Fletcher and Munson had proved, low frequencies need to be louder than high frequencies to sound balanced to us. Yet Dorrough saw that many engineers still operated as though our hearing was "amplitude flat," meaning they thought loudness was loudness, regardless of frequency. If you were to make a recording of a singer accompanying someone playing a bass drum, you would naturally record the bass drum at a higher level so that it would balance out the singer. When you turned that tape into a record, or played that recording on the air, those higher-level low frequencies would trigger the limiter and pumping would occur.

But if there were a way to separate the frequencies—to instruct the system to clamp down on the low frequencies while letting the high frequencies spike higher—you'd eliminate pumping. Working at home on his kitchen table, Dorrough, who became a staff engineer at Motown and then RCA, built a prototype of something he called a "discriminate audio processor." The DAP could take an inputted signal, separate it into three bands—low, medium, and high—and feed each into its own processor. Dorrough discovered that for the signal to sound "transparent," the bands had to overlap slightly. But the real tricky part was reconstructing the outputted signal. Our psychoacoustics dictated that the total power of the output had to be identical to the total power of the input. So if the low frequencies were limited by a factor of x, the mids and highs had to increase by x.

Dorrough had planned to market his DAP to recording studios, but he discovered that radio stations, while generally skeptical (they thought the DAP compromised the integrity of the records), were more receptive. His big break came in 1972, when he sold two DAPs to KYNO, a trendsetting Top 40 station in Fresno, California. One advantage of multiband processing was that it made stations sound cleaner and stronger, and people began to notice that stations that were "DAP-tized," as Dorrough put it in his sales pitch, often experienced a ratings boost. "Suddenly out of nowhere we started selling processors to all kinds of rockers all over the place," he says. "I remember one fellow saying, 'I thought you were just a hippie with a one-shot.' "

One day in the mid-1970s, Dorrough brought his DAP to WPLJ, an album-oriented rock station in New York City. WPLJ's program director, Larry Berger, had grown up listening to WABC and studied electrical engineering in college, which gave him a technical knowledge most program directors lacked. After working at stations around the country, Berger returned to New York in the fall of 1974 to take the job at WPLJ. The first thing he did when he checked into his hotel was turn on his portable radio. "I'm scanning the different stations," he recalls, "and I hear bip . . . bip . . . bip . . . and then—" he makes a barely audible sound. That was WPLJ. It wasn't that the signal wasn't clear; it just wasn't very loud. Berger decided that a louder signal would help the station make a splash, and would also make it sound better on the mediocre receivers he figured his target audience was using. "We were a struggling station going after teenagers and young adults," he says. "We were competing with 99X, a Top 40 station. They were the ones who, when I went across the dial in my hotel, were 'BEHHHHHH' and we were 'bluhhhhh.' I felt that in order to make a good first impression we needed to get louder."

What Berger had in mind was a station that sounded like Spector's wall of sound, particularly the neo-Spectorian production on records like Bruce Springsteen's *Born to Run*. Dorrough understood that the DAP, by being a multiband peak limiter, could give him the dense signal he was looking for. He could compress the dynamic range to nearly nothing. Dorrough came to WPLJ, and in the middle of the night he and Berger gave the newly DAP-tized signal a trial run by playing Elton John's "Benny and the Jets." The song begins with staccato piano chords set against a backdrop of what sounds like crowd noise. The chords stand out in stark relief to the crowd noise, which is placed low in the mix. The needle of a VU meter should shoot up when the chord is struck, and then fall sharply back down again before the next chord is struck. But that's not what Berger had in mind. With the help of engineer Bob Deutsch, he and Dorrough adjusted the DAP so that there was virtually no contrast. "The modulation monitor just quivered," Berger says. "It just hung around 99 or 100 percent. It was like there were cobwebs at the lower end."

Wasn't Berger concerned that all this compression might backfire by causing listener fatigue? "Nah, that's bullshit," he says. "We were going for a young audience and we weren't concerned about fatigue. I just don't see it in the ratings. I think that the trade-off even if you're driving down a highway today with the windows open and you have a radio station on and it has wide dynamic range, as opposed to WPLJ which had no dynamic range, you stand the risk of losing a listener during a low passage."

Dorrough had begun to see more of this sort of thing, a trend that dismayed him. The point of the DAP had always been to increase clarity and bring out the full body of the music, not squash all dynamic range in a quest for loudness. "It used to drive me crazy [how much] they wanted to compress," Dorrough says. "Anytime you turned on WPLJ, it just had to *pour* out of the radio."

And so, while the Loudness War in recording began to die down as records got longer, it began to heat up in radio, as FM began to rival AM's popularity. In 1975, Orban introduced an audio processor for radio called the Optimod. It wasn't a multiband processor, but it was designed specifically to address some problems inherent in processing an FM signal, and put many functions in one box. The Optimod was a huge success and gave stations another loudnes weapon.

Berger's gamble paid off for WPLJ, which became New York's leading rock station for the rest of the decade. "So there we are, we're cooking along with this very unique and very compressed sound," he says. "And then in the early eighties, rock and roll started to splinter off into new wave, classic rock, heavy metal, and suddenly AOR [album oriented rock] was an endangered species." To pursue an older, more female demographic, ABC, WPLJ's corporate parent, decided to switch the station to an "adult Top 40" format in the summer of 1983. Across the country, many stations were doing the same thing. Top 40, traditionally an AM format, was colonizing the FM dial, in reaction to the fractured rock audience and the rise of MTV.

Malrite Communications, a Cleveland-based company, decided to get in on the Top 40 juggernaut in a big way. The company purchased WVNJ, a failed New York beautiful-music station, and announced it was flipping it to Top 40 and renaming it WHTZ, or Z-100. WPLJ's format change was incremental; the station began gradually introducing Top 40 acts while still nominally a rock station. "We are preparing ourselves for the future," Berger said of the change, denying that the flipping of WVNJ had influenced WPLJ's decision that Top 40 was FM's future. Malrite, however, may not have known when it decided to plunge into the country's biggest radio market that it would be competing with New York's biggest rock station. Resentment over this unpleasant discovery would certainly explain why Z-100 so publicly made WPLJ its sworn enemy.

Berger chuckles. "Then the wars were on, okay?"

Scott Shannon was a program director at a rock station in Tampa, Florida, who had recently made a splash in the industry by developing the highly successful "morning zoo" format, correctly surmising that what people wanted to hear during their morning commute was two or more grown men acting like imbeciles. When Malrite came calling, he had no desire to leave Tampa, but he was intrigued by Malrite's seemingly quixotic goal to take its new station "from worst to first" in the biggest market in the country. He also saw the new station as a potential laboratory for ideas he had about radio—how a station could be programmed and packaged, but also how it could sound. He took the job and also agreed to go on air in the mornings as part of Z-100's zoo crew.

Shannon found a kindred spirit in Frank Foti, Malrite's choice of engineer for the new station. "From the moment we met I knew he was the guy to bring to life what I heard in my head," Shannon says. "He was crazy. He was just fuckin' crazy. He had a strange look in his eye. His mouth couldn't keep up with his brain, with the things he had to say. It was almost like he had to stutter because he couldn't get everything out."

Foti had in mind something loud but different from WPLJ's hyper-compressed approach, which just sounded "constipated" to him. The drums on a WPLJ-broadcast song reminded him of empty coffee cans. "New York radio has always been very processed, and for years a lot of that was dictated by PLJ," he says. "They had this really heavily compressed sound that sounded very fatiguing to my ears." Foti had an ideal sound in his head, so clear he could practically see it. "I know that sounds weird, since we can't 'see' audio, but I could see something that would give me the loudness that I need, but also the quality I need. I remember thinking that if we had the loudness, we'd have an attention-grabbing thing, and if we had the quality, we'd know we weren't giving people a subliminal reason not to stay with us."

Z-100's studios were located in the fetid, body-burying swamps of Secaucus, New Jersey, just across the Hudson but a world away from Manhattan. (Shannon: "I was happy about being in Secaucus, because I looked at it like we were in the ocean and Manhattan was Europe.") By the time Shannon, with Foti and the rest of the Z-100 staff standing next to him, told the statistically zero listeners to "GET OUT OF THE WAYYY" and blasted these hypothetical people out of bed with "Eye of the Tiger," Foti hadn't quite perfected the sound of the station. Playing around with compressors, clippers, limiters, and other processing toys, he would experiment with the station's sound late at night—first on a closed-circuit system, and then on the air.

At 4:00 a.m. one morning, a few weeks after the launch, Foti heard what he wanted. "I remember hitting the button and it getting louder and cleaner, and thinking I must be doing something wrong because that can't be happening," he says. Thinking it must be a fluke, he put the old configuration back on the air, and then switched back to his new creation, again hearing the sound appear to get bigger—but also cleaner—before his very ears. Foti switched it back, went home, grabbed some sleep, came in the next day, called Shannon into the engineering room, and turned on his new setup for Shannon and all of Z-100's listeners to hear. Shannon's eyes lit up. "Don't touch it!" he said. "Leave it alone!"

Foti had daisy-chained together a series of components—including something called a Texar Audio Prism, an EXR Exciter, an Optimod 8100, and a composite clipper—but even Foti couldn't explain exactly how it worked. "There was a lot of science involved, but some of it was black magic," he says. Somehow, this setup, and the way Foti tuned the machines, made the station sound loud but without the pinched sound of loudness achieved through hypercompression. The sound was clean and open and bright, with a touch of echo—"to kind of remind you of that WABC sound," Shannon says. Its sheen was as suited to the early digital age as WABC's had been to the era of transistor radios.

"I heard this sound and I said, 'What the hell is that?'" says Paul Sanchez, who first heard Z-100 while at a fellow engineer's house. "We were like, 'Okay, that raised the bar.' We aggressively went after it, trying to figure out what Frank was doing, so we could match it or beat it."

Sanchez wasn't alone. Word began to spread through the engineering world about this new station that had found the magic sweet spot of non-fatiguing loudness. "I can honestly tell you that my phone would ring at least three times a week," Foti says. "Program directors would be in New York on vacation or traveling through, and they'd be saying, 'I had to call you, man, I don't know how you get Z-100 to sound like that, but no one else can achieve it.'" The Z-100 receptionist was under strict orders to give the engineers a heads-up when anyone visited the studio, so that they could make sure to close the engineering-room door. Foti took the extra

precaution of placing a shade in front of the board, with a sign that warned
BEHIND THIS SHADE IS THE THRESHOLD OF PAIN.

The short version of what happened after that fateful "Eye of the Tiger" is
that Z-100 did indeed go from worst to first, overtaking WPLJ and topping
the ratings by the end of the year. Radio had never seen (and still never
has) a turnaround happen that quickly in a major market. From his post as
head of the morning zoo team, Shannon personalized the rivalry with WPLJ
via a recurring character named "Larry Booger," program director of
"WIMP-FM." WPLJ mostly remained above the fray—"I kind of saw us as
the good guys with the white hats," Berger says—which was just as well,
since WPLJ's occasional foray into the fray, such as its "Zit-100" campaign
("There is a scourge on the face of your tuner . . .") lacked a certain formal
commitment.

While the tristate area was transfixed (or not) by the programming
rivalry between "Zit-100" and "WIMP," a guerrilla war was being fought on
the battlefield of loudness. The fact that Z-100 was so loud, yet sounded so
uncompressed, convinced the city's radio engineers that Foti had to be
overmodulating. There was simply no other logical conclusion they could
draw. "We'd get complaints from other radio stations—'you're too loud,
you're overmodulating, you're breaking the law,'" Shannon says. "But we
weren't! It just sounded like it. And the more complaints we got, the more
we liked it!"

Across the dial, stations began to up their modulation in a wan attempt
to sound like Z-100. Not wanting to be one-upped by a bunch of loudness-
come-lately stations, Z-100 started pushing the modulation envelope
themselves. Soon enough, Z-100 and WPLJ were engaged in open loudness
warfare. While Berger avoided having anything to do with the man behind
Larry Booger, he wasn't shy about confronting Foti. "Yeah, Frank Foti was
my nemesis," Berger says, laughing. "We'd yell and scream about one or
two percent differentials." There was a pulpish, comic-book symmetry to
this rivalry: the program director with an engineer's technical smarts versus
the engineer with a program director's sense of creativity. Each enjoyed
solitary walks through malls, in search of stores playing the radio, priding
himself on being able to tell within seconds, just by the sound, if it was his
station. (You can almost imagine the two doing battle atop the Empire State

Building, trying to sabotage each other's transmitters while saying things like, "You know, we're really quite alike, you and I . . .")

"For a while, everyone in New York did it," says Foti of the overmodulation epidemic, "and the worst offender was WPLJ. So if they jack it up, I jack it up, and if they jack it up some more, I jack it up some more." (Berger denies overmodulating, saying ABC's strict rules forbade it.) Knowing that the FCC was unlikely to be monitoring anyone over the weekend, Foti would juice the station's modulation before leaving on Friday afternoons, which drove Berger nuts. "I had in my office a multifrequency modulation monitor, so I could push a button and see my modulation, his modulation, other competitors' modulation," he says. "I would come in once in a while on weekends, and I could see what was going on."

What Berger didn't know was that Foti had rigged up an easy way to make Z-100's modulation levels fluctuate wildly on demand. So when Berger called to accuse Foti of overmodulating, Foti, sitting at his desk, would simply twist the dial up and down as he listened to Berger complain. Across the river at WPLJ's offices, Berger's meter would start to jump all over the place. "He'd say, 'Wait, something's wrong with my meter,' " Foti recalls. "And I'd say, 'You stupid idiot!' and hang up the phone."

"It got so competitive," Foti says, "that one time they were really pushing their modulation, so we called up and said, 'C'mon guys, back off.' 'Yeah, we will.' You know, they were just giving us lip service. So I looked up who in New York and New Jersey was at 95.3 and 95.7"—WPLJ's neighbors on the dial—"and called up one of those stations and said, 'Sir, I'm from Z-100, and I happen to be driving through, and it sure sounds like your radio station has a lot of interference.' 'It does? Why do you think that is?' 'Well, I think the people at 95.5 in New York are causing you some interference.' 'They are? I'll sue those sons of bitches!' Two weeks later, their modulation was right back down."

Eventually the New York radio Loudness War got the attention of the authorities. At a radio trade show, an FCC official was examining a new modulation monitor. Scanning the dial, he discovered that a huge chunk of the FM dial was a morass of overmodulation. He told the guy behind the booth to start spreading the word: all the clownish engineers making a mockery of the FCC had exactly two weeks to tie up their little Loudness War games; after that, fines would be levied.

Foti's boss, recognizing that Z-100 and WPLJ were the two superpowers in this war, urged Foti to organize a summit. Foti called the city's engineers and invited them to lunch to discuss a cease-fire. Tensions were high. A WPLJ engineer made some crack about Z-100 copying WPLJ's sound. Foti, who suspected that WPLJ had a mole at Z-100 who had passed along Foti's setup, couldn't believe it. "Copy you?" he asked incredulously. "You guys have been chasing our ratings since we went on the air!"

The New York radio Loudness War in the eighties pretty much ended in a draw. Hostilities intensified a bit with the debut of the R&B station Hot 97 in 1986, but eventually the loudness race reached diminishing returns. "Every one of us were vying for that last tenth-of-a-dB of loudness," Foti says.

By the early eighties, Dorrough had stopped making his DAP, partly out of disappointment over the loudness craze he had unwittingly set in motion. Orban, whose Optimod now dominated the radio processing business, was similarly disillusioned about how his products were being used. "As soon as you give people the ability to achieve more loudness, they will use it and abuse it," he said in 1985. "Radio has started sounding worse again . . . but after ten years of fulminating about it, I despair of doing anything." Whenever he was in New York, he could hardly believe what he heard. "In the eighties, I couldn't stand to listen to virtually anything on the New York FM dial, because it was so distorted," he says today.

Foti, however, was just getting started. Program directors never stopped asking him how they could get the Z-100 sound at their station, so he decided to start a company, Omnia, to produce it on a mass scale. One digital Omnia processor could house all the functionality of that clumsy array of analog effects he'd put together for Z-100. More important, the one box could let stations perfect their own unique sound.

Foti's advances were as much conceptual as purely technical. The lesson he took from his years on the processing front lines was that people don't just tolerate sonic corruption—they crave it. "I've had many professional debates with people where I've argued that we're used to hearing certain amounts of natural distortions," he says. "Walk into a recording studio that's been tuned for no reflection at all"—that is, a completely dry room—"and it sounds 'wrong,' even though technically you're in a sterile sonic room. To me, that proves that human beings are accustomed to hearing things that aren't 'pure,' that aren't perfect."

Foti aggressively explored the outer limits of human psychoacoustics.

In any processing, the final step, the one designed to really get the edge of loudness over competing stations by reducing dynamic range, is some sort of audio clipper. The clipping that pop and R&B stations typically employ is so aggressive that on its own it would make the signal sound grossly distorted. Foti decided that a listener can typically withstand up to 5 percent of harmonic distortion on a tone without noticing any unwanted artifacts, and designed his processors' clipping capabilities to guard against overshooting this limit.

For the Loudness War, the most important thing about Foti's machines is that they are very sophisticated multiband processors. Foti took Dorrough's breakthrough and ran with it, allowing users to divide a signal into six different bands to be processed separately. When Dorrough first began to travel around the country with his DAP, the most common criticism he received from skeptical stations was that his machine would alter the intentions of musicians and producers who had decided that a record should sound a certain way. By the nineties, this concern seemed quaint. Radio began to get louder and louder. And then a funny thing happened. CDs began to sound like the radio.

Thomas Edison hated the way radio made people think that its microphone-driven electrical gloss was the way recorded music should sound. The cycle began anew in the late eighties. Radio increasingly sounded like Z-100, and then CDs tried to mimic radio, covetous of radio's glorious compression powers. "My understanding is that that's when the mastering world started to experiment with multiband compression and multiband limiting," Foti says. "And that changed everything."

There was actually evidence that Top 40 radio was moving away from the loudness insanity of the eighties—"a backing off from the balls-to-the-wall attitude," as Garnet Drakiotes, the chief engineer of Seattle's KUBE, put it in 1991. This was partially due to Foti's products. Multiband processing now made extreme loudness easier to achieve, but it also gave stations more options for developing custom sounds; a station's Omnia settings were often guarded with the same secrecy that made Foti put a shade in front of his setup at Z-100. But as radio's Loudness War became a more low-level affair, the idea of loudness as power migrated virally into the recording world, along with some of the toys.

Multiband processors didn't make their way into every mastering studio, and even today many mastering engineers take a dim view of them. But all mastering engineers had to grapple with the expectation among their clients that CDs had to sound like the radio in order to be played on the radio—and, on a more symbolic level, had to sound like the radio in order to be considered a serious commercial product. "There's a certain sound that compression makes on the ear where it kind of sounds like you're listening to it on the radio," Calbi says. "So if you're a label trying to hype up your promotion department and you're playing something that sounds like a mix and they're used to hearing stuff that sounds like it's on the radio, there's that sound."

"I would get people telling me that they wanted [their CD] to sound like it was on the radio," says Feathered. "They wanted it loud, that thick compressed sound." Soon enough, there was real business incentive for mastering engineers to make a CD—which, remember, has a potential dynamic range of 96 dB—and compress it so that its range was a "radiofied" 55 dB. "You had to smash the life out of these things. But people loved it, because finally their CD sounded, when you put it in the boom box, like it was coming out of the radio."

First the high-end mastering houses got compression tools. But then the price began to drop. "It became more egalitarian out there," Feathered says. "So now you had the hacks. They didn't have the ears, they didn't have the [correct] monitoring situation—pretty much their sole weapon to justify getting money from the client was, 'Look, I can make it as loud or louder than this Metallica record you guys like so much.'"

Every mastering engineer has a slightly different story of the digital tool that really pushed the war into overdrive. For Feathered, it was the L1 Ultramaximizer by a company called Waves. For Gray, it was the Apogee, which had a setting that could compress a signal by 9 dB, and took off in the hip-hop world. "Within a year everyone was doing the nine-decibel thing on rap records," he says. "The next thing I noticed it was happening in dance music. That started going real real loud too. Pretty soon it filtered into everything, including jazz."

For Ludwig, it was the Finalizer, which advertises itself as capable of providing "that 'radio ready' sound." Ludwig was mastering an album for the Canadian band the Tea Party and gave one of the members of the band a reference disc. "He said he preferred his own version, which had been run through the newly developed Finalizer, with one of the brutal stock settings," Ludwig recalls. "It was twice as loud as my reference, but that's how he liked it. I ended up mastering the record through it in order to incorporate the sound he wanted. That was a horrible day."

Then CDs began to break the clipping barrier, a practice that until recently had been so taboo that Philips and Sony expressly forbade it. "There used to be a spec in the Red Book [the CD system's manual of technical specifications] that prohibited having anything going over level," Gray explains. "Up through 1990 or so, that rule was pretty hard and fast. Then around 1991 you would have to send an affidavit to the plant saying that the producer, the engineer, and the artist had approved the fact that there were over-levels. And then by about 1994 or so, nobody cared anymore. It just wasn't an issue."

After 1994, there was no turning back. With each passing year, CDs got more compressed. More waveforms were slammed up against that 0 dBFS barrier. In 1999, the Loudness War reached a crisis point.

They called it "the year of the square wave," in tribute to the flat-topped waves that had donated their transients to the cause of loudness. It wasn't just CD buyers that were feeling the onslaught of digital-era loudness. Responding to complaints that movie previews were being produced at ear-splitting levels to command theatergoers' attention, the Trailer Audio Standards Association announced that trailers would be run through a "soundtrack loudness meter" developed by Dolby Laboratories. The meter would ensure that a trailer's "annoyance factor"—a measure of the duration of loud sounds in relation to the total length of the trailer—did not exceed 87 dB. But in the music world, where the only guidelines were voluntary, anarchy reigned. Everybody had a favorite example of loudness gone wild. Was it Ricky Martin's "Livin' La Vida Loca"? Cher's "Believe"? Rage Against the Machine's *The Battle of Los Angeles*? Santana's *Supernatural*?

There was one CD that everyone could agree was loud beyond the call of duty. The Red Hot Chili Peppers' *Californication* is so filled with loudness-inducing compression that even casual listeners were noticing it. From the opening fuzzed-out bass riff of "Around the World," the album just pummels you. Clipping abounds, but the CD goes beyond clipping to something much more perverse. This is a picture of a brief moment of "Get on Top."

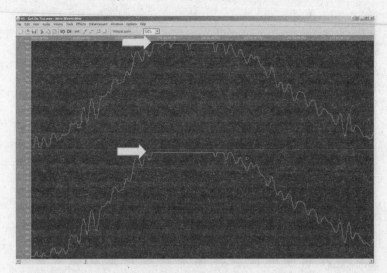

The arrow is pointing to a flatlined wave, but notice that the wave is *not* bumping up against the 0 dBFS ceiling. This suggests that the signal was compressed violently enough to clip; and then, to reduce dynamic range further, this flat-topped signal was compressed once more.

" 'Get on Top' is probably the worst-clipped song in the history of human endeavor," says Simon Howson. "It's absolute craziness." Howson is not a mastering engineer or any kind of audio professional. He was a film history graduate student in Australia, and a huge Chili Peppers fan who knew nothing about mastering or loudness when he first heard *Californication*, but he knew something didn't sound right. In fact, he found himself never wanting to listen to it. He discovered Rip Rowan's seminal article on the compression atrocities inflicted on Rush's *Vapor Trails* and realized that *Californication* exhibited the same symptoms. Comparing the album with exquisitely remastered albums by Miles Davis and John Coltrane further radicalized Howson to the crimes of hypercompression.

The Chili Peppers' next album, *By the Way*, was released three years later. By then, CDs had begun to creep back down from the 1999 loudness extremes. But it was still very loud. Inspired by a Warner Bros. decision to reissue *Vapor Trails*, partly as a response to the complaints of Rowan and other Rush fans, Howson began an online petition to urge the label to reassess its Chili Peppers catalog. "The main objective is to release new versions of the albums that do not contain excessive compression, and are free of digital distortion (clipping) that is sadly prevalent on current CD, and even LP, copies," the petition reads. "The music should not be mastered simply to make all of the songs sound as loud as possible when broadcast on radio."

By the fall of 2006, the petition had just over seven hundred signatures. That's not exactly a groundswell of opinion, especially compared with the momentum Rowan started with his article. But as Howson points out, Rush's fan base is older than the Chili Peppers' and more likely to own the sort of high-end stereo equipment that highlights the scourges of compression. Rush fans can remember what music used to sound like; for the youngest of the Chili Peppers fans, hypercompression is all they've known. But the impassioned, pleading comments left by some signatories ("Be trend-setters and say 'NO MORE' to the loudness race") suggest a growing awareness of the high musical cost of loudness and compression.

More than any other album before or since, *Californication* touched off a debate within mastering circles about the limits of loudness. How hot was too hot, and had *Californication* crossed that line? One of the mastering engineers pondering that question was Tardon Feathered. Although Feathered isn't one of the more high-profile mastering engineers, he's one of the few left who actually *is* a mastering engineer, as the job has traditionally been defined. In the analog era, the mastering engineer produced the final product, the disc from which others were cut. For CDs, the actual stamper disc is fabricated (authored) at the CD factory, so most mastering engineers are really premastering engineers. Today they don't even have to send a digital tape to the plant; they just transmit the music electronically to the person who authors the master disc. When DVDs became popular in the nineties, many of the people who authored discs at CD factories were lured to Hollywood to author DVDs. Rather than replace them, factories began outsourcing authoring duties to freelancers like Feathered, who runs a small mastering house in San Francisco called Mr. Toad's. These people are in the unique position of hearing the handiwork of mastering engineers around the world.

Because he was constantly hearing premasters from different engineers, Feathered knew that ideas of what constituted an acceptable level of loudness varied greatly among mastering engineers. He followed the debates that raged over *Californication* on the Mastering WebBoard. "Numerous people were complaining, 'This record is so loud, it redefines bad,' " Feathered recalls. "Mastering engineers were ripping the CD digitally, and counting the number of places they found clipping." It occurred to Feathered that even if there was a general consensus that *Californication* was too hot, there was no consensus whatsoever about what the acceptable threshold of hotness was. The first step toward rectifying the negative effects of the Loudness War was being able to codify—if not quantify—what they were. And so the What Is Hot? project was born.

The Bay Area band Applesaucer agreed to be Feathered's test case. In the summer of 2000, he sent an unmastered version of the band's dreamy, midtempo "Angeline" to anyone on the board who wanted to participate. The instructions were simple: make a master of the song and send it back. Twenty people took up the challenge. As Feathered expected, the amount of hotness varied greatly among the versions. Arranging them in order from softest to loudest, Feathered discovered that, to his ears, the very softest and very loudest were a disaster ("proving that all engineers make some mistakes"), versions two through eight were passable, nine through twelve sounded great, and everything from thirteen on contained audible artifacts caused by very hot mastering.

Feathered sent out a compilation of twenty versions to anyone on the board who asked. Then he went one step further. Robert Orban, the radio processing guru who lamented the Loudness War in radio during the Z-100 days, took an interest in the project. He ran all twenty, plus the original unmastered mix, through some of his company's Optimod FM processing gear on a few settings. In doing so, he was approximating how the various masters would sound if they were played over the radio. The results were interesting, if not very surprising to people who, like Orban and Feathered, had been paying attention to the Loudness War. "What we found was that nine through twelve stayed pretty big," Feathered says. "The bottom line was that not only did the ones in the middle sound fine, but the ones that were hotter were negatively impacted even more." In some cases, the combination of the superhot mastering and FM processing resulted in a phenomenon called "inversion," meaning that the loud parts actually sounded tinier and more pinched than the softer parts.

"So now we knew there was a ceiling up to which digital sounded good, based on the way current FM processing gear handled it," Feathered says.

This wasn't necessarily an eternally binding rule. As Feathered points out, what was true about the effects of dynamic range compression in 1999 isn't necessarily true today. Changes in technology affect the interplay between the sound of recorded music and the sound of transmitted music. Still, it was a powerful demonstration that the Loudness War had real observable consequences. "At the very least, by all of us discussing the same thing, for a brief period of time we could all agree that there were indeed negative artifacts, and that things were compromised by going too loud," Feathered says. "Relative to what FM broadcasting was putting out, the only conclusion we could draw was that if you had any realistic hope of getting on the radio, you shouldn't do this to your record, because it won't sound good on the airwaves."

It was a simple but powerful theorem: the more one applies technology designed to make records sound big on the radio, the smaller they will sound when they are played on the radio. It was an important enough conclusion to unite two of the three unwitting architects of the Loudness War.

You could argue that Dorrough, Orban, and Foti, through their pioneering work in radio processing, have collectively had as much influence on the way music sounds today as any musician. Like the members of the Manhattan Project, whose feelings regarding their life's work were complicated and conflicted after Hiroshima and Nagasaki, the Loud Three have a complex relationship with the war they set in motion. Disenchantment with the Loudness War was one of the reasons Dorrough left the radio processing business. His company's current signature product, the Dorrough Meter, is a tool that lets audio engineers simultaneously monitor an audio signal's peak level and average levels. There's something utopian about the Dorrough Meter, in the way it tries to reconcile the sonic model of the analog world (average) with that of the digital world (peak) that almost feels like penance from somebody who never meant to start a war.

Orban and Foti have remained in the business, though they each have a very different temperament and outlook. Orban, who was there from the beginning of FM, tends to have a more detached, dispassionate attitude toward the processing game, while Foti, more a product of the latter period of radio's Loudness War, still maintains an aura of the upstart. "He's sort of a rock and roller, and I came from a more classical background," Orban says. Foti thinks Dorrough has never gotten the credit he deserves and believes Orban's aggressive business tactics were part of the reason Dorrough receded into the background. "Bob can be a bit of a surly guy," Foti says. "He's got a bit of arrogance about him that gets on my nerves."

But these two rivals found common cause in the wake of What Is Hot? to issue a joint statement that implored their clients to use the tools of loudness more responsibly. The radio processors that their companies made had been designed for a recorded music environment that had ceased to exist in a very short period of time. The products simply weren't designed for the boundless pursuit of hypercompression that had gripped the recording industry. "Broadcast processing is complex and sophisticated, and was tuned for the recordings produced using practices typical of the recording industry during almost all of its history," they wrote. "In this historical context, hypercompression is a short-term anomaly, and does not coexist well with the 'competitive' processing that most pop-music stations use." The result was a broadcast climate dominated by "musical wallpaper," sounds squelched by processors that were just doing their job.

One could argue that the record companies just as easily could have told the radio processing companies that the onus was on them to catch up and adapt to the new hypercompressed musical world. But it was a start. The sound of radio was just one casualty of the Loudness War, but at least one component of the industry was officially taking the position that enough was enough.

The Loudness War never really ended, though it has subsided a bit since its fin-de-siècle peak. "For the first time in a long time, I can finally say that on *occasion*, a client will request less compression than before, which is a good sign," says Ludwig. "Still, most clients want things loud, often to the degradation of the music." Just as Neil Young warned that one day we'd look back on the digital age and wonder what that music really sounded like, maybe we'll listen to the output of the nineties and wonder what it would have been like if it hadn't been compressed to within an inch of its life. "Engineers who squash their mixes may rue the day they did, if supercompression falls out of style," Ludwig warns. "There is no way to get the dynamics back."

One shorthand way of assessing the Loudness War is considering it through the prism of the Red Hot Chili Peppers, whose improbably long career forms a microcosmic view of the conflict. The following chart, using data compiled by Howson, compares the "replay gain" of the band's studio albums.

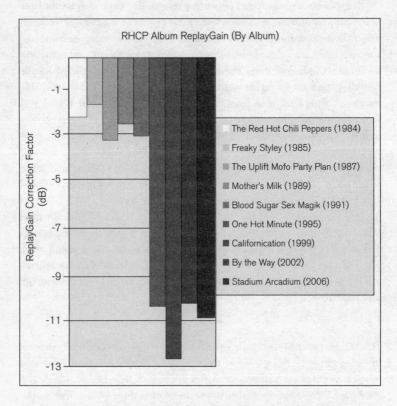

Replay gain is a proposed standard for normalizing the volume of computer audio files. This chart shows the degree to which each album's average volume would have to be decreased so that they were at the same level. Thus the longer the bar, the greater the necessary decrease, and the louder the mastering. Notice that their self-titled debut in 1984 is actually a bit louder than their follow-up the next year. *The Uplift Mofo Party Plan*, released in 1987, shows a considerable increase. Two years later, *Mother's Milk* drops the level again, and then at the dawn of the nineties, the band's breakthrough, *Blood Sugar Sex Magik*, raises it to the 1987 level. By 1995, with *One Hot Minute* the level suddenly becomes steroidal, signifying that we're now immersed in the war, as digital limiters enter the market. *Californica-*

tion, comeback number two, takes things to a ludicrous height, as the industry begins to crash and burn with the rise in downloads and decline in CD sales. Then the hangover: *By the Way* drops way down (though nowhere near the early nineties levels). *Stadium Arcadium* rises again, proving the war is far from over.

To this day, *Californication* remains a bête noire for the anticompression crowd. A version of the album purported to be the final mix in its unmastered form (the sequencing is the same, and the songs seem identical to the official version, although some of the vocals are incomplete) was leaked onto the Internet, presumably by members of the anti–Loudness War underground, though the source of the leak could be closer to home. One person involved with the album's production says that in its premastered form, it was the best-sounding recording he had ever worked on. Even some of the band's supporters at Elektra Records, the Chili Peppers' label, were said to be openly dissatisfied with the way the album turned out.

The unmastered *Californication* isn't exactly a smoking gun. Whoever leaked the songs probably had them as MP3s, converted them to WAV files, and burned the music onto CD-Rs. The discs circulated as bootlegs, until somebody decided to post them on the Web, a process that would entail yet another conversion to MP3 or a similar format. That's a lot of converting, most of it crude.

Nonetheless, the difference is still noticeable and at times striking. That leadoff track, "Around the World," doesn't sound nearly as distorted, for example. As a whole, you do get a sense of more breathing space from *Unmasterfication*.

The visuals tell a more concrete and discernible story. Just compare the respective pictures of "Right on Time." Here is the CD version.

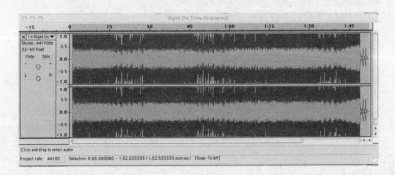

And here is the unmastered version.

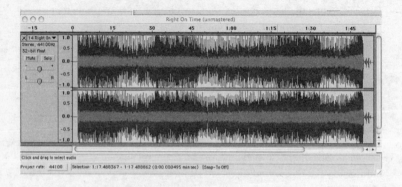

As the pictures make clear, *Californication* underwent a big transformation during the mastering process. It was mastered by Vlado Meller, among the half dozen or so most elite mastering engineers working today, and the one with the biggest reputation for excessive hypercompression. That's not an entirely fair rep. Besides a slew of rock and hip-hop albums, Meller's many credits include acts as unrock as Harry Connick Jr., Botticelli, and others whose albums he doesn't give the loud treatment for obvious aesthetic reasons. But the fact remains that Meller is among the top ten mastering engineers in the world—on any given week, a Meller-mastered album is likely in the Top 10 in a few countries—and within that select group he's the one most likely to bring the Hammer of Thor down on the music he masters. Some anticompression advocates practically accuse him of committing Loudness War crimes. "His work is very bad," one mastering engineer told me. "He defaults to 'stun.'"

Longtime Chili Peppers producer Rick Rubin,* who has a reputation as something of an audiophile, is a big fan of Meller's mastering. Michael Fremer, in a 2004 interview with Rubin on MusicAngle.com, brought up the Mars Volta's *De-Loused in the Comatorium* album, which was produced by Rubin, and perfectly captured the tenor of the anti-Meller contingent.

---

*Rubin was at the center of a controversy regarding Metallica's 2008 album *Death Magnetic*, which he produced. Fans complained about the hypercompressed sound of the album and discovered that the version used for the video game *Guitar Hero* actually had more dynamics than the commercially released version. Ted Jensen, the album's mastering engineer, claimed that what he was given to master was already so compressed that there was little he could do to it.

RR: The guy who does my mastering at Sony in New York . . .

MF: Vlado Meller?

RR: Yeah.

MF: Now somebody smashed the Mars Volta record.

RR: Him.

MF: WHY?????

RR: *(chuckling)* That's what he does.

MF: He shouldn't have done that! That sounds like it could have been a great recording. It was a great recording but he squeezed the dynamics out of it . . . Something has to be done about that. Can't you control the mastering guy? "Vlado, lay off!"

Later in the interview, Rubin says, "We do shoot-outs all the time. I master with as many as five different mastering engineers mastering the same album, and then we [compare] them, and it's interesting, Vlado wins nine out of ten times, and he claims it's not him. He's got technology in that room that's a 2 million dollar mastering suite that other people don't have."

A magical room where records go through some sort of alchemical hotness process? Presided over by a modern-day Vlad[o] the Impaler who sucks the lifeblood (dynamics) from his victims (records)? This I had to see.

I found that room—Meller's spacious mastering suite—on the ground floor of Sony Music Studios on Manhattan's West Side. Meller turned out to be an unassuming guy wearing shorts and a yellow golf shirt. "I have certain tricks to make records sound loud," he admitted, with a pronounced Eastern European accent, though he insisted he never engaged in "squashing" the music he mastered.

Meller grew up in a Jewish family in Czechoslovakia. His father worked as a refinisher of pianos, and Meller learned the violin as a child. He had his first exposure to Western music while studying electrical engineering at the University of Prague. At nights he would tune in to Radio Luxembourg, picking up the faint sounds of the Beatles, Chubby Checker, and Dave Clark, when the signal managed to elude the Communist Czech government's signal jamming. "I'd listen between the noise," he recalled. "I said to myself, 'Wow, there's life on the other side of the fence, and it sounds so good!' " He took weekend trips to Yugoslavia, where the Communists had a more lax attitude toward Western culture, to buy 45s, concealing his purchases when he recrossed the border for fear of being arrested.

Meller managed to escape Czechoslovakia in 1968 and eventually wound up in the United States, unemployed and unsure of his future. He met somebody who worked for CBS Records, who mentioned that the label had a recording studio. Although Meller knew very little about recording, the studio hired him as an assistant in December 1969. Eighteen months later, he was promoted to staff mixer and eventually transitioned into mastering. Over the years, he worked on albums by everyone from Paul McCartney to Public Enemy. Meller stayed with the company through all its corporate permutations. (Sony acquired CBS in 1988.) With Meller's reputation, he could certainly thrive on his own, but he's always liked the job security he has at Sony. In an extremely volatile industry, Meller has managed to hold down the same job for almost forty years.

I'd always thought of the Loudness War as a very American phenomenon—like Tardon Feathered says, capitalism rules—but talking to Meller suddenly made me feel like *complaining* about the Loudness War was embarrassingly American. It felt slightly ridiculous, like the way I imagine it would have felt to argue about the problems of late capitalism with the recently defected Meller in 1969. I could just picture him thinking that only in America, where the streets are paved with gold and loudness, could somebody complain about such abundance. "Today's kid has a $40 MP3 player, and guess what—it sounds fuckin' great!" he said. "Many people will say, 'It sounds better on vinyl.' That's total fuckin' nonsense. These people know nothing about recording."

For Meller, making hot records is about giving the audience what it wants. "Today's generation likes to listen to CDs which are loud," he said. "Most people listen to music in their cars, and they don't have to turn it up. They expect you to make it loud. If it's not loud enough, they'll take it out and put in something else. This is the game we play now. You can still preserve the dynamics. I wouldn't say you're squashing the program or killing the program, because you can put these CDs on, and they sound okay. They sound nice . . . It's one thing to have a theory in your head—dynamics and all these beautiful things—and another thing to be able to play it on a portable player or in your car."

On the sound of *Californication*, a topic he'd clearly been over many times, he said, "Yeah, it was a super-hot CD, but you know what? It sold—what is it, 9 million? They like a loud sound, they like it in-your-face. Yeah, maybe *Californication* was a little over the top, but everybody loved it."

As for his critics, "I would withhold my comments on Bob Katz," he said, though he soon offered them freely. "Bob Katz likes to analyze everything. I respect his opinions, but it's out of his league over here. I master more records in one week than he's done in five years!" (Not true, though Meller does more high-profile records than Katz.)

"If you take three people and play them the same three CDs with three different levels, they'll pick the loudest one," he continued. "It doesn't matter if it's an audiophile, a kid who's fourteen, or someone who's fifty-nine. The louder will sound better. If I go to Carnegie Hall to hear a concert, I'd kill the guy behind the stage if he ran the sound through a compressor. I want to hear the whole thing. But [CDs] are for the listening enjoyment of people who are driving cars, who have MP3 players, who are jogging. Some of them have stereos at home, but what's the setup? The dog is barking, the wife is banging dishes in the kitchen, the kid is crying in the bedroom. Are they worrying about dynamics? What dynamics? I work with classical people. They want dynamics. It's absolutely gorgeous. I know how to do that. But that's not what the Chili Peppers want, that's not what Puddle of Mudd wants, and it's not what Limp Bizkit wants. It's a totally different world.

"You go to a rock concert—it's unbearable! It's unbearable for me to sit there and listen to the levels they're playing at. The CD doesn't even come close. But this is how they want it! It's a rock-and-roll concert, and if you don't like it loud, then go to fuckin' Carnegie Hall and listen to Beethoven. The people who criticize loud records are probably the ones who never listen to them. If you like Shostakovich, you don't buy Chili Peppers CDs. If you like Metallica, you don't listen to Miles Davis. There are very few people who like classical music and heavy metal at the same time. Go to any college, gather two hundred kids, and ask them if they like loud records. I guarantee all two hundred will. Are they 'fatigued'? Nonsense."

Meller's hypotheticals were interesting, because Howson, the Chili Peppers fan who launched the petition, was a student whose antiloudness epiphany came when he began to listen to Miles Davis reissues. I mentioned Howson. Meller bristled. "Another techno-freak," he said. "I say get a life, get a job, and do some real mastering. Then I'll talk to you. Sitting at home analyzing my sine wave on an oscilloscope—I don't call that mastering. I tell you right now—all these people who criticize and send me e-mails, if you want to do mastering, go ahead, see how many clients you get."

When I left that afternoon, and I was back on West 53rd, it struck me

that the Hudson River was just down the street, and that Secaucus, the
original home of Z-100, was very close to the riverbank on the other side.
Z-100 has long since migrated to Manhattan, but I imagined them on the
other side, combining with Meller's mastering room to form a sort of "loudness corridor" in the lowest reaches of the Hudson, with ships piled high
with loudness streaming into the ocean and the world beyond. We may not
make many things in this country anymore, but we can still export the loud.

8

Tubby's Ghost

Ricky Martin's "Livin' La Vida Loca," one of the biggest songs of 1999, was the perfect song for the end of the millennium. Its internationalist rhythms and intuitive Spanglish offered a model of casual multiculturalism, evoking a world of porous boundaries. Heard today, the song still sounds uprooted and unmoored. Like the song's narrator, who wakes up and discovers that he has somehow been teleported to New York City, the sounds themselves seem to jet by, as though movement through time and space were their birthright.

Martin, a former member of the Latin boy-band sensation Menudo, worked on his first solo album, from which "Livin' La Vida Loca" was taken, with several producers. One of them was Desmond Child, who ran a studio called the Gentlemen's Club out of the garage of his Miami home. Besides the sofas, saltwater fish tanks, and tasteful cabinetry that housed the recording equipment, there was one other aspect of the Club that belied its garage origins: it contained hardly a scrap of analog tape. While the twenty-four-track tape machine gathered dust, Child favored a 24-bit, sixty-four-track hard-disc recording system called Pro Tools.

Child was particularly obsessive about vocals. Before he began working with Pro Tools, one of his favorite tricks, which he'd learned from the legendary recording engineer Tom Dowd, was to execute quick cross-fades between two performances of the same vocal line, thus avoiding the subtle artifacts caused by cutting and splicing tape. What he liked most about Pro Tools was that it made editing both simpler and more precise. He could see the sounds as digital waveforms on a computer screen, and move them around with the click of a mouse. He could repeat parts as much as he wanted with no loss of fidelity. He could try ten variations of an edit, and decide which worked best.

"That's what Desmond got into—the fact that he could invent a vocal performance that he was hearing in his head," says Charles Dye, a staff engineer at the Gentlemen's Club during the making of the Martin album. "That's what he realized he could now do in Pro Tools. He could even take syllables and move them around. If he felt a syllable should be phrased just a bit back in time, he'd cut it and move it ever so slightly because phrasing is where the emotion is. You set up the expectation with the groove, and then you lay back on one line or come in a little earlier on another. It subtly changes the emotion of the listener, because things aren't happening exactly where you imagine they would."

By the late nineties, the idea of digital recording wasn't new. Digital audiotape (DAT), a technology that Sony and Philips originally conceived as the next step after the compact disc, and then vigorously promoted as a professional recording standard when the piracy-averse music industry decided not to cooperate, was an affordable digital alternative and a common feature of many recording studios. Although Pro Tools had been around since a Silicon Valley company called Digidesign introduced the first version in 1991, the idea of using hard-disc recording to make a professional record was considerably more exotic. The conventional wisdom was that to do so required something like the Post Pro, a huge (twenty-four cubic feet) and hugely expensive (at least $250,000) hard-disc recording system manufactured by New England Digital, the company that had created the Synclavier, the first all-digital synthesizer, in the seventies. The Post Pro was a particularly advanced version of what people were now calling "digital audio workstations" (DAWs), hardware and software that allowed musicians to record, edit, and mix sound in the digital domain.

Throughout the decade, as the cost of memory decreased and processing speed increased, and digital signal processors grew more sophisticated, DAWs had become more common. At first they were mostly used to edit music that had been recorded on digital or analog tape. Then they began to creep into the recording process. In 1997, Dye did a shoot-out between the Sony 3348, the company's leading 16-bit DAT recorder, and the latest version of Digidesign's Pro Tools. The DAW won. "I realized that for $20,000, including interfaces, you could get something that sounded better than a $250,000 machine," he says.

It was clear you could edit music using Pro Tools, and the idea of recording directly into Pro Tools was gaining currency, but mixing remained an unconquered realm of the analog frontier. Since the seventies, recorded music had developed around the idea that mixing required a massive amount of sound processing. You needed to add compression, EQ, delay, reverb—not to mention artfully combining twenty-four tracks or more into two stereo channels—and to do all this to professional-grade standards required the vast acreage of knobs and faders provided by an analog SSL (or comparable) console.

It was possible to mix "in the box," using a DAW's digital controls in lieu of an analog console, especially as plug-ins were becoming available that could offer credible alternatives to these analog effects. But mixing in the box was used almost exclusively either for demos or by musicians who had no access to a recording studio. The virtual interfaces were a poor substitute for the intuitiveness of row upon row of physical controls. A bigger problem was the enormous amount of sound processing required for a multitrack mix, enough to make DAWs prone to glitches. Even when they worked well, they couldn't match the subtlety and expressiveness of an analog board.

In the late nineties, a newer generation of sound engineers who had come of age in the era of digital sampling began to question this orthodoxy. Much more than their predecessors, these engineers considered postproduction and mixing to be a crucial step in itself, not some adjunct to the recording process. People like Dye idolized the Power Station vet Bob Clearmountain, who had done more than anyone to make "mixing" a specialized skill. "Like every other recording engineer, I wanted to be a mixing engineer," Dye says. "The only reason I had a leg up was that I was at Desmond's place. I had Pro Tools in front of me, and those were the only tools I had. If I was going to do record-quality mixes, I would have to do it on that gear, because nobody was gonna pay for a $1,000-a-day room for me to figure out how to mix."

"Livin' La Vida Loca" began as a demo banged out on keyboards and recorded onto a boom box by Martin and his collaborator, Robi Rosa. In the new world of DAWs, this demo was more than just a guide to what the song would become. Because it was saved in Pro Tools, it became the literal seed of the song. "From the beginning, the demo was the record," Dye explains. Using Pro Tools, a programmer named Randy Cantor assembled percussion, acoustic guitar, and keyboard parts. During one session, it was decided that a gong should be heard a few bars into the second verse. Percussionist Rafael Solano didn't have one, so engineers recorded him hitting his largest cymbal with a soft mallet. They dropped the pitch of the cymbal by two octaves in Pro Tools, and combined the sound with the original cymbal crash, creating a reasonable facsimile of a gong. To add a sense of depth to the vocals, Dye used a Pro Tools plug-in to split the signal, delaying one split by eighteen milliseconds and the other by twenty-four milliseconds.

Throughout the whole process, Dye made rough mixes in Pro Tools. When the song was finished, it was sent to New York to be mixed on an analog console, along with one of Dye's Pro Tools mixes as a guide. When he was finished, the engineer in New York played the result over a high-fidelity phone line for Child and Rosa in Miami. Something didn't sound right.

"Didn't you listen to the rough mix?" Child asked.

"Yeah," the engineer replied. "It's all distorted."

He was right. Dye's mix did sound distorted—too much so for a final mix—but it had a naturalistic quality that the New York mix lacked. The tracks mixed on the analog board had come back too clean, too digital. Dye, working with Pro Tools, had digitally shaped the sound into something that sounded analog.

Rosa thought Dye had the right idea and asked if he'd like to try doing a final mix at Miami's Criteria Recording Studio, or perhaps at Emilio Estefan's Crescent Moon Studios, two places with fancy analog consoles. Dye said he'd like to stick with his Pro Tools rig. Although Child was okay with that, "it made everyone else on the planet skeptical," Dye says. "They thought it was nuts, because there was this inertia of working in million-dollar rooms, and this belief that a $250,000 console with a $250,000 tape machine and another $100,000 worth of outboard gear was the only way to mix a record."

Dye struggled to get the exact mix he heard in his head. "At first, I was really frustrated and didn't think it sounded good," he says. "But I learned to use plug-ins that allowed me to get a more analog sound. I was able to be a lot more precise than I could be on an analog mixing console. I could make things pop out for a moment and then tuck them back into the mix. I could zoom in on a snare drum, a single hit, and turn it up louder at a certain point because it seemed to make sense that the drummer would pop out and play a fill there in a really exciting way."

"Livin' La Vida Loca" went on to be the first number-one song made completely in the box. For the first time, the chart in *Billboard* that lists the equipment used to record the week's chart-toppers had the same entry ("Pro Tools") in every column, "recording console," "recording medium," "mixing console," and "mix medium."

Dire Straits' *Brothers in Arms*, recorded in 1984 and released the following year, is often cited as the first major album made for the digital era because it was a "fully digital" recording. It was recorded on digital tape, mixed with a two-track digital tape machine, and then mastered onto CD: "DDD." But it wasn't—not really. The problem is the second D. Digital audio technology was not advanced enough to mix the album fully in the digital realm. Neil Dorfsman, the album's recording and mixing engineer, mixed *Brothers in Arms* on an SSL G series console. The output from the digital tape had to pass through a D/A converter so that the signal could be mixed on the analog console. Once mixed, the signal passed through an A/D converter and was once again encoded on digital tape. The exposure to the analog world was brief, and the analog signal never touched magnetic tape, but there was nonetheless a small break in this all-digital chain.

Just as "Livin' La Vida Loca" was probably not the very first commercial release mixed with Pro Tools, *Brothers in Arms* was not the very first DDD release. But each was a defining moment in digital audio history. The Dire Straits album fulfilled the promise of the compact disc: digitizing a sound at its source and keeping it digital all the way to the end product (the brief conversion in the mixing stage notwithstanding). The goal was sonic purity. The Martin song more truthfully embodied the promise of digital—it was nothing but code all the way down the line—but it also inverted the promise of the CD. The goal was not so much to preserve a sound in crystalline form, but to achieve maximum flexibility—to sully it, take it as far from its original form as the musician/engineer wanted it. Where there is no gong, a gong shall be.

What the word processor did for the written world, Pro Tools—and other DAWs such as Logic, Cubase, and Reason—does for sound. Audio can be recorded directly onto a hard drive, stored on separate tracks, moved around with a mouse, and manipulated through various plug-ins. "Pro Tools has replaced the multitrack recorder," says the mixing engineer Tom Lord-

Alge. "More or less, every bit of recorded music these days is recorded into a DAW. It gives you the option of changing arrangements and using plug-ins to really fine-tune performances. It opens a whole new creative door for people. I call it a 'tape machine on steroids.' "

"Digital editing and Pro Tools multitracking have completely changed everything," says Chris Lord-Alge, Tom's brother and also a mixing engineer. "Now you can move audio around, organize it, duplicate, flop it around in a much easier fashion."

"In the old days it was trial and error," Tom says of the laborious process of mixing. "We would mix sections of the song, print to two-track, listen to it, and say we have to make an adjustment here and here. By the end of the day, the two-track had thirty edits in it. You were never able to sit down at the console and listen to the whole song if you had to make arrangement changes. Now it's instant gratification. It has definitely changed 100 percent how I mix."

Musicians value Pro Tools for the same reason as engineers. "The thing I like about it is that you can try out ideas so much more quickly now," says the Flaming Lips multi-instrumentalist Steven Drozd. "I can do ten parts of orchestration at my fingertips, or I can try crazy hip-hop beats. Ten years ago, it would have taken forever to do something like that on a four-track, or even an eight-track, whereas now you can try all these options, decide whether or not they're good, discard them, and move on."

In the DAW age, the recording studio is no longer necessarily the locus of all music production. Pro Tools is the reason a jet-setting hip-hop producer like Just Blaze can mix a song on a transatlantic flight. And it's the reason why musicians, recording straight to disc and judiciously using plug-ins and samples, can make records in simple home studios—or even bedrooms. "The big thing that Pro Tools did, which we recognized right away, is that at the time there was a big divide in the music business," says Evan Brooks, who cofounded Digidesign, the company that makes Pro Tools, in the eighties. "You couldn't play this game as a professional unless you were able to produce material that was of high enough quality, sonically, to be able to be played on the air. At that time, the only way to do that was in a professional recording studio. What we did was remove the barrier."

The democratizing impulse of DAWs is both their selling point and their chief criticism, something even Pro Tools' godfathers recognize. "Pro

Tools was all about egalitarianism, bringing those capabilities to literally anybody," Brooks says. "Unfortunately, if you allow anybody to make music, anybody will make music, which is a whole other set of unintended consequences."

The most common charge is that DAWs have dealt a fatal blow to the idea of musical spontaneity. Why get it right the first time when you can always fix it through plug-ins or judicious editing? "Personally, when I hear a produced pop tune where everything is highly quantized, highly pitch-corrected, with high-gloss perfection, it's just not interesting to me," says Peter Gotcher, Brooks's Digidesign partner. "To me, it's all the idiosyncratic qualities and faults in a human performance that make music interesting. One thing I regret about Pro Tools is that it's being used to manufacture a product that I personally am not all that enamored of. But it really is just a tool, and there are plenty of ways to make bad records on tape machines."

In fact, ever since multitrack tape recording became the norm, it's been possible to employ all manner of trickery to make music sound better. DAWs just make it a lot easier. "With analog, you don't have the ability to perfect things into an artificial reality, so it forces you to keep some of the humanity," Dye says.

"You create a lazy musician who will play a mediocre part and then enhance it with tuning or plug-ins," says Chris Lord-Alge. "I definitely hear mediocre performances becoming takes, whereas back in the day we'd have them resing or replay it until it was perfect," Tom agrees. Sometimes while mixing a record, Bob Clearmountain adds, "I'll hear something and think, why did they even bother? Why didn't they get someone who could play it? There are amazing musicians out there, who can play in time and sing in tune, so what's the deal? Why are these losers having their records made?"

Even certified nonlosers risk falling victim to the allure of DAWs. Just as the downside of the digital video revolution in documentary filmmaking has been that directors, freed of the expense of film, find themselves bogged down in the editing room with hundreds of hours of film, DAWs free musicians from the physical constraints of tape while overwhelming them with choices. The producer Ron St. Germain once spent a week just preparing one song for mixing because the band had given him two hundred tracks to work with.

A particularly vivid example of the effect DAWs have had on recording was on display in 2007 in a BBC documentary made to commemorate the fortieth anniversary of the Beatles' *Sgt. Pepper's* album. Geoff Emerick, the Beatles' recording engineer, supervised a remake of the album, with several acts—mostly youngish British bands—each recording a song at Abbey Road Studios. The goal was to use the original recording equipment, and to record the songs utilizing the same methods as the Beatles. That meant using the original four-track console and analog tape, a setup foreign to some of these groups.

The first band to record were the Kaiser Chiefs, who tackled "Getting Better." The documentary catches them arriving at the studio and realizing what they were in for. With four tracks of analog tape, overdubs would have to be minimal. If a mistake was made, the band would have to start over. "Normally, what we do is five or six takes, and then if there's one thing you really like from take four that isn't on take six, you can take that bit in Pro Tools and just drop it in," drummer Nick Hodgson tells the interviewer. "It's easy and it takes one second."

"You can get lazy, but it's much more convenient doing it the digital way," keyboardist Nick "Peanut" Baines adds.

As they play the basic tracks, you can see Emerick wearing a perplexed look in the control room. Something isn't quite right. The band is competent, but they're not really nailing it. "No," Emerick says, and calls them into the control room. They look sheepish. They ask the cameras to be shut off and spend two hours conferring. They manage to get through the song to Emerick's satisfaction, and afterward reflect on the experience.

"It took us something like twenty takes," Hodgson explains, looking as though he can't believe they did it. "We've never done that before."

Singer Ricky Wilson also describes the experience in revelatory terms. "It sounds more lively and it sounds more live, and it doesn't sound like instruments playing separately," he says. "I can actually hear the difference, which I didn't think I'd be able to do. People talk about tape and analog recording and digital recording, and everyone says analog is so much better, and you kind of think these people are stuck in the past, but they're not. They're right. Listen to the old folks. They know what they're talking about. Respect your elders."

A few months later, at an Audio Engineering Society convention, Emerick elaborated on the experience, describing the difficulty the band had doing harmony vocal overdubs without the crutch of Pro Tools. He told them that they'd each have their own mike, and that they'd have to look at each other while they sang, and only one person should say *s* and *t* sounds. And then, of course, there was the problem of singing out of tune, which took a while to iron out. "Eventually, they nailed it," Emerick recalled. "Well, after four and a half hours of this they were so appreciative, and almost in tears that someone had actually told them how to do it together. It was the most amazing feeling. They said, 'No one ever told us before.' It was just unbelievable."

It is fitting that mixing became the last step of the Pro Tools revolution, because as the Kaiser Chiefs' experience demonstrates, mixing (and editing), as opposed to recording (and letting it be), is the dominant mode of music today. The rise of DAWs is of a piece with the rise of sampling and sequencing, as well as digital sound files and iPods, all of which contribute to music's reduction into a universal code that can be recombined at will. Call it the Pro Tooling of the world, a musical condition of which Pro Tools itself is merely the most obvious example. Noting that "the recording mixer, which started out as just some slide controls and some knobs, is now in a sense a musical creation device," digital-sampling pioneer Roger Linn recently observed that computer-based interfaces and "control surfaces" used to create music are examples of "the mixer as metaphor."

We could trace the origin of this metaphor all the way back to Les Paul's sound-on-sound experiments, if not the musical enhancements of Stokowski and Bell Labs. But the person who wrote the first modern narrative to employ this metaphor in all its glory was a former electronics repairman in Jamaica named Osbourne Ruddock, known to most of the world as King Tubby. From the early seventies to the early eighties—reggae's initial roots period and the first part of its dancehall phase—Tubby was arguably the single greatest force driving the music. Tubby was not a singer or deejay, or a musician in any traditional sense. He was not even really a producer.* He was a recording engineer, though he rarely recorded anything besides vocals. Tubby made his living mixing records, something he did so

---

*The Jamaican music industry at the time was organized around what Steve Barrow has called an "auteur" framework. Producers wrote the music or solicited it from others, recruited musicians—often working with their own house band—and hired singers. The producers usually retained control of the recordings.

well that his name, like Edison's decades earlier, was often featured more prominently than the artist's on a record's label.

Producers would bring to Tubby's small voicing studio completed instrumental tracks recorded elsewhere. Tubby would overdub vocalists, and sometimes some additional instruments, and then mix the songs. He would then rework the instrumental songs into "dub" versions. Using the mixing board, he would manipulate the individual tracks, sometimes including the vocals, moving them in and out of the mix and adding additional effects. Bass, drums, rhythm guitar, vocals, and anything else on the tracks were dramatically recombined. A track could suddenly vanish or sound like it was shooting into the stratosphere. These dubs would become the B sides of the songs on which they were based, although the B sides were often what sold the records.

Dub—and, by extension, King Tubby—is often credited as the foundation of hip-hop, techno, and other types of music steeped in the idea of the remix, which is true enough but really sells Tubby short. He began the Pro Tooling of the world by turning his tiny studio into a musical instrument. He forged an aesthetic based on the idea that the recording of music—that initial capturing—wasn't so much unimportant as a historical given. There were recorded sounds out there already, just waiting to be reshaped.

One of the first all-dub albums was *Blackboard Jungle*, a 1973 collaboration between Tubby and Lee "Scratch" Perry, using rhythms* from Perry's house band, the Upsetters. On the song "Dub Organizer," a deejay named Dillinger pays tribute to Tubby: "Rock-and-roll like you never knew before / While King Tubby's at the controls." "Organizer" might seem like an oddly stale sobriquet for a groundbreaking musician, like calling a great artist a "paint-mixer," but Dillinger had it right. Tubby was a predigital Pro Tools prophet precisely because he had a preternatural ability to organize sound.

That's why Tubby's legacy extends far beyond the musical genres most closely linked to dub. The salient point about Tubby is not that he invented the remix (although he did). It's that the concept of the remix reinvented modern music.

---

*In the context of Jamaican music, a "rhythm" refers to a specific bass line and drum pattern combination. Since the emergence of rocksteady, the music that evolved into reggae in the late sixties, rhythms have been continuously "recycled." That can mean using the actual backing tracks for several songs, or making a new recording of the rhythm.

One night in Kingston in the late sixties, King Tubby's sound system was in full swing. His deejay,* Ewart "U-Roy" Beckford, was toasting over a rhythm called Stalag 17. He held the mike in his hand and shouted, "You're now listening to King Tubby's Hi-Fi!"

That's what he said, but what the crowd heard was *"You're listening to King Tubby's Hi-Fi-fi-fi-fi-fi . . ."* Tubby had engineered a slap-back echo by splitting U-Roy's vocal feed and delaying one of the feeds.

The crowd erupted. They cheered, they fired shots in the air. Philip Smart, an apprentice engineer at Tubby's studio who was there that night, remembers people finding Tubby and lifting him up on their shoulders. "It was the first time anyone in Jamaica had heard delay," he says. Although nearly everyone had heard it on records, "nobody knew how to get it in the dance. Tubbs secretly designed that, and nobody knew. After that dance, all the sound systems came by with orders for amplifiers. We couldn't fill them all. We were building amplifiers for months."

As with Edison's tone tests, it's impossible for us to comprehend fully what it was about hearing sound appear to hover in the air that made the crowd so excited. But it probably had something to do with the shock of having the world of recordings suddenly appear in the world of lived experience. Most of those people didn't know exactly how a reverb effect was achieved on a record, but they understood implicitly that recordings were fictions, not unmediated documents. In the real world, the microphone was supposed to be transparent.

It had been twenty years since Alan Lomax fantasized about giving recording machines to the unheard masses whose voices were being drowned out by "our commercially bought-and-paid-for loudspeakers." By now Lomax was beginning to wonder if that was such a good idea after all, since the larger one-way communication apparatus that those loudspeakers symbolized was colonizing all sonic space, obliterating local expression

---

*In Jamaican music, a deejay is not someone who spins records. (The term for that is "selecter.") A deejay is a vocalist distinct from a singer, though the difference can be hard to detect for someone new to the music. Deejays were initially akin to emcees at outdoor dances called "sound systems." They would fire up the crowd and often improvise lines over the music the selecter was playing, a practice known as "toasting." In the early seventies, deejays took their trade out of the dance hall and into the recording studio, and their styles became less "talky" and more keyed to the music.

with "the smog of the phoney." In Jamaica, the question was moot; the loudspeaker had won. The popularity of sound systems fostered a cottage industry in amplifier and loudspeaker design. The goal was to make sound travel far—sound systems were outdoors, so sound dissipated easily—and clear, something that Tubby excelled at.

Like Moses Asch, Tubby began as an electronics repairman, working with everything from televisions to refrigerators, and became steadily infatuated with the possibilities of amplified sound. Where Asch had his epiphany in midtown Manhattan, as FDR's voice bounced off the buildings, Tubby's canvas was the Jamaican night air.

Before his rise to fame, Tubby sometimes serviced the equipment in a modest one-mike recording studio called Treasure Isle run by Duke Reid, a popular producer. Reid had an arrangement with Rudolph "Ruddy" Redwood, a record-store owner and sound-system operator. Reid would give Redwood acetates, and Redwood would report back to Reid on which songs went over best with the crowd. The story—perhaps apocryphal—is that one day when Redwood was picking up music at Treasure Isle, he asked Reid's engineer, Byron Smith, to cut him an acetate of "On the Beach" by the Paragons. While making it, Smith realized he'd forgotten to include the vocals, but Redwood asked him to keep it the way it was. That night he cued up the normal version on one turntable, and the instrumental on the other. "I said, 'I'm gonna turn this place into a studio, and switch over from the singing part to the [instrumental] part, cut down the sound,' and you could hear the dance floor rail, man," Redwood later recalled.

Redwood persuaded Reid to release an instrumental version of the song. Realizing that he could double the amount of music he released without having to record more songs, Reid began releasing Treasure Isle singles with instrumental versions as the B side, with an overdubbed sax or organ carrying the vocal melody. Between 1968 and 1970, as the brief rocksteady era faded into the earliest reggae, other producers began putting instrumentals—now known simply as "versions"—on their B sides, until the practice became standard.

Tubby was friends with Bunny "Striker" Lee, a producer who often used Treasure Isle to record his music. In 1968, he took Tubby to one of Redwood's dances. Tubby noticed the electrifying effects the versions had on the dances and decided to upgrade his own fledgling Home Town Hi-Fi sound system. For his deejay, Tubby recruited U-Roy, who had made some records with Lee.

Tubby soon had the island's preeminent sound system. Part of the reason for its success was Tubby's technical innovations, such as separate tweeter boxes, little steel horns sprinkled throughout the dancers that accentuated the high-frequency slice of hi-hats and the crack of snares. As his sound system took off, Tubby began to build his voicing studio at a house his mother owned in the Waterhouse section of Kingston. Around 1971 or 1972, he began to experiment seriously with the creative possibilities of versions. The craft was growing. Other engineers, particularly Errol Thompson at a studio called Randy's, were beginning to play a more creative role, experimenting with manipulating the tracks and creating what soon came to be known as dub. Tubby's epiphany was discovering a way to import the sound of his dances onto a record.

It was clear that Tubby had a comprehensive, almost intimate understanding of the tools he used to mix, down to the level of the circuits. But how he achieved his sound, not even his assistants—Smart, Lloyd "Prince Jammy" James, and Overton "Scientist" Brown—understood exactly. "There was a few things that was done that nobody knew how it came about," Smart says. "There was talk from the other studios that Tubby souped up the board. I never really discussed it with him, if he added something to enhance the EQ. I don't think he did, but rumor had it at the other studios that Tubby's changed the resistors or whatever, and that's why the EQ sound like that." Tubby's most easily identifiable innovation was that he installed faders on his board, which allowed him to glide tracks in and out of the mix. Thompson's board only had buttons, so he was limited to punching tracks in and out abruptly.

The general arrangement that Tubby had with producers was that they paid him to mix their records and then left the tapes with him to do whatever he wanted. He would do dubs of them, which he would sell to sound-system operators. It was good promotion for the producers, since their rhythms gained a wider audience.

Tubby worked particularly closely with Bunny Lee. Lee's rhythms were well suited for dubbing. Carleton "Santa" Davis, the drummer for Lee's house band, the Aggrovators, had developed a "flying cymbal" sound inspired by the Philly bump rhythms of Kenny Gambell and Leon Huff. It was a hissing hi-hat, open on the upbeat and closed on the downbeat, a high-frequency sound that cut through the mix and abetted Tubby's intense high/low frequency segregation.

Lee urged Tubby to get creative behind the board, reminding him that the crazier the sounds, the more the crowds at the dances liked them. Bunny Lee helped develop Tubby's distinctive echo/delay effect, using one tape player feeding back into another. He also seized on Tubby's use of a high-pass filter, which became probably the most powerful effect in his arsenal. A high-pass filter removes low frequencies from a sound. Isolated on one word, or even one syllable, it had the effect of making the sound seem to shoot into space, draining its low end as it got farther away. Combining the filter with a reverb effect compounded the trippiness. "It sounded like madness, like a horror movie," Bunny Lee recalls. "But people like it. People like strange things, y'know."

"That was the secret weapon, and no other studio could figure out how we did it," Smart says.

Tubby and his crew treated the studio itself as a musical instrument. "Everything was live," Smart says. "All the drops and everything was done live over and over again. I'd be cutting twenty, thirty, or even forty dubs in a day. It was all improv, because we had the vibe, the feel. We didn't even have to think about it. You would hear [the finished dub] and go, 'Whoa, I didn't even know I did that one.'"

Tubby's most astonishing dub appeared in 1976. For "King Tubby Meets Rockers Uptown," he collaborated with Augustus Pablo, a producer and instrumentalist whose signature sound, usually built around his melodica, was hypnotic, almost drowsy. The root of "King Tubbys Meets Rockers Uptown" is a Pablo instrumental called "Cassava Piece," featuring a mournful minor-key melodica riff, a particularly heavy bass line, and drumming by Carlton Barrett that's so forceful it's practically the lead instrument. Tubby's mixing effects on "Cassava Piece" are subtle—mostly some reverb and delay on the melodica.

"Cassava Piece" became the foundation of "Baby, I Love You So" by Jacob Miller, a singer who recorded for Pablo's Rockers label. That song has an oddly off-kilter quality. It has no chorus, and the verses seem to resolve themselves randomly. "Baby, I Love You So" became "King Tubbys Meets Rockers Uptown." Nothing stays put in "King Tubbys Meets Rockers Uptown." It's a perfect example of what the writer Steve Barrow calls "the sense of continuous mutation" contained in a great Tubby dub. Miller's word fragments fly through the air, Barrett's drums reverberate, and then the reverberations reverberate some more. Listen closely and you'll hear every strike of the hi-hat echo almost imperceptibly in the right channel. The melodica and guitar are drenched in reverb. The song is too big to be contained in one room. Like much of Tubby's work, it evokes an outdoor sound system, but even that forum seems too small. Really, the song sounds too big for Earth. All the mutating elements seem to be orbiting one another, or maybe orbiting the song itself, as though the song were the sun and the various parts were planets.

It's not just space that seems larger. The song seems to stretch time, like U-Roy's delayed voice in the dance. The weaving in and out of Miller's voice is like the eternities implicit in one moment, the huge machinations of emotions and synapses and electrical charges behind a simple, nervous declaration: Baby, I love you so.

"King Tubbys Meets Rockers Uptown" sounds infinite. It is this sense of the mixer as metaphorical conjurer of eternity that Tubby brought to music. "I don't think that song was as big in Jamaica as it was abroad," Smart says. "It's probably what really made the international market listen to dub music. After that, everyone wanted Tubbs to mix their dubs." For much of the world, "King Tubbys Meets Rockers Uptown" was the first glimpse of a Pro Tooled future.

During the years that Tubby began to dub seriously, violent conflicts often erupted between factions loyal to Prime Minister Michael Manley's People's National Party and the more conservative Jamaica Labour Party. Tubby's studio on Dromilly Avenue was in a sort of no-man's-land between PNP and JLP areas. After a while, the soldiers at the roadblocks began to realize what was going on at Tubby's. "They would respect us," Smart says. "They'd say, 'Yes, engineer, go through!' "

Tubby often liked to work at night, when the streets outside became battlefields. "I remember [producer] Bertram Brown talking about how he'd leave his home, in a PNP area, and get to Tubby's around nine o'clock," Barrow says. "Tubby would come by after dinner, and they'd lock themselves in for the night. Sometimes they'd hear gunshots outside, but they wouldn't go out. They'd just mix dub after dub after dub, and leave around four or five in the morning, as it got light and all the factions had gone to bed. All of that went into the music. What you're hearing in a Tubby's mix is a nation at political war with itself."

The chaos of a Tubby mix—the unexpected dropouts and surges and distortions—is indeed analogous to the political chaos outside those studio doors. But the real metaphor embedded in those dubs is embodied by the image of a man locked inside behind a mixing board as the bullets fly outside, his studio a neutral zone where you made your own laws. You can't unfire a gun. The act of firing it is like a one-take live-in-the-studio recording. You live or die with what you get, and you can't remix the past. Late at night at Tubby's, you could imagine a better world, one where you had complete control—a place where even if the bullet had been fired long ago, you had an eternity to decide its trajectory.

In 1971 and 1972, the same years Tubby's craft began to flourish, laying the conceptual groundwork for the Pro Tooled world, others were beginning to lay the technological foundations. Two pairs of high school pals—Dave Rossum and Scott Wedge in the Bay Area, and Kim Ryrie and Peter Vogel in Sydney, Australia—were beginning collaborations and founding companies (E-MU Systems and Fairlight) that would profoundly influence the digital future. But the first people out of the gate were two Ivy League academics trying to find out if a computer could play music.

By 1963, Dartmouth College had become the first school to implement a centralized time-sharing computer that could be accessed from terminals around campus. It was a pet project of the school's president, John Kemeny, a brilliant mathematician and computer scientist (during graduate school at Princeton, he had been Albert Einstein's assistant), and another mathematician, Thomas Kurtz. The duo would create the computer language BASIC a year later.

Jon Appleton, a Dartmouth music professor and experimental composer, wondered if the time-sharing computer might solve a problem related to the school's Moog synthesizer. Early analog synthesizers like the Moog were modular systems, a series of boxes that accomplished various effects and were connected by patch cords. Since Dartmouth's Moog was shared by many students, its settings were constantly changed to get the sound the player wanted, a process that could take up to half an hour or more. Appleton's idea was to somehow connect the Moog to the time-sharing system so that the computer could store individual settings. That way, a player could begin a practice session by typing some commands on a terminal, and the computer would instantly do the work of all those patch cords.

In 1971, Appleton mentioned the idea to Sydney Alonso, a digital electronics specialist at Dartmouth's engineering school. They looked into it but decided that the power necessary to translate between the computer's digital data and the Moog's analog signal would unfairly tax the time-sharing system. Alonso had a better idea: remove the Moog from the equation. "Screw it," he said. "Why don't we just do the whole thing digitally?"

Nobody had ever built a completely digital synthesizer before, but Alonso and Appleton took inspiration from Max Mathews, a Bell Labs engineer who, in the late fifties, had written MUSIC, the first computer program that synthesized sound. Mathews is to digitally created music what Thomas Stockham is to digitally recorded music: the earliest pioneer who truly understood the technology's potential. In a famous article published in *Science* the same year that Dartmouth launched its time-sharing computer, Mathews had predicted that "soon, a computer will be able to make music." The Dartmouth team figured the time had come.

Alonso could build the hardware and Appleton could bring a musician's sensibility to the design of the instrument, but they still needed someone with enough programming acumen to write software. As it happened, they had a student in common. Cameron Jones was a freshman engineering major, as well as a double-bass player studying counterpoint with Appleton, and he had a prodigious aptitude for writing software. He jumped at the chance to work with Appleton and Alonso. "Once I discovered a hybrid between technology and engineering and music, I was sucked into it," Jones says. "Basically, that became my whole life. I was having a blast, and by the end of the summer, we had something that caught people's attention."

What they had doesn't seem like much by today's standards. It was a hybrid system programmed with exercises to help music students recognize notes and scales. The oscillators that created the sounds were controlled by a 16-bit minicomputer made by a company called Computer Automation. The music and verbal data were stored on the time-sharing computer. A user would log in and type a command to select an exercise, and the time-sharing computer would download information to the minicomputer so that it would generate sound and begin the program. The device used very simple computer logic to make the oscillators generate sound waves. "It showed the principal of a computer-controlled sound-generating device— which is sort of what Jon asked for—that could evolve to be fully digital in nature," Alonso says.

The first semiconductor memory chips became commercially available in the early seventies, making it theoretically possible to build a synthesizer with digitally sampled sounds. But each one-square-inch chip held only 256 bytes, making a sampling synthesizer a practical impossibility. Instead, for the next version of their machine, completed in 1974, the Dartmouth team turned to FM synthesis, an algorithm that had been discovered, somewhat accidentally, by John Chowning, a graduate student at Stanford. For sound produced by FM synthesis, one oscillator produced a stable "carrier" tone and another produced a variable "modulator" tone. This combination, when done correctly, could produce, with very little memory, sounds with rich palettes of frequencies and harmonics. The 1974 machine used chips programmed with "wave tables" that provided information to the oscillators.

The problem now was that the machine was still shackled to a noisy, refrigerator-size Data General minicomputer. "At that point Sydney realized, 'You know, I could make a computer that fits on one tiny circuit board'—tiny being about the size of a breadbox—'but if I'm gonna do that, I need some software, and oh my god if we do this maybe we can come up with a portable musical instrument!'" Jones recalls. By the following year, Alonso had designed a small processor that fit on a five-by-eight-inch circuit board, and which didn't require a noisy cooling fan. Jones, who was still in school, spent a summer writing an operating system for the processor.

Whatever its musical applications, the Dartmouth team had developed a powerful all-purpose computer, which they called the ABLE. When Jones graduated, they formed a company to market it, called New England Digital (NED), with offices in an old Victorian house across the Connecticut River in Norwich, Vermont. Their client list soon included the U.S. Navy, who used ABLE to monitor antisubmarine sensors around U.S. waters.

Meanwhile, they continued their research in synthesized music. The goal now was to create sounds that were "musical." When a trumpeter holds a note, even for one second, the cycles of the sound wave change in minute ways that we can't consciously hear but which contribute to the musicality of the sound. A synthesized musical sound needed to include these subtle variations in order to sound musical, which is why analog synthesizers, though they produced interesting sounds, lacked the subtlety of musical instruments. Digital sampling could provide a solution, but one megabyte of RAM still cost several thousand dollars. NED's solution was to first record a note, and then use software Jones wrote to extract three cycles of the wave—near the beginning, middle, and end. Each cycle would be translated into a wave table, and the combined output of the three wave tables re-created the note. This was not digital sampling as such; NED was just isolating three moments and artfully joining them together. "Combined with software that changes the volume of the playback over a period of time, you can begin to take steps that will reproduce a sound that comes closer, from a perception point of view, to what the original was," Jones explains.

Perfecting this process took a few years. In 1977, they connected their new synthesizer to Alonso's suitcase-size processor to create the first computer-based synthesis system that could reasonably be called portable. It had a short keyboard with a vertical control panel behind it, like a piano with the lid raised. In June 1978, they drove to Bell Labs to show off their machine to Max Mathews. A few weeks later, after considering the name Clavisyn—a portmanteau that combined "clavier" and "synthesizer"—they decided to call their machine the Synclavier (usually pronounced SINK-la-veer). Its sounds could be altered in real time by pressing buttons indicating what was to be changed—such as pitch, harmonic content, or the index of FM modulation—and then turning a spring-loaded master knob to one of a thousand settings to indicate the degree to which the effect should be implemented. "At that time," Appleton remembered, reflecting on Alonso's achievement, "digital synthesizers had to be addressed through a language at a terminal. What a thrill it was, therefore, to be able to change the sounds as one played them, just as one does an acoustic instrument." Appleton finally had the performance instrument of his dreams. He soon began presenting solo Synclavier performances on the Vermont bank of the Connecticut River, playing to crowds who sat on the New Hampshire side.

The aspect of the Synclavier that garnered the most attention was something NED had included almost as an afterthought. It was a sixteen-track "sequencer," a device that stored sounds as simple "on/off" commands and could play them back on command. It was not the first sequencer ever invented, but it was the first to use multiple tracks so that a piece of music with several "instruments" could be replayed at will. It was, in a sense, the first DAW. Even among professionals at the annual Audio Engineering Society convention, where the Synclavier made its public debut in 1978, the sequencer caused confusion. "A lot of people couldn't believe it,"

Appleton recalls. "They thought it was a tape recorder that you played and instantly rewound."

FM synthesis works best with sound waves that describe a tidy circular symmetry, like the waves generated by a pebble dropped in a pond. One of the easiest instruments to imitate with FM synthesis is a gong—a large circular object—and instruments with a ringing quality, such as pianos and organs, also work well. Drums, with their chaotic transients and jumbled harmonics, are the least suited to FM synthesis, so it's not surprising that the quest for "realistic" synthetic drums resulted in the first successful musical-creation device based on digital sampling.

When the Synclavier debuted in 1978, Roger Linn was a semiprofessional guitarist in Los Angeles with an interest in computers and an affinity for computer programming. Linn had a small home studio, but he wasn't much of a drummer and found it difficult to record drums well. He was dissatisfied with the analog drum machines that companies like Roland were making, which worked by generating white noise and removing certain frequencies. Linn knew the basic principles of digital sampling and figured that a programmable drum machine built on digital samples of drums would offer more realistic sounds.

Like everyone who worked with digital instruments, Linn knew that the high cost of memory made sampling a difficult proposition. But it occurred to him that the nature of percussive sounds meant he could sample at a very primitive level and still get sounds that were realistic enough. "My thought was, jeez, if you can store sound as numbers, a drum doesn't have to be that much," he says. "So instead of storing an entire [rhythm], since drums are repetitive why not just store one strike of the bass, one strike of the snare, and one strike of the hi-hat?"

Linn began by hooking up his computer to the voice generator of a Roland analog drum machine, and writing a program that displayed an on-screen grid that plotted time against "drum events." To construct a rhythm, a player would put "stars" on the grid; hitting the space bar would play back the pattern. Next came the actual recording of the drum sounds, most of which were played by Art Wood, a housemate of Linn's. Now Linn had to sculpt these sounds into usable samples. The way sounds are edited today—through visual representations of the waves—was practically unheard of, so Linn had to stare at line after line of hexadecimal code (combinations of the numerals 0 through 9 and the letters *a* through *f*) that represented the audio data.

Partly out of aesthetic concerns, and partly because of his relative inexperience with engineering, he took liberties with the Nyquist-Shannon sampling theorem, that supposedly inviolable principle of digital audio. Since he was sampling at 27 kHz, his Nyquist frequency—the point at which all higher-frequency sounds should be filtered out—should have been 13.5 kHz. That was within the range of many people's hearing, and the inevitable stray signals that slipped by the low-pass filter could cause audible aliasing. But Linn thought that filtering made the drums sound dull, so he let some of the higher frequencies through, deciding that the distortion had the "sizzle" of real drums. Linn even programmed in further "imperfections." His "shuffle" function made the space between sixteenth notes just slightly irregular, to give the drums a more human feel.

By 1979, Linn had a prototype of the first programmable drum machine that used sampled sounds, which he called the LM-1. It wasn't cheap ($5,000, mostly due to the high cost of memory), but word spread quickly. Some members of Fleetwood Mac bought one after Linn demonstrated it at a party. Orders came in from two polar-opposite keyboard-playing musicians: Stevie Wonder and Daryl "the Captain" Dragon from the Captain and Tenille. Prince bought one, which he used for several albums, even after more advanced drum machines became available.

At the same time that Linn was building the LM-1, Kim Ryrie and Peter Vogel were conducting their own experiments with digital sampling in Australia. Their goal was to build a hybrid synthesizer, with analog oscillators controlled by digital circuitry. In December 1975, Ryrie and Vogel founded a company called Fairlight, operating out of the basement of Ryrie's grandmother's house on Sydney Harbour. (The company took its name from the hydrofoil that ran past the house.) After six frustrating months, they met Tony Furse, a consultant for Motorola who had built a fully digital synthesizer that used two Motorola microprocessors to synthesize single-cycle waveforms.

It was a clunky machine that took two hours to boot up (using paper tape and a teletype machine), consumed massive amounts of power, and became very hot. Because of its crude wave-table synthesis, the sounds it produced were dull and lifeless. But it was fully digital, which impressed

Ryrie and Vogel enough that they licensed the design from Furse. The Fairlight duo spent the next two years struggling to build a machine with sophisticated digital synthesis, but they couldn't make the sounds as realistic as they wanted. Then it dawned on them what they could do with the small amount of RAM they had built into their machine. "What we realized was that by having sixteen kilobytes of RAM there, it was possible to actually sample a real sound into memory," Ryrie recalled years later. "So Peter designed an eight-bit A-to-D [analog-to-digital] converter, and lo and behold, that solved our sound-quality problem."

They called it the Fairlight CMI (computer musical instrument), and in the end it wound up being as complex as the Synclavier, if not as elegantly designed. With a price tag of at least $25,000, it was aimed at the same high-end customers. The Fairlight did have two things the Synclavier did not. It included a CRT display and a light pen that allowed the user to "draw" the waveform to change the sound. It also had a tiny built-in digital sampler. The sampling rate was very low, and if you wanted a sound more than one second long, the rate was even lower. Since the samples were only 8 bits long, the sounds were very crude. Still, in time-honored tone-test fashion, the CMI, when it was introduced, garnered praise for imitating instruments so well that you couldn't tell the difference.

Meanwhile, times were tough at New England Digital. A year after introducing the Synclavier, with a price tag of $13,000, NED had sold only about a dozen. Only one had been purchased by a musician, a British engineer and producer named Mike Thorne. The rest had gone to universities and research institutions. The machines were expensive to assemble, and the company was nearly broke.

Across the country, Denny Jaeger was a successful musician, composer, and analog-synthesizer enthusiast in the Bay Area who made a living writing advertising jingles and scoring films. He had recently been hired to score a movie for the king of Saudi Arabia. Jaeger's instructions were to compose music that blended Western and Middle Eastern motifs. He wanted to use many different sounds for his score, which he was able to do with his large modular synthesizer setup. The problem was that he wanted to play all the music himself, and there was no way to do so without playing every sound on cue, since there was no way for him to store all the settings.

"I'd be using, like, fifty-two patch cords, twenty-nine knobs, filters, all the stuff, and it was just driving me up the wall," he says. "And then the owner of the studio where I worked put the manual for the Synclavier I on my desk and said I should call these people."

In late 1978, he contacted Alonso, who invited Jaeger out to Norwich to look at a Synclavier. "When I came to meet Sydney, it was a winter's day, very cold," Jaeger recalls. "I arrived a little early, and I'm standing around this building that looked like Betsy Ross had knitted her first flag there." Alonso pulled up in a rusty Valiant, invited Jaeger inside, and showed him some specs for the Synclavier. The more he learned, the more Jaeger realized how potentially powerful the Synclavier was, and also what needed to be improved. He told Alonso that NED should hire him to redesign the Synclavier.

Actually, Alonso said, NED was thinking of closing up shop. "The basic feeling there was just total defeat," Jaeger says. He made Alonso an offer: let him take a Synclavier back to California, and give him two weeks to tinker with it. "I'll send you programs, in your own machine, that you can play," Jaeger told them. "If they don't knock your socks off, I'll send back the machine, prepaid, and we're done.

"Cameron and Sydney had a certain style of doing things that came out of the academic community, and I had a certain style of doing things that came out of the entertainment industry," Jaeger says. "To me, a sound could either bring tears to your eyes and send shivers down your back, or it was useless. To them, it was ones and zeros. And I'm not being critical, because that's a perfectly rational way of looking at it. But the music industry was not interested in ones and zeros. They didn't even know what ones and zeros were."

Jaeger spent the next two weeks developing sounds. Impressed, NED gave him the go-ahead to continue working on improving the Synclavier. "Cameron started writing code, and Sydney started redesigning the hardware," Jaeger says. "They would send me some new things, and it was really kind of a beautiful way of working, because they could download stuff onto discs, which they'd send to me, and I could download them into the machine, and then it was kind of like, 'Welcome to the digital age!' " He made recommendations for redesigns, talked it up to people in the music business, and continued to come up with sounds for it, using the works of Max Mathews for inspiration. "I studied Max like a Bible," Jaeger says.

Mathews had devoted much of his synthesis research to studying the behavior of three instruments: violin, trumpet, and flute. Jaeger was particularly intrigued by Mathews's violin work. "Mathews talked about how a violin bow excites the string in such a way that it creates a certain waveform at the front, which we'll call an 'attack,'" Jaeger explains. "The harmonic content is almost inharmonic there. There's no normal harmonic series there because the volume is so loud at that moment in time." In other words, the initial moment of a violin note—the moment the bow meets the string—is radically different than the rest of the note, and should be treated as such in any attempt to synthesize a violin.

Jaeger decided that any sound made by the Synclavier would have to be divided into four parts—one for the attack and the other three for the rest of the sound. He called it the "four partial timbre method" and urged Alonso and Jones to adopt it. "There was really fine work that was already there," Jaeger says of the first Synclavier. "But I built a whole world on it, a world that worked. And so they wrote this code, and they made the four partial timbres work."

There was just one nagging problem: Jaeger still hadn't cracked the problem of the perfect string sound. "And so I just worked night and day," he says. "I can't tell you how many weeks went by. And then I hit it! It happened. I called Sydney up in the middle of the night—it was early in the morning in Vermont—and I played him a little violin piece. He said, 'Get on a plane, come here right away.'"

"Denny came up with a really credible violin sound," Alonso says. "Like, incredibly credible."

"And so I went back to Vermont, and I played these strings," Jaeger says, "and it was like you could see flares shooting up in the sky, with the excitement that went into that evening."

Jaeger called the completed machine, the Synclavier II, "the most advanced digital machine in the world." Hyperbole aside, the Synclavier II was an extremely sophisticated device. It came with 256 preset sounds—some imitated specific instruments, while others were just interesting sounds that Jaeger had developed. You could combine them to create an infinite sonic palette. The Synclavier II could even translate a piece of music played on it into standard notation and print it out. The sequencer could now store up to fifty-four minutes of music. It would be several years before the term was used, but the Synclavier II was a true DAW.

NED's new Synclavier made its public debut in May 1980 at the Audio Engineering Society convention in Los Angeles, a gathering that had an enormous effect on the Pro Tooled future. Linn's LM-1 drum machine had its official unveiling, as did Fairlight's CMI. (That this was the same conference where Dr. John Diamond caused a ruckus by decrying the toxicity of digital audio lends the event a nice little ironic historical curlicue.)

Jaeger remembers the event as a wildly successful coming-out party. "I'll never forget this for as long as I live," he says. "We had a suite upstairs in the Hilton. The line for our demo started at the elevator shaft at the far end of the hotel. We were the hit of the show."

Fairlight's CMI was also a big hit. Although it was targeted to the same high-end market as the Synclavier, the CMI was in many ways a less advanced machine. But the Fairlight's light pen that could "draw" sound was a huge crowd-pleaser. It's easy to understand why. Many in the audience had probably never seen a computer monitor up close, let alone one that served as a tablet for sound. This was a cool trick, but from a practical, musical, and scientific standpoint it was just a novelty. A graph of a complex wave that just plots time against amplitude, without any frequency information, provides no indication of how that wave sounds.

Fairlight's stunt still irks Alonso. "Fairlight, our competition, used some kind of quackery, a magic show, where people could take the light pen and 'draw' the wave and instantly hear it," he says. "Well, that's nice, but it's sort of misleading. It was just gimmickry. It pissed us off."

"Using a light pen to draw a visual representation of a sound wave is kind of like using a pencil to draw a high-resolution JPEG image," Jones adds. "That's why we concentrated on harmonic synthesis, where the user could specify the amplitude of each harmonic directly. That model perfectly matches how the human ear hears things."

Similarly unmoved, Linn says, "It was completely useless, a stupid idea, because you're only going to get very odd and bad harmonics, which was emphasized by the fact that Fairlight's sampling rate and bit width was so low. It was a feature they kept talking about, like you could 'make any sound,' but imagine making any sound by drawing a waveform. It's just impossible."

There were at least two people at the convention who were impressed by the Fairlight while understanding that the light pen was a gimmick. Dave Rossum and Scott Wedge, founders of E-MU Systems, were there to promote their newest analog synthesizer. What intrigued them was the Fairlight's sample-based technology. They recognized the Synclavier as the more sophisticatedly expressive machine, but it also seemed like nothing new. But sampling, which they also noticed was used on Linn's LM-1, sounded like the future. "We knew that all of these products were fairly hot, and of interest to most musicians, most of whom couldn't afford them," Wedge says. "Being the sort of people who didn't mind borrowing other people's ideas, we said, 'It sounds like this digital sampling idea is ripe. Someone should come in and do it right.' "

Wedge and Rossum had known each other since high school, when they hung out together in science clubs and rocket clubs. Rossum, two years older than Wedge, went to Caltech, and on a whim built an analog synthesizer in the summer of 1971. It was so much fun that he continued dabbling with synthesizers while pursuing a graduate degree at the University of California at Santa Cruz. He dropped out of graduate school and persuaded Wedge to leave UC Berkeley, where he was an undergraduate. They began E-MU out of a Berkeley garage. (One of their first orders of business was to find an IBM Selectric typewriter that had a key for the Greek letter "mu.")

As E-MU grew over the years, the company became known for creating hybrid synthesizers that ran on a combination of analog and digital technology. For example, the sounds themselves might be generated through analog methods (manipulating voltages), while the keyboard integrated digital circuitry for better control. They were commissioned by the Grateful Dead to create an analog keyboard that could interface with a computer, using software written by Wedge. Most important for the company's future, they licensed their keyboard technology to Sequential Circuits for use in the popular Prophet-5 synthesizer, earning E-MU a nice dependable revenue stream.

By the late seventies, E-MU was operating out of a Victorian house in Santa Cruz. When Peter Baumann, who had recently left the German ambient synthesizer group Tangerine Dream, asked them to custom-build a machine, they decided to create the greatest analog synthesizer of all time. It was the size of a refrigerator, used special E-MU software, and had sixteen programmable "voice cards." "With sixteen sounds," Wedge says, "you have a small orchestra."

After completing Baumann's machine, Rossum and Wedge decided to turn it into a marketable product. The result was the Audity, a computer-controlled analog synthesizer that included a digital sequencer and editing capabilities, which was hailed by Robert Moog himself as "the last great analog project." Wedge and Rossum made plans to show the Audity at the 1980 Audio Engineering Society convention in L.A., where they were wowed by Fairlight's CMI.

During the drive back to Santa Cruz, the two talked about what was right and wrong with the CMI and figured out they could probably make a comparable product that wasn't merely for the high-end user. "On the way home, Dave invented the circuits that we could use in the Emulator for a fraction of the cost," Wedge recalls. "At the same time, I was working on the business model. The Audity was going for $70,000 or $80,000. We were never gonna sell more than three on the entire planet. I was saying, if we had a standard product that could support our habit of noodling with all this fun technology, that would be a good thing to do."

The main problem with the Fairlight, as they saw it, was that despite all it could do, it was a very inefficient machine. "It had that built-in sequencer, so it was sort of like an all-in-one workstation, the only instrument you'll ever need," Wedge says. "But it really was a totally insane design. Each channel had its own memory, so each channel was essentially its own independent synthesizer. It was like, how to throw money at a problem, rather than actually solve it.

"So Dave has the idea for the circuitry for the Emulator, I've got the business thing," Wedge says, "and when we get home we get a letter from Sequential Circuits saying, 'We've decided to stop paying royalties on the Prophet.'" (Sequential's move touched off a legal battle with E-MU that stretched on for years and was eventually settled amicably.) Without the revenue stream from Sequential, making the Audity was no longer realistic. They needed a more affordable product. The idea they'd been kicking around in the car would have to become a reality. "People were paying a lot for Fairlight sampling, which we thought we could do as well or better for less money," Wedge says. "So we said, 'Let's go for it.'"

By the end of 1980, they were ready to begin manufacturing their digital sampler, which they called the Emulator. It was a portable but formidable machine, eighty pounds encased in rolled steel. It allowed for six seconds of digital sampling. Built-in pitch-shifting turned any sampled sound into a musical note that could be played up and down the keyboard. The Emulator would retail for about $10,000, less than half the cost of a Fairlight.

The Emulator made its public debut in January 1981, with Stevie Wonder getting the first one. (It was originally supposed to go to Daryl "the Captain" Dragon, but when they learned of Wonder's interest, E-MU thought he made a more auspicious first customer.) But over the next few months, only twenty were sold, and by the end of the year, sales had dropped off completely.

"People didn't know what to make of it," says Marco Alpert, then E-MU's marketing director. "People who had Fairlights knew, but there weren't that many people who had Fairlights. And there wasn't a paradigm yet that everyone was familiar with. It had a slow build. It took about a year, and it was really our introduction of a sound library that you could get along with it that helped out. So you could take it out of the box, put a few discs in, and have a bunch of useful sounds right then and there, rather than having to go out and figure out how to do it yourself."

Part of the slow build was probably the cost—though $10,000 may have been cheaper than a Fairlight, it was still a lot to pay for a musical instrument. It says a lot about how weird and radical an invention the Emulator was that although it allowed you to capture any audible sound in the world and make that sound musical, it didn't take off until people were given samples in the form of sound libraries. In our sample-happy Pro Tooled era, it's odd to think that there was a time not long ago when people not only had to be taught how to sample but also why they should sample.

New England Digital and E-MU were headquartered on opposite coasts, and each company's ethos reflected its surroundings: puritan New England versus laid-back Santa Cruz. NED was Alonso not suffering fools and Jones churning out code while still an undergraduate. E-MU tested their sampler's looping function by sampling the sound of someone peeing (the "big bladder simulator"). E-MU gave off a distinctive West Coast hacker/prankster vibe. They could take what you did and figure out a better way to do it—on the ride home! "I remember coming to see Scott Wedge and Dave

Rossum," says Jaeger, a valued E-MU customer during his pre-Synclavier days. "They were in a little apartment, hot as blazes, building E-MU modules on the carpet. They came from the tiniest roots, and they were quirky and fun and really creative. Sydney and Cameron came from a very stoic kind of academic world, and they never understood the music world. Never."

The fun extended to E-MU's marketing. A magazine ad for the first Emulator pictured a turkey, with the caption PLAY A TURKEY, a pun on musician slang for a bad note, and a reference to the Emulator's ability to make every sound potentially musical. When informed that the pun wouldn't play overseas, they made their British ads read FROM FARTS TO PHILHARMONICS. Ads for the next-generation Emulator had, in mind-numbingly small type, a list of features, including the ability to insert secret satanic messages. "The phones went crazy, and we got hate mail from all over the place," Wedge recalls. "People would say they really wanted to buy our $10,000 product, but they couldn't support a company that advocates worship of the devil."

A more significant difference between NED and E-MU was what their products said about the evolution of music as it moved toward its Pro Tooled future. The Synclavier was the ultimate synthesizer. The Emulator was an electronic keyboard-based instrument, but it was not a synthesizer. It was a sampler. (The Fairlight, which never really caught on in the United States, was mostly a synthesizer with a bit of sampler thrown in.)

Synthesizers and samplers do exactly what their names imply. A synthesizer manufactures a new sound, a sonic alloy synthesized via the machine's circuitry. A sampler grabs sounds that have already been made.

What's interesting about this distinction is that many of the people who built synthesizers and samplers did not grasp it at the time. E-MU initially did not think of their product as a sampler. ("I think we called it a 'digital audio instrument' or something," says Alpert.) Before somebody at E-MU realized that adding "lator" to the company's name perfectly described what their new creation did, the Emulator was known in-house as "the sampler," but not because that was its function. The nickname was a geeky pun that referenced the Whitman's Sampler chocolate assortment (since the machine was "box of sounds") and the Nyquist-Shannon sampling theorem, that computational backbone of digital sampling. In E-MU's view, sampling was the engine that drove the Emulator, not an act that described how people would play it.

Fairlight's Ryrie and Vogel were even more disconnected from the implications of the small sampling capability they had built into their machine. They saw it as a failure of sorts. "We regarded using recorded real-life sounds as a compromise—as cheating—and we didn't feel particularly proud of it," Ryrie said. "We wanted to digitally create sounds that were very similar to acoustic musical instruments, and that had the same amount of control as a player of an acoustic instrument has over his or her instrument. Sampling gave us the complexity of sound that we had failed to create digitally, but not the control we were looking for. We could only control things like the attack, sustain, vibrato, and decay of a sample, and this was a very, very severe limitation of the original goal that we had set ourselves."

As for New England Digital, they certainly had the know-how to integrate a digital sampler into the Synclavier II. But that wouldn't happen until the next-generation Synclavier, because the limitations of memory and processing power at the time the Synclavier II was released meant that people could make only low-quality samples. "We were interested in recording full fidelity, which meant 50 kHz and 16-bit, and you just couldn't record that to a computer hard drive for any useful amount of time," Jones says. "The Emulator group was doing 8-bit sampling at 12 kHz, and then 20 kHz. They were really struggling with fidelity, but they were recording right to semiconductor RAM. You load your samples into memory, and my goodness, you can call up a trumpet on the keyboard, although it won't sound like a trumpet. When polyphonic sampling came in 1984"—with the Emulator II, which allowed for eight simultaneous "voices"—"that really started selling. People were saying, 'Well, the Synclavier is great, but monophonic sampling is for the birds.' "

In a way, a Synclavier sampler would be beside the point. People loved the Synclavier because it could make such startling new sounds, and because the Synclavier itself, like any well-crafted musical instrument, had its own sound. It was those round, bell-like tones, a product of FM synthesis and the Synclavier's unique circuitry, that had an almost analog warmth.

The Synclavier had a sound, but the Emulator had no sound—or, if you like, it had every sound. People would use Emulators to sample Synclaviers.

"The Emulator really was designed to emulate things," says Jaeger. "Whereas the people I talked to who were using the Synclavier, I don't think they cared at all about emulating anything. They wanted to create a newness, and the Synclavier was the most powerful newness creator on Earth."

This isn't just idle boasting from the Synclavier camp. E-MU's Wedge remarks that the greatest achievement of the Synclavier was its "expressivity." To understand what he means, think of an electric guitar solo or somebody singing an a cappella line. These soloists can, in a split second, make minute changes that are almost undetectable—a slight bend of the string or catch in the throat—but which change the music dramatically. The Synclavier was such an advanced sound creator and allowed for so much subtle tinkering, even in real time as a note was sounded, that it made a valiant stab at that expressivity. "The Synclavier's strong suit was its ability for the sound to evolve during a note, to make something big and shimmery," Wedge says. "The Emulator, you would more 'orchestrate.' Orchestral musicians don't do a lot of expressive playing. The music is more worked out through who is playing and how loud they're playing. There's a little more of that in the violins and some of the horns, but it's more about the mix, as opposed to that single vocal line from an opera singer, where one note can make you cry."

In other words, the move to samplers presaged music's eventual Pro Tooled emphasis on "the mix." Just as a conductor "mixes" an orchestra, building a unified sound that subsumes individual expressivity into something greater, the Pro Tooled world that was birthed with the first samplers privileges the mixing of sounds, rather than the recording of sounds.

"You start with a pure sine wave," Jones says of the expressive capabilities of the Synclavier. "Then you add harmonics, you put in an unrelated modulating frequency, change the index of modulation over time, and you get these distorted-sounding bell sounds or horn sounds, and you turn those into a hit. Michael Jackson turned that into a billion-dollar record."

He's talking about Jackson's *Thriller*, released in 1982, containing arguably the most famous Synclavier-generated sound ever. It's that "gong" that opens "Beat It." Producer Quincy Jones apparently lifted those tones directly from *The Blue Record*, an NED promotional disc made to show off the Synclavier's capabilities. ("It was the exact melody and the exact sound," Jaeger says of the song's intro. "I had a copyright on that, and they just took it.") It's just a couple of repeating notes. If you haven't heard the song in a long time, it would be natural to edit them out of your memory, since what follows is one of the most recognizable opening guitar riffs in music history. But you remember them because the sound is so odd. The way the note decays sounds organic, as though someone were striking a surface like an oil drum. Yet its unsettlingly synthetic. It sticks in your mind because it really does sound like nothing else.

An Emulator also appears on the album, played by session musician Michael Boddicker, one of the earliest Emulator users. Where the Synclavier created something wholly new, the Emulator created something new out of existing real-world sound. For "Human Nature," Boddicker created a melodic line from samples of Jackson's backup vocals. On "Thriller," he used the Emulator to play wolf howls that were sampled from a sound-effects record, which were then mixed with "real" howls voiced by Quincy Jones. "He was 'emulating' the sound-effects record," Boddicker says.

Although the Emulator's debut marked the beginning of the sampling revolution that eventually led to Pro Tools, synthesis by no means vanished. Yamaha, which owned the patent for FM synthesis, used it for its affordable DX-7 synthesizer, which became massively popular in the eighties.

The rise of the DX-7 and the gradual encroachment of the Emulator put New England Digital in somewhat of a bind. Now you could get an FM-synthesis-powered machine that was good enough for most people and cost a lot less than a Synclavier. Or you could get an Emulator and use it to sample a Synclavier—again, not nearly as good as the real thing, but better than nothing. Rather than compete with these new products—"I sort of tried to ignore it," Alonso says of the Emulator—NED responded by making their product even more rarified. A fully tricked-out Synclavier with maximum memory, disc space, sequencing, and sampling capability could cost nearly $1 million. Musicians who could afford one, like Michael Jackson, Pete Townshend, and Frank Zappa, were almost evangelical in their support of what was essentially the first DAW. Sting, who used the Synclavier to make records in his living room, lauded NED "for making me a whole person, not just a mind."

Eventually, the Synclavier evolved into the Post Pro, an enormously powerful DAW used by high-end recording studios. It also became widely used for postproduction sound on big-budget Hollywood movies. There were even rumors that the Synclavier's sophisticated synthesis was adapted for top-secret voice-recognition purposes. "It was used by government agencies like the CIA," says the Synclavier expert and former NED employee Mitch Marcoulier. "I can't tell you more than that."

What was perhaps the grand finale for synthesis, before sampling took over, was unknown to many people outside of Jamaica. As with Tubby's groundbreaking mixes in the previous decade, the island nation once again heard the future, and once again it involved Tubby, albeit tangentially. Prince Jammy, one of Tubby's original apprentice engineers, became a well-regarded producer. In 1985, Prince Jammy produced a song called "Under Me Sleng Teng," by Wayne Smith. The music, which sounded like a robotic version of Eddie Cochran's "Something Else," was created almost entirely on a Casiotone, a cheap Casio keyboard that used very simple and crude synthesis.

"Under Me Sleng Teng" debuted on February 23, 1985, at a sound clash between Prince Jammy and Black Scorpio, and the crowd's response was not unlike that of the crowd who heard Tubby's reverberating Stalag 17 some fifteen years earlier. The song quickly became a huge smash in Jamaica, and suddenly the "Sleng Teng" rhythm was everywhere, on dozens of songs. From that moment on, Jamaican pop-music production practices became almost completely digital. "A lot of people were already using drum machines, but nobody had had a dancehall hit with computers until that one broke," says Philip Smart, Prince Jammy's former colleague at Tubby's. "It was the hit that changed the whole business. It sounded like it happened overnight, because it was the starting of a new era."

As Tubby had done with dub, Jammy's dancehall explosion provided a glimpse of the future. Soon enough, it would seem like all the world's music was powered exclusively by computers.

Meanwhile, the early Emulator users were building the sampled world from the ground up. Boddicker remembers Saturday afternoon "sample parties" at Westlake Studios in L.A. "It was like trading cards," he says. "People would go, 'Here, I recorded this string sound,' or 'Here, I recorded this vocal sound' or whatever, and you'd go, 'Oh, here, I'll give you two dog barks and a cat sound." Jaeger, the Synclavier II architect, built his own sample library by flying to Cleveland and sampling the entire string section of the Cleveland Philharmonic. Mindful that musicians unions were already beginning to grumble about the use of samples, Jaeger had the musicians sign releases and maintained a low profile. "We were so underground that nobody knew we were doing this, because it was so politically sensitive," he says.

The most immediately noticeable effect of the Emulator (and the most insidious) came from a new generation of recording engineers who dreamed of joining the small ranks of mixing engineers—people like the Lord-Alge brothers. "When the Emulator first came out, it was like, 'Okay, sampling vocals, who cares? Let's sample some drums in there!' " Chris says. "As soon as you could sample anything, the first thing I said is, 'Where's that Zeppelin record—let's sample that kick and snare. Let's get the freaking "Levee Breaks" kick and snare in there *now*, and let's see if we can figure out a way to sample it, truncate it, and use it.' Lo and behold—*boom!*"

Boom is right. Sampling drums was a way to create something as big and powerful as the ambient drum sounds that had emerged from studios like the Power Station and the Townhouse, without actually being in those hallowed spaces—much like Sam Phillips engineered "fake reverb" because he didn't have the vast physical space that let Columbia record "real" reverb. Engineers like Chris and Tom Lord-Alge began to scour albums for open kicks and snares to sample. Besides "When the Levee Breaks," Phil Collins's Townhouse drums were a favorite, especially his own "In the Air Tonight" and Frida's robotically minimalist "I Know There's Something Going On." The engineers didn't use these samples as complete rhythms to be looped, in the manner of hip-hop DJs. Instead, they would isolate one drum hit and blend it with the sound of the drums on an album they were mixing. "My brother and I were trying to see who could make the snare drum louder, who could get away with the wackiest sample," Tom says. "I remember starting with the first Emulator, figuring out how to make it trigger drum sounds."

Today, software makes it easy to program a Pro Tools system to trigger a sample, so that, for example, every snare hit automatically generates the sample the engineer wants to add to it. In the early days of sampling, however, triggering required ingenuity. Sometimes the only way to do it was to trigger the samples manually, having the engineer "play" the Emulator along with the song, a painstaking process that could take hours to get right. Meanwhile, as the sampled drum sounds piled up and reproduced themselves on records, the sampled class observed the proceedings with a mixture of bemusement and horror. Says Hugh Padgham, the engineer whose creative use of the SSL console helped birth that sound, "Phil and I talked about this in the late eighties, and realized what a mistake it had been to have open drums with no other music going on."

Why go to so much trouble to make the drums so big? To emulate the master, of course, the one who was creating such a big sound on albums like David Bowie's *Let's Dance*, Bryan Adams's *Cuts Like a Knife*, and Hall and Oates's *Big Bam Boom*. "It was Clearmountain," Tom says. "There's no doubt that we bowed down to Bob. The dude was on the money. Chris and I listened to those records, and we wanted ours to sound like that, or even better. We were definitely using Bob's records as templates and trying to go a little overboard. We were just seeing if we could get more obnoxious than his mixes. He was our competition at the time, and we wanted those gigs."

"Yeah, we tried to 'clear the mountain,' " Chris says. "Bob would come out with these drum sounds, and we'd be like, 'Damn, we gotta get something like *that*.'" Chris carried out much of his triggering experiments on hip-hop songs and dance remixes. To hear the sound of not only clearing the mountain, but also *clear-cutting* it, listen to the twelve-inch dance remix of Bruce Springsteen's "Dancing in the Dark," which was produced by Arthur Baker, mixed by Chris Lord-Alge, and engineered by Clearmountain.

When they could, they'd go straight to the source. The record that really put Tom on the map as an engineer and mixer was Steve Winwood's 1986 *Back in the High Life* album. Tom was pleased to discover that one of the musicians was Mickey Curry, the drummer who had played on the Bryan Adams and Hall and Oates records. "I remember the first session I did with him, I was really excited, because he came up and played the drums and it was *that sound* that Bob used for those records," he says. "That fuckin' snare drum. I remember going, 'All right, I've got it now! Now I have the sample.' "

As intrigued as E-MU's Wedge and Rossum had been by the Fairlight they saw at the 1980 AES convention, they were even more impressed with Linn's LM-1 drum machine. "It was the more profound and competent instrument," Wedge says. "It fit a purpose dead-on and really broke things open for digital sampling. But it had the same naïveté in its design as the Fairlight." Like the Fairlight, the LM-1 used a separate piece of memory for each output, a very expensive design. Wedge and Rossum figured they could do for the LM-1 what they had done for the Fairlight: simplify the design and bring the cost way down. At the same time that they were working on the Emulator II, they built a drum machine that used five chips—four to store the sounds and one that served as a map for the system to locate the sounds. The result, released in 1983, a year before the Emulator II, was the Drumulator. (E-MU's slogan: "Never a Beat Off." Nyuk, nyuk.)

Many of the Drumulator's samples came from a drummer whose snare sound the E-MU guys liked, Bill Gibson of the soon-to-be-famous Huey Lewis and the News. Gibson, who didn't completely understand what he was being hired to do, was surprised to discover that his "playing" would consist of single hits of his drums. "Those were some really strange record-ing sessions," Wedge says.

One thing the Drumulator and the LM-1 had in common was that neither offered a user-sampling function. The machines could only play the sampled drum sounds they came with (although the LM-1 had a pitch-shifting function, which let users tune the sounds to their liking). This nat-urally led some drummers, mindful of all the sampling that was going on elsewhere, to wonder if they could somehow turn the Drumulator into a sampler.

One of them was Peter Gotcher, a recent graduate of UC Berkeley, who was working nights as an assistant engineer at a Bay Area recording studio and building his own studio by day.

He played in a Police/English Beat–inspired band with his friend Evan Brooks. Gotcher and Brooks had both been double majors in electrical engineering and computer science at Berkeley, though Gotcher eventually abandoned the computer-science part. "I ended up kind of hating it, because my Apple II was way cooler than Fortran and punch cards," he says. "So Evan stuck it out and I didn't."

Gotcher was impressed with the way the Drumulator improved on the LM-1's "brute force" design but wished it had a bigger selection of sounds. Brooks thought there might be a way for them to modify the machine to sample other sounds, but when he examined the Drumulator he was stumped. So Brooks and Gotcher took the unusual step of calling E-MU and asking them how to hack their drum machine. "We might have been able to reverse-engineer it," Gotcher says. "But E-MU at the time was a bunch of hippies living in Santa Cruz. We called them and they were like, 'Yeah, cool . . .' "

"E-MU was very friendly, very 'Santa Cruz,' " Brooks adds.

"We were small enough and ad hoc enough that when Peter and Evan showed up and described what they wanted to do with the Drumulator, it seemed like, 'Oh, that's cool,' " E-MU's Alpert says. "The main question we had was are these guys capable of doing this? I mean, they were two guys in their apartment talking about doing their own recording, and building these boards. But I had a gut feeling that they could probably do it, so we pitched it to Dave and Scott."

Gotcher and Brooks were told that the first thing they had to do was buy an Emulator—which took about all the money they had—and use it to sample Gotcher's drums. With an operating system provided by E-MU and software written by Brooks, they could transfer the samples from the Emulator to a computer Brooks had built, so that the sounds could be edited. The maximum size of an Emulator sample was 8 kb, which made it difficult to make the sounds seem "real," especially with a sound with a long decay, like a cymbal. As Linn had done while editing sounds for his LM-1, editing these sounds meant staring at rows of hexadecimal code. Although Brooks and Gotcher were aware of systems that allowed for editing the visual waveforms, such as Soundstream's machine, the Synclavier, or the SoundDroid— a high-end system launched by George Lucas's company—"all those things were either proprietary to an educational institution, were being used inhouse, like the SoundDroid, or were being sold for several hundred thousand dollars," Brooks says. "It was like talking to someone about buying a rocket ship. So we were stuck with editing screenfuls of gobbledygook. But the good news was it was all digital, so when we wanted to do something like brighten up the sound of the drums we had digital EQ software that we had written. We would run it on the sound and then listen to it."

Listening to sounds while tweaking them presented another problem, related to what Brooks calls our "modified listening cycle." "If you're working in an analog recording studio, you listen to a sound in real time—if you want to add high end you grab the EQ knob for 'high,' and turn it up," Brooks explains. "You tweak and you keep on tweaking until your brain tells you to stop. It's a cyclical process between your hands and your brain." The computer Brooks and Gotcher used needed time to process an edit, so by the time they heard the new sound, it was difficult to remember how it compared with the old sound.

After they had made some chips with their perfected sounds, Gotcher and Brooks drove to Santa Cruz to present their handiwork. A few minutes into their presentation, E-MU's vice president for sales left the room. When he returned twenty minutes later, he announced that he'd already secured some sales of the chips from some of the larger music-store chains. "Evan and I drove back over the hills from Santa Cruz saying, 'Jeez, maybe this is a business,' " Gotcher recalls.

They called their two-man venture Digidrums and went into business selling drum chips to Drumulator users. They'd stay up all night programming a thousand of them, send off the orders COD, and use the money they made to buy more chips. E-MU designed a sound card that allowed them to connect a Sony digital recorder to Brooks's computer, eliminating the need for the Emulator. "We could also audition the sounds in real time back through those same D/A converters," Brooks says. "Suddenly, we had our ears back."

One of Digidrums' most popular chips was the "ambient rock drum set," which provided the sort of booming eighties sounds that people like the Lord-Alges were taking to the next level. "Every Tears for Fears and Howard Jones song had it," Gotcher says. He laughs. "Sometimes you feel like you've unleashed something into the world that you shouldn't have."

The remaining years of the eighties were a weird time for the architects of digital sampling. They had designed their projects under the impression that people would use them to grab small bits of sound and use them as building blocks for something larger. A sample of a single kick-drum blast, combined with a single snare hit, could create a rhythm; a sample of a flute could become a melody on the keyboard. What the sampler godfathers didn't realize was that people would want to sample entire passages from records, and repeat them to build a song. They didn't want just the sound of John Bonham's kick drum, they wanted to loop and repeat the whole "When the Levee Breaks" intro.

"On the Emulator I, for demos, we had the archetypical James Brown 'hit me's, but we didn't even have enough memory to record four bars of music," says E-MU's Alpert. Linn was surprised to discover that people were using the sampling function of his Linn 9000 drum machine, released in 1984, to build loops. "I thought it was kind of odd, because there was only something like five seconds of memory, because memory was so expensive" he says. "But people would squeeze in a loop in five seconds and just overdub something on top of that."

Especially as hip-hop developed, loops became a valued musical commodity. Steve Ett, a recording engineer who worked with several hip-hop artists in the eighties, including Public Enemy and the Beastie Boys, was known for going to great lengths—literally—to satisfy his clients' desire for loops. The music for "Public Enemy No. 1," on Public Enemy's debut album, *Yo! Bum Rush the Show*, began as a "pause tape," which is made by stringing together bits of records recorded onto cassette. You keep the tape on Pause, and release the button when the record gets to the part you want; the moment that part passes you hit Pause again, turn back the tape's reel a tiny bit, and cue up the next part.

By the time the song was ready to record, the music amounted to a passage of thirty-eight to forty seconds that needed to be looped enough to last for the duration of the song. Ett placed a microphone stand in every corner and sent the tape spinning around the room, held aloft by the tension of the tape against the stands. The tape would flow over the playback head, and then around the circumference of the room, and then back to the tape machine to start the journey over again.

Although he didn't see it coming, Linn embraced the idea of building music around looped samples and even gave the practice a name: "object oriented composition." "I thought it was great," he says. "It was a very pleasant surprise. After sixty years of recordings, there are so many prerecorded examples to sample from. Why reinvent the wheel?" Linn was so comfortable with this new world of music that he folded his drum-machine company in 1986 and went to work for Akai, where he designed the MPC line of digital samplers, which became hugely successful among hip-hop musicians.

For E-MU, Linn's fellow pioneers in the early days of digital sampling, the evolution of music-making was more disconcerting. They followed up the Drumulator with the SP-12 drum machine. The SP-12 contained a small amount of RAM so that people could use their own drum samples, but most of the memory was ROM, devoted to built-in sounds designed by Gotcher and Brooks of Digidrums. It turned out they had it backward. Alpert recalls, "Everyone was ignoring the built-in sounds and going, 'We want more memory to do it ourselves.' "

Heeding those demands, E-MU ripped out the ROM and quintupled the RAM for their next user-sampling drum machine, the SP-1200. E-MU wasn't thrilled with the final product. "It was okay for a drum machine, but it had cheesy pitch shifting," Wedge says. "It got away from the fidelity and quality we aimed for." The SP-1200 was so named because it was a 12-bit system at a time when many competing drum machines were still using 8 bits. But 12 bits still guaranteed an inherent amount of distortion, and with the quickly declining cost of memory, machines with 16 bits would soon be possible. Surely, E-MU reasoned, that's what people would really go for.

But the SP-1200 was a huge success. Hip-hop producers loved that it had enough memory for loops, and they loved its gritty sound. "I designed the user interface for the SP-1200, and while I would like people to think I was so prescient as to think it would be a cool tool for rap and hip-hop people, it was totally by accident," Alpert says. "None of us had any idea that what we were doing would be used in that particular way. But people loved that interface. The SP-1200 was very approachable and intuitive and immediate. And then we couldn't even kill it."

Why kill such a successful product? For one thing, the SP-1200's parts were increasingly hard to find. Who wanted 12 bits, when 16 would soon be the new 12? "We searched the world, but the technology had moved on," Alpert says. "We'd have to hunt around on the after-market and go through discontinued-parts brokers to get the pieces to keep building them. But every time we announced we were discontinuing it, there would be this hue and cry, with people offering twice as much as retail for them."

"The SP-1200 was expensive to produce, and sales had kind of trickled off, so we sort of discontinued it," Wedge says. "But we kept hearing rumors that used ones were selling for more than we had been selling them new, and that was really weird."

As technologists, the E-MU crew was baffled by their customers' attraction to the SP-1200 and its inferior technology. As mild-mannered Santa Cruz neohippies, they were even more flummoxed by what their customers were doing with the SP-1200. "We tried to stuff it back in the closet," Wedge admits. "Rap had a bad . . ." His voice trails off. "Politically, it was really ugly stuff. We kind of pulled [the 1200] out of retirement, but when we learned that what it was being used for was this rap music, we went, 'Well, let's discontinue it, maybe that'll stop it.'"

Needless to say, putting the SP-1200 out to pasture did not have the desired effect. The hip-hop world embraced it, for reasons that, in terms of sonics, were as puzzling to E-MU as hip-hop's political bent.

It's fitting that the hip-hop album that more than any other explored the intersection of politics and sonics, Public Enemy's *It Takes a Nation of Millions to Hold Us Back*, released in 1988, helped put the SP-1200 on the hip-hop map. The sound of that album was an explicit rejection of the traditional ideas of fidelity—both in and out of the hip-hop world. The intricate abrasiveness of the music mirrored the pervasive lyrical theme of "noise"—both as something politically desirable in an Attali/Adorno sense (Chuck D challenging black radio on "Bring the Noise") and as a perpetual miasma that hides the truth ("don't believe the hype"). There is a low end to these songs, but it bubbles to the surface at odd times, like a subway rumbling under the sidewalk. The goal of the record, explains Hank Shocklee, who led the Bomb Squad, Public Enemy's production crew, was "to take everyday life, and say, 'Okay, what is the difference between the noise you hear out there, and music?' There is no difference. It's all sound frequencies."

"Noise," of course, was a concept redolent of the analog era, something that digital audio was supposedly in the process of eradicating—hence the glorious move from 12 bits to 16. As Shocklee points out, it wasn't until digital audio that a recording artist could experiment with total silence, since analog tape always had a "floor-bed of noise." Yet even as they made music based on the newly accessible science of digital sampling, Public Enemy wanted not to jettison noise but rather to "bring" it. This seeming contradiction is at the heart of the uses to which the Bomb Squad put the SP-1200, almost all of which were "wrong."

"It was a sampling percussion machine, so what they were expecting you to do was to go in there, sample a kick, sample a snare, a hi-hat, that kind of thing," Shocklee says of the SP-1200. "That was pretty much the only way to use it. They never intended it to be used for audio." The maximum duration of an SP-1200 sample was just 2.5 seconds, but Shocklee and others found a way around that limitation. When sampling sounds from an LP, they'd play the record at 45 rpm, rather than 33⅓—thereby fitting a bigger block of sound into those 2.5 seconds—then pitch-shift the sample down to compensate for sampling it at the wrong speed. Now the maximum duration of each sample was around 5 seconds. "The way we stretched time, you lose a little fidelity that way," Shocklee says. "But back then, who cared about fidelity?"

But using the SP-1200 was about more than just taking E-MU's lemons and making sampled lemonade. People like Shocklee valued the SP-1200 for its unique sonic characteristics. For example, if you hit one of the pads to trigger a sample, and then hit another to trigger a second sample before the first one was finished, the first sample would be truncated. This was an "unmusical" trait—if you're playing a piano, you don't want one note to cancel out the preceding one—and it was a function of the SP-1200's lean-and-mean design, the type of flaw E-MU wanted to move beyond. But it also happened to dovetail perfectly with developments in hip-hop during its unfolding golden age in the mid- and late eighties. The music was moving away from a more traditional R&B-derived sound and toward an aesthetic rooted in the concept of the DJ. Producers like Shocklee's Bomb Squad, Pete Rock, Marley Marl, and DJ Premier built tracks out of jagged, inter-locking shards of sound, beats that "slammed" as much as they swung, and musical motifs built on almost punishing repetition—think of the sax loop on Rock's "They Reminisce Over You (T.R.O.Y.)." For them, the SP-1200's mechanistic feel was perfect. "It quantized sound very abruptly," Shocklee says. "It was the thing that gave the SP-1200 its soul."

Used judiciously, the SP-1200 lent a performative aspect to hip-hop producing. "It felt more like DJing," Shocklee says. "You had more control of the sound on a performance level. Your samples could be defined by your performance, not by a fixed length. You could basically trim off unwanted information." The Bomb Squad exploited that capability to its fullest. Many of the sounds on *It Takes a Nation of Millions to Hold Us Back* were trig-gered manually, like a band playing together.

The results of all this experimentation were so sonically arresting, and the music so singular, that the Bomb Squad's work on *It Takes a Nation of Millions to Hold Us Back*—as well as its follow-ups, the "Fight the Power" single and the *Fear of a Black Planet* LP—added up to the era's most pow-erful iteration of the ethic that King Tubby had inaugurated fifteen years earlier, the transformation of previously recorded sounds into something new. You couldn't ask for a better example of the idea of music as "mix." Public Enemy might have been consciously reaching backward to a noisier predigital era, but their music heralded the Pro Tooled future.

Tubby himself never saw that future. He had gracefully ridden out his own era of dominance. While no longer as relevant, he was revered as an engineer emeritus in Jamaica. In the all-digital "Sleng Teng" world pio-neered by Prince Jammy, there was less use for the complex and mysterious analog mastery Tubby had pioneered. Sensing the tide turning, Tubby built a digital recording studio and tried his hand at producing. In 1985, he had a sizable dancehall hit with Anthony Red Rose's "Tempo." He had begun to work with a deejay named Ugly Man, who would later change his name to Ninja Man and go on to stardom.

On February 6, 1989, while returning from a session, he was shot and killed outside his home in what was probably a robbery attempt. (Nobody was ever charged with the crime.) I like to think his spirit migrated to the United States, a reverse of the process by which ghostly faint radio transmissions from American stations had been heard in Jamaica, in the late sixties, by the musicians who created a Jamaican version of those sounds. There would be a certain logic to this journey by Tubby's ghost, because shortly before he died, a company called Digidesign (formerly Digidrums) gave the world something called Sound Tools, Tubby's ghost in software form.

When Apple released its first Macintosh computer in 1984, Gotcher and Brooks, who had a nice little business going with Digidrums, recognized that the computer's famous graphical interface could change everything. "That was catalytic, having a Macintosh," Brooks says. "We thought, wouldn't it be great to be able to show a picture of the waveforms, because then we could see exactly where to make the bloody edits. It would be 100 percent more precise, and so much easier than looking at screens full of ASCII characters."

At first, they just used the Mac for editing samples, not for the actual signal processing. "But if you're sitting there, manipulating the sound with a mouse, why not just do it all there?" Brooks says. "That was the genesis for a program called Sound Designer, which was to sound files was MS Word was to text files—essentially an editing environment that allowed you to view, edit, and process sounds."

Brooks and Gotcher initially considered Sound Designer to be an in-house tool, not a salable product. But they reconsidered when E-MU began making user-sampling drum machines, a move that spelled the end of Digidrums, since anyone could now grab a drum sample. For all its awesome power, the Emulator only had a small LCD screen for its interface, so Gotcher and Brooks began marketing Sound Designer as housekeeping software that allowed Emulator users to edit samples on the Mac.

Sound Designer had the capability to be more than just an editor. The problem was the computer. The first Macs did not have an analog/digital converter, so they couldn't be used for sampling. They did, however, have a digital/analog converter, which could be used to preview sounds, but it was mono and used just 8 bits, so it was difficult to make subtle changes to the sound. The computer wasn't powerful enough to process changes in anything close to real time, so editing meant dealing with that same frustrating ear-to-brain disconnect that Gotcher and Brooks endured when making those first Digidrums sounds. "So here we were in 1985, maybe 1986," Brooks says. "We had all this capability with Sound Designer to do digital processing and editing of sounds. [But we thought,] 'God, this modified listening cycle is so long, and the sound is still crappy because we have to listen to it with the output of the sampler, which is bad, or the output of the Mac, which is even worse.' "

Then Apple released the Macintosh II, which contained some key improvements: card slots, more memory, and a hard disc. Gotcher and Brooks designed hardware that allowed Sound Designer to work with CD-quality sound. They wrote software that allowed a user to get up to two channels of audio coming out of the Mac. "That lit up our eyes," Brooks says, "like oh my god, do you realize what this means?" What it meant was that suddenly it seemed possible to turn the Mac into something resembling a portable recording studio.

Motorola announced it was developing a digital signal processor for the Mac that would be ideal for audio and invited Digidrums to be part of the process. By December of 1988, beta versions of the processors were available. Brooks built a circuit board for the processor and then wrote software that tied it to Sound Designer. The result was a program called Sound Tools.

Sound Tools debuted on January 20, 1989, at the National Association of Music Merchandisers (NAMM) annual convention. Brooks and Gotcher, who had renamed their company Digidesign, played a continuous stream of 16-bit audio, while using the Mac to manipulate the EQ and add various effects in real time. "Compared to an analog studio, it was no big deal, but compared to what anybody could do before with something like Sound Designer, it was unheard of," Brooks says. "We were showing people that you could stream audio endlessly off a hard drive and do very fast non-destructive edits to it. It was a huge hit."

If you could do all these things in real time, you had the makings of a powerful music-manipulating device. "Suddenly, Sound Designer was no longer just an editor," Brooks says. "It was what people today would call a digital audio workstation. We had successfully integrated the entire recording studio into the box."

Gotcher and Brooks discussed with E-MU the possibility of integrating Sound Tools into the Emulator III, released in 1987, to create a full-fledged DAW. E-MU was distracted by some business problems, so Rossum and Wedge passed, and the two companies amicably ended what had been, in terms of its lasting effect on recorded music, the most fruitful collaboration between hardware and software companies.

"That's where Digidesign and E-MU's special relationship went off in different directions," Alpert says. "Peter and Evan decided that to control their own future, they had to design the hardware. And that was really the start of Digidesign as we know it today."

Digidesign advertised Sound Tools as "the first tapeless recording studio." Because it was only a two-track system, Sound Tools was mostly used as a mix-down and mastering program for people working with DAT. Hard drives had a difficult time keeping up with Sound Tools, which meant that too many edits could cause glitches. Whatever its flaws, Sound Tools was a huge breakthrough, bigger even than what came next.

The next goal was to increase the number of tracks. As they always did, Brooks and Gotcher waited for computer technology to advance and then evolved Sound Tools accordingly. "Processors were getting faster, which allowed programs to be richer, including the visual interfaces," Brooks says. "The DSPs [digital signal processors] we used were getting larger and faster, and hard discs finally became fast enough for us to do four channels. Suddenly we were able to make the leap from it being a mastering editor to doing real multitrack recording." He laughs. "So we had gotten to where we were thirty years before that with magnetic tape." To mark the milestone, Digidesign changed their product's name to Pro Tools.

The first version of Pro Tools, released in 1991, had four tracks and sold for $6,000. It didn't set the music world on fire, and word spread that it was buggy. Successive versions began to gain adherents. Digidesign added a sequencer. The Pro Tools hardware eventually had enough interfaces to record a full band. The sound reached CD-quality level (16 bits, 44.1 kHz). It was the 24-bit, 48-track version, released in 1997, that really began the migration of Pro Tools into professional recording studios. Producers like Desmond Child and engineers like Charles Dye made the final leap, using Pro Tools not just as a recorder and editor but also as a mixer.

Not surprisingly, Miami was the first city where Pro Tools as a studio standard really took off after "Livin' La Vida Loca." Robi Rosa, Ricky Martin's collaborator and the executive producer of his album, became a Pro Tools believer and spread the word around town. By 2000, as using Pro Tools became standard practice, musicians and engineers began keeping their rough mixes in Pro Tools rather than using a studio's huge console. That way, once you were done for the day you could save the mix in Pro Tools, and you wouldn't need to "rebuild" it on the console the next day by getting the settings exactly as they were the day before. Until you did the final mix, you needed only two tracks on the console, one for each stereo channel. "Everyone was doing all their production prior to the mixing stage with just two faders up on the board," Dye says. "Eventually, that started to happen across the country, but in Miami it happened a bit earlier."

This was a subtle but enormous change in the way music had always been recorded. For musicians who could afford them, the big draw of high-end recording studios, aside from the sonic characteristics of their rooms, was access to the consoles. But now most music wasn't recorded to emphasize the sound of musicians in a room, so the rooms were less of a draw, and if you needed only two of forty-eight tracks prior to mixing, there was less need for the consoles. If Pro Tools could be used at home, why not record at home? Especially since Pro Tools was becoming more powerful and was able to handle more plug-ins that could control aspects like EQ, compression, and effects. Home studios began to flourish, and business began to drop off at high-end studios.

"Their business model was based on the fact that they were renting you a million dollars worth of equipment," Dye says. "But for ten days of studio time, at $2,000 a day, you could buy your own multitrack studio and work at home. That really propelled Pro Tools forward. Studios had amazing acoustic environments, and you can't take that away from them, but what lured everybody to those rooms was the fact that you could work on a console that you couldn't work on anywhere else."

Since most people still didn't want to mix in the box, the expensive recording studios were increasingly used just for mixing. "Pro Tools was catching on, but not everybody was willing to abandon their analog SSL and Neve consoles, because they do sound amazing," Dye says.

Meanwhile, the music industry's business model was also ailing. The decade-plus boost caused by people replacing their records and tapes with CDs was ending. Napster revived the old "home taping is killing music" hysteria. There was a reluctance to invest in expensive projects of any sort, including superstar albums requiring million-dollar recording sessions. The appeal of Pro Tools increased.

"What really kicked it into overdrive was 9/11," Dye says. "Every business based out of New York froze. The record industry stopped production on all projects. When they finally did begin production again, they had smaller budgets and fewer artists, so now you had fewer projects for less money. Before that, you already had this Pro Tools juggernaut that wasn't stopping. They kept improving the technology, the sound, addressing all the complaints that everybody had." Digidesign had been working on its crowning achievement, Pro Tools HD, all through 2001 and announced its official release at an NAMM show four months after 9/11. It had more tracks than any musician could ever need, and it cost just $12,000, or $20,000 with the full interface.

The record labels saw a way to cut costs. "They would say, 'Look, here's your recording budget—we'd like to encourage you to rent a warehouse and we'll buy you a Pro Tools system,' " Dye says.

The trend also affected the huge corps of freelance professional recording engineers who didn't have their own studios. "Engineers found that since the budgets were so small, they could either continue to work in a big recording studio but charge less money, or they could buy a Pro Tools system," Dye says. "They could charge what they used to charge per hour, and basically throw the studio services in for free [by using Pro Tools]. And of course, the people who were hiring the engineers also bought Pro Tools, too."

As mixing in the box became more accepted, the last rationale for using expensive studios vanished. "This is what really started the downturn of recording studios, because they had SSL boards, expensive tape machines, and a huge-ass mortgage," Dye says. "Most of them went out of business. Very few survived. Classic studios, where amazing records were made, closed down. Almost every major studio in Miami has closed.

"The next barrier was mixing," Dye says of Pro Tools in the post-9/11 period. "It just didn't happen in 2001. It happened more in 2003, 2004, and 2005." By 2007, between 70 and 80 percent of all pop music (and probably nearly 100 percent of all hip-hop, R&B, and dance music) was mixed in the box.

Pro Tools is to the post-9/11 era what magnetic tape was to the immediate postwar period. And yet . . .

More than two decades after they tried to out-do Bob Clearmountain in percussive obnoxiousness, Tom and Chris Lord-Alge have both reached the same upper echelon as Clearmountain in the mixing world. All three credit Pro Tools with transforming the nature of their jobs.

Just as they did in the early days of the Emulator, Tom and Chris use samples to beef up the drums on music they mix, though Pro Tools has made the process much simpler. "I hate to say it, but nowadays, when I start a mix, if I turn on the bass drum and it's not punchy and aggressive, rather than even trying to get it to sound that way, it's so much easier for me to retrigger it with a sample that I already have dialed in and ready to go," Tom says. "Especially with bass drums. A lot of times I'll retrigger the bass drum and take all the dynamics out so that it hits at the same volume every time. It makes the song sound more aggressive. I generally don't replace a snare drum. I just add to it, so a sample will give it more attack or more tone. And sometimes the toms as well. They're tricky to record, or the guy doesn't hit them hard enough, so sometimes it's just easier to put a sample on there. If I hear that I can get the sound from what was recorded, I don't bother. But more times than not, I'm replacing the bass drum, before I even start."

Most top-tier mixers use DAWs on drums to similar effect, though not always so overtly. Andy Wallace, for example, rarely replaces drums with samples, but he will often have drums trigger samples of room ambiance— sounds taken from microphones hung around the recording room rather than close-miked on an instrument—so that the drums are trailed by some tightly controlled reverb.

None of these engineers, however, mixes in the box. Although they assemble the sounds in digital form, they then run the signal through a D/A converter so that they can mix on an analog console, the same way Dire Straits' *Brothers in Arms* was mixed in the early DDD days. "I really think its weakest point is mixing within it," Tom says of Pro Tools. "It can be done and it can sound good, but when you hear a similar thing coming discretely through forty-eight channels of an audio console, it creates more depth and imagery than you can get out of a digital box."

"For me, mixing in the box just isn't going to work, and I'm probably not going to change, because I need the analog gear to bend the digital signal in an analog way," Chris says. "No matter what you do in the box, it still sounds like it's in the box. I [use] a twenty-year-old SSL, because I don't think they've improved the sound since then."

"There's something about the sound of an analog desk that just beats mixing digitally," Clearmountain says. "I can mix so much faster on an analog desk because they're all dedicated controls. You don't have to tell the control what it's supposed to be controlling."

What Clearmountain is referring to is the intuitive nature of an analog console. Each track has the same row of controls, and each control means the same thing for each track. Digidesign and other DAW companies have responded to these complaints by making control surfaces that closely mimic what it's like to work on an analog console. That still leaves the issue of sound quality. When SSL consoles first began to infiltrate recording studios, some engineers bemoaned their effect on sound. Today, the SSL sound is considered "classic," while Pro Tools is still greeted with suspicion for its effect on mixing. The DAW makers have to resort to the same defense that digital advocates have been mounting since Tom Stockham: look at the numbers.

"There was a long phase of Digidesign's history when people claimed the mixing engine in Pro Tools radically changed the sound," says Gotcher. "We were able to do mathematical proofs where we would take some files, process them through Pro Tools, and prove that the actual bits that came out were identical to what went in. It was a complete hallucination. I thought we definitely proved it, but that's one of those arguments where somebody claims to be this 'golden ears' person who can hear things no one else can hear. It's an unwinnable debate."

When people talk about the huge effect Pro Tools has had on the way music is made, what they usually mean isn't so much Pro Tools itself but rather the plug-ins, which are made by companies other than Digidesign. Some of the most popular try to model the sound of analog audio, to undercut some of the harshness of hard-disc recording. Others are designed for extremely precise editing. Beat Detective, one of the more popular plug-ins, allows users to quantize rhythms to exact specifications. If the drummer for your favorite band sounds a lot looser onstage than on a record, there's a good (or better) chance that's because the drums have been run through Beat Detective. By far the most influential plug-in, and the most controversial, has been Auto-Tune, a program that corrects the pitch of vocals, and which owes its existence, oddly enough, to the oil industry.

Andy Hildebrand, the inventor of Auto-Tune, was a flute player who went to college on a music scholarship and later earned a PhD in electrical engineering. He went to work for the oil industry, performing signal processing on seismic data. Drilling for oil involves setting off dynamite charges, recording the way the sound reflects off the subsurface layers of the Earth, and producing an image of those layers that provides clues as to the possible existence of oil. After eighteen years of this work, Hildebrand went back to school to study musical composition at Rice University. He experimented with synthesizers and found that the looping functions were typically bad. Looping solo instruments worked fairly well, but problems arose when trying to loop collections of sounds that formed a complex waveform, such as a string section. Hildebrand wrote his own algorithm to solve this problem and in the early nineties began marketing a looping program called Infinity.

At an AES convention in 1996 or 1997, Hildebrand was speaking with the wife of one of his distributors. She was a choral singer and mentioned that it would be great to have a device that would make her sing in tune. Hildebrand realized that the same type of processing that he had used in the oil industry could be put to work as a pitch corrector. A year later, at a trade show, Hildebrand showed off the first version of Auto-Tune, at Digidesign's booth, by running an out-of-tune singer's voice through the program. "People couldn't believe what they were hearing," he says. "I had trouble convincing several of them that I wasn't pulling the wool over their eyes."

What Auto-Tune could do was not entirely new. Very skilled engineers could correct pitch with various methods, including sampling the voice and manually manipulating a sort of pitch wheel. But as with other facets of the Pro Tooled world, Auto-Tune made a formerly difficult task so easy anybody could do it. You tell the program what scale and key to use as a reference point, and it continuously samples the singer's voice and decides which of the correct notes is closest, adjusting accordingly.

Although Auto-Tune was designed as a corrective device, it broke into the mainstream as a creative sound processor. While working with Cher on the song "Believe" in 1998, producers Mark Taylor and Brian Rawling discovered that if they set Auto-Tune on its most aggressive setting, so that it corrected the pitch at the exact moment it received the signal, the result was an unsettlingly robotic tone. When "Believe" became a huge world-wide hit, Taylor and Rawling initially tried to keep their Auto-Tune trick a secret, although word soon got out and the "Cher effect" became a ubiquitous production tool over the next few years.

At the same time, Auto-Tune was steadily infiltrating the recording world in more insidious ways. For obvious reasons, producers and musicians often don't admit that they use Auto-Tune to fix voices that are out of tune, but it's obviously used to make singers out of people who cannot actually sing. The Spice Girls, who broke out around the same time, were clearly Auto-Tuned to the gills. Since then, Auto-Tune has done as much as Pro Tools itself to change the sound of pop music. Today it's used on "pretty much every fuckin' record out there," Tom Lord-Alge says.

As with Pro Tools in general, Auto-Tune has decreased the importance of getting something right in the moment. "I see some producers use it to fix bad performances, when they should really have the singer come in and do it again," Tom says. "I'm guilty of doing it as well, but I never use Auto-Tune as my savior. I will only use it to fix the absolute minimum of notes."

Once you start to really pay attention to how voices sound when they've been Auto-Tuned, it's impossible not to hear the program doing its work. "The advent of Auto-Tune really created the 'car horn effect,' " says Chris Lord-Alge. "A lot of pop stuff, and even some country, every note they hit is perfect, and when they do it in harmony, it sounds like a car horn. I've never understood why people like that."

"You'll have the lead vocal track be Auto-Tuned, and then on the chorus they might add another vocal track that's been run through Auto-Tune," Tom elaborates. "Now you have two tracks, holding notes in perfect pitch. It's impossible to do that as a singer. It just doesn't happen, because of the inflections of the voice. So when you have two notes from two different performances Auto-Tuned, it sounds like a car horn. And then you add harmonies to that, and it starts to sound like baby seals honking.

"Yeah, it's the seal tooting the horns," Chris says. "Everything's perfectly pitched, so sometimes you get 'em hitting harmonies and no one's bending. It just sounds so fake."

"I get tracks that have been through Auto-Tune, and you can actually hear it working," Tom says. "It's a nightmare."

Denny Jaeger, the man whose FM-synthesized string sounds helped jumpstart the Synclavier II, remembers meeting future Digidesign mogul Peter Gotcher several years before the Pro Tooling of the world had begun. "I think he was still a teenager," Jaeger says. "He was looking at the Synclavier, all wild-eyed."

If history had played out a little differently, we might now be experiencing the Synclaviering of the world. What Gotcher and Brooks did with Digidesign—bring the DAW to the masses—New England Digital could have done with the Synclavier, and many of the Synclavier faithful were hoping that this was the route NED would take. "I really wanted to build an inexpensive Synclavier," Jaeger says, wistfully.

For a while, NED's plan to make the Synclavier the highest of high-end music machines worked. "In a deserved monopoly position, the company complacently marketed to just high-end consumers, leaving them vulnerable to economic pressures from upwardly mobile domestic equipment, and it collapsed in 1992," producer Mike Thorne wrote in his online history of recording studios. "A constructive and creative revolution in wide studio practice was bungled."

Thorne is in a unique position to talk about the Synclavier's history. He edited the British journal *Studio Sound* in the early seventies, and then went to work for EMI as a staff producer and talent scout. It was Thorne who signed the Sex Pistols to EMI, thus setting in motion the band's infamous "great rock-and-roll swindle." Although he didn't produce the Sex Pistols debut album, *Never Mind the Bollocks . . . Here's the Sex Pistols*, he did produce what would arguably become an even more influential British punk album from the era, Wire's *Pink Flag*.

Mike Ratledge, keyboardist for Soft Machine and a friend of Thorne's, showed him "an advert for this funny machine" in the back of *Computer Music Journal*. Intrigued, the two arranged to preview a Synclavier. Thorne immediately fell in love. He became the first—and only—musician to buy the Synclavier I. "It was just a new sound," he says. "I heard those FM synthesis cathedral bell tones, and said, 'I want one.'"

Thorne was also attracted to the nonlinear editing capability of the Synclavier, still an exotic prospect in the pre–Pro Tools era. He used the machine to sequence parts and layer tracks, doing just about everything in the box. "It was one thing to generate new sounds, which was wonderful," he says, "but it also meant that you could flip things around—and not just drum beats but whole sections." Thorne points to "Love in a Vacuum," the first song on 'Til Tuesday's 1985 debut album, which he produced. The opening vocals were inserted from elsewhere in the song—something that could easily be done today with Pro Tools, and which could have been done in 1985 by "flying in" tape, a much more laborious process.

His Synclavier was put to good use on Soft Cell's "Tainted Love," a huge international hit in 1981 that has endured to become a synth-pop "Stairway to Heaven." Like the Synclavier tones that begin Michael Jackson's "Beat It," "Tainted Love" sounds both machine-driven and organic. Part of that feel is a result of Thorne's production choices. He integrated room ambience to give the song a live feel. Most of the mixing was in fact done live, in one session, with band, producer, and engineers lunging across the console to apply effects at the desired moment. "When we were mixing, we were dancing in the control room without even realizing," Thorne says.

But a large part of what makes "Tainted Love" one for the ages is the sounds the Synclavier generated. Like Jaeger says, the Synclavier was a "newness creator." You can't quite place these sounds as belonging to any particular place or time, so the song continues to sound simultaneously retro, futuristic, and completely of the moment. "Tainted Love" is your life.

Thorne continued to use a Synclavier after he moved to New York and opened up the Stereo Society, a small recording studio in Greenwich Village. When New England Digital shut down in 1992, Thorne was instrumental in forming the Synclavier Company to continue operations and provide maintenance for the world's remaining Synclaviers. The company held together only for four years, but even then Thorne continued to use his Synclavier, as did the small but passionate coterie of users worldwide for whom Pro Tools and other DAWs were poor substitutes.

When I dropped by the Stereo Society early in 2007, Thorne was still using a Synclavier setup. He had recently looked at the newest version of Pro Tools and decided it still didn't measure up to the Synclavier. His reservations about Pro Tools were similar to what Scott Wedge had said about the limited "expressivity" of DAWs, how even the best couldn't mimic the sort of subtle real-time changes that a singer can make in the moment. The Pro Tooled world was all about arrangements, orchestrations, the mix—not so much about playing and recording. What Synclavier true believers loved about the machine that blazed the first trail to Pro Tools was that it was as much an instrument—with all the multitudes of possible expressive capabilities that designation implies—as it was an editor. "They seem a little too oriented toward the pure recording itself, and the manipulation of that," Thorne said of Digidesign and Pro Tools. "It's still better at audio manipulation than as a compositional tool. It's not quite there yet."

Later in the year Thorne reconsidered. He decided that the new version of Pro Tools finally gave him what the Synclavier had always provided. The first musician to buy a Synclavier was putting his out to pasture.

The question was what to do with it. Thorne was wondering if a museum might want it. But it had to go, if for no other reason than that its massive appetite for power was inflating the Stereo Society's electric bills. On the other hand, the days were getting shorter, and the massive setup would soon have another use. Thorne pointed out that the power-guzzling Synclavier is a good space heater in the winter.

Outro: "Testing, Testing . . . (Reprise)"

By the second half of the first decade of the twenty-first century, signs of the crumbling recording-industrial complex were everywhere.

In January 2005, at the annual National Association of Music Merchandisers convention in Anaheim, California, Digidesign showed off its ICON digital console. It was touted as combining "the familiar feel of a professional mixing console with the power and flexibility" of Pro Tools. Brian Wilson, interviewed at the convention, credited Pro Tools with giving him the means to complete *Smile*, the intricately constructed, unfinished Beach Boys album that had literally driven Wilson insane during the analog cut-and-splice era. The next week, the famous Cello Studios in Los Angeles, where the Beach Boys, tape pioneer Bing Crosby, and luminaries like Nat "King" Cole and Frank Sinatra had cut albums, closed its doors. It was hard not to see a simple cause-and-effect at work.

The dominoes kept falling in February. The casualties included Muscle Shoals Sound Studio in Alabama, one of the most famous recording facilities in the world, an American landmark where Wilson Pickett, Aretha Franklin, Bob Dylan, Paul Simon, and the Rolling Stones had made records; New York's venerable Hit Factory, birthplace of records by Bruce Springsteen, Madonna, Michael Jackson, Notorious B.I.G., and just about every other multiplatinum act; and the Royaltone Studios in Hollywood. Also that month, following a debate among the stakeholders over the future direction of the company, SSL announced it was for sale. Quantegy, the last major manufacturer of analog magnetic tape, filed for bankruptcy and ceased production, forcing tape aficionados worldwide to hoard their stocks and scramble for alternative sources.

Some of these institutions managed to hold on in one form or another—at least temporarily. Peter Gabriel became a co-owner of SSL. Songwriter and producer Linda Perry purchased Cello and turned it into a studio for her own projects. Quantegy started making tape again, and then stopped—for good, the company said—in the spring of 2007. That left the Recording Media Group International, a Dutch company with roots in DuPont and Philips, as the last tape manufacturer in the world. There will always be a need for professional recording studios, large studio consoles, and even, for the foreseeable future, magnetic tape. But the commercial studios that survive today are mostly lean operations. The era of the big recording studio, and everything the concept implied—privileged access, centralized production, the "aura" of hallowed ground—is over.

For what it said about the state of the music industry and the practice of recording, the Hit Factory's demise was the most significant. The name itself evokes a bygone industrial era and an outmoded one-way communication model. Once the jewel of New York studios, the Hit Factory is now emblematic of the decline of the city as a capital of recording. Mike Thorne estimates that the number of "truly first-class, general-purpose recording studios" in New York has declined more than 80 percent since the dawn of the digital age, from about twenty-five in 1980 to fewer than five today.

The swift collapse of the Hit Factory serves as a parable of the changing recording industry. As recently as 2000, it had been hailed by *Billboard* as "far and away, the biggest music studio operation in the world." Two years later, the Hit Factory expanded its facility, adding two more rooms stocked with SSL consoles. "There's always going to be a place for the small, technologically advanced recording equipment that keeps coming out," said the Hit Factory's Troy Germano, paying lip service to Pro Tools, "but I think that to make records that are special [and] cutting-edge, you need to be in a studio like the Hit Factory, whether it's in New York or somewhere else." When the Hit Factory went under three years later, one report blamed "technological advances that have made it cheaper and easier for stars to record in their own state-of-the-art facilities, often in their own homes."

What happened to the Hit Factory can't be blamed solely on DAWs, which were part of the fabric of interrelated factors—including downloads, new entertainment options, general consumer dissatisfaction over the price of CDs (and perhaps even their wearying loudness-abetting compression, if you believed what a lot of studio pros were quietly saying)—that roiled the music industry. For years, the Hit Factory had been plagued by rumors of the sort of rock-and-roll excess and graft that appeared increasingly misguided in the scaled-down music world. The studio's reputation for doing whatever it took to make its customers happy (supposedly, they once filled a room with hay to placate a country singer) surely caught up to it. Troy Germano, for his part, denied new technologies had anything to with the studio's closing. He blamed his mother, Janice Germano, who took over operations when her husband, Hit Factory founder Ed Germano, died in 2003, for running the studio "into the ground." Troy announced he was building new studios in the United States and Prague, because "there has to be a place where Eminem can bump into Mick Jagger in the hallway."

The Hit Factory's afterlife was as symbolic as its downfall. Germano moved the operation to Miami—the city where Pro Tools began its infiltration into commercial recording studios—and changed the name of Criteria Recording Studio, which he owned, to Hit Factory Criteria. Back in New York, the Hit Factory building on West 54th Street was sold to developers, who announced plans to turn it into luxury apartments. I visited the Hit Factory Condominiums a few months before renovations were complete. As it happened, that morning Sony Music Studios, located a block away and home to Vlado Meller's mastering suite for many years, had announced its imminent closing. The reason, according to an internal memo: "hard times in the recording studio business."

One obvious appeal of occupying one of the Hit Factory's twenty-seven apartments is the idea that you can live your life where the magic happened. The condo's literature plays up this angle, describing the Hit Factory as "a legendary place and a state of mind," but aside from the gold records hanging in the lobby, there isn't much about the building that would remind former tenants of its previous life. It's not like anyone could claim their bathtub is where Madonna laid her vocal tracks. But if you know something about the Hit Factory's layout, the building's four deluxe duplex penthouses hint at the studio's former grandeur. Collectively they fill a space that was once a recording room large enough to handle a session with 150 musicians.

The Hit Factory isn't the only recording-industry relic to get the living-museum treatment. On the banks of the Delaware River, ninety-five miles away in Camden, New Jersey, the former footprint of RCA Victor is undergoing changes that say just as much about the state of the music industry, and even more about the state of industry itself. "Building 17," Victor's former Victrola factory and one of just two original Victor buildings still standing, was reborn in 2004 as The Victor, an apartment building with 341 luxury lofts. The lobby contains a working Victrola. Residents can hold functions in the nearby Caruso Room, named after the recording industry's first megastar. On the roof, right above the private gym, developers have restored Building 17's most distinctive feature: a stained-glass rendering of Victor's famous mascot, Nipper the dog, peering into a Victrola as he hears "His Master's Voice."

During RCA Victor's heyday, Camden was one of the nation's busiest ports and a thriving city of sycamore-lined streets spread over nine square miles. Besides RCA Victor's mammoth operation and the huge cannery that produced Campbell's soup, Camden had three hundred working factories. In the years following World War II, deindustrialization and the loss of relatively well-paying blue-collar jobs hit Camden even harder than most Midwest and Rust Belt cities. RCA Victor and Campbell's moved most of their operations elsewhere (though Campbell's still maintains a Camden office), and the closing of Camden's New York Shipyards in 1967 destroyed what was left of the port's huge shipbuilding trade. Four years later, a police killing sparked devastating race riots. White flight to nearby suburbs transformed Camden's demographics, and the arrival of AIDS and crack cocaine in the eighties devastated the area.

By the end of that decade, just 50,000 people remained in Camden—less than half the prewar population—with only one hundred households earning more than $50,000, the amount that Eldridge Johnson, founder of the Victor Talking Machine Company, had paid for Emile Berliner's disc recording patent. Once a city of families, Camden was now a ghost town full of lost children, with 42 percent of its population under 18 and 62 percent of them living below the poverty line, the highest rate of child poverty in the United States.

Much of the money the state of New Jersey has spent on civic renewal has gone into Camden's waterfront, where The Victor is located. Similar to projects in other faded riverfront cities, Camden's largely involves the development of public attractions designed to lure visitors from affluent suburbs a few minutes' drive away. These include the privately run New Jersey State Aquarium and Campbell's Field, a minor league baseball stadium with luxury boxes, a picnic pavilion, and an amusement area called the Acme Fun Zone (shades of the 1915 expo's Joy Zone?). The Campbell's Soup Company has offered to build a Camden office park, partly financed by the state, contingent on the demolition of the downtown Sears building, one of the last remaining vestiges of old Camden and a fixture of various historical registries.

Victor's own odd contribution to the postindustrial reinvention of Camden is L-3 Communications Systems–East, housed in a large, low-slung building across Market Street from The Victor. In the eighties, General Electric acquired RCA and sold 75 percent of the RCA Victor music division to the German conglomerate Bertelsmann AG, which already owned the other 25 percent. GE sold RCA's defense and aerospace contracts to the company that became Lockheed Martin, which in turn transferred them to a new company called L-3 Communications. With 1,000 employees, L-3's Camden office is the city's largest employer, and the last distant corporate descendant of Eldridge Johnson's Victor Talking Machine Company on the Camden waterfront (a connection the company boasts of on its Web site). Much of what goes on in that building is shrouded in secrecy—"almost all the work we do here is classified," an L-3 rep told the *Philadelphia Business Journal*—but the L-3 East's known projects include network encryption for the National Security Agency, data collection systems for the U.S. Navy's Space and Naval Warfare Systems Command, and the U.S. Army's Remotely Monitored Battlefield Sensor System.

There is a certain logic to Victor's weird corporate trajectory in Camden. Against the Edisonian ideal of music as something ineffable, impervious to any attempts to reduce or adduce it, Victor pioneered the idea of music as "information," data to be communicated, amplified, attenuated, and broadcast far and wide. With its horizontally integrated operation pumping out records, record players, radios, and televisions, not to mention its roster of artists and its on-site recording studios, RCA Victor was the quintessential communications corporation of its era—a true "hit factory." L-3 takes the communications paradigm to its logical conclusion for the age of the national security state.

Across Cooper Street on the other side of The Victor is a building owned by Rutgers University that was once a beautifully appointed public library built by Johnson. There is a stop there for the River Line, part of the Camden revival, a light rail that runs from downtown Philadelphia, through the streets of Camden and its suburbs, all the way to Trenton. The day I visited,

I rode the River Line with two elderly couples I'd met while touring The Victor. They were former Camden residents and employees of Victor who'd worked at Building 17 and were curious to see what had become of it.

There's a weird Disneyland-monorail feel to the River Line. A few blocks from the fresh-scrubbed Camden waterfront, Camden is still Camden: boarded-up buildings, vacant lots, urban desolation. My new friends pointed out the former locations of the theaters and clubs they'd haunt on Saturday nights. I kept waiting for an animatronic Eldridge Johnson to board the train and start talking about Camden's glory days.

On March 9, 1952, an essay appeared in *The New York Times* with the curious headline "High Fidelity—Does It Exist?" The author was the audiophile's audiophile, Emory Cook, who was about to set the high-fidelity world on fire with *Rail Dynamics*, his album of train recordings. The question was both rhetorical and a call to arms. Of course high fidelity was real, but Cook felt the term was being diluted beyond recognition by unscrupulous manufacturers of audio components who slapped the label on everything.

"There can be no question as to what constitutes high fidelity," he wrote. It was a recorded sound that faithfully reproduced the original—not just the sound but the environment in which it appeared. Cook urged readers to attend a concert, and to listen "less for enjoyment" and "more for memory." They should use that memory to determine whether the system rebuilt the concert hall in their living rooms. Though he didn't use the word in his piece, Cook was advocating for the high-fidelity Holy Grail: "presence."

That Cook's question was considered worth asking in such a mainstream forum underscores the popularity of the original high-fidelity movement. The quest for presence made sense within the context of postwar modernism, when no frontier seemed unconquerable—something that many obsessive audiophiles understood. "The thing we're seeking is a method of packaging human experience in such a fashion that we can unpackage [*sic*] it anywhere, anytime, and enjoy it," John Campbell wrote in *High Fidelity*, comparing this quest to the nascent frozen-foods industry. "Unfortunately, spring peas don't exist everywhere, at all times, so it behooves us to find means of packaging them, making the pleasure of eating them universally available. 'High-fidelity' packaging is improving; modern frozen peas are getting hard to distinguish from the garden-fresh article."

There was every reason for Cook and his fellow audiophiles to believe that this packaging would continue to improve. The science of recording and reproducing a sound would advance until there was no discernible difference between the real and the represented. Total presence would happen in our lifetime.

What Cook didn't know was that the days of high fidelity as he defined it were already numbered. Magnetic-tape recording, a technology that made high fidelity possible, contained the code of its destruction. Tape's capacity for editing spelled the end of the quaint notion that recordings were only linear recordings of real-time events. Multitracking destroyed the idea that recordings documented actual performances. Soon enough, the creative use of multitracking—all the myriad effects you could apply to individual tracks—ended the idea that the sound of recordings bore any relation to a real-world event. And for a while there in the seventies, multitracking led to a dry, bloodless (literally—there was no bleeding to disrupt the sanctity of the tracks) sound, as studios became dead rooms, the sound of which Cook believed was "like dying."

Multitracking not only destroyed the idea that records recorded something that actually happened. Many of the major technological advancements compromised the pure art of recording while increasing the capacity for creative manipulation of sound. Tube-driven eight-track consoles yielded to transistor-driven solid-state sixteen-track models. When the twenty-four-track consoles came, jamming eight extra tracks onto the same two-inch tape, the decreased bandwidth lessened the tape's frequency response and ability to capture transients. The SSL consoles, those enormously complex conflagrations of analog and digital technology, contained integrated circuits that corrupted the sound. And once digital recording became the norm, DAWs exploded the flexibility of sound, but many engineers think they are a step backward in terms of fidelity.

In the digital age, playback technology began to deviate from the high-fidelity arc of progress. CDs arrived and "perfect sound forever" became the new "high fidelity"—the buzzword of the age. But the only ways in which CDs were undeniably better than records were the lack of surface noise and the dynamic range. A noiseless recording medium was one of Cook's dreams—he claimed the audible pops and clicks of recordings made him physically ill—but by the time he died in 2002, the Loudness War was in full swing. And whatever you think of the effect that aggressive rampant dynamic-range compression has had on music—even if you don't think it's a problem—the fact remains that compressed recordings, technologically speaking, are a step backward. The typical dynamic range of a contemporary CD is smaller than that of the recordings made in the pre-digital era.

Meanwhile, the proliferation of iPods means that much of the music we hear is *literally* compressed, into digital formats such as MP3 and AAC. Much of it is heard through cheap ear-bud headphones or small, tinny computer speakers. The high-fidelity ideal of re-creating the concert hall in the living room has little relevance when the living room is no longer the place where most recorded music is heard. "With audio and music right now, it's all about convenience, not sound quality," Chris Lord-Alge says. "That's why there's Pro Tools, that's why there's MP3s, that's why there's iPods." Digidesign cofounder Peter Gotcher, whose company gave the world Pro Tools, expresses similar reservations: "The interest in high-fidelity playback systems on the consumer side is disappointingly weak. The reality is that the generation coming up may never own a stereo."

Talk to recording engineers and music producers, particularly ones old or experienced enough to have worked in the analog era, and you'll invariably hear some sort of regret expressed regarding what current technology has done to the sound of music. Tracing the decisive moment back to the twenty-four-track changeover, Ron St. Germain says, "The backsliding had begun, which has now mushroomed into plague-like proportions with the 'MP Free' that we are now saddled with and which we, with shame and embarrassment, must call state-of-the-art." Sandy Pearlman, the legendary producer who once bragged about how many guitar parts he was cramming onto the Clash's *Give 'Em Enough Rope*, told me in 2007 that he doesn't even see the point of making well-crafted records anymore. Why bother, when they are destined to become compressed digital sound files played on laptops through bad speakers?

Many pros express extreme ambivalence on the subject of what Pro Tools has done to and for music. They value DAWs as tools that make their jobs easier while multiplying the creative possibilities of sound manipulation and even laud the democratizing effect these tools have had on music, but they also feel that something ineffable has been lost to a generation that both makes and consumes music that has never been outside the digital domain. As Tony Bongiovi puts it, using drums as an example, the sounds of percussion on records all seem tapped from the same source. "Everybody has the same box of drums," he says. Having sounds in a box means never having to know how to create and capture them in a recording studio.

Some engineers take a fatalistic approach to this trend. "I don't see engineering as a career anymore," says Charles Dye, the engineer who helped popularize in-the-box mixing via his work on "Livin' La Vida Loca." "It's simply a skill set of being a musician. I'm part of a dying profession. And it really did happen because of DAWs."

Bongiovi, who has taught audio-engineering classes and is a big proponent of DAWs, likes to play old records for his students, especially recordings made at places like Columbia's 30th Street Studio. "I know you've never seen a tape recorder, but listen to what these records sound like," he tells them. "We can't do this today. We can't get this sort of rich quality. There's a certain clarity and brightness that you can't replicate in the digital domain."

At the London recording studio where Hugh Padgham first worked as an engineer, he recalls finding an artifact from an early-seventies Yes recording session. It was a "track split sheet" that the engineer and coproducer Eddie Offord had used to allocate sounds to the sixteen tracks. "These were quite sophisticated arrangements, and it was unbelievable the skills he had going from one thing to another on the same piece of tape—how the lead vocal on one track would become a saxophone or something," he says. "People like that just do not exist anymore. If you told someone today to make a record like that with that equipment, they just wouldn't be able to do it, full-stop."

It's not just people steeped in the rock world who lament the passing of certain recording skills. At a panel discussion held at an Audio Engineering Society convention in 2007, I heard Young Guru, an engineer known for working with Jay-Z and other hip-hop acts, talk about how fortunate he was to have received formal training and studio mentoring experience in the years just prior to the spread of Pro Tools. He felt he had a facility with—and an appreciation for—the art and science of recording that too many young engineers lacked.

There are signs that some of this malaise is spreading beyond the engineering world. Though the Loudness War has never returned to its turn-of-the-century peak, awareness is more widespread. Although vinyl records never went away, they've made a comeback in recent years. Vinyl may still account for less than 1 percent of total music sales, but in 2007 vinyl sales jumped 30 percent from the previous year, a significant development in an industry whose overall business model is probably doomed. One fifteen-year-old quoted in *Time* credited "bad sound on an iPod" as the reason people his age were returning to analog.

It was Bob Dylan who, in his inimitable way, best summed up the malaise in a 2006 interview with Jonathan Lethem:

> The records that I used to listen to and still love, you can't make a record that sounds that way. Brian Wilson, he made all his records with four tracks, but you couldn't make his records if you had a *hundred* tracks today. We all like records that are played on record players, but let's face it, those days are *gon-n-n-e* . . . I don't know anybody who's made a record that sounds decent in the past twenty years, really. You listen to these modern records, they're atrocious, they have sound all over them. There's no definition of nothing, no vocal, no nothing, just like—*static*. Even these songs probably sounded ten times better in the studio when we recorded 'em. CDs are *small*. There's no stature in it. I remember when that Napster guy came up across, it was like, 'Everybody's getting music for free.' I was like, 'Well, why not? It ain't *worth* nothing anyway.'

"They have sound all over them." That's where we've arrived a half century after Cook urged the public to rescue high fidelity. We have an extreme facility with sound—it has become so flexible that even a novice can access, manipulate, and slather it all over a record. But we've lost something along the way. Ours is a lo-fi world.

This sense of loss is built right into the language of audio compression codecs, the programs that drive the iPod-ed world, which are classified as either "lossless" or "lossy." As the name implies, lossless codecs are where we really live the dream of having our digital cake and eating it, too. They basically function by figuring out how to recode a digital bitstream to express the exact same information with fewer bits. The process is somewhat analogous to the way Morse code assigns fewer bits (dots and dashes) to letters like *E* that are common in the English language, and more bits to letters like Q that are less common. The total number of bits in a Morse code message is less than if each letter was represented by the same number of bits (you'd need five bits to represent twenty-six combinations, the number of letters in our alphabet), but the message is exactly the same. Lossless codecs analyze a signal, determine which are the more common elements, and recode them using fewer bits, creating a signal with exactly the same informational component but which requires less storage space.

Common formats like MP3 integrate some lossless technology, but it is mostly used in high-end formats such as Super Audio CDs (SACD). To really shrink music enough to stuff thousands of songs on an iPod, you need lossy algorithms. When music on a CD is converted to MP3 or AAC (the iPod default), between 80 and 90 percent of the music is simply discarded. We (supposedly) don't notice because of the psychoacoustic phenomenon called masking. You experience masking every time you're having a conversation on a crowded street and a fire engine's wailing siren temporarily makes your speech inaudible. This often happens in spoken language; plosive consonants (sounds made by restricting airflow, such as t or k) are often masked by louder vowel sounds that precede them. Another variation, called postmasking, occurs when a loud sound makes the hair cells in the inner ear stiffen; during the few milliseconds it takes for them to regain sensitivity, you can miss what comes next. More bizarre is premasking, in which a loud sound actually masks a softer sound that precedes it by up to twenty milliseconds. This occurs because loud sounds require less time for the brain to process.

The type of masking that fuels lossy codecs occurs because of a quirk in how we perceive individual frequencies. The membrane that bisects the cochlea—that grape-size snail-shaped organ in the inner ear—is divided into twenty-four areas, each corresponding to a range of frequencies. Nerve receptors determine which frequencies are present by noting which of the twenty-four areas are vibrating. But since these areas correspond to groups, rather than individual frequencies, a strong frequency in one group can mask a weaker frequency from the same group occurring simultaneously. Music typically contains multiple frequencies at any given moment. Every codec has a "psychoacoustic model" built into its algorithm that determines which frequencies are masking others, and eliminates the information corresponding to the weaker ones.

More than anything, it is the billions of songs encoded in lossy formats that are making Emory Cook's world a distant memory. High fidelity barely exists today, not so much because recordings don't attempt to document reality anymore but because the fundamental ethic governing recorded music has been reversed. Presence implies capturing *everything*. Today, we try to capture as little as possible while fostering the illusion of everything. We don't want everything. We want just enough.

I was sitting in a specially designed listening room, trying to quantify how annoying I found a clip of a Dire Straits song, as per the instructions of a subjective listening test. It was a more difficult task than I'd expected. So far, the answer was: no more than usual.

The room was in the basement of the Communications Research Centre Canada (CRC), a government research institution in Ottawa that sits on an idyllic plot of land next to a Canadian Forces weapons range. CRC is one of only a handful of places around the world that are equipped to conduct the kinds of rigorous tests that determine how successfully a codec fosters the illusion of everything while delivering just enough. CRC doesn't build codecs, but it determines if they are ready for the world.

The room's construction satisfied requirements set by the International Telecommunications Union in Geneva, including being "symmetrical relative to the vertical plane on the mid-perpendicular of the stereo base" and "shaped like a rectangle or a trapezium." To eliminate unwanted vibrations, the ceiling and walls formed a shell that disconnected the room from the building around it. Every precaution had been taken to ensure that this room was the best spot in the world to measure listening behavior. It was where the "just enough" world of audio was put through its paces.

The origins of this world extend back to Leonardo Chiariglione, an Italian engineer who in the mideighties organized the Moving Picture Experts Group (MPEG) to establish a global standard for digital video. Chiariglione felt that video standards in the past had suffered from the influence of conservative corporate interests, so he built some free-market competitiveness into the process. MPEG standards mostly applied to the specific makeup of the bitstream, while allowing considerable leeway regarding how that bitstream was generated. The result is that MPEG-ready decoders are fairly uniform, but encoders can take many forms. This guaranteed a constant evolution toward new and better encoders and had the unlikely effect of creating an audio standard that blindsided the music industry, partly because the music industry had no influence in blocking its development.

The first job of the MPEG group was to establish a standard for moving images on CD-ROM. In 1988, a subcommittee met to discuss the audio component of the standard. After considering several audio compression algorithms and conducting extensive listening tests in Stockholm during the summer of 1990, the group came up with an audio model for first-generation MPEG devices (MPEG-1) based on three "layers" of audio coding. All MPEG-1 devices had to be able to play at least the first layer, while the most complex could play all three.

The third layer—MPEG-1 Audio Layer 3—was a combination of two codecs: MUSICAM, developed by Phillips, and ASPEC, which grew out of work done by Karlheinz Brandenburg and was now being developed by Germany's Fraunhofer Institute of Integrated Circuits; the French company Thomson; and Lucent, a Bell Labs descendant. Brandenburg was a brilliant electrical-engineering graduate student at Erlangen-Nuremberg University who was part of a European Union–funded collaboration between the university and Fraunhofer.

The three layers became official in 1992, and for the next few years Brandenburg and others continued to tweak Layer 3. They aggressively pushed the limits of compression, finding new ways to use fewer bits. Besides just eliminating frequencies that were totally masked, they experimented with "coarse quantization"—doing a very simple representation of frequencies that were audible but buried. "This lets you code large parts of the frequencies with just one or two bits," Brandenburg explains. "The coarse presentation will mean an error, but if the error is masked, that's okay." Coarse quantization saves space but can also cause a problem called time-smearing, an effect especially noticeable with dry percussive instruments like maracas. Their attack sounds normal, but the decay sounds strange, almost as though the sound were preceded by its own echo.

As Brandenburg experimented with ways around these sorts of problems, his ultimate proving ground became the a cappella version of "Tom's Diner" by Suzanne Vega. The dry production and the lack of any instruments besides Vega's voice minimizes the psychoacoustic mileage you can get from masking. Everything is right out in the open, no sounds hiding behind other sounds. Over and over, Brandenburg tweaked the same twenty seconds of the song.

Eventually the song sounded okay, and Brandenburg began to think that Layer 3 might have a life apart from just being the MPEG-1 audio standard. As the nascent World Wide Web developed, standard formats like Real Audio sounded increasingly weak. "I remember a meeting in late '94 where we internally said, 'Look, we have a window of opportunity to make Layer 3 the Internet audio standard,' " he recalls. Far removed from the music industry, Brandenburg wasn't thinking about the consequences of peer-to-peer file sharing, but others were, like Ricky Adar, a British entrepreneur who had an idea for selling music on the Internet. "He looked at what we could do, and I still remember him asking, 'Do you know that you will destroy the music industry?' I said, 'That's not our intent, and I don't think we'll do it.' " Fraunhofer began to see newsgroups with information about Layer 3, which the company was now calling MP3.*

Adar was right, of course. Once college students began to play around with MP3s around 1997, the music industry's century-old business model fell apart. MP3 was very good to its developers, however. By 2005, MP3 licensing was bringing in more than $100 million annually to the Fraunhofer Society, the company's applied research institution. In 2007, a federal court ordered Microsoft to pay Lucent (now Alcatel-Lucent) $1.5 billion for infringing on MP3 patents.

By the time Napster really pushed MP3 over the top, Brandenburg and a team of researchers from Sony, AT&T, Dolby, and other companies were working on the next phase of lossy compression, AAC ("advanced audio coding"). In 1997, AAC was put through two major tests. The first was a joint effort between the BBC and Japan's NHK network. The second and more extensive test was conducted by CRC.

AAC was one of six codecs included in the CRC's test. The codecs came in a variety of bit rates, so there were seventeen test items in all. The CRC appointed a panel of three "expert listeners" who spent three months evaluating possible sounds to use for the test. The companies whose codecs were being tested were also invited to submit suggestions. The CRC narrowed the possible pool to eighty audio selections, each of which was processed through all seventeen codecs. The listening panel evaluated the

---

*As the MPEG group developed MPEG-2 and subsequent standards, MP3 was often confused with MPEG-3. To further confuse matters, there is no MPEG-3: after developing MPEG-3 as a standard for high-definition television, the MPEG group discontinued it after discovering that tweaking MPEG-2 worked just as well.

results and winnowed the eighty possibilities down to twenty, choosing ones that best represented a cross section of the types of audible artifacts that had shown up in the 1,360 clips.

Semiformal listening tests then narrowed the twenty down to a group of eight, each a few seconds long, that collectively highlighted the biggest problems encountered by each codec: a bass clarinet arpeggio, a harpsichord arpeggio, and a bowed double bass, all taken from a library of test sounds maintained by the European Broadcasting Union; "Ride Across the River," from Dire Straits's *Brothers in Arms*; a snippet of music and rainfall from an Indiana Jones movie; a pitch pipe; a muted trumpet; and that old codec chestnut, the a cappella "Tom's Diner," to which the sound of tinkling glass balls was added as an extra hurdle for the codecs. Eight sound clips and seventeen codecs meant a total of 136 test items.

CRC recruited twenty-four test subjects—twenty men, four women: seven musicians, six broadcast or recording engineers, three piano tuners, two codec developers, and three everyday civilians. Past experience had taught CRC that subjects could handle about forty-five test items in one day, broken up into three blocks with long breaks between them. Any more, and fatigue and boredom tainted the results. That meant it would require three days for each subject to get through the complete trial. On the morning of each test day, the subjects, in groups of two, were given an orientation at the CRC that included playing them some of the items they would hear that day so that the subjects could become acclimated and ease into the listening process.

The test the CRC uses is double-blind and triple-stimulus. Subjects are presented with a sound clip played in normal CD-quality uncompressed audio. They then hear two more versions of the same clip. One of these is exactly identical to the first version. The other has been compressed using a codec and bit rate unknown to the subject. Subjects first choose which of these two they believe is the compressed version. Then they assign to it an "annoyance" rating based on how distracting they find the audible artifacts that influenced their choice, using a five-point system: "imperceptible," "perceptible, but not annoying," "slightly annoying," "annoying," and "very annoying." Subjects use a numerical system to express gradations. For instance, a 1.7 rating means "somewhere between 'very annoying' and 'annoying,' but closer to 'very annoying.'"

The tests allow for subjects to go at their own pace. They can take as long as they like to compare all three clips, bounce back and forth among them, and even isolate small sections. Although subjects never know which codec they're hearing, the order isn't completely random. From consulting with a psychologist who studies test-taking behavior, the CRC learned that front-loading too many difficult selections—codecs encoded at a high bit rate that makes them harder to distinguish from the CD-quality versions—discourages subjects and makes them doubt their ability to perceive differences.

When the results were in, the overall winner was AAC, encoded at 128 Kbps, with an average score that placed it firmly in the "not annoying" territory. The big surprise wasn't that AAC at 128 Kbps beat MP3 at 128 Kbps, or even that this same version of MP3 also lost to AAC at 96 Kbps. It was that AAC vanquished some highly touted proprietary codecs at larger bitrates. AAC at 128 Kbps beat Lucent's PAC at 160 Kbps, and even performed as well as Dolby's AC-3 at 192 Kbps.

Nearly ten years later, AAC is everywhere. The CRC agreed to give me the same test that had demonstrated AAC's lossy superiority. I wasn't so much curious about whether AAC would triumph over the others, but rather how difficult it was to tell the CD-quality clip from the compressed version. I assumed it wouldn't be difficult at all.

To take a subjective listening test at CRC, you sit in a chair and stare slightly downward at a monitor between two speakers. When you toggle back and forth to compare selections, the testing software makes sure the transitions are completely seamless. Every aspect of the test is designed to isolate the act of listening—"to eliminate every variable, except for this," said the CRC's Michel Lavoie, a member of the institute's Advanced Audio Systems Group, pointing at his ears. "Ideally, there would be a brain implant. Even having to look at the monitor means your brain is processing, when you should just be using it to listen."

Before administering the test, Lavoie made it clear that he wouldn't give me the results, a policy the CRC strictly observes. Since so many of the people whom the CRC recruits for subjective listening tests are professionally involved in audio, they all assume they'll ace the test. But one thing the tests can reveal is that people who think they have golden ears really have nothing of the sort. Subjects may consistently misidentify which selection is the codec and which is the original. They may hear all kinds of phantom artifacts in what they mistakenly think is the codec choice and wind up giving an "annoying" rating to the original. "People always want to know how they did," Lavoie said. "But no good can ever come of it. It either strokes your ego or demolishes your ego. If people don't do as well as they thought, and word gets out, it's just bad news."

Lavoie gave me a very abbreviated version of the pre-test-training the subjects received, which involved playing selections they would hear during the test. It was immediately apparent that this wasn't going to be nearly as easy as I thought. Lavoie started me off with the bass clarinet arpeggio. I listened to A, and then toggled between B and C and realized, with a small twinge of panic, that all three selections sounded the same to me. How could I not hear the difference between a codec and a CD? "Listen to the envelope," Lavoie said. "Listen for frequencies. Try to hear if there is filtering." He played a bit of the Suzanne Vega song and told me to concentrate on how the sound of the glass balls interacted with the music. For the snippet of music and rain from *Raiders*, he urged me to get a "global impression" of the sounds, but all I could think about was how the rain sounded like cicadas in both clips.

It was time for the test. "All I'm interested in is what's happening between your two ears," Lavoie said before he left the room. I realized quickly that I didn't know myself. The first selection, the bass clarinet, threw me; I could only hope that this was one of the more sophisticated codecs. When the pitch pipe came up, it was easier to detect the codec because the high frequencies clearly taxed it, creating a sound that I could easily describe as "annoying." I found it helpful on the single-instrument selections to make loops of the highest notes, since the differences were more likely to be perceptible. The music and rain continued to trip me up, however. I just couldn't separate the two, and the more I tried the less confidence I had in my choices.

The whole experience was oddly disorienting. How could the "just enough" world be so hard to hear? I understood why the CRC keeps the test results secret. I'm happy to spend the rest of my life not knowing how I did.

According to Lavoie, my response was common among test takers at the CRC. "It humbles you," he said. "You lose your preconceived notions, and you're walking blind."

High fidelity still exists in some unlikely places. One of them is the three-hundred-seat theater at the Museum of Tolerance in Los Angeles, which has one of the most advanced sound systems of any theater in the world,

installed by Iosono, a German company founded by Brandenburg. The reason that a museum commemorating the Holocaust, as well as racism and
prejudice throughout history, has such a fancy theater is mainly due to
some of its wealthy filmmaker benefactors, such as Stephen Spielberg, who
wanted to do private screenings of their films in a perfect sonic environment. Also, the rabbis who run the place "are total audio freaks," Uwe Kar-
benk, Iosono's director of marketing, told me as I stood in the empty
theater. "They wanted a system that would still feel new in fifteen years."

Brandenburg formed Iosono to capitalize on wave-field synthesis, a
technology that Louis Thibault, the CRC's manager of advanced audio systems, described as "the future of audio reproduction." The technology's
theoretical underpinnings stretch back to work done by the Dutch scientist
Christiaan Huygens in the seventeenth century. Huygens proposed that any
point on a wave can be thought of as containing a smaller wave, and that
the sum of these smaller waves is identical to the larger wave. In the 1980s,
Augustus Berkhout, an expert in seismics and acoustics at Holland's
Delft University of Technology, applied the Huygens principle to the problem of pinpointing the exact location of deposits in oil fields. His method
involved detonating many small explosions on a field and studying the
behavior of the waves they generated to construct a larger picture of where
the oil lay.

Brandenburg and other audio researchers essentially applied
Berkhout's methods in reverse. Wave-field synthesis begins with a large
"picture"—the way sound waves generated by an event would behave in a
specific environment—and physically rebuilds them piece by piece. The
walls of a listening room equipped with a wave-field synthesis system are
covered with dozens of tiny speakers laid end to end. The system makes
each speaker vibrate in the correct way at a precise moment so that the sum
of the vibrations perfectly reconstructs the complete "wave field" of the
sounds it reproduces. The waves are physically rebuilt, piece by piece. For
the man who brought the world the MP3, wave-field synthesis represents a
massive conceptual shift. Rather than capture just enough, wave-field synthesis aims to snare everything. We're back in the realm of re-creating the
concert hall in the living room.

Brandenburg conceives of wave-field synthesis as a natural progression
after the MP3. "If you look at how high-fidelity technology evolved, there's
always been two goals," he says. "One is to have the fidelity of the signal

itself, and the other is to re-create ambiance, that feeling of being some-where else. MP3 advanced the first part with the lowest bit rate possible, and wave-field synthesis clearly advances the other task. It's an old dream."

The upshot of wave-field synthesis is that the designer has maximum control over high-fidelity sounds. Every wave-field synthesis system can handle up to thirty-two discrete sounds. Iosono chose thirty-two partly for reasons of processing, but also because thirty-two is twice the number of discrete sounds that a blind person can pick out of a noisy environment. (The sighted can typically identify no more than thirteen.) Using a mouse, these sounds can be "placed" anywhere in a room. If you wanted to do the concert-hall re-creation trick, you could build a virtual stage at the front of the room, placing the singer in the center, the guitarist to the right, the drums in the back, and so on. You could even make the musicians wander around the "stage." The system handles directionality so well that no mat-ter where you are in the room, the geometric relationships hold. If you walk from one side of the room to the other, you never lose the sense of where the musicians are, because the system knows how the complete "wave field" would behave in this space and physically builds it, piece by piece.

A typical audio setup, whether it's a simple two-channel stereo setup or 5.1 "surround sound," is optimized for one spot in the room, the so-called sweet spot. A concert heard through a wave-field-synthesis system is de-signed so that every spot in the room may not be an equally good place to sit—in the same way that a spectator at a real concert may not want to sit directly in front of the guitarist's amp—but, no matter where you are, you still perceive the geometric setup.

That's the theory, anyway. I stood in a small soundstage at Disney Imag-ineering in the San Fernando Valley town of Glendale, hearing a jazz con-cert reproduced through an Iosono system. As I walked around the room, the illusion was indeed convincing, though not absolutely lifelike. But just as I began to wonder whether I wasn't willing myself to be blown away, and maybe thinking about the sound a little too hard in hopes of hearing the perfect illusion, a cell phone went off to my right. I instinctively turned to see whose it was and realized that it belonged to a phantom audience mem-ber at the virtual jazz club I was in. Then I started to notice clinking glasses and people having discussions at the "tables."

More impressive was a demonstration of how wave-field synthesis can dispense with the "real" altogether. Iosono located its American office in Los Angeles to be near the entertainment industry; at the moment most of Iosono's clients are amusement parks. The room at Disney was being used to design sounds for a haunted-house attraction at Disney World. Tanja Linssen, Iosono's director of product development, made the room fill with what sounded like disembodied figures hyperventilating. It was a truly spooky, unsettling sound. Then she directed me toward an X marked on the floor, and now the voices were right on top of me, and then inside my head as though I were wearing headphones. I could actually feel a twitching sensation in my ear, as though my inner ear were trying to figure out what it was hearing and where it was coming from.

"Your brain goes ape-shit," Linssen said. "It's trying to figure out what's going on."

Linssen cued up another file, and techno music filled the room. Iosono is also trying to get wave-field synthesis adapted by DJs at clubs. It would be a fun tool, making music slice across the room, in and around and even through dancers' heads. ("Nobody would need any drugs," Linssen pointed out.) And of course, even in 2008, it wouldn't be a high-fidelity demo without train sounds. (In fact, it was in Glendale that Ross Snyder and Bill Cara made their stereo recording of trains that wowed everyone at the 1953 audio fair in L.A.) The Iosono team had made a recording of two trains in nearby Altadena, and now I heard them both coming toward me and then veering off on either side of me.

Later on that day I was walking around the screening room at the Museum of Tolerance, listening to an Iosono-produced recording of a mixture of environmental sounds. The sounds were coming from speakers lining the walls, most of them partly obscured by mesh that hung from the ceiling. I heard wild animals stalking through a jungle, intermittent rain, buzzing insects. And it was true: no matter where I walked in the room, I could perceive the totality of the scene. Sometimes insects would buzz my ear or an animal would stalk in front of me. There were people, too—ghosts forming some sort of drum circle that was closing in on me.

When that was over, they played a video of a Boz Scaggs concert with the sound remixed for the wave-field-synthesis environment. Sure enough, I could hear the placement of the various musicians. The sound was indeed perfect, but I had to admit that I wasn't sure it would pass a tone test. I asked the Iosono people listening with me what they thought would happen if a curtain was placed over the stage, and an audience was told that there were live musicians—Boz Scaggs himself!—behind the screen. I was expecting an unhesitatingly affirmative response. Of course it would work. These were physically reconstructed waves we were talking about. But that wasn't the answer I got. "We can capture a lot," Tanja said. "We can even capture the waves bouncing off the musicians. But we can't capture the electromagnetic field that surrounds everybody in the room." She paused. "What we're missing is the presence."

There is something about the sound of the human voice that hits us on an instinctive level. Our auditory system has evolved to be most sensitively attuned to the frequencies present in that sound. Throughout the history of recording, the sound of the voice has been a proving ground. It was a recording of Edison's voice, reciting "Mary Had a Little Lamb," that demonstrated that recording was possible. More than a century later, Karlheinz Brandenburg used a recording of Suzanne Vega's unaccompanied voice to demonstrate that massive audio compression and decent fidelity were not incompatible. If the voice could be captured, whether engraved on wax paper or wrung through an algorithm, there was no limit to what it could do.

Our facility with perceiving the voice sometimes vexes our attempts to record it. The sound of sampled voices on the early Emulators sounded "wrong"—more like chipmunks than human beings—because the simple pitch-shifting that was sufficient to turn virtually any other sound into a musical scale was not enough for the voice. What our ears perceived to be missing was the filtering effects of the resonating cavity—a person's head—from which the voice emerges. Even as we change the pitch of our voices, that filter remains fairly constant, and our ears have evolved to recognize the filtering and the pitch as independent phenomena. The pitch-shifting Emulator moved everything up or down without maintaining that constant. It was almost as though the context of the voice, the condition that identified it as human, was missing. Today, the makers of the Emulator, and all similar devices, are still looking for a way to process sound, in real time, that can match the same precise changes that a singer can effect from moment to moment.

Even as the voice remains a final frontier for recording, one recording engineer thinks that nobody managed to solve the problem of the voice quite like Edison. Peter Dilg, a collector and dealer of vintage phonograph equipment, isn't a typical engineer. He's one of the last living practitioners of the art of acoustic recording on wax cylinders. The "wax" that covers these cylinders is really more like a metallic soap, a special resin concocted by one of Dilg's friends. Otherwise, Dilg makes records the same way people did in the predisc days. He uses an Edison lathe made in 1889 that records sound by running a cutting head—a glass diaphragm attached to a sapphire stylus—across a cylinder spinning at 100 rpm, the speed the nascent recording industry settled on after experiments with 120 and 144. These are purely acoustic recordings. The only electricity involved is the current that drives the motor that rotates the cylinder. Sound energy channeled through a protruding horn vibrates the glass, and the sapphire etches 98 grooves per inch.

There is more demand for Dilg's services than you might expect. He is sometimes hired for corporate events. He's pointed his horn at Hillary Clinton ("We played it back and she was amazed by it") and recorded a wax cylinder at the Edison National Historic Site in New Jersey. He recorded They Might Be Giants on *The Daily Show* and played the cylinder over the closing credits. He's recorded scores of amateur musicians who are curious to hear what they would have sounded like on record a hundred years ago. Wynton Marsalis cut a cylinder to confirm a suspicion he had that contemporary recording methods were hurting rather than helping the sound of music. "I wanted . . . to see if we'd sound more like jazz musicians, and I discovered that yes, it was true," he said.

Dilg said he gets this reaction all the time when he records people, especially singers. Many claim that for the first time they're hearing themselves sound like they always thought they did. The slight unease that most of us who aren't singers feel when we hear the sound of our recorded voice—do I really sound like that?—is a testament to recording's age-old difficulty with the human voice. Dilg was suggesting that something about the acoustic process does away with this unease by giving those who sing into the horn a version of themselves they'd always sensed but never quite heard outside of their own heads.

To see if this was true, I booked a session with Dilg. He's lived all his life in Baldwin, a Long Island, New York, town that has its own unique connection to recorded history. A few blocks away from where Dilg lives is a home that belonged to Billy Murray, a singer who was one of the biggest stars of the acoustic era. (Like Caruso, Murray had an almost intuitive sense of how to project his voice for the acoustic recording process.)

"Let me show you around," Dilg said, leading me into an attic crammed wall-to-wall with phonographs, gramophones, Graphophones, disembodied recording horns, cutting heads with glass diaphragms, cutting heads with cork diaphragms, and other accoutrements. Dilg has been accumulating this stuff since he was four or five, when he became enthralled with the Victrola used by his grandmother, a dance instructor, in her studio.

What drives Dilg is the idea at the root of recording, the crystallization of a found moment. It adds an extra dimension to the urge to hold history that drives any collector. "This is one of my best machines here," he said, pointing to an Edison Class M cylinder machine modified by Gianni Bettini—one of the earliest audiophiles and a recording pioneer—that he'd picked up at a local antiques store. "I got this when I was a kid, and it's got the name of a guy, 'F. B. Glover,' on it. I thought that some day his name would turn up. One day I'm reading the local Baldwin paper, and it has something about the main events in Baldwin one hundred years ago. It said, 'Invention of the Century,' and talked about 'Mr. Frank B. Glover playing his wonderful phonograph' at the church across the street! This is it!"

One thing Dilg has learned over the years is that Edison was right about a lot of things. Like the Diamond Disc, for example, the record player that launched a thousand tone tests. "They sound so much better than the electrical ones that came later on," he said. "Even if those had more bass response and all that."

Not that Dilg's an acoustic purist. He remembers the day as a kid when he dragged out of someone's trash a fully functioning Orthophonic—the Victor gramophone that, although acoustic in its operation, was built to handle electrical recordings—and being amazed at the sound that came out. "I heard it and couldn't believe it was mechanical," he recalls. "But in a way it doesn't count, because the Edison machine was acoustic, and all the records were acoustic. But for a lot of people [the Orthophonic] was a *sound*. They had never heard bass before, and then everybody wanted *bass*. I look at that as like, 'Here comes radio.'"

Dilg also thinks that Edison had the right idea sticking to the vertically cut hill-and-dale method over Victor's lateral cutting technique. Like Edison, Dilg thinks one advantage of vertically cut records was that the stylus could be connected directly to the diaphragm, whereas the lateral process required that the two be connected by a lever, thus increasing the chance that some vibrations would get lost. Also, by cutting side to side, the lateral cutter always risked dispersing some energy into a neighboring groove, which could cause a subtle pre-echo effect. In other words, Edison was solving a problem that would plague compression codecs a hundred years later.

Making an acoustic recording is by its nature an imprecise task. Dilg has learned which of his many cutting heads will work best with which instruments, and he's learned a lot about how to please the fickle recording horn, but he can never be sure how a recording will turn out. There are no levels to monitor, no objective signs that all is going well, although he can get a pretty good idea just by looking at the grooves in the finished cylinder. It's a good sign if he can see vibrations within the vibrations. "There was a guy here who imitated Al Jolson, and we did about ten cylinders," he said. "I looked at the record and said, 'Wow, it looks like Jolson—the groove patterns look like a Jolson record.' There's a certain way his grooves look. I said, 'You passed the sight test!' "

After all this time, Dilg still speaks of the act of recording with a reverence that borders on mystical. Even today, he can hardly believe the acoustic recording process works as well as it does. He recalled making cylinder recordings at the Grammy Awards a few years ago. "It just came out so clear and beautiful," he said, almost whispering. "Maybe it was because we were underground, but it almost sounded electrical. I was onstage in front of the whole academy. Why that day? *Why that day?* Was the wax warm for just long enough? Was it because the gods were watching me—all the old-time guys? I have no idea. I have no idea . . .

"It's like recording someone's soul, in a way," he continued. "It's different, I'm telling you. But we're gonna do you, so you'll see what I'm saying."

It was time for me to make a record. It occurred to me that I really had no idea what to say on it. Dilg took a blue cylinder and placed it under a glow lamp to soften up the wax. While we waited, Dilg gave me pointers. "You have to project," he said, putting his face close to the horn. "You need to really use the energy. You gotta push all that sound out."

Dilg judged the wax to be softened up just enough. He put it on the lathe, turned it on, announced the date, and then introduced me. He had suggested that I talk about why I was interviewing him, and what I was writing about. So I did that for a minute or so, and then, on a whim, I sang what I could remember of "Hawai'i Pono'i," the Hawaii state anthem, which I had to sing every morning in elementary school, and which was written three years before Edison recorded "Mary Had a Little Lamb."

When I was done, the cylinder was covered with little white wormlike shavings. Dilg burnished the disc, and then said, "Let's see how it turned out."

It turned out well. As with the Caliburn turntable, Dr. John Diamond's push test, the unmastered version of *Californication*, and the subjective listening test at the CRC, I can't guarantee that the sound I heard wasn't affected by prior expectations, but I can say that I know what people mean when they say the wax cylinder makes them sound like themselves. Making a sound recording may be the ultimate narcissistic act. You're capturing something that wasn't meant to be captured, in a form that is absolutely meaningless without some sort of technological actualization to play it back, and you call it reality. And if you can honestly say it sounds like you wanted it to, that it gives back the voice exactly as you hear it in your head, then it's perfect. Forever. "You engraved this," Dilg said, holding up the cylinder. "This is you."

He gestured around the room. "You don't make money at this," he said. "All this equipment cost me thousands. But just to hear what you just heard, on a permanent record like that. It'll be around long after we're gone, you know? It's kind of neat that there will still be people listening to it, because it's so mechanical."

This was a surprise. It had never occurred to me that these wax cylinder recordings were anything other than fragile, ephemeral wisps of a moment. But Dilg said that as long it was kept in a cool, dry place, it could last hundreds of years.

Not that Dilg thinks that cylinders are the only way to freeze time. He mentioned that he owns a small house built on the oceanfront marshland nearby. You need a boat to get to it. "In that house is an old Sonora phonograph, all beat up like that one over there," he said. "And we have some CDs there, and they're all going bad. But the 78s have been under the water during two hurricanes. And we saved them. If there's ever a big bomb, they're gonna find little piles of these 78s. And they'll listen to them, ten thousand years from now. Everything else will be dead."

Notes

All direct quotations not cited are from in-person and telephone interviews conducted by the author between 2004 and 2008. Quotations from e-mail exchanges are noted. For material that was drawn from a combination of author interviews and secondary sources, both sources are cited.

Intro: "Testing, Testing ..."

3 " 'The turntable of the talking machines . . .' " Theodor W. Adorno, "The Curves of the Needle," in *Essays on Music*, edited by Richard Leppert (Berkeley: University of California Press, 2002), 275.

3 "It also conducted sound . . ." Robert Roy Britt, "Early Universe Bears Imprint of Big Bang's Echo," MSNBC.com (January 13, 2005), available at www.msnbc.msn.com /id/6817399/.

4 "The concert was by invitation only . . ." William Maxwell, *The Edison Sales Laboratory* (Orange, NJ: Thomas A. Edison, Inc., 1915, private printing), 23–24.

6 "The crowd went wild." To re-create the tone test of September 17, 1915, I tried to be as accurate as possible, though some details were inferred from consulting several sources. Date, time, location, musicians, attendance: "Supreme Triumph of the Edison Diamond Disc Phonograph," *The Edison Phonograph Monthly* 13, 11 (November 1915). Selections played: Emily Thompson, "Machines, Music, and the Quest for Fidelity: Marketing the Edison Phonograph in America, 1877–1925," *The Musical Quarterly* 79 (Spring 1995): 131–71; and Maxwell. Structure of tone tests, layout of stage: George L. Frow, *The Edison Disc Phonographs and the Diamond Discs: A History with Illustrations* (Sevenoaks, UK: G. L. Frow, 1982).

6 ". . . the most famous tone test . . ." Thompson, 153.

7 " 'I remember I stood . . .' " Interview with Anna Case, September 19, 1972, in John Harvith and Susan Edwards Harvith, *Edison, Musicians, and the Phonograph: A Century in Retrospect* (New York: Greenwood Press, 1987), 44.

7 "The many minds that developed . . ." For a thorough review and description of the Caliburn, see Michael Fremer, "Continuum Audio Labs Caliburn and Cobra

Turntable," *Stereophile* (January 2006), available at http://stereophile.com/turn tables/106con/.

12 "**. . . declared the LP to be . . .**" Glenn Gould, "The Prospects of Recording," *High Fidelity* 16, 4 (April 1966): 46–63. Available at www.collectionscanada.ge.ca/glenngould/028010-5021-e.html.

14 "**'. . . sound and its intention.'**" Edward Rothstein, "The Quest for Perfect Sound," *The New Republic* (November 17, 1985): 30–42.

14 "**'. . . recording consciousness . . .'**" H. Stith Bennett, *On Becoming a Rock Musician* (Amherst: University of Massachusetts Press, 1980). Helmut Rösing has offered a similar analysis of what happens when we listen to music. Learning how to listen to recordings requires one to grasp the "sign-like meanings" of sound events and the "semantic system" in which they operate. See Helmut Rösing, "Listening Behaviour and Musical Preference in the Age of 'Transmitted Music,'" *Popular Music 4: Performers and Audiences*, edited by Richard Middleton and David Horn (Cambridge, UK: Cambridge University Press, 1984), 119–49.

15 "**When a sound wave . . .**" See Peter B. Denes and Elliot N. Pinson, *The Speech Chain: The Physics and Biology of Spoken Language* (New York: W. H. Freeman and Company, 1993), 17–28.

17 "**The inner ear is . . .**" See Denes and Pinson, 128–31.

18 "**. . . 140 million times smaller . . .**" Measuring SPL is easier than measuring intensity, so intensity is typically inferred from SPL. The 140 million figure is from Denes and Pinson, 98. The hydrogen molecule example is from Mark Ballora, "You've Got the Power," *Electronic Musician* (September 2004), available at http://emusician.com/mag/emusic_youve_power/.

19 "**. . . perception of music is an evolutionarily ancient neural skill . . .**" Robert Zatorre, "Music, the Food of Neuroscience?," *Nature* 434 (March 17, 2005): 312–15.

20 "**. . . chills-down-the-spine feeling . . .**" Ibid. See also Daniel J. Levitin, *This Is Your Brain on Music: The Science of a Human Obsession* (New York: Dutton, 2006), 185–86.

22 "**. . . absolutely meaningless unless it is played.**" See William Pietz, "The Phonograph in Africa: International Phonocentrism from Stanley to Sarnoff," *Post-Structuralism and the Question of History*, edited by Derek Attridge, Geoff Bennington, and Robert Young (Cambridge: Cambridge University Press, 1987), 270–85. He writes: "The recording surface of the phonograph record is not a recording surface encoded with signifiers in the manner of speech. Rather, it is inscribed with singular lines which can be *decoded*, but which do not *represent* what they record"; 263.

22 "**. . . Gould said it best . . .**" Gould.

23 "**'What held them back . . .'**" Walter Murch, "Hyser Memorial Lecture," Audio Engineering Society 117th Convention, October 30, 2004, San Francisco.

24 "**. . . the artistic 'big bang' . . .**" Randall White, *Prehistoric Art: The Symbolic Journey of Humankind* (New York: Harry N. Abrams, 2003), 8–16.

25 "**. . . study of the Kaluli of Papua New Guinea . . .**" Steven Feld, *Sound and Sentiment: Birds, Weeping, Poetics, and Song in Kaluli Expression* (Philadelphia: University of Pennsylvania Press, 1982, second edition), 30–31.

1: The Point of Commencement

29 **". . . opened the door of Machinery Hall . . ."** "Exposition to Be Opened by Radio," *San Francisco Chronicle*, February 20, 1915; "How President Opened Fair" and "President Opens Fair by Wireless," *The New York Times*, February 21, 1915.

30 **"The Tower of Jewels was the centerpiece . . ."** The details of the expo were mostly drawn from Donna Ewald and Peter Clute, "The Enchanted City," *American History Illustrated* 27 (July–August 1992), 46–57; and Gray Brechin, "Sailing to Byzantium: The Architecture of the Fair," in Burton Benedict, *The Anthropology of World's Fairs: San Francisco's Panama Pacific Exposition of 1915* (Berkeley, CA: Lowie Museum of Anthropology and Scolar Press, 1983), 99.

30 **" 'It will be set . . .' "** Brechin, 101.

30 **" '. . . height of the tide . . .' "** "New Standards Have Been Set for the World," *San Francisco Chronicle*, February 21, 1915.

30 **"The Joy Zone . . ."** " 'The Mysterious Orient': Cowboys and Indians Meet Two Princesses," *San Francisco Chronicle*, February 19, 1915.

31 **". . . 'a place that could not possibly be real.' "** Ewald and Clute, 47.

31 **" 'a white-haired man of peace . . .' "** "Thomas A. Edison Accorded Greatest Ovation of Year by Enthusiastic Throngs," *San Francisco Chronicle*, October 22, 1915.

31 **" 'From the day that he first made . . .' "** "The Edison Diamond Disc and Its Inventor's Voice Are Heard from the Atlantic to the Pacific (and Vice Versa) on Edison Day," *The Edison Phonograph Monthly* 13, 11 (November 1915), 9–10.

34 **" 'The phonograph knows more . . .' "** Andre Millard, *Edison and the Business of Innovation* (Baltimore, MD: Johns Hopkins University Press, 1990), 66.

34 **"The first of Edison's creations . . ."** A. M. Kennedy, "The Birth of the Phonograph and a Comparison of Edison and Berliner Methods," *The Edison Phonograph Monthly* 13, 9 (September 1915), 11–12.

34 **" 'This is my baby . . .' "** Paul Israel, *Edison: A Life of Invention* (New York: John Wiley & Sons, 1998), 147.

34 **". . . record as well as reproduce . . ."** Millard, 184.

34 **". . . his proposed uses . . ."** Israel, 147.

34 **" 'As it may be filed . . .' "** Thomas Edison, "The Phonograph and Its Future," *North American Review* (May/June 1878), 527–36.

34 **". . . a real celebrity . . ."** Israel, 154.

34 **". . . liked to demonstrate . . ."** Walter L. Welch and Leah Brodbeck Stenzel Burt, *From Tinfoil to Stereo: The Acoustic Years of the Recording Industry, 1877–1929* (Gainesville: University of Florida Press, 1984), 20.

35 **" 'It seems to me . . .' "** Letter of June 27, 1888, from William Henry Meadowcroft to Thomas Edison, Folder D8847, Thomas Alva Edison Papers Project.

36 **" 'In the phonograph . . .' "** Thomas A. Edison, "The Perfected Phonograph," in *Description of the Phonograph and Phonograph-Graphophone by Their Respective Inventors: Testimonials as to Their Practical Use* (London: The London Phonograph and Gramophone Society, 1973, originally published 1888), 4.

36 **" '. . . many stupid persons . . .' "** William Lynd, "On Tour with the Phonograph," *The Phonogram* 1, 1 (May 1893), 7–8.

37 **". . . coin-operated phonographs . . ."** Welch and Burt, 33.

37 **". . . sales increased tenfold . . ."** Millard, 164.

37 ". . . first commercially available recordings . . ." Israel, 150.

37 ". . . easier to mass-produce . . ." Millard, 207.

37 ". . . more durable . . ." Israel, 424.

37 ". . . artists signed to Victor's record division was Enrico Caruso . . ." Millard, 209.

38 " 'Victrola' became a colloquial term . . ." Millard, 210–11.

38 ". . . Edison remained popular in rural areas . . ." Israel, 424.

38 ". . . Thomas Alva Edison, Inc. (TAE) . . ." Ibid., 427.

38 ". . . stylus was attached to the diaphragm . . ." Kennedy, 12.

39 ". . . 2,300 different styli." Israel, 431. "A Brief Chronology of Edison's Life," http://edison.rutgers.edu/brfchron.htm.

39 " '. . . Mr. Edison weighs . . .' " Allan L. Benson, "Edison's Dream of New Music," *Cosmopolitan* 54 (May 1913), 797.

39 " 'What a pity . . .' " "The Care Used in Producing Edison Records," *The Edison Phonograph Monthly* 13, 9 (September 1915), 8–9.

39 "Edison leaned over . . ." Benson, 798.

40 " 'Nobody realizes how much music . . .' " Ibid., 798.

40 " 'Forty percent of the sounds . . .' " Ibid., 799.

41 " 'If music is worth anything . . .' " Ibid., 797, 799.

41 ". . . Anna Case decided to pay . . ." William Maxwell, *The Edison Sales Laboratory* (Orange, NJ: Thomas A. Edison, Inc., 1915, private printing), 18.

42 ". . . East Orange's two hundred most . . ." Ibid., 23–24.

43 " 'It was intended . . .' " Ibid., 26.

44 ". . . Edison phonograph dealers . . ." "A Rousing Two-Day Dealers' Convention at the Edison Factory," *The Edison Phonograph Monthly* 13, 9 (September 1915), 2–4.

45 "As word got around . . ." "Supreme Triumph of the Edison Diamond Disc Phonograph," *The Edison Phonograph Monthly* 13, 11 (November 1915), 3, 7.

45 " 'A new baby . . .' " "Cylinder Exclusively Hereafter," *The Edison Phonograph Monthly* 13, 12 (December 1915), 1.

45 ". . . had invented yet another . . ." Millard, 211–12.

46 " 'We are trying . . .' " "Cylinder Exclusively Hereafter," 3.

46 ". . . peaked in 1915 . . ." Millard, 293.

46 ". . . sales were strong . . ." Ibid., 292.

46 ". . . sales declined . . ." Ibid., 293.

46 ". . . could play only on . . ." Ibid., 298.

46 "Score: Amberola 12 . . ." "Score: Amberola 12; Talking Machine 1," *The Edison Phonograph Monthly* 14, 7 (July 1916), 3.

46 ". . . cartoon of two phonographs . . ." "Knockout at End of Three Rounds—New Diamond Amberola Gets Decision," *The Edison Phonograph Monthly* 14, 12 (December 1916), 3–4.

46 " 'We are looking . . .' " "A Warning," *The Edison Phonograph Monthly* 15, 1 (January 1917), 2.

47 ". . . interest in spiritualism . . ." Austin C. Lescarboura, "Edison's Views on Life and Death," *Scientific American* 123 (October 30, 1920), 446.

47 ". . . 'emotional effects' . . ." George L. Frow, *The Edison Disc Phonographs and the Diamond Discs: A History with Illustrations* (Sevenoaks, UK: G. L. Frow, 1982), 247, 249.

47 ". . . Mood Change Chart . . ." Ibid., 247–48.

47 " 'Last year, when you were . . .' " Millard, 300–301.

47 ". . . affecting what people wanted . . ." Ibid., 301.

47 ". . . 'volume fad' . . ." Ibid., 308.

48 " 'I tried it . . .' " "Edison Still Busy on Phonograph," *The New York Times*, July 19, 1922.

48 ". . . 'straight phono company.' " Millard, 308.

48 ". . . begin marketing 12-inch 78 rpm records . . ." Ibid., 305.

48 ". . . Edisonic machine . . ." Ibid., 308.

48 ". . . TAE released its last records." *The Edison CD Sampler, 1877–1984* (West Orange, NJ: Edison National Historic Site, Sony Corporation of America, 1984).

49 " 'Mr. Edison put . . .' " "The Edison Diamond Disc . . ."

49 " 'Very successful,' Verdi Fuller wrote . . ." Ibid.

2: From the New World

50 ". . . walked onstage at Carnegie Hall . . ." "Super-Volume Concert Records Scare Audience," *New York Herald Tribune*, April 10, 1940; and "Sound Waves 'Rock' Carnegie Hall as Enhanced Music Is Played; Stereographic Reproduction Demonstrated by Bell Laboratories—Tones Near Limit That the Human Ear Can Endure," *The New York Times*, April 10, 1940.

53 ". . . the machine that . . ." Roland Gelatt, *The Fabulous Phonograph, 1877–1977* (New York: Collier Books, 1977), 219–23.

53 " 'Every tone is preserved . . .' " "Science Again Comes to the Aid of Music," *The Musician* 30 (November 1925), 9.

54 " 'I wonder if . . .' " "Electric Reproducers," *The Gramophone* (April 1928), 475.

55 " 'Whatever may have been . . .' " Walter L. Welch, "The Six Great Limitations of the Gramophone," *The Gramophone* 10 (January 1933), 116.

55 " 'As the great war . . .' " John C. W. Chapman, "Electrical Recording and Value for Money," *The Gramophone* (March 1929), 469.

58 "In the early 1920s . . ." Origins and by-products of Bell's research from Bell Labs press release, 1980, Stokowski collection, University of Pennsylvania; and "Hi-Fi Is Old Hat," *Bell Labs Reporter*, 24–27. Information about 2.5 octaves is from Robert Conley, "The Pioneers of the Audio Trail," *The New York Times*, November 16, 1958.

59 " 'A singer unable . . .' " Emile Berliner, *The Gramophone: Paper Read Before the Franklin Institute, May 16, 1888* (Washington, D.C.: The United States Gramophone Company, 1894). One of Berliner's other visionary ideas was that one could compress a life into one record—"a tone picture of a single lifetime," from a baby's first words to the deathbed utterances: "Will it not be like holding communication even with immortality?" See also Gelatt, 62–63.

59 "When Western Electric . . ." Hans Fantel, "50 Years Ago—Musical Stereo's First Disk," *The New York Times*, January 11, 1981.

59 " 'It is clear . . .' " "Merger Is Approved by RCA and Victor," *The New York Times*, January 5, 1929.

59 " 'Every dramatic performance . . .' " David Sarnoff, "Where Opportunity Beckons," *The New York Times*, September 22, 1929.

60 ". . . was an industrial giant . . ." Frederick O. Barnum III, *His Master's Voice in America* (Camden, NJ: General Electric, 1991), 124.

60 ". . . 'no musician of our time . . .' " Glenn Gould, "In Praise of Maestro Stokowski," *The New York Times Magazine*, May 14, 1978.

60 " 'The first step . . .' " Leopold Stokowski, *Music for All of Us* (New York: Simon and Schuster, 1943), 229.

60 ". . . 'completely meaningless criterion . . .' " Robert C. Marsh, "Conversations with Stokowski," *High Fidelity* (April 1961), 44–47, 162–63. On Stokowski and the physicality of music, see also Hans Fantel, "Custom Tailored Sound for the Home," *The New York Times*, November 18, 1979.

61 " 'Sometimes, after a . . .' " Irving Kolodin, *The Musical Life* (New York: Knopf, 1958), 198–209. Kolodin also compares Stokowski to Toscanini this way: "If the inner tension of music has rarely been realized so fully as in some of Toscanini's interpretations, so the outer, surface sheen has rarely been polished so glowingly as in [Stokowski]."

61 ". . . arranged for an elephant and other zoo animals . . ." Howard Taubman, "Strenuous Maestro Stokowski," *The New York Times*, April 16, 1941.

61 ". . . performed in Guatemala . . ." Oliver Daniel with Bert Whyte, Stokowski papers, University of Pennsylvania.

61 ". . . 'for some mysterious reason . . .' " Gould.

61 ". . . 'the "natural" sound . . . ' " Leopold Stokowski, "New Vistas in Radio," *The Atlantic Monthly* 155, 1 (January 1935), 9.

61 " 'Don't be shocked . . .' " Gould.

62 " 'the Stradivarius of orchestras' . . ." Arthur Bronson, "Leopold Stokowski," *The American Mercury* 59 (October 1944), 405.

62 " 'the juiciest sound in the world.' " Taubman.

62 " 'the rhythm of our life . . .' " Stokowski, "New Vistas in Radio," 12.

62 " '. . . yet another piece of evidence . . .' " Compton MacKenzie, review of *Danse Macabre*, Philadelphia Orchestra, conducted by Leopold Stokowski, *The Gramophone* (November 1926), 245.

62 " 'the most ambitious electrical recording . . .' " Lawrence Jacob Abbott, review of Antonín Dvořák's Symphony No. 9, "From the New World," Philadelphia Orchestra, conducted by Leopold Stokowski, *The Outlook* 89 (May 5, 1926), 36.

63 " 'No one controls Stokowski's . . .' " Preben Opperby, *Leopold Stokowski* (New York: Hippocrene Books, 1982), 38–39.

63 ". . . worked closely with Charles O'Connell . . ." Abram Chasins, *Leopold Stokowski: A Profile* (New York: Hawthorn Books, 1979), 135–36.

65 ". . . invited the Bell engineers . . ." Fantel, "50 Years Ago—Musical Stereo's First Disk." Also Bell press release, 1980, Stokowski papers, University of Pennsylvania.

65 " 'the bellow of a bull . . .' " Quoted in "Supervises Pick-up for Two Outstanding Programs," *The Erpigram* (November 1, 1931), 8.

65 " 'Listening monaurally . . .' " Fantel, "50 Years Ago—Musical Stereo's First Disk."

66 " '. . . kind of electric ear' . . ." Stokowski, "New Vistas in Radio." Note that Stokowski was not claiming that binaural sound would replicate the live experience, merely that it would help the listener at home have an experience that was as "satisfying" as the live experience.

66 ". . . 'auditory perspective.' " Conley.

66 " 'Six violins . . .' " Oliver Daniel interview with Harvey Fletcher, Stokowski papers, University of Pennsylvania.

66 " 'You have heard . . .' " "Up Hill and Down Dale," Western Electric newsletter (date unknown).

67 " 'You would have to hear . . .' " Ibid.

67 " 'Opera today . . .' " "Stokowski Testing Singerless Opera," *The New York Times*, May 3, 1932.

68 " 'What you've just witnessed . . .' " Conley.

68 ". . . 'impossible for one listening . . .' " Robert E. McGinn, "Stokowski and the Bell Telephone Laboratories: Collaboration in the Development of High-Fidelity Sound Reproduction," *Technology and Culture* 24 (January 1983), 55.

69 ". . . 'a loudness almost great enough . . .' " "The Reproduction of Orchestral Music in Auditory Perspective," *Bell Laboratories Record* 11, 9 (May 1933), 254–61.

69 " 'If a gold mine . . .' " Stokowski, "New Vistas in Radio," 8.

70 " 'We must enlarge . . .' " McGinn, 56.

70 "Bell's solution was a system . . ." Ibid., 64.

71 "The *Fantasia* story began . . ." Opperby, 68, 69–70; also "*Fantasia* Restored," *Musical America* 3 (March 1991), 72–73.

72 " 'Why don't you give . . .' " Bronson, 406.

72 " 'You had to know . . .' " Bert Oliver interview with Tom Shepherd, Stokowski papers, University of Pennsylvania.

73 " 'The contributions of electronics . . .' " Leopold Stokowski, "Music and Electronics," Stokowski papers, University of Pennsylvania, 1958.

73 ". . . he felt like he'd . . ." Hans Fantel, "Stokowski: A Pioneer of Sonic Splendor," *The New York Times*, December 9, 1979.

73 "His ideal of the perfect world . . ." Stokowski, "New Vistas in Radio," 15.

3: Aluminum Cowboys: A Pretape Parable

77 " 'It is always . . .' " John A. Lomax and Alan Lomax, eds., *Our Singing Country: Folk Songs and Ballads* (Mineola, NY: Dover Publications, 2000 [1941]), xxvi.

77 ". . . the summer of 1933 . . ." Ibid., 40–46.

77 ". . . 'intensely American and flagrantly . . .' " Nolan Porterfield, *Last Cavalier: The Life and Times of John A. Lomax, 1867–1948* (Urbana: University of Illinois Press, 1996), 339.

77 ". . . armed with an Edison cylinder machine . . ." Alan Lomax, "Saga of a Folksong Hunter," *HiFi/Stereo Review* 4, 5 (May 1960), in Ronald D. Cohen, ed., *Alan Lomax: Selected Writings, 1934–1997* (New York: Routledge, 2003), 173–86.

79 " 'I realized then . . .' " Alan Lomax, "Folk Music in the Roosevelt Era," in ibid., 92–93.

79 "Alan retold this story . . ." Story of Blue and the Lomaxes reconstructed from four slightly different versions: Alan Lomax, " 'Sinful' Songs of the Southern Negro," *Southwest Review* 19, 2 (January 1934), 105–31; Alan Lomax, "Saga of a Folksong Hunter"; *Folk Music in the Roosevelt White House: A Commemorative Program Presented by the Office of Folklife Programs at the National Museum of American History* (Washington, D.C.: Smithsonian Institution, 1982), 14–17; and Alan Lomax, *The Land Where the Blues Began* (New York: New Press, 1993), xi.

80 ". . . 'most unlike those . . .' " Porterfield, 298.

80 " 'So it was that . . .' " Alan Lomax, " 'Sinful' Songs of the Southern Negro," 120.

80 ". . . 'almost supplied the deficiency.' " Porterfield, 300.

80 ". . . 'sensitive audience for . . .' " From a 1992 interview in Charles Wolfe and Kip Lornell, *The Life and Legend of Leadbelly* (New York: Da Capo, 1992), 160.

81 " 'He really understood . . .' " Gene Bluestein, "Moses Asch, Documentor," *American Music* 5, 3 (Autumn 1987), 299.

82 " '. . . my prize record' . . ." Porterfield, 389.

82 ". . . listening to the distant strains . . ." Porterfield, 17–18.

82 ". . . enamored of the cowboy mystique . . ." Wolfe and Lornell, 10–11.

82 ". . . forced to sell . . ." Porterfield, 8.

83 ". . . already playing guitar . . ." Wolfe and Lornell, 38–45.

83 ". . . one thousand copies . . ." Porterfield, 119.

84 "By hitting the road . . ." Chronology of the Lomaxes, Office of Folklife, Library of Congress. See also John Lomax, *Adventures of a Ballad Hunter* (New York: Macmillan, 1947), 77.

84 " 'I have preserved . . .' " Ibid., 61–62.

85 ". . . kept his promise . . ." Wolfe and Lornell, 84–87.

85 " 'Immediately my imagination . . .' " Bluestein, 294.

85 ". . . last year of high school . . ." Peter D. Goldsmith, *Making People's Music: Moe Asch and Folkways Records* (Washington, D.C.: Smithsonian Institution Press, 1998), 52.

86 " '. . . when I got back . . .' " Robert Palmer, "How a Recording Pioneer Created a Treasury of Folk Music," *The New York Times*, May 29, 1983.

86 ". . . a lot of work for . . ." Goldsmith, 67.

86 " 'We even kicked out . . .' " Bluestein, 296.

86 "He returned to . . ." The details of the incident that eventually got Lead Belly sent back to jail aren't clear. Wolfe and Lornell do a good job of piecing together what probably happened. See Wolfe and Lornell, 97–99.

87 ". . . embarked on a tour . . ." John Morthland, "Folk Hero," *Texas Monthly* (November 1988), 72; Porterfield, 273–81.

87 ". . . named honorary consultant . . ." Ibid., 194.

87 ". . . the portable machine . . ." Porterfield, 301.

88 ". . . Lead Belly was a free man." Although there was no evidence that the record had anything to do with this—Lead Belly was actually eligible for release under a law that required him to serve out the rest of his sentence if he was ever convicted of another crime—the story spread, and the Lomaxes, who wound up looking like record-makers with inordinate clout, were always willing to support it implicitly. See for example John Lomax, *Negro Folk Songs as Sung by Leadbelly* (New York: Macmillan, 1936), 33; Alan Lomax, "Saga of a Folksong Hunter"; and Alan Lomax, "Leadbelly's Songs," in *Alan Lomax: Selected Writings*, 198.

89 ". . . sing at the upcoming . . ." John Lomax, *Negro Folk Songs*, 38; Porterfield, 342; John Lomax, *Negro Folk Songs*, 45.

89 ". . . performed at a Greenwich Village apartment . . ." Ibid., 48.

89 " 'Northern people hear . . .' " Wolfe and Lornell, 2; Lomax chronology, Library of Congress.

89 *"The New Yorker* published . . ." William Rose Benét, "Ballad of a Ballad-Singer," *The New Yorker*, January 19, 1935.

89 " 'I am distressed . . .' " Jess Tyehimba, "Lomax *v.* Leadbelly in New York: Letters to Home, 1934," *Callaloo* 27 (2004), 2.

89 ". . . relocated to a cottage . . ." John Lomax, *Negro Folk Songs*, 50.

90 ". . . conducted extensive sessions . . ." Lomax chronology, Library of Congress.

90 ". . . Lead Belly and John played . . ." For the script for the March of Time newsreel see Wolfe and Lornell, 164–66.

90 " 'I suffered intense . . .' " John Lomax, *Negro Folk Songs*, 63.

90 ". . . checked to make sure . . ." Exchange between Alan Lomax and Lead Belly taken from "Monologue on Square Dances or Sookey Jumps," Lead Belly, *Go Down Old Hannah: The Library of Congress Recordings*, vol. 6 (Rounder Records, 1994).

90 ". . . invariably sensationalistic." "Bad Nigger Makes Good Minstrel," *Life*, April 19, 1937.

92 " '. . . pull Lead Belly off the stage . . .' " Sean Killeen, "Far Above Cayuga's Waters: Lead Belly at Cornell," *Lead Belly Letter* 4 (Winter 1994), 1, 3, 8.

92 ". . . a letter to Alan . . ." Benjamin Filene, *Romancing the Folk: Public Memory & American Roots Music* (Chapel Hill: University of North Carolina Press, 2000), 73.

92 " 'The idea was . . .' " Wolfe and Lornell, 221.

92 ". . . consensus opinion on the song . . ." Ibid., 17.

94 ". . . last of the nineteenth-century World's Fairs . . ." See Gray Brechin, "Sailing to Byzantium: The Architecture of the Fair," in Burton Benedict, *The Anthropology of World's Fairs: San Francisco's Panama Pacific Exposition of 1915* (Berkeley, CA: Lowie Museum of Anthropology and Scolar Press, 1983), 99.

95 " 'My astonishment and chagrin . . .' " Alan Lomax, *The Land Where The Blues Began*, 45–46.

95 ". . . a twenty-six-year-old singer and guitarist . . ." Robert Palmer, *Deep Blues* (New York: Penguin, 1981), 2–15. As Palmer notes, Muddy wasn't the first Delta blues guitarist to "go electric," but with the band he formed in Chicago in the mid-forties, he "did more than anyone to adapt the electric guitar to a rawer form of blues, rather than just using it to make themselves heard over large bar audiences."

96 ". . . its public apotheosis . . ." Jac Holzman and Gavan Daws, *Follow the Music: The Life and High Times of Elektra Records in the Great Years of American Pop Culture* (Santa Monica, CA: FirstMedia Books, 1998), 119–22.

96 " 'As time goes on . . .' " Gary Kenton, "Moses Asch of Folkways," *Audio* (July 1990), 46.

97 " 'You never see me . . .' " Goldsmith, 293.

97 " 'My practice has . . .' " Ibid.

97 " 'My philosophy . . .' " Ibid., 42–44.

98 ". . . 'the producer reconstructs . . .' " Ibid., 42.

98 " 'We had ten people . . .' " Ibid., 43.

99 " '. . . Lead Belly and I were brothers' . . ." Bluestein, 299.

99 ". . . time was passing him . . ." Porterfield, 421, 444.

100 " 'I'm scared of . . .' " Interview of February 1948 with Ira Peck, *New York Daily Compass*, November 7, 1949.

100 " 'He smiles, and . . .' " Frederic Ramsey Jr., "At the Vanguard, and After," in *Jazz Music: A Tribute to Huddie Ledbetter*, edited by Max Jones, Albert McCarthy, and Frederic Ramsey, Jr. (London: Jazz Music Books, 1946), 7.

101 " '. . . Lead Belly as their tool . . .' " Sean Killeen, "Fred Ramsey (1915–1995)," *Lead Belly Letter* (Winter–Spring 1995), 11.

101 " 'He gives it to you . . .' " Ramsey, "At the Vanguard," 8.

102 " 'It just flowed . . .' " Killeen, "Fred Ramsey," 11.
102 ". . . last song of the third session . . ." My account of Lead Belly's sessions with
     Ramsey are taken mostly from listening to the CD reissue of *Lead Belly's Last Sessions*
     (Smithsonian Folkways, 1994) and reading Sean Killeen's liner notes. The CD also
     contains a useful reprint of an article Frederic Ramsey wrote about Lead Belly for the
     November–December 1953 issue of *High Fidelity*. The scene of Ramsey first dis-
     cussing the project with Lead Belly came from a recording, not included with the CD
     reissue, that is part of the Folkways archives at the Smithsonian Center for Folklife and
     Cultural Heritage.
103 " 'It is all very pat . . .' " Quoted in Goldsmith, 255.

4: Pink Pseudo-Realism

105 ". . . asked Crosby for the tiny piece of tape . . ." The story of Ken Carpenter
     saving the tiny piece of tape was recounted by Jack Mullin during a talk he gave at an
     Audio Engineering Society event in Los Angeles on June 18, 1994. As Mullin tells it,
     he had this encounter with Carpenter "after recording the first or second show," and
     the line they fixed was "The new Philcos gives . . ." It probably did not happen exactly
     as Mullin remembers. None of the several Philco commercials delivered by Carpenter
     during the first ten shows of the 1947–48 season contains the line "The new Philcos
     give." In those first couple of months, Mullin amply demonstrated the full extent of
     magnetic tape's editing capabilities, so it's doubtful that Carpenter would have had that
     reaction after that initial period. Mullin was probably getting the chronology right but
     the details of the commercial wrong. For Mullin's talk, see volume one of *A Chronology
     of American Tape Recording*, a VHS tape issued by the Audio Engineering Society.
107 ". . . remarkably durable." Marvin Camras, *Magnetic Recording Handbook* (New
     York: Van Nostrand Reinhold, 1988), 37–38.
107 ". . . something dark and shadowy about magnetism . . ." Ibid., 15–16.
108 ". . . a mechanical engineer named Oberlin Smith . . ." S. J. Begun, *Magnetic
     Recording* (New York: Murray Hill Books, Inc., 1949), 2.
108 "Valdemar Poulsen is sometimes . . ." Ibid; Peter Hammar, "Jack Mullin: The
     Man and His Machines," *Journal of the Audio Engineering Society* 37, 6 (June 1989),
     496.
109 ". . . built a prototype machine . . ." Heinz H. K. Thiele, "Magnetic Sound
     Recording in Europe up to 1945," *Journal of the Audio Engineering Society* 36, 5 (May
     1988), 398.
109 ". . . formation of the American Telegraphone Company . . ." Camras, 5–8.
110 ". . . the United States began extensive research . . ." Peter Hammar and Don
     Ososke, "The Birth of the German Magnetophon Tape Recorder, 1928–1945," *DB: The
     Sound Engineering Magazine* 16, 3 (March 1982), 48.
110 ". . . a British version called the Blattnerphone . . ." Thiele, 399.
111 ". . . he completed a working prototype . . ." The historian Friedrich Engel
     called Pfleumer's machine "the first tape recorder in the modern sense." See Friedrich
     K. Engel, "The Introduction of the Magnetophon," in *Magnetic Recording: The First
     100 Years*, edited by Eric D. Daniel, C. Denis Mee, and Mark H. Clark (New York:
     IEEE Press, 1999), 48.
111 ". . . its public debut in 1935 . . ." Thiele, 396.

112 " '. . . a total revolution . . .' " Engel, 64.

114 ". . . liked to listen to the radio . . ." Peter Hammar, "Jack Mullin: The Man Who Put Bing Crosby on Tape," *Mix* 23 (October 1999), 87.

115 ". . . playing about 5,000 kilometers of tape . . ." H. J. von Braunmuhl, "The Magnetophon: Its Properties and Field of Use," in *The Magnetophon Sound Recording and Reproducing System,* translated by J. G. Arengo-Jones and M.J.L. Pulling and included as Appendix IV, reported by M.J.L. Pulling, British Intelligence Objectives Subcommittee, London, BIOS Trip No.: Rat 43, BIOS Final Report No. 951, 1945.

115 "At a very young age . . ." Paul Laurence and Bob Rypinski, "Interview with Les Paul," *Audio* (December 1978), 40.

116 ". . . sent to newly liberated Paris . . ." John T. Mullin, "Capturing the Craft of Tape Recording," *High Fidelity and Musical America* 26 (April 1976), 62.

116 ". . . when Mullin and a lieutenant got there . . ." Hammar, "Jack Mullin: The Man and His Machines," 500; and author interview with Hammar.

117 " 'I couldn't tell . . .' " Mullin, 62–63.

118 ". . . to procure two K-4s . . ." Mullin, 64.

119 " 'It is not ideology . . .' " Theodor W. Adorno, *Prisms,* translated by Samuel and Shierry Weber (Cambridge, MA: MIT Press, 1981), 32.

120 ". . . 'a kind of pink pseudo-realism . . .' " Theodor W. Adorno, *Essays on Music,* edited by Richard Leppert (Berkeley: University of California Press, 2002), 381. See also Leppert's commentary on pages 388–89.

120 ". . . 'kneaded by the same modes . . .' " Adorno, "On Popular Music," in *Essays on Music,* 438–39.

120 " 'stems from an era . . .' " Adorno, "The Curve of the Needle," in *Essays on Music,* 272.

121 " 'a practiced ear . . .' " Karl Pflaumer, "Notes on the Manufacture of Magnetophon Tape," in *The Magnetophon Sound Recording and Reproducing System,* translated by H. J. von Braunmuhl and included as Appendix 1, reported by M.J.L. Pulling, British Intelligence Objectives Subcommittee, London, BIOS Trip No.: Rat 43, BIOS Final Report No. 951, 1945.

122 ". . . Crosby's show was recorded onto 16-inch transcription discs." Mullin, 64–65.

123 ". . . Ampex had built the tape reels . . ." "Record of Development of Magnetic Tape Recorder, Ampex Electric Corporation, San Carlos, Cal.," manuscript 1230, box 66, Ampex Corporate Records archives, Stanford.

124 ". . . became a more skilled editor . . ." Hammar, "John Mullin: A Recording Pioneer."

125 ". . . ABC eventually ordered twenty Ampex machines . . ." Hammar, "John Mullin: A Recording Pioneer."

127 ". . . sketched out the entire arrangement . . ." Liner notes, *Les Paul with Mary Ford: The Best of the Capitol Masters, 90th Birthday Edition* (Capitol Records, 2005).

127 ". . . hatched a plan . . ." Author interview with Ross Snyder; and Howard Sanner interviews with Ross Snyder for the Ampex Virtual Museum and Mailing List, available at http://recordist.com/ampex/mp3/.

5: Presence

129 " 'The first to discover . . .' " John S. Wilson, "Percussion Discs Launch New Trend," *The New York Times*, December 11, 1960.

129 " 'We developed a small . . .' " Charles Young, "The Ramones Are Punks and Will Beat You Up," *Rolling Stone* (August 12, 1976), available at www.rollingstone.com/artists/theramones/articles/story/6485054/the_ramones_are_punks_and_will_beat_you_up.

129 " '. . . If it doesn't sell . . .' " All quotations and information regarding the making of *Hysteria* were taken from the DVD *Classic Albums: Def Leppard—Hysteria* (Eagle Rock Entertainment, 2002).

132 ". . . Sarnoff was in a . . ." "RCA's Sarnoff Tangles with Rosenman" and "Speed Battle Talk Rises as Rumors Fly," *The Billboard* (May 13, 1950).

135 ". . . announced that LPs would soon go on sale." "LP Disk Secret Open to Market, Columbia Says" and "Columbia Diskery, CBS Show Microgroove Platters to Press; Tell How It Began," *The Billboard* (June 26, 1948). See also Roland Gelatt, *The Fabulous Phonograph, 1877–1977* (New York: Collier Books, 1977), 290–91.

136 " 'In many respects . . .' " Joe Csida, "Lowdown on New RCA Disk," *The Billboard* (January 8, 1949).

136 " 'R.P.M. Peace Plan . . .' " "R.P.M. Peace Plan Flops; Each Company on Its Own," *The Billboard* (June 30, 1949).

137 ". . . 'plain disgusted.' " "Constant Disc Bally Is Needed," *The Billboard* (April 16, 1949).

137 " '. . . biggest potential disk market . . .' " "12 Million Phonos Put Out Since War Give the Diskers Biggest All-Time Potential," *The Billboard* (January 7, 1950).

137 ". . . theorized that 'the so-called . . .' " "Wax Boom May Go to Spring," *The Billboard* (December 17, 1949).

137 ". . . 'sheer listening comfort . . .' " Howard Taubman, "Speeds, Competition over Revolutions per Minute Was the Highlight of 1949," *The New York Times*, January 1, 1950.

138 ". . . 'major cultural phenomenon' . . ." John Conly, "Hi-Fi for All," *The Atlantic Monthly* (September 1954), 89.

138 ". . . 'major American enthusiasm' . . ." Herbert Brean, "The 'Hi-Fi' Bandwagon," *Life* 34 (June 15, 1953), 146.

138 " 'So assiduously has the term . . .' " Daniel Lang, "Ear-Driven," *The New Yorker* (March 3, 1956).

138 ". . . 'the final link . . .' " J. G. Mitchell, "The Ultimate Fi," *The Atlantic Monthly* (June 1960), 148–49.

138 ". . . 'give to psychiatry this useful word . . .' " "Audiophilia," *Time* (January 14, 1957), 44.

139 " 'Ever and always . . .' " James Hinton Jr., "Promise and Problems," *The Nation* (December 1953), 182.

139 ". . . event hosted by Briggs . . ." Edward Tatnall Canby, "Mr. Briggs and the Concert Hall," *Harper's Magazine* (December 1955), 109–10.

140 " 'growing human flood . . .' " John M. Conly, "The Higher-Fi," *The Atlantic* (December 1956), 112.

141 "His space was mobbed . . ." Lang.

144 " 'Stereo tape and the lunatic fringe . . .' " Roland Gelatt, "Stereo Sound Comes into the Home," *The Reporter* (January 24, 1957), 37.

144 " 'Wives are like that . . .' " Ibid., 37.

144 ". . . a system designed by Westrex . . ." For more on the two stereo disc-cutting systems, see Ralph W. Wight, " 'I See What You Mean!' How the Westrex 45/45 System Was Adopted by the Record Makers," *Audio* (March 1975), 24–30; and H. E. Roys, "The Coming of Stereo," *Journal of the Audio Engineering Society* 25, 10–11 (October–November 1977), 824–27.

145 " 'Stereo wasn't getting . . .' " John S. Wilson, "Percussion Discs Launch New Trend," *The New York Times*, December 11, 1960.

146 " 'There are ninety million . . .' " Ibid.

148 " 'You have a single signal . . .' " "Pseudo Stereo," *Time* (January 20, 1961).

148 " 'young man with a good ear.' " "Young Man with a Good Ear," *Life* (September 22, 1961), 33.

149 ". . . Laico received some of his training . . ." David Simons, *Studio Stories: How the Great New York Records Were Made* (San Francisco: Backbeat Books, 2004), 22–46.

150 ". . . most famous origin stories . . ." John Lewis, "Ike Turner: Interview," *Time Out London* (July 31, 2006), available at www.timeout.com/london/music/features/1766.html.

152 " '. . . trying to improve on it.' " On the use of reverb in old rock-and-roll records, see Peter Doyle, *Echo and Reverb: Fabricating Space in Popular Music Recording, 1900–1960* (Middletown, CT: Wesleyan University Press, 2005), 184.

153 " 'What everybody strives for . . .' " Mick Brown, *Tearing Down the Wall of Sound: The Rise and Fall of Phil Spector* (London: Bloomsbury, 2007), 118.

153 " 'I thought I'd discovered. . .' " "Joe Remembers," included on *Joe Meek: Portrait of a Genius: The RCM Legacy* (Castle Music, 2005).

154 ". . . 'the one record that epitomizes . . .' " Ibid.

156 ". . . the story really begins . . ." The story of the Sel-Sync was put together from the following sources: author interview with Ross Snyder; Howard Sanner interviews with Ross Snyder for the Ampex Virtual Museum and Mailing List, available at http://recordist.com/ampex/mp3/; and Ross H. Snyder, "Sel-Sync and the 'Octopus': How Came to Be the First Recorder to Minimize Successive Copying in Overdubs," *ARSC Journal* 34, 2 (2003), 209. See also George Petersen, "Ampex Sel-Sync, 1955," *Mix* (October 2005), available at http://mixonline.com/mag/audio_ampex_selsync/.

157 ". . . seemed 'like heaven . . .' " Mark Lewisohn, *The Beatles Recording Sessions: The Official Story of the Abbey Road Years 1962–1970* (London: Hamlin, 2004 [1988]), 6.

158 "Now consider how 'Penny Lane' . . ." Ibid., 91–94.

159 "George Harrison's 'While My Guitar . . .' " Ibid., 145.

160 " 'Abbey Road was the first . . .' " "Geoff Emerick," *Mix*, October 1, 2002, available at www.mixonline.com/recording/interviews/audio_geoff_emerick.

6: Perfect Sound? Whatever

185 " 'Nothing since Edison's . . .' " Peter K. Burkowitz, "The Sound Revolution . . . Demystifying the Technology," *Recording Engineer/Producer* (April 1983).

185 " 'From the early 1980s up till now . . .' " Neil Young, "The CD and the Damage Done," *Harper's Magazine* (July 1992), 23–24.

186 ". . . recorded some songs at home . . ." Daniel Keller, "Bruce Springsteen's *Nebraska*: a PortaStudio, Two SM57's, and Inspiration," available at www.tascam.com/

Press/UserStories/Bruce_Springsteins_Nebraska.html (link disabled as of October 2007).

186 **"An opposite fate awaited . . ."** I reconstructed the details of the manufacture of the *Born in the U.S.A.* CD and the early days of Sony Digital Audio Disc Corporation from phone interviews with Mike Mitchell on January 20 and 31, 2006, and from in-person interviews with Mitchell and Ed Proffitt at Sony DADC, Terre Haute, Indiana, on January 27, 2006.

190 **". . . had praised Springsteen's 'message of hope' . . ."** Jon Pareles, "Bruce Springsteen: Rock's Popular Populist," *The New York Times*, August 18, 1985.

191 **"a set of positive and reliable techniques . . ."** John Haugeland, *Artificial Intelligence: The Very Idea* (Cambridge, MA: MIT Press, 1985), 53.

191 **". . . a model of precision and complexity. . ."** On the technical specifications of the compact disc, see Senri Miyaoka, "Digital Audio Is Compact and Rugged," *IEEE Spectrum* 21, 3 (March 1984), 35–39. The best example of a more technical overview was written by two Philips engineers on the CD team. See J.P.J. Heemskerk and K. A. Schouhamer Immink, "Compact Disc: System Aspects and Modulation," *Philips Technical Review* 40, 6 (1982), 157–64. Other useful articles for understanding CD technology are John Monoforte, "The Digital Reproduction of Sound," *Scientific American* (December 1984), 78–84; Peter Mitchell, "Inside the Compact Disc System," *High Fidelity*, Musical America edition (July 1983), 39–44; and David Ranada, "Digital Debut: First Impressions of the Compact Disc System," *Stereo Review* (December 1982), 61–69. For a very early brief description of the proposed system, before it was fully developed, see John Free, "Laser Plays Super Hi-Fi from Pocket-Size Disc," *Popular Science* (October 1979), 111.

193 **" 'These semantic aspects . . .' "** Claude Shannon, "A Mathematical Theory of Communication," *Bell Systems Technical Journal* 27, July–October 1948, 379–423, 623–56. See Solomon W. Golomb, "Claude E. Shannon: 1916–2001," *Science* (April 20, 2001); and Shannon's bio at NYU Linguistics Department Web site, available at www.nyu.edu/pages/linguistics/courses/v610003/shan.html.

194 **". . .'perfecting approximation.' "** Quoted in Edward Rothstein, "The Quest for Perfect Sound," *The New Republic* (December 30, 1985), 29–37.

195 **" 'Listening to a CD is like . . .' "** Young, 23–24.

196 **" 'The future belongs . . .' "** Liner notes, Big Black, *Songs About Fucking* (Touch and Go Records, 1988).

196 **" 'This recording is meant . . .' "** Liner notes, Slint, *Spiderland* (Touch and Go Records, 1991).

197 **" 'When, in five years . . .' "** Liner notes, Big Black, *The Rich Man's Eight Track Tape* (Touch and Go Records, 1992).

197 **" 'Every time I hear a CD . . .' "** Urge Overkill, "What's This Generation Coming To?" *The Urge Overkill Stull EP* (Touch and Go Records, 1992).

197 **" 'See this needle . . .' "** Pearl Jam, "Spin the Black Circle," *Vitalogy* (Sony, 1994).

198 **". . . articles appearing in sound engineering journals . . ."** Ken Pohlmann, "What Is Reality?" *Stereo Review* (June 1990), 52.

198 **" 'Progress is not always . . .' "** P. B. Fellgett, "Naturalness and Artificiality in Sound Recording," *Studio Sound* (April 1981), 40–41.

198 **" 'The record industry . . .' "** H. Wiley Hitchcock, "Response to *Address* by John Cage," in *The Phonograph and Our Musical Life: Proceedings of a Centennial Conference*, 7–10 December 1997, edited by H. Wiley Hitchcock (New York: Institute for

Studies in American Music, Department of Music, School of Performing Arts, Brooklyn College, City University of New York, 1980), 5.

199 " 'Is this intensification . . .' " Roger Reynolds, "Thoughts on What a Record Records," in *The Phonograph and Our Musical Life*, 28–35.

199 " '. . . the unique quality of experience . . .' " Ibid.

199 " 'A gray-out is in progress' . . ." Alan Lomax, "Appeal for Cultural Equity," *Journal of Communications* 27 (Spring 1977), 125–26.

201 ". . . led the team that examined . . ." Nicholas Wade, "Watergate: Verification of Tapes May Be Electronic Standoff," *Science* 182, 4117, 1108–1110.

203 ". . . decided to restore some old Enrico Caruso . . ." Thomas G. Stockham Jr., "Restoration of Old Recordings by Means of Digital Signal Processing," presented at the 41st Audio Engineering Society Convention, October 5–8, 1971, Audio Engineering Society reprint 831 (D-4).

209 " 'It is not outrageous . . .' " Thomas G. Stockham Jr., "Records of the Future," *Journal of the Audio Engineering Society* 25, 10–11 (October–November 1977), 895.

210 " '. . . somebody had removed a veil . . .' " William Aspray oral history with Heitaro Nakajima, IEEE History Center (New Brunswick, NJ: Rutgers University, 1994).

211 ". . . it was the Philips engineers . . ." Heemskerk and Immink, "Compact Disc: System Aspects and Modulation," 163–64.

211 ". . . presided over a press event . . ." Philips press release, May 26, 1981.

212 " 'Last month the world of audio . . .' " Hans Fantel, "Listening to the Digital Future," *The New York Times*, June 26, 1981.

212 " '. . . our big surprise.' " Suzuki quoted on a radio report on the twentieth anniversary of the CD, reported by Jessica Smith and broadcast by Minnesota Public Radio, September 30, 2002.

213 ". . . he'd 'barely escaped physical . . .' " John Nathan, *Sony: The Private Life*, (Boston: Houghton Mifflin, 1999), 143.

213 " 'I fear what the hardware people . . .' " Mike Hennessey and Peter Jones, "Bright Days Ahead, Say Execs At IMIC," *Billboard* (May 8, 1982).

214 ". . . calling the CD 'small and beautiful.' " Ibid., 58.

217 " 'At each company, there was someone . . .' " Trudi Miller, "CD's Launch: The Hidden History," *Billboard* (September 26, 1992).

218 ". . . to judge from his digital hi-fi setup . . ." Susan Spillman, "Compact Discs on the Marketing Beam," *Advertising Age* 56, 25 (April 1, 1985), 84.

219 " '. . . heard a single compact disc . . .' " Rothstein, 35.

220 " 'In the private opinion of many on the studio side . . .' " Association of Professional Recording Studios, "Digital, Slightly Digital, or Not Digital at All," *Studio Sound* (July 1983), 36.

220 " 'I have no argument . . .' " Roger Lagadec, "The High End," *Stereo Review* (August 1985).

221 ". . . the fastest-growing home entertainment product . . ." Ken Terry, "1982–1992: Talkin' 'Bout a Revolution; How Compact Discs Changed the Music Industry Forever and (Mostly) for the Better," *Billboard* (September 26, 1992).

221 " 'The change from 78 RPM . . .' " Alan Kilkenny, "The Compact Disc," *Studio Sound* (November 1981), 66–67.

222 " '. . . except for the use of a finite number of digits . . .' " Stockham, "Records of the Future," 893.

222 ". . . a ' "transmission system" . . .' " Heemskerk and Immink, "Compact Disc: System Aspects and Modulation," 157.

222 " '. . . Sony turns your living room . . .' " Marianne Meyer, "Compact Discs: On the Charts, with a Bullet," *Marketing & Media Decisions* 28 (March 1985), 65.

222 " '. . . walk out with a *perfect duplicate* . . .' " Glenn Kenney, "Digital Audio Today," *Stereo Review* (October 1992), 54.

222 ". . . 'now ensures that the electronic encoding . . .' " Andrew Goodwin, "Sample and Hold: Pop Music in the Age of Digital Reproduction," in *Rock, Pop, and the Written Word*, edited by Simon Frith and Andrew Goodwin (New York: Pantheon, 1990), 259.

223 " '. . . through the last two decades . . .' " Peter K. Burkowitz, "The Sound Revolution . . . Demystifying the Technology," *Recording Engineer/Producer* (April 1983).

224 " '. . . another step in an exciting new age . . .' " Kilkenny, "The Compact Disc."

224 ". . . designing the CD . . ." Kees A. Schouhamer Immink, "The CD Story," *Journal of the Audio Engineering Society* 46, 460.

226 ". . . Stockham had argued that the . . ." Thomas G. Stockham Jr., *A-D and D-A Converters: Their Effect on Digital Audio Fidelity*, presented at the 41st Audio Engineering Society Convention, New York, October 5–8, 1971, Audio Engineering Society reprint 834 (D-1).

226 " 'The reductionists will say . . .' " Author e-mail interview with Akin Fernandez. See also Akin Fernandez, "Why CD Is a Con or, The Preservation of the Analogue Infrastructure," Irdial-Discs, available at www.irdial.com/original_analogue_vs_digital_essay.htm.

228 " 'This is a matter of . . .' " Daniel Levitin, "Pioneer Addresses Digital Debate," *Billboard* (January 22, 1994), 74.

229 ". . . differences arise from 'euphonic effects of . . .' " E. Brad Meyer, "The Romance of the Record," *Stereo Review* (January 1996), 67–70.

230 " '. . . not like perfect sound . . .' " Rothstein.

230 ". . . a specially designed solar-powered . . ." Richard Leiby, "A Place in the Desert for New Mexico's Most Exclusive Circles," *The Washington Post*, December 15, 2005; and *20/20*, December 20, 1998.

233 ". . . wrote up his findings . . ." John Diamond, "Human Stress Provoked by Digitalized Recordings," *Journal of the Audio Engineering Society* 28, 9 (September 1980), 613.

7: The Story of the Band That Clipped Itself to Death (and Other Dispatches from the Loudness War)

237 "Every station had its own . . ." Frank Foti and Robert Orban, "What Happens to My Recording When It's Played on the Radio," in Bob Katz, *Mastering Audio: The Art and the Science* (Oxford: Focal Press, 2002), 271–72, available at www.omniaaudio.com/tech/mastering.htm.

246 ". . . sounds described in terms of decibels . . ." For an explanation of decibels, see Peter B. Denes and Elliot N. Pinson, *The Speech Chain: The Physics and Biology of Spoken Language* (New York: W. H. Freeman and Company, 1993), 40.

248 " '. . . correlated with what happens outside . . .' " Llewelyn S. Lloyd, "The Loudness of Pure Tones," *The Musical Quarterly* 33, 4 (October 1947), 489.

248 " 'If you tune your dial . . .' " Author e-mail interview with Bob Ludwig, May 16, 2006.

249 " 'I cannot say this enough . . .' " Rip Rowan, "Over the Limit," Prorec.com (August 31, 2002), available at www.prorec.com/Articles/tabid/109/EntryId/247/Over-the-Limit.aspx.

255 " 'It's this flatness, this clipping . . .' " Nick Southall, "Imperfect Sound Forever," *Stylus* (April 1, 2006), available at www.stylusmagazine.com/articles/weekly_article/imperfect-sound-forever.htm.

255 " 'The music we listen to today . . .' " Bob Speer, "What Happened to Dynamic Range?" CD Mastering Services, available at www.cdmasteringservices.com/dynamicrange.htm.

255 " 'Every single CD was squashed . . .' " Roger Nichols, "Another New Year's Resolution," *EQ* (January 2002), available at www.rogernichols.com/EQ/EQ_2001 _12.html.

256 ". . . sounded 'relentlessly loud . . .' " John Atkinson, "Overcooked Floyd," *Stereophile* (June 2003), available at www.stereophile.com/asweseeit/851/.

257 "Stations tweak their processing . . ." Robert Orban, the founder of Orban, another company that provides audio processing equipment for radio, offers this general advice for its customers: "Very dense audio is generally appropriate for stations looking for maximum loudness and dial impact. However, it tends to be fatiguing in the long-term, so it is usually most appropriate for formats that emphasize cume over time-spent-listening." See Robert Orban, "Evaluating FM On-Air Processors," available at www.orban.com/brochures/white_papers_faqs/How%20to%20Evaluate%20FM%20On -Air%20Processing%20for%20PDs.pdf.

257 " 'I am unaware of any studies . . .' " Author e-mail exchange with Stephen McAdams, July 11–13, 2006.

261 ". . . albums like *Californication* . . ." Four million people bought *Californication* during its first year of release. It took four years for *The Wall*, released in a very different era, to sell that many albums, but by 1999, the year *Californication* came out, *The Wall* was selling on average a million copies each year. *Californication* added another million four years after its release, and that's where it stands now.

261 "It's gratifying . . ." Chris Johnson, www.airwindows.com.

266 " 'One interesting facet of broadcasting . . .' " Frank Foti, "Audio Processing: A Retrospective," Omnia Audio, available at www.omniaaudio.com/tech/retrospective.htm. See also Robert Orban, "A Short History of Audio Processing," Soundpro cessing.nl, available at www.soundprocessing.nl/hisbob.html.

274 ". . . had daisy-chained together . . ." Frank Foti, "Z-100: How a Flamethrower Ignited New York City Radio from Worst to First," Omnia Audio, available at www.omniaaudio.com/buzz/clippings/Z100.pdf.

277 ". . . the loudness craze he had unwittingly . . ." Author interview with Mike Dorrough; and "Boosting the Beat of a Different Drum," *Broadcasting* (August 5, 1985).

278 ". . . 'a backing off from the . . .' " Craig Rosen, "Are Stations Pumping Down the Volume? Engineers Say Trend Is Toward 'Cleaner' Sound," *Billboard* (February 16, 1991).

280 ". . . 'It was twice as loud . . .' " Author e-mail interview with Bob Ludwig.

280 ". . . movie previews were being produced at ear-splitting levels . . ." Perry Sun, "Thundering Trailers," *Film Journal International* 102 (May 1999), 36.

281 **". . . began an online petition . . ."** To read or sign Howson's petition, go to www.petitiononline.com/RHCPWBCD/petition.html.

285 **" 'Broadcasting processing is complex . . .' "** Foti and Orban, "What Happens to My Recording When It's Played on the Radio."

285 **" 'For the first time in a long time . . .' "** Author e-mail interview with Ludwig.

287 **". . . isn't exactly a smoking gun . . ."** The un-mastered *Californication* can be downloaded at www.megaupload.com/?d=FBKM7IOB.

288 **". . . in a 2004 interview with Rubin . . ."** Michael Fremer, "The Music Angle Interview: Producer Rick Rubin, Part 1," MusicAngle.com (May 1, 2004), available at www.musicangle.com/feat.php?id=38.

8: Tubby's Ghost

293 **"Martin, a former member of . . ."** The description of the making of Ricky Martin's "Livin' La Vida Loca" was taken from an author interview with Charles Dye; and from Dan Daley, "Recordin' 'La Vida Loca': The Making of a Hard Disk Hit," *Mix* (November 1999), available at http://mixonline.com/mag/audio_recordin_la_vida/index.html. The description of the Gentlemen's Club was taken from Dan Daley, "The Gentlemen's Club: Desmond Child's Virtual Aesthetic," *Mix* (February 1999), available at http://mixonline.com/mag/audio_gentlemens_club_desmond/index.html.

297 **". . . made completely in the box . . ."** Paul Verna, "Pro Tools Takes Recording, Mixing, Editing Worlds By Storm," *Billboard* 111, 36 (September 4, 1999), 58.

297 **". . . the first major album made for the digital era . . ."** Blair Jackson, "Classic Tracks: Dire Straits' 'Money for Nothing,' " *Mix* (February 1999), available at http://mixonline.com/mag/audio_classic_tracks_dire/.

300 **"A few months later . . ."** Emerick's recollections are from a presentation he gave at the 123rd Audio Engineering Society Convention, New York, October 6, 2007.

301 **". . . 'the recording mixer, which started out as . . .' "** "Mr. MPC: Roger Linn," *Remix* (January 2007), available at http://remixmag.com/more_stuff/roger_linn/.

304 **" 'I said, "I'm gonna turn this place . . ." ' "** Quoted in Steve Barrow and Peter Dalton, *Reggae: The Rough Guide* (London: The Rough Guide, 1997), 201.

305 **". . . discovering a way to import the sound . . ."** Author interview with Steve Barrow; and Barrow and Dalton, 199–206.

309 **" '. . . just do the whole thing . . .' "** Sydney Alonso, Jon H. Appleton, and Cameron Jones, "A Special Purpose Digital System for Musical Instruction, Composition, and Performance," *Computers and the Humanities* 10, 4 (July 1976), 210; Max Matthews, "The Digital Computer as a Musical Instrument," *Science* 142 (November 1963), 553–57; and Jon Appleton, *21st-Century Musical Instruments: Hardware and Software*, Institute for Studies in American Music Monographs: Number 29 (Brooklyn: Conservatory of Music, Brooklyn College of the City University of New York, 1989), 21–28.

314 **"They called it the Fairlight . . ."** On the Fairlight, see "Fairlight: The Whole Story," *Audio Media* (January 1996), available at www.anerd.com/fairlight/fairlight story.htm.

316 **". . . an extremely sophisticated machine . . ."** Jon Appleton, "A Complex Tool for Performance, Teaching, and Composition," *Music Educators Journal* 69, 5 (January 1983), 67.

319 ". . . 'the last great analog project.' " Mark Vail, *Vintage Synthesizers: Ground-breaking Instruments and Pioneering Designers of Electronic Music Synthesizers* (San Francisco: GPI Books, 1993), 137.

320 ". . . Stevie Wonder getting the first . . ." Ibid., 201.

322 " 'We regarded using recorded real-life sounds . . .' " "Fairlight: The Whole Story." I have rearranged one sentence in this quote for clarity.

324 ". . . 'making me a whole person' . . ." Bill Stephen, "Sting: The Technological Evolution of a Musician/Composer," *Music, Computers & Software* (February–March 1988), 22. Available at www.sting.com/news/interview.php?uid=3700.

338 ". . . the first city where Pro Tools . . ." Dan Daley, "Miami's 'Ground Zero' for Pro Tools," *Billboard* 113, 23 (June 9, 2001), 59–60.

344 " 'In a deserved monopoly position . . .' " Mike Thorne, "The Recording Studio: The Rise and Fall of an Institution," Stereo Society, available at www.stereosociety .com/recordingstudio.html.

345 " 'When we were mixing . . .' " Mike Thorne, "Soft Cell: 'Tainted Love,' " Stereo Society, available at www.stereosociety.com/taintedlove.html.

Outro: "Testing, Testing . . . (Reprise)"

354 " 'The backsliding had begun . . .' " Author e-mail exchange with Ron St. Germain, September 19, 2008.

356 "It was Bob Dylan who . . ." Jonathan Lethem, "The Genius of Bob Dylan," *Rolling Stone*, August 21, 2006, available at www.rollingstone.com/news/story/ 11216877/the_modern_times_of_bob_dylan_a_legend_comes_to_grips_with_his_ico nic_status/1.

357 ". . . the psychoacoustic phenomenon called masking . . ." For an introduction to masking, see Brian C. J. Moore, "Masking in the Human Auditory System," in Neil Gilchrist and Christer Grewin, eds., *Collected Papers on Digital Audio Bit-Rate Reduction* (New York: Audio Engineering Society, 1996). On premasking, see E. Zwicker and H. Fastl, *Psychoacoustics: Facts and Models* (Berlin: Springer, 1999).

358 ". . . organized the Moving Picture Experts Group . . ." William Sweet, "Chiariglione and the Birth of MPEG," *IEEE Spectrum* 34 (September 1997), 70–77.

359 "The third layer—MPEG-1 Audio Layer 3 . . ." For a detailed description of MP3, see Karlheinz Brandenburg and Gerhard Stoll, "ISO-MPEG-1 Audio: A Generic Standard for Coding High-Quality Digital Audio," in Gilchrist and Grewin, eds., *Collected Papers on Digital Audio Bit-Rate Reduction*, 23.

360 ". . . the next phase of lossy compression . . ." For a comparison between MP3 and AAC, see Steve Church, "On Beer and Audio Coding," available at www.telos -systems.com/news/reprints/rw_092601_aac.pdf.

Acknowledgments

With the standard caveat that anything wrong in these pages is on me, this book really was a collaborative effort. So I thank the many people who took the time to tell me their stories or guided me through the technological waters when I was way out of my depth:

Robbin Ahrold, Steve Albini, Sydney Alonso, Marco Alpert, Jon Appleton, Clete Baker, Mark Ballora, Steve Barrow, Larry Berger, Jules Bloomenthal, Michael Boddicker, Tony Bongiovi, Karlheinz Brandenburg, Evan Brooks, Chris Byrne, Greg Calbi, Danny Cancavvo, Joe Carducci, Leonardo Chiariglione, Bob Clearmountain, Jack Clement, Wayne Coyne, Michael Devecka, John Diamond, Peter Dilg, Mark Doehmann, Mike Dorrough, Steven Drozd, Bob Ezrin, Tardon Feathered, Akin Fernandez, Marc Finer, Frank Foti, Michael Fremer, Neil Gilchrist, Mick Glossop, Peter Gotcher, Kevin Gray, Lee Groves, Peter Hammar, Rick Harte, Andy Hildebrand, Kees Schouhamer Immink, Denny Jaeger, Gary Jarman, Ross Jarman, Ryan Jarman, Chris Jenkins, Chris Johnson, Cameron Jones, Alex Kapranos, Bob Katz, Eddie Korvin, Roger Lagadec, Michel Lavoie, Bunny Lee, Roger Linn, Tanja Linssen, Chris Lord-Alge, Tom Lord-Alge, Bob Ludwig, Mitch Marcoulier, Stephen McAdams, Vlado Meller, E. Brad Meyer, Randy Michaels, Tim Midgett, Mike Mitchell, Ray Moore, Robert Orban, Hugh Padgham, Sandy Pearlman, Ed Proffit, Tom Ray, Ron St. Germain, Paul Sanchez, Doug Sax, Michael Schulhof, Scott Shannon, Art Shifrin, Hank Shocklee, Philip Smart, Jack Somer, Ross Snyder, Jens Spille, Walt Stinson, Joe Tarsia, Louis Thibault, Mike Thorne, Harry Tuft, Phil Wagner, Andy Wallace, Scott Wedge, Bob Weston, and Bob Woods.

Several of these people have done their own writing on the topics covered in this book. Readers are urged to seek out the sources in the notes section, and I want to highlight a few. Although Bob Katz's *Mastering Audio: The Art and the Science* is aimed at audio pros, novices can still enjoy his discussion of dynamic range compression and the overall philosophy of recording. The book also contains the seminal essay by the radio processing kingpins Frank Foti and Robert Orban, "What Happens to My Recording When It's Played on the Radio?" Mike Thorne brings an insider's perspective in "The Recording Studio: Rise and Fall of an Institution." It deserves a book-length expansion, but for now it can be found at www.stereosociety.com/recordingstudio.html. Peter Hammar has done as much as anyone to keep the history of magnetic tape alive. The articles he's written, and the hours he gave me in interviews, helped me immensely.

I thank Simon Howson for showing me what loudness looks like and letting me reprint his images, and the denizens of the electrical.com forum, who responded to my many pleas. Susan Waltzman was a fount of audiological wisdom. Alissa Kleinman provided life-saving research and transcriptions.

Paul Israel's *Edison: A Life of Invention* and Andre Millard's *Edison and the Business of Innovation* are great overviews of Edison's work. Charles Wolfe and Kip Lornell's *The Life and Legend of Lead Belly*, Nolan Porterfield's *Last Cavalier: The Life and Times of John A. Lomax*, and Peter D. Goldsmith's *Making People's Music: Moe Asch and Folkways Records* are excellent biographies of figures whose effect on modern music is incalculable.

These people provided crucial help: Reinel Adajar, Mitzi Angel, Mike Brown, Scott Budman, Peter Burkowitz, Lizzy Burns, Tara Callahan, Peter Cho, John Chowning, Chantal Clarke, Steve Cody, Ric Coppola, Dan Crewe, Joe D'Ambrosio, Alan Douches, Gerald Fabris, Alia Fahlborg, Jessica Ferri, Jon Fine, Jessica Forman, Anne Galperin, Rick Gershon, Jerimaya Grabher, Richard Griscom, Rick Hashimoto, Paul Heine, Dave Hoeffel, Raette Johnson, Uwe Karbank, Henning Koehler, Pablo La Rosa, Eleanor Logan, David McCormick, Brian McKenna, Martin McQuade, Jim Murphy, Jo-Ann Nina, Michael Paoletta, Gail Parentau, Al Parker, Jeff Place, Ron Ricardo, Dave Rossum, Rob Roy, Gary Ruderman, Tricia Ryan, Adam Sohmer, Sue Stopps, Han Tendeloo, Paul Verna, Peter Vogel, Daniel Weiss, Don Wershba, Aaron Wilhelm, Geoffrey Wright, and Robert Zattorre.

These companies, organizations, and institutions came through, big-time: Antares Audio Technologies, the Audio Engineering Society, the Communications Research Centre Canada, Dorrough Electronics, the Illinois Institute of Technology, Iosono, the Library of Congress American Folklife Center, Mr. Toad's Recording, the New York Public Library, the Smithsonian Center for Folklife and Cultural Heritage, Rutgers University's Thomas A. Edison Papers Project, Sony DADC, Stanford University's Ampex Corporate Archives, and the University of Pennsylvania's Leopold Stokowski Collection.

For the right word at the right time: Michael Azerrad, Joe Berlinger, Doug Brod, Melissa Checker, Henry Corra, Robert Christgau, Jon Dolan, Chuck Eddy, Rob Garfield, Andy Gensler, Harry Goldstein, Will Hermes, Sean Howe, Chuck Klosterman, John Leland, Robert Levine, Alan Light, Melissa Maerz, Mike Mathog, Sia Michel, Jonah Murdock, Andrew O'Hehir, Rob Sheffield, Laura Sinagra, Marc Spitz, Paul Wagenseil, and Patrick Whalen.

Daniel Greenberg understood this project immediately, and was the best advocate I could hope for. Denise Oswald expertly steered the book, while tactfully asking questions about the long periods of radio silence. Bella Shand and Matt Weiland also provided excellent editing advice.

Ross Snyder, the force behind the first multitrack tape recorder, is an unsung hero of recording history, and I'm sorry he didn't live to see this book. Morgan Cowles was a stellar human being for so many reasons, including his impeccable musical taste. What can I say—he was the reason I first heard Mission of Burma and the Meters.

I thank Van Halen, Steely Dan, Creedence Clearwater Revival, the Minutemen—and many others too numerous to mention—for making timeless music, and Richard Meltzer for cowriting "Burnin' for You."

Neal, Joy, and Joanna Milner have given me so much help and support along the way, I don't know where to start. Kimo Nichols also helped get it started a long time ago.

And then there's Julie Taraska, whose keen editing eye is merely the most obvious way she helped make this project happen. Her love, patience, and tolerance for hearing about arcane audio trivia during the making of this book was boundless. In the end, it's all for her.

Index